ANNALS OF THE
LIVERPOOL STAGE

ANNALS OF THE
LIVERPOOL STAGE

FROM THE EARLIEST PERIOD
TO THE PRESENT TIME

TOGETHER WITH SOME ACCOUNT OF
THE THEATRES AND MUSIC HALLS
IN BOOTLE AND BIRKENHEAD

BY

R. J. BROADBENT

AUTHOR OF 'STAGE WHISPERS'
'A HISTORY OF PANTOMIME'
ETC.

WITH ILLUSTRATIONS

LIVERPOOL

EDWARD HOWELL

1908

PREFACE

It is not a whit surprising that although the annals of most of the other provincial theatres of importance have long been published, no one hitherto has written any record of the Liverpool stage. The difficulties of the task lie in the fact that data are at once too sparse and too abundant. Owing to the incompleteness of the collection of playbills in the Liverpool Free Library, there are many gaps in the story of the Liverpool Theatres which it is well-nigh impossible to fill. This is all the more regrettable as the remoter period in the annals of our local drama is much more individual and characteristic than the record of the last half century. Of the era which came in with the dawn of the touring system data are superabundant; on the whole the period is colourless and unpicturesque, and its records call for rigid compression and deft selection. It has been my aim to take a rapid bird's-eye view of the whole panorama, noting everything vital, and preserving vivid colour where it presented itself. I cannot hope under the serious limitations of matter and space to have fully succeeded in my labour of love. My fellow-townsmen must take the will for the deed.

Ample acknowledgment must be frankly and freely made to those who lent a willing hand in furtherance of the task. My gratitude is due to that learned stage historian, Mr. W. J. Lawrence, for his great assistance in kindly furnishing a mass of valuable material, as well as for his expert advice on many moot points. I also extend my thanks to Mr. Ronald Stewart-Brown, Mr. E. R. Dibdin, Mr. Peter Entwistle, Mr. George T. Shaw, and to Mr. Peter Cowell and the assistant librarians of the Liverpool Free Library, for much help kindly and courteously given.

R. J. BROADBENT.

LIVERPOOL, *November*, 1908.

CONTENTS

CONTENTS

CONTENTS

THE VARIETY STAGE.

Annals of the Liverpool Stage

THE EARLY THEATRICAL HISTORY OF LIVERPOOL.

Long before the Norman Conquest there stood at West Derby, Liverpool, an ancient castle, whose origin is lost in antiquity. Probably it was there when the Danes were driven out of Lancashire by Athelstane and Edmund, the grandsons of Alfred the Great. The site of this old castle, and of the manor house which succeeded it in the reign of Henry III, can yet be identified. It is on the north side of the lane—now known as Meadow Lane—leading from West Derby Village towards Croxteth Hall. Curiously enough, the ground upon which the old castle was built is known to this day as ' Castle Field.'

To the Castle of West Derby during Danish, Saxon, and Norman times, doubtless, came wandering minstrels, who sang to their own accompaniments stirring songs of chivalry. There, also, in all probability, the jester played his merry pranks, and with his ' quips and quiddities' caused the old oaken rafters to ring again with the loud laughter of the Baron and his retainers.

A few years after the Norman Conquest, Earl Roger de Poictiers (according to Camden's ' Britannia ') is said to have erected in 1073, on a portion of the site now occupied by the Queen Victoria Memorial, a baronial castle. There is no evidence to support this assertion. It seems more feasible to infer that the castle occupied (but not erected) by Roger de Poictiers was that of the ancient Castle of West Derby. ' It was, probably,' says Baines,* ' the chief place in the district during the Danish as well as the Saxon dominion '; and, I may add, during the early part of the Norman period.

Here Earl Roger, doubtless, kept his minstrels, and in imitation of his royal master, a jester. The Conqueror's life,

* 'History of the Commerce and Town of Liverpool,' p. 54

B

when Duke of Normandy, was saved by his jester, Goles. The accounts of the household expenses of our kings contain many payments and rewards to jesters, both foreign and domestic.   These early disciples of Thalia excited the mirth of kings and beggars—the hovel of the villein and the castle of the baron were exhilarated by their jokes.   The names of many of these buffoons are still preserved; for they were associated with the English court down to a late period.

The religious mystery series of plays—out of which grew our English drama—inaugurated in the year 1110 by the monks of this country to bring home with dramatic effect to untaught minds the solemn truths to be deduced from that unique and grand inspirational tragedy enacted on the hill of Golgotha, were, for several centuries, given in the neighbouring city of Chester.   It is not unlikely that these performances were largely attended by the inhabitants of Catholic Liverpool and neighbourhood, for their spiritual welfare.   That this was so, is highly probable, as for many years, the Priors of Birkenhead Priory* sat in the Parliaments of the Earls of Chester, and the monks had considerable intercourse, both commercially and otherwise, with Liverpool town.†   Again, the monks of St. Peter and St. Paul, Shrewsbury, had continuous association with Walton, for at one time they held the advowson of that place.   Evidence of their connection with Wavertree and Childwall can also be traced.   Be it noted, also, that through Liverpool pilgrims journeyed to the shrine on Hilbre Island, and that Liverpool's first known ecclesiastical building— St. Mary's del Key—was of monastic origin.

The Chester Mystery plays usually began on Whit Monday, and continued until the following Wednesday.   In the fourteenth century permission to perform them in English had more than once to be asked of Pope Clement, who granted an indulgence of a thousand days, and the then Bishop of Chester a further indulgence of forty days to 'every person resorting in peaceble maner with good devotion, to heare and see the sayd playes, from tyme to tyme as oft as the shall be played within the sayd citty.' ‡

* Founded 1150 by Hamon de Mascl, third Baron of Dunham, the remains of which— thanks to the Corporation of Birkenhead—are still in an excellent state of preservation.
† They had the right of ferryage from Liverpool to Birkenhead for over two hundred years.
‡ Harleian MSS., 2013.

The pageant, or mumming-play of *St. George and the Dragon* had a prominent place in the Mystery plays of the fourteenth and fifteenth centuries. This mumming-play supplemented the festivities of our forefathers at Christmas and Easter. It was known not only in Lancashire (and, of course, Liverpool), but also in other counties. The Easter or Pace-egg play—so called from its being performed in connection with the well-known custom of pace-egging—was generally on the subject of *St. George and the Dragon*. Its origin can be traced to Pagan times. It is, in fact, an example of the skill with which the Church supplanted the Pagan Pantheon. Thirty years ago I saw several performances of the old Pace-egg play at Kirkby, in Lancashire, where it had been annually performed for many years.*

The number of characters in the play varied from six to a dozen. They included St. George, Slasher, Prince of Paradine, Doctor, King of Egypt, Hector, Fool, Beelzebub, Devil-Doubt, and one rejoicing in the singular name of ' Toss-Pot.' The performance commenced with one of the characters drawing a circle with a wooden sword, and all that followed took place within that circle. After the various characters had been introduced in a song with a doggerel rhyme there was a fearsome combat between St. George and Slasher, in which the latter was wounded. The Doctor then revives Slasher and bids him fight again. This was the sum and substance of the play as I saw it.

At the Castle of Liverpool (erected early in the thirteenth century), during its occupancy by the Molyneux family, and at the Tower (built *circa* 1252), in Water Street, formerly belonging to the Lathoms of Lathom, afterwards to the Stanley and Derby families, theatrical entertainments to amuse the ' lord and his lady,' their retainers and neighbours, were, doubtless, given by players and others when passing through Liverpool on their way to Chester, and the southern towns. As late as 1734 James, the tenth Earl of Derby, entertained at the Tower. ' It is ascertained,' mentions J. G. Underhill in his unpublished MSS., in the archives of the Liverpool Free Library, ' that at a remote period, probably in the days of Queen Elizabeth, an apartment in the Castle was fitted up for the performance of

* An interesting account of the Pace-Egg Mummers will be found in J. Harland and T. T. Wilkinson's volume, ' Lancashire Legends,' p. 101.

plays for the amusement of my lord Constable and the officers of his retinue.   It is also most likely that out of courtesy the mayor and the principal inhabitants were occasionally invited to partake of these diversions, but it does not appear if this primitive hall of Thespis was open for all who chose to resort thither.'

That Liverpool in the middle ages favoured itinerant performers is shown by the bestowal of the name Juggler upon one of the then principal streets of the town.   With reference to the derivation of the name that erudite historian, Mr. W. Fergusson Irvine says : ' The only one the writer has ever heard of is that, as a large empty space lay on the west side of the street, it gained its name from the *jongleurs* who performed for the edification of mediæval Liverpool.'*   It is from the poet-musicians of the Normans, formerly comprehended in France under the general title of *jongleurs*, that we derive the word juggler.   Juggler Street was situated on the east side of the present Town Hall.   The street formed the junction between Castle and Tithebarn Streets, and was in a direct line with Old Hall Street.   Juggler Street is first mentioned in a deed dated August 18, in the sixteenth year of the reign of Henry VI.†

After the dissolution of the monasteries there came the dissolution of the four chantries in connection with Liverpool's first-known ecclesiastical building, St Mary's del Key, which was situated on the quay-side in close proximity to the Tower in Water Street.   In 1552 a list was made of the sacred vessels and vestments belonging to St. Mary's.   These chattels and properties were not then appraised, and they were, probably, left for disposal by the Corporation of Liverpool, who afterwards instituted an enquiry as to what had become of certain of the vestments, which, apparently, had been misappropriated. In connection with this one finds the following entry in the Corporation Records :—' John Rile alsoe beyng Scholem' in this Towne acknowledgyth hym to have in his custodie Mor twoe Coops the wheche he made in Apparrell for M'· Maior's Sonne Willi ͣ Cross & Thom's Burscough w ͭ ͪ others to playe theyr *paidances* in —more not.'   ' Paidances ' it is conjectured, mean ' plai-dances,' so that these copes once used in Catholic times for Divine Service were afterwards requisitioned for stage dresses for the acting of children's plays.*

The Corporation Records for the year 1571 contain the following entry : ' Item. We agree that no players of interludes, jugglers, gesters, or wandering people bryngyng into this towne any monstrouse or straunge beasts, or other visions voyde or vayne, to theyre lucre and distresse of the q^{ns} subjects without licence of Mr. Maior tyme beyng.'

It is stated in the Records that some unlucky itinerants described as ' the wanderers with the hobby horse,' were ordered to be put in the stocks at the High Cross.† Apparently they had given a performance ' without licence of Mr. Maior tyme beyng.'

In Queen Elizabeth's reign other itinerant performers met with a similar, or, perhaps, worse treatment. At that time ' Stage players, were declared to be Rogues and Vagabonds by the three Estates of England met in Parliament, and ordered to be sent to the House of Correction to be imprisoned, set on the Stocks, and whip'd, and if they continued to Play notwithstanding, that they should be *burnt with an Hot Iron of the breadth of an English Shilling with a great Roman R in the left shoulder which should there remain as a perpetual mark of a Rogue.* If they continued obstinate they were to be *Banished*, and if they return'd again, and continued incorrigible *they were to be executed as felons.*' The italics are mine. Yet to this and other Acts, both before and after, the law gave exceptions, as in the case of the companies of Royal players, and to those who were specially licensed to perform as servants of the several noblemen, such as the Earls of Leicester, Essex and others.

According to the Corporation Records for the year 1571 ' pleyes of dawnsyng ' were given in the ' comyn hall,' called ' (as) of old time Lady Hall '‡ in order to supplement

* The John Rile referred to was John Royle, who was appointed about 1592 master of the free grammar school of Liverpool. Money at that time was somewhat scarce, as, in addition to being the schoolmaster he was required to act also as the ' clerk and ringer of the curfew,' at the reduced stipend of £7 14s. 8d. The school, which was for ' poore chyldren y^t have no socour,' was afterwards held in the disused chapel of St. Mary's del Key. This chapel was in existence before 1257. Chapel Street, which has always been associated with St. Nicholas's, was really so called in connection with St. Mary's, long before St. Nicholas's was built.
† The High Cross was located near the site of the present Town Hall.
‡ Porte Mote, I, 14.

wedding and other festivities * The following is the entry
referred to : ' We fiynd necessarie for the upholdyng better and
long continewyng of oure comyn hall of this towne in good
order of reperacion of the same, that noe licence be or shall be
granntyd and gyvyn to make any weddyng diners or *pleyes of
dawnsyng* therein to the damagyng, decayng, or falling of the
floore of the same, and if it chaunce upon any urgent cause
or earnest request not deniable, any licence to be gyvyn
therein, that there by the same licence the partie or parties soe
obteyning licence shall pay to the comyn cooffer for everie such
licence fyve shilyngs usual money.'   And in the following
year this charge was made and received for four ' Brydalls '
In 1555 the charge made for a wedding dinner in the hall was
3s. 4d., and in 1558, 1s. 4d.

' Pleyes of dawnsyng ' were those primitive masques
which were frequently given in those days in connexion with
the marriages of the better classes. This is proven by the
fact that a masque was the only sort of ' play ' of dancing
that could be given on the floor of the hall. All other sorts of
plays required a raised platform.†

At court, even so late as 1630, all the dancing in the
masque took place on the floor of the hall. This is all the more
curious seeing that masques at that time had a regular stage
with movable scenery, and a proscenium front. All the
characters appeared first on the stage, and spoke there, but
they came down subsequently by fronting steps to dance on
the floor   The King and Queen were ranged at the other end
of the hall. But in 1571, and thereabouts, the masques had
not yet attained to the dignity of a stage, and everything was
done on the floor of the hall

Theatrical performances during the sixteenth century
seem to have been regularly given before the Derby family at
Knowsley and Lathom, but, notwithstanding the magnificence
of Edward, the third Earl of Derby, his household had no
company of players like other great nobles of his time.

In the diary‡ of William ffarington, comptroller of the
household to the third and fourth Earls of Derby§ one finds

* This was the second Town Hall, and like its predecessor, the religious hospice of
the Blessed Virgin Mary, was also situated on the east side of Juggler Street, afterwards High Street
† A picture of a wedding masque can be seen in the National Portrait Gallery, the
festivities being in celebration of the marriage of Sir Henry Unton, who died in 1596.
‡ Chetham Society's publications, vol 31
§ Margaret, wife of Henry, the fourth Earl of Derby, was the patroness of two distinguished writers of the time—Thomas Lupton and Robert Greene.

the following entries relating to theatrical performances at Knowsley :—

September, 1589—'Queen's players came, and played at nyghte, my L? of Essex's came.'

September, 1589—' Sondaie, Mr. Leigh preached and the Queen's Players played in the afternoone, and my L. of Essex's at nyghte.'

February and June, 1590—' Players again at New Park and Knowsley.'

Although ffarington does not mention that the Earl of Leicester's company played at Knowsley, it is very probable that they did, as the diarist states that they twice performed at Lathom House, Lathom, near Ormskirk, in July, 1587. It is well known that Shakespeare was a member of the Earl of Leicester's company, and it is, therefore, not impossible that he, together with the Burbages and other players of the period, visited, and performed in Liverpool. Charles Knight in the second edition of his ' Shakespeare '* gave it as his opinion that the poet must have seen ' The Nine Worthies '† a pageant peculiar to Chester. To reach Chester from this part of Lancashire, Shakespeare would probably pass through Liverpool as being the nearest point for departure.

The mention of Shakespeare reminds me that many good people relying upon internal evidence and alleged ciphers, cling tenaciously to the idea that Sir Francis Bacon wrote our poet's plays. Bacon, it is interesting to note, represented Liverpool in Parliament from 1588 to 1592.

Shakespeare's connexion with the house of Stanley is shown by an epitaph on the monument erected to the memory of Sir Thomas Stanley, Knight, second son of Edward, third Earl of Derby, in Tong Church, Salop, and attributed to the English Sophocles on the authority of Sir William Dugdale. Sir Thomas Stanley died December 21, 1576. The inscription referred to is on the east end of the monument, and is as follows :

'No monumental stone preserves our fame
Nor skye-aspiring pyramids our name.
The memory of him for whom this stands,
Shall outlyve marble, and defacer's hands,
When all to time's consumption shall be geaven,
Standley, for whom this stands, shall stand in heaven.'

* Vol. I, p. 317.   † Love's Labour's Lost, Act V, Sc. 2.

On the west side of the monument :—

> 'Ask who lyes here, but do not weep ;
> He is not dead, he dooth but sleepe.
> This stony register is for his bones,
> His fame is more perpetuall than theise stones ;
> And his own goodness, with himself being gon,
> Shall lyve when earthlie monument is none.'

The beginning of the first line, ' Ask who lyes here,' is reminiscent of that on Combe—' If any man ask who lies in this tomb.' That the writer knew his 'Shakespeare' is shown by a similar sentiment which the Bard of Avon has introduced into *Henry VIII* :—

> ' Ever belov'd, and loving may his rule be !
> And when old time shall lead him to his grave,
> Goodness and he fill up one monument '

However, Eyton, the great Shropshire antiquary, doubts if the last six lines were from the pen of Shakespeare He considers that they were the work of an inferior poet.' The monument to Sir Thomas Stanley was not erected until long after his death.   It is also a monument to his son, Sir Edward Stanley, who died about 1632, in which year the monument was probably erected, for it speaks of his daughters, Frances and Venetia, as ' yet living,' and the latter died in 1633.

It is well known, that Ferdinando, Lord Strange, took great interest in the drama and lent his patronage and his name to a troop of actors.   When he became fifth Earl of Derby, he still kept up his company of players, and allowed them to ply their calling in other counties besides Lancashire

In 1579 Lord Strange's players performed in Shakespeare's own town of Stratford-on-Avon, as the following account shows : ' Item paid to my Lord Strange men the xi[th] day of February at the comaundement of Mr. Bayliffe . . . v[s].' This sum was paid out of the funds of the Corporation of Stratford for theatrical performances.   Lord Strange's men were a little better paid than ' my Lord of Worcester's players ' at Stratford in 1577, as they only received three shillings and fourpence.

In 1579 the gratuity bestowed at Stratford-on-Avon upon
' the Countys of Essex's players ' was fourteen shillings and
sixpence, but in the following year ' The Earle of Darbyes*
players' only obtained eight shillings and fourpence.   In
1569, when John Shakespeare (our poet's father), was chief
magistrate of Stratford a payment of nine shillings was made
to the Queen's players, and of twelve pence to the Earl of
Worcester's Players.   In 1573 the Earl of Leicester's players
received six shillings and eightpence, and the following year
(1574) Lord Warwick's company received as much as seventeen
shillings. † It must, of course, be remembered that money then
had at least five or six times its present purchasing power.

About 1590 the players who performed under the patronage of Ferdinando, Lord Strange, appeared in a play, entitled
*Fair Em, the Miller's Daughter of Manchester: With the Love
of William the Conqueror.* The author of this ' pleasant comedie '
is unknown, but it has been attributed to Shakespeare.   In
Act III, Sc. 4, of the play, Mountney, one of the characters,
says : ' Since fortune hath thus spitefully crost our hope, let
vs leaue this quest and harken after our King, who is at this
daie landed at *Lirpoole*.'   This, it is interesting to note, is the
earliest reference in an English dramatic work to Liverpool.   It
is also worthy of note that Shakespeare was a member
of Lord Strange's company.   This is shown by an account of
the year 1593, belonging to the Treasurer of the Chamber, in
which our poet's name appears after that of Kempe, and before
that of Burbage.

Robert Greene, the dramatist, dedicated to Ferdinando,
Earl of Derby, his poem *Ciceronis Amor. Tullies Loue.*   To
this nobleman and his Countess, Spenser, Nash, Harrington,
Davies, Marston, and at a later period Milton, all recorded
their attachment and respect.

Ferdinando died in 1594—a victim, it was believed, to
the potent powers of witchcraft, but he was more probably
poisoned.   He was succeeded by his brother, William, the
sixth Earl of Derby,‡ who was not only a patron of the drama,
but also a writer of plays.   To the latter one finds a very interesting reference in a letter from George Fenner to his

* Henry, fourth Earl of Derby.
† Accounts of the Chamberlain of Stratford-on-Avon.
‡ Elizabeth, wife of Earl William, performed in Marston's entertainment at Ashby-de-
la-Zouche in 1607 : and in Ben Jonson's masques of *Blackness* (1605), *Beauty* (1608),
Queens (1609), and in *Tethys Festival* (1610).

partner, Balthazar Gybels, at Antwerp, under date June 30, 1599. It is as follows :—' Our Earl of Darby is busye in penning commodyes for the commoun players.'*

Earl William has been claimed by James Greenstreet in ' The Genealogist 't as the author of Shakespeare's most important plays. Of the truth of this statement Mr. Greenstreet felt fully convinced after painstaking research among the State Papers.

Bidston Hall, Cheshire, was built by Earl William soon after he succeeded to the estates. Subsequently he made over the most of his property to his son, Lord Strange, and passed the summer months at Bidston Hall, and the winter at Chester, until his death in 1642.

In 1630, Lord Strange, performed in Ben Jonson's masque of *Love's Triumph Through Calipolis*, and in the same year Charlotte de la Trémoille, Lady Strange, was one of the fourteen nymphs in the masque of *Chloridia* by Ben Jonson. After he had become the seventh Earl of Derby this member of the family played a prominent part in the Civil War, and closed his noble career on the scaffold at Bolton. The name of his Countess is familiar to most of us as the brave defender of Lathom House.

Prince Rupert, who engineered the siege of Liverpool in 1644, had, it is interesting to note, several players in his army. Three of them were Burt, Shatterel, and handsome and dignified Charles Hart. The latter was to become the first lover of ' pretty, witty ' Nell Gwyn. This was before Mistress Gwyn became the favourite of Charles II. Hart, who was Shakespeare's grand-nephew, had been the apprentice, or ' boy,' of one Robinson—an actor contemporary with Shakespeare—who met his death at the taking of Basinghouse in 1645.

A theatre is mentioned by Troughton ‡ as existing in Liverpool as early as the seventeenth century. He says :—' During the reign of Charles the First, a small building for the exhibition of dramatic entertainments stood in a court at the bottom of St. James Street; but at the time of the Civil War it was shut up, and continued unoccupied until the Res-

* State Papers, Domestic Series, Elizabeth, Vol. 271, No. 34.
† *Vide* 'A Hitherto Unknown Noble Writer of Elizabethan Comedies' (Vol. VII, Part 4); ' Further Notices of William Stanley, sixth Earl of Derby, K.G., as a Poet and Dramatist' (Vol. VIII, Part 1); ' Testimonies against the Accepted Authorship of Shakespeare's Plays ' (Vol. VIII, Part 3).
‡ ' History of Liverpool,' p. 98.

toration.' Sir James Picton* denies Troughton's assertion, simply because no such named street existed in the reign of Charles I. It is quite true that James Street and St. James Street were not in existence in the time of Charles I, in fact, they were not made until some considerable period later.

Now Troughton's ' Liverpool ' is dated 1810, and at that time James Street had been some years in existence. Therefore, when he referred to a theatre which ' stood in a court at the bottom of *St.* James Street,' I think he intended to convey the idea that it was located near the bottom of what is now known as James Street. That Troughton meant James Street, and *not* St. James Street, is shown in his reference to the great storm of 1768, when he states that the cellars of the houses in Water Street, Moor Street, *and St.* James Street were flooded, all these streets being in close proximity to one another.

Stonehouse in his ' Streets of Liverpool '† says that ' in or about the time of Charles the First there was an uncovered theatre of some sort, at the bottom of Redcross Street. It stood on the site of part of the Carron Iron Warehouse in James Street.' As a matter of fact the Carron Company never had an establishment in James Street.

Stonehouse in an article on the ' Dramatic places of Amusement in Liverpool a Century ago'‡ further elaborated Troughton's original statement by maintaining that ' The first theatre, or building devoted exclusively to dramatic performances, of which there is any positive mention made, was erected about 1641 (*temp.* Charles I), on the ground now (1852-3) occupied by a portion of the Coalbrookdale Company's premises, at the back. It stood between the present James Street and Redcross Street, or Tarleton's New Street, as it was formerly called. This building, of which, however, we have but very imperfect notice, was constructed of frail materials, and was only used by strolling companies, who came to Liverpool from the north on their road to Chester and other places. The interior of this theatre would present to view the same aspect as do all the prints of the Globe (?) on the Bankside, where we find the most distinguished of the audience seated in a sort of boxes at the

* 'Memorials,' Second edition, Vol. II, p. 90.
† Third edition, p. 58.
‡ Transactions of the Lancashire and Cheshire Historic Society, Vol. V, p. 192.

side, or on chairs on the stage, while the pit is unboarded, and
the audience there are standing on the bare ground.'*

The hypothetical Liverpool theatre dealt with by Stonehouse is also referred to in the Annals in 'Gore's Directory'
as being in existence in 1640. All these uncorroborated
statements have been based on the few lines written by
Troughton. Apart from the fact that neither Troughton
nor Stonehouse gives any authority for his statements I am
of opinion that there was no structure in Liverpool *exclusively*
set apart for the exhibition of dramatic entertainments at
the period dealt with.

About the middle of the seventeenth century the three
streets of the town towards the river side, Moor Street, Water
Street, and Chapel Street, were but scantily covered with buildings Redcross Street was not opened until about 1674, and
James Street not for some years later. Troughton's statement
gives one the impression that there were a goodly number of
buildings in and about James Street That the theatre, if it
ever existed, should have been in a court when there was
plenty of vacant ground thereabouts is not very conceivable.
Besides, at that time there was no need for the establishment
in the town of a permanent Temple of Thespis, as Troughton
presumed it to have been Visiting players were glad enough
to perform anywhere. All they wanted was a remunerative
audience. That the town possessed an early, but primitive
theatre, I shall endeavour to prove. But like the first theatre
in Drury Lane, London,† its primary institution was not due
to a love for the drama, but to a taste for the ancient sport of
cockfighting.

THE COCKPIT YARD THEATRE.

In 1567, it was ordered by the local authorities that ' For
further and greater repair of gentlemen and others to this
town we find it needful that there be a handsome cockfight-
pit made.' ‡

* Stonehouse must have drawn upon his imagination for some of his facts No authentic
view of the interior of the Globe is known of by the most expert stage historians.
† This theatre was called the Cockpit When it was first used as a playhouse is not
known. It was a private, and, therefore, an aristocratic theatre. On Shrove Tuesday,
1616-17, the London apprentices sacked and set fire to the house. It was afterwards rebuilt, and named the Phœnix.
‡ Corporation Records.

The cockpit referred to is identical with the one which was located in Cockpit Yard, between Moor Street and the Old Ropery.* Cockpit Yard, I may mention, was a thoroughfare between the end of Drury Lane and Moor Street,† afterwards built up.

Sir James Picton observes in his 'Memorials'‡ that ' on taking down some old buildings at the top of Shaw's Brow, in 1868, the remains of a cockpit, having a sunk area, with tiers of benches round, cut in the rock, were laid bare. This may probably have been the relics of the one in question.' As a matter of fact, the cockpit ordered to be made in 1567 was for the ' further and greater repair of gentlemen and others to this *town*.' The town at that time, and for many years afterwards, did not extend eastward as far as Shaw's Brow. That the town was only of small extent in 1567 is proven by the following entry in the Corporation Records :—' The Cattle Market to be held at the Castle, and *not in the town*.'

When the cockpit in Cockpit Yard was first used for dramatic entertainments I am unable to say. It may have been so employed as early as the sixteenth century, certainly not later than the seventeenth. Mains continued to be fought as a relief to Thalia and Melpomene until a late period.

According to that mine of information, the unpublished MSS. of John Holt and Matthew Gregson,§ the Cockpit Yard playhouse *was the first humble building in which were exhibited theatrical entertainments.* The italics are mine. It is significant that these authorities make no mention of the theatre referred to by Troughton and others as being in a court at the bottom of James Street in the reign of Charles I.

The size of the Cockpit Yard Theatre was 50 feet by 20 feet. It had a gallery, while further accommodation, as in other early English theatres, was provided by benches placed

* ' This Cockpit ' says John G. Underhill in his unpublished MSS. in the Liverpool Free Library, ' was in Moor Street. After it fell into disuse, a more commodious place was provided in Cockspur Street, Vauxhall Road.'
† ' In this street,' mentions W. G. Herdman in his ' Pictorial Relics of Ancient Liverpool,' ' dramatic entertainments were exhibited soon after the reign of the first Charles.' Herdman infers that performances took place in a large mansion in Moor Street. Dramatic entertainments may have been given in the house referred to by Herdman, but there is no evidence to show that it was ever used as a regular theatre.
‡ Second edition, Vol. I, p. 56.
§ The MSS. are now in the Liverpool Free Library. John Holt, who was schoolmaster of Walton, was born in 1743 and died in 1801. He bequeathed his collections for a local history to Matthew Gregson, who died in 1824, aged 75.

on either side of the stage The walls of the auditorium were whitewashed, and candles were the only illuminants used.

It may have been the Cockpit Yard Theatre that Nicholas Blundell, the Squire of Crosby Hall, visited on May 13, 1706 In his diary* he does not state where the theatre was situated, but simply records his visit in the following manner . ' My wife and I went to Leverp : and saw Acted *The Earl of Essex*. We came home about two of yᶜ clock in yᵉ morning.' On July 29, 1708, he ' saw yᵉ *Souldier's Fortune* Acted in Ri: Harris: Barn,' (Crosby)† On August 13, 1708, ' the actors of *The Souldier's Fortune* came hither (Crosby) and sung the Gigg.' On May 27, 1709 : ' *The She Gallats* was Acted imperfectly in ye Hall' (Crosby). In Liverpool, on June 15, 1710, he witnessed *Sephonisba ; or Haniball's Overthrow*. The entry for February 25, 1712, states that ' *The Souldier's Fortune* was Acted at Mrs. Ann Rotherwell's in this Town (Crosby). My wife went with me both to ye Play and Gigg. The actors of ye Play were Thos. Farer (Sir Davyd Dunce), Wᵐ Marrow (Captain Bewgard), Watty Thelw : (Sir Jolly Jumble) &c.' On April 21, 1712, ' My wife and I saw part of ye Play called ye *Schoole of Compliments*‡ Acted at He : Bushell's by a Company as came from towards Scarisb(rick).' Here we have direct evidence that Lancashire in the early eighteenth century was occasionally visited by itinerant players.

June 23, 1712.—' I went to Leverp : and saw Acted in ye Castle the Play called ye *Yeoman of Kent*.'§ This performance doubtless took place in that portion of the Castle which was used as an assembly room. This is the first time the diarist records the place where he saw a play acted in Liverpool. He also records that on October 12, 1714, ' One from Leverp : brought a Ticket for my Wife of the Play as is to be acted there to-morrow.' To bring a ticket for the Squire's wife was perhaps an ingenious ruse on the part of the players to secure the patronage and presence of the Squire himself at their performance. On the following day (October 13), he writes : . . .

* ' Blundell's Diary,' edited by the Rev. T Ellison Gibson, Liverpool, 1895.
† *The Soldier's Fortune* was a comedy by Thomas Otway (1681)
‡ *The School of Compliments* was a comedy by James Shirley (1658). Its original title was *Love Tricks ; or the School of Compliments*. For details of the plot see Genest's ' Some Account of the English Stage,' Vol IX, p. 545.
§ P. 103.

' Then went to ye New Market where we saw a Play Acted called *Mackbeth.*'[*] The New Market was formerly the Old Castle of Liverpool, then altered for the purpose of a market.

The Cockpit Yard Theatre was, probably, the old crazy warehouse, referred to by Charles Lee Lewes in his 'Memoirs.'[†] Lewes also mentions that a company under the leadership of John Heron, of intriguing memory, performed in Liverpool. He further tells us that ' the company's success was great, exceeding the receipts of any former season.   During a run of *The Tempest* for five nights, they seldom took less than twenty pounds ; and at the benefit of Tottenham Wright, a favourite actor, the receipts amounted to twenty-seven pounds fourteen shillings and sixpence.   I am afraid my readers will imagine I cannot be serious in this relation, but there are several now living who will subscribe to the truth of it.   But lest I should be suspected of advancing anything which might induce the present generation to form any idea of a sordid disposition in the wealthy inhabitants of that hospitable town (Liverpool), I declare it as my opinion, that neither lack of spirit or taste was the cause of such scanty receipts at their theatre in those days.   On the contrary it was an eminent proof of their true taste and discernment, by their soon after giving great encouragement to Mr. Gibson,[‡] who brought a regular company to their town.'

The Cockpit Yard playhouse remained standing for a number of years, and was used as a theatre even after a more commodious one was opened in the Old Ropery.   Afterwards it was used as a cowhouse by one Lees. ' The beam which supported the gallery,' says the Holt and Gregson MSS., ' is yet to be seen, also a door through which it is probable the spectators ascended out of the street into the gallery.   There is also some remaining whitewash in small parts on the walls.' Apparently the building was in existence as late as the commencement of the nineteenth century, as it is referred to by Troughton as being still ' frequently used for a cockpit.'[§] At a later date Gregson in his MS. additions to Enfield's 'History of Liverpool' states that the Cockpit Yard Theatre

* P. 129.
† ' Memoirs of Charles Lee Lewes ' (1805), Vol. I, p. 43.
‡ William Gibson.
§ Troughton's ' Liverpool ' (1810), p. 98.

' behind a house in Moor Street,* where Mr. Hesketh lived, and leading into Drury Lane, has now been pulled down, and a corn warehouse built upon the site.'

THE BLACKBERRY LANE THEATRE.

This early playhouse, according to the Holt and Gregson MSS., was more generally known by the name of Hugh Davies's Cockpit, which, in a word, suggests its origin. The theatre was situated on the left-hand side of Blackberry Lane, coming from Dale Street. Blackberry Lane was afterwards called William Street, and is now known as Eberle Street.

' Mr. Houlston '† says the Holt and Gregson MSS., ' remembered that a company of players performed here in *The Tempest* for thirty nights without intermission, that the machinery was good, and that the performances gave great and general satisfaction.'

Sir James Picton in his ' Memorials '‡ refers to an Irish company of players, who, in 1745, performed in this theatre. Picton, I think, obtained his information from the Holt and Gregson MSS. In the MSS., no exact date is given (except the vague one of ' fifty years ago '). Holt and Gregson first say that the Irish players appeared at the Blackberry Lane Theatre, but this statement is corrected later on and the actual place of performance shown to be the Old Ropery Theatre. The players referred to were those that came over from Dublin for Preston Guild. The only date at all applicable for their appearance in Liverpool is 1742, which was a Guild year—not 1745, as Picton has it.

Beyond the fact that the theatre was afterwards converted into a warehouse, I have never been able to discover any further particulars, and am, therefore, unable to state when the playhouse terminated its career.

THE OLD ROPERY THEATRE.

This structure, which consisted of two large rooms, was built by Alderman Thomas Steers, the constructor of the Old

* Curiously enough the majority of the Liverpool historians erroneously state that the theatre was *in* Moor Street.
† Probably Dr. Houlston, author of a treatise entitled ' Liverpool Spa Water ' (1773), and other works.
‡ Second edition, Vol. II., p. 91.

Dock. The theatre was situated on the ground floor, and the rent of the room was about £25 yearly. The room above the theatre was used by a Mr. Carson as a dancing academy. The theatre itself was also used as a dancing-room, and as an assembly room, where wire dancers occasionally exhibited, and finally, as a Roman Catholic chapel.*

When the theatre was first opened I cannot say with certainty, but am inclined to think its genesis dates from *circa* 1740. That this surmise is not mere guesswork is shown by a letter, one of a series, written by an intelligent Londoner, in 1741, to several friends, and published anonymously in Dublin in 1746. The title page of the little work in question records that it is :—'A Tour Through Ireland in several Entertaining Letters Wherein The present State of that Kingdom is considered; and the most noted Cities, Towns, Seats, Rivers, Buildings, etc., are described. Part I. Humbly Inscribed to the Physier-Historical Society. Dublin : Printed for Peter Wilson, at Guy's Head, opposite the Spring Garden, in Dame Street. MDCCXLVI.'†

The extract referred to is as follows :—' They (the Liverpolitans), have their Musick-Meetings, Assemblies, etc., and a neat theatre that maintains a set of comedians for four months in the year very well.'

How the foregoing particulars came to be written was owing to the writer having to wait at Parkgate for a favourable wind to take him to Ireland. It appears he had exhausted all the sights of Chester, and then bethought himself of Liverpool, of which he gives‡ the following pen-picture :—

' The obstinacy of the wind made time hang heavy on our hands, therefore we resolved to take a cursory view of Liverpool. We set out at Four o'clock in the morning, and got over the Ferry at six ; though it was so early we found every shop open, and almost as busy as the Exchange in London at noon. The first Person we saw . . . was Mr. F. . . . and while Dinner was preparing shewed us the most remarkable Places in this opulent Town, and which I am of opinion few of our Cities, after the Metropolis, can exceed in size. It is not orbicular, as Chester is, but, I am sure, more extensive in its irregularity of Buildings. It is divided into two parts, the one called the Old, and the other the New. The last has many well-built

* Holt and Gregson MSS.
† Probably an earlier edition of the work was published in London.
‡ P. 33.

C

Structures. The Quay is also very spacious, and has a Face
of Business that seems surprizing. There was a Man-of-War
on the Stocks, almost finished, that is to mount fifty guns, to
which this town, they say, is to stand Godmother and give
her its own Name . . . We were informed their Malt Liquor is
chiefly brewed with Salt Water, which to us seemed strange,
yet I could not distinguish it by the taste.'

The warship referred to was christened the ' Liverpool.'
According to the Admiralty Records she was a vessel of 40 guns,
and was built here by Mr. Okill. Building operations were
commenced on June 2, 1740, and the launch took place on
July 19, 1741.

At the end of August, 1742, an excellent company of
players arrived in Liverpool from Dublin on their way to
perform at Preston Guild. ' Faulkner's Dublin Journal,' for
August 24, 1742, says :—' Yesterday Messrs. Delane, Garrick,
and Arne, and Mrs. Cibber embarked for England ; and the
Company of Comedians belonging to Smock Alley Theatre will
sail for Liverpool this day in order to entertain the nobility
and gentry at Preston at the Jubilee, which is said to be held
there once in 20 years.'*

Peg Woffington had just been acting in Dublin with Garrick.   At the end of the Dublin summer season, she had to
return to London to open in the autumn at Covent Garden.
Why then did she not go back with Garrick, seeing that Davy
and she were then lovers ?   The inference would be that she
had been persuaded by the Smock Alley Company to accompany them to Preston Guild, from whence she could easily
repair to London.   If she had not made this arrangement I
see no reason why she should not have returned with Garrick.

The Smock Alley Company were detained by contrary
winds on their passage over, consequently they arrived in
Liverpool too late for the Preston Guild festivities, which commenced that year on August 30, and lasted a fortnight.   The
finances of the Smock Alley Players being exhausted on their
arrival in Liverpool, they obtained permission from the Mayor
of Liverpool to perform in the Old Ropery Theatre, and to
solicit the gentry in the town to patronise their performances.

* Garrick sailed from Dublin on August 23, 1742, on board ' The Lovely Jane,' for Parkgate ; so he, Delane, and the rest did not intend to go to Preston. Probably the engagement
only extended to the ordinary stock company of the Smock Alley Theatre.

Success so attended their efforts that they were induced to come here the following year.*

Apropos of charming Peg Woffington's appearance with the Smock Alley Company at the Old Ropery Theatre in 1742, the Holt and Gregson MSS. mention that ' Mrs. Williamson (mother of Captain Ralph Williamson), the reigning Queen of the Assembly,† bespoke the play of *The Fop's Fortune.*' In this play Peg Woffington had acted the part of Angelina at the Smock Alley Theatre, during the season of 1742.‡

The Smock Alley Company in 1742 included Messrs. Elrington, Giffard (formerly of Goodman's Fields), Wetherilt, Henry Delamain (a dancer), Tom Walker (the original Captain Macheath), Mrs. Furnival, a brilliant actress, and Mrs. Chetwood, wife of William Rufus Chetwood, the famous prompter. This is only a selection ; there were, of course, several others. The company re-opened in Dublin on November 8, so their stay in Liverpool must have been limited to only a few weeks.

I cannot say if the Smock Alley Company came after 1743. They may have done so, but I cannot find any account of their having appeared again in Liverpool. I have, however, long been of opinion that in the early period of the Liverpool stage there was some connection between it and the Dublin stage. Curiously enough, Liverpool had a Smock Alley. It was a court off Chorley Street.§

The absence of play-bills and newspapers of the period unfortunately prevents us from knowing the names of the players who appeared in the Old Ropery Theatre. Hitchcock however, in his ' Historical View of the Irish Stage,' states that during the summer of 1759 the majority of the players of the Crow Street Theatre, Dublin, crossed over to England in a body and visited Chester, Manchester, Liverpool, etc. The period would be between the end of June and the beginning of October, the usual Dublin recess at that time. Among the itinerants Hitchcock only makes mention of Mr. and Mrs. Dancer,

---

* Holt and Gregson MSS.

† The Queen of the Assembly held her court in the Town Hall, then known as the Exchange. Derrick, in a letter dated August 2, 1760, to his patron, the Earl of Cork, says : ' The Assembly Room, which is also upstairs, is grand, spacious, and finely illuminated : here is a meeting once a fortnight to dance and play cards ; where you will find some women elegantly accomplished, and perfectly well dressed. The proceedings are regulated by a lady styled the Queen, and she rules with absolute power.'

‡ Genest's ' Some Account of the English Stage ' Vol. X, p. 317.

§ The Improvement Act of 1786 gave power to do away with Smock Alley, mentioning it by name. This, and other courts, between Castle and Chorley Streets were swept away when Brunswick Street was made.

Mr. and Mrs. Jefferson, Mr. and Mrs. Kennedy, Isaac Sparks, and Mr. Carmichael. Mrs. Dancer was afterwards Mrs. Spranger Barry, and finally Mrs. Crawford. The Jeffersons were, I believe, ancestors of the celebrated Joe, of Rip Van Winkle fame. Isaac Sparks was an excellent low comedian of the W. J. Hill and Harry Monkhouse build.

Hitchcock does not mention where the Crow Street players performed in Liverpool. It is quite possible that they played in the Old Ropery Theatre, inasmuch as the principal theatre in the town, the one in Drury Lane, would at that time be occupied by other players. The Crow Street itinerants could of course, have performed in the Cockpit Yard Theatre, or in the one in Blackberry Lane, but I think it rather unlikely that they did. The Old Ropery Theatre was subsequently made into a warehouse.

THE DRURY LANE THEATRE.

Drury Lane was so called in emulation of the metropolitan Temple of Thalia and Melpomene of that name, and for a similar reason the style and title of Covent Garden was bestowed upon an adjacent thoroughfare. The first Drury Lane Theatre in Liverpool was opened in 1749 or 1750.* It was situated on the east side of a new thoroughfare called Drury Lane, between the Old Ropery and what is now known as Brunswick Street, and was a plain brick building about 27 yards long and 16 yards broad.

The house had a pit and gallery, but no boxes. Admission to the pit could be obtained on payment of two shillings, and to the gallery for one shilling. The gallery extended some distance over the pit, and was the best place for witnessing the performance. Over the proscenium there was painted *Totus Mundus Agit Histrionem.*

As in the Cockpit Yard playhouse there were seats on either side of the stage for the accommodation of the more privileged spectators. The stage and auditorium were lighted by candles fixed in circular wooden frames, suspended from the ceiling and snuffed between the acts. When Garrick went to France and

* Holt and Gregson MSS.

Italy he found the stages there lighted by oil lamps stationed behind the wings. On his return to London he introduced this hidden mode of lighting into the metropolitan theatres. Candles, however, continued to be used at the local Drury Lane Theatre until the opening of the Theatre Royal by Letters Patent, in Williamson Square.

The players had no dressing-room accommodation at the local Drury Lane Theatre, and they had to attire themselves as best they could. Needless to say there was no Green Room ; in fact they had no other place of resort than a bench behind the scenes.*

According to the metropolitan custom of the time, two soldiers taken from a regiment stationed in the town were hired at one shilling each per night, to stand on either side of the stage to keep order. They took up their positions immediately before the performance, and with hands resting on their firelocks stood like statues until the final fall of the old green curtain.

Sir James Picton erroneously states in his ' Memorials 't that the theatre had boxes from the very outset, and that it was opened with the comedy of *The Conscious Lovers*, and the farce of *The Lying Valet*. It is also important to note that the majority of our local historians and annalists are inaccurate with regard to the date of the initial performance.

' In June, 1759, the Drury Lane Theatre was opened with the tragedy of *The Orphan*, but it is certain that about the middle of the last century, and several years before 1759, a theatre, or a building used as a theatre, existed somewhere in Liverpool.'—Brooke's ' Liverpool,' p. 81.

' In the beginning of June, 1759, the new theatre was opened in Drury Lane.'—Troughton's ' Liverpool,' p. 141.

' The theatre, Drury Lane, opened with the tragedy of *The Orphan*, 1759.'—' Gore's Directory Annals.'

' In 1759, a new theatre, erected in Drury Lane, was opened on the 8th of June, with the tragedy of *The Orphan*.'—Smithers' ' Liverpool,' p. 323.

' This theatre was opened in 1759.'—Stonehouse's ' Streets of Liverpool,' third edition, p. 57.

Clear proof of the existence of the house prior to 1759 is afforded by ' Williamson's Liverpool Memorandum Book,'

* Holt and Gregson MSS.   † Second edition, vol. II, p. 91.

for 1753, in which it is definitely referred to as the ' Playhouse in Drury Lane.'

Liverpool was for many years a popular seaside resort, and to the ' good old town ' numerous well-to-do families came for the bathing season. The floating population in the dog days was, therefore, greatly augmented. This fact was known to the players generally, and the Theatres Royal in London, being closed during the summer months, the players used to journey here to turn an honest penny in their off season.

The joint managers of the theatre for some years were Messrs. Gibson and Ridout, both members of the London Covent Garden Theatre company. I am unable to say when Gibson first became associated with local theatricals. Lee Lewes, who knew him personally, says that Gibson 'was bred a Quaker, and brought up in the most rigid discipline of that sect till the pomps and vanities of this world drew him off from the precise rules by which he had been hitherto used to square his life. The many hotbeds which are to be found in Covent Garden, and the purlieus thereof, soon ripened in him the seeds of degeneracy, and, as he became a constant visitor to both the theatres, the spirit gave way to the flesh, and soon rendered him a proselyte to the doctrines of Otway, Dryden, etc. The simplicity of his original discipline was not so wholly erased, but that the Quaker was still legible, and rendered him a ludicrous mixture of gravity and stage buffoonery. He had been for some time weaning himself from the peculiarities of the speech and garb of the Quaker, and with facility both dressed and spoke like a man of the world. The stage, with all its fascinating charms, was looked forward to by young Gibson, but with the same impediment which hindered Farren* from an engagement at Liverpool, lay in the way of Gibson in London. But getting acquainted with Messrs. Bridgewater and Hippisley at a tavern in the Garden, and the houses being near their closing for the season, they were far from discouraging our new made Christian, they rather commended his spirit, and the droll Hippisley, being upon the eve of opening his theatre at Bristol, he offered him a situation in his *corps*, with a promise of instruction and protection, while he should remain with him. The old gentleman kept his

* George Farren, father of Elizabeth Farren, afterwards Countess of Derby.

word ; and when he was recalled to his town engagement, he
gave the young man a letter of recommendation to Mr. Dennis
Herbert, with whom he remained a considerable time.   His
figure was a good one, and he was blessed with a prepossessing
countenance, which gained him much applause, especially in
the soft-sighing lovers.   Particular circumstances induced
him to apply for a London engagement, which he without
difficulty obtained from Mr. Rich, where he remained for a
long course of years, performing a respectable line of business
    . . . he was a man universally respected, and remarkable for
his probity and philanthropy.'* In a foot-note, Lewes jus-
tifies his employment of the epithet, ' new made Christian,'
by pointing out that Gibson had never been baptised until he
was received into the Church of England at an age bordering
on thirty.

Genest† states that Gibson made ' his first appearance in
a public theatre ' at Covent Garden, on September 17, 1739,
when he played Bellmour in *The Old Batchelor*. This, I think,
is an error, as Gibson must have served some apprenticeship
to the stage before he trod the boards of Covent Garden
Theatre. The reference is, I think, to Gibson's *first* appearance
in a London theatre. Gibson was a member of the Covent
Garden Company for many years. When Peg Woffington
made, under tragic. circumstances, her last appearance on
the stage on May 3, 1757, at Covent Garden, in *As You
Like It*, Gibson was in the cast as Adam. Hugh Kelly in
his ' Thespis ; or, A Critical Examination into the minds of
all principal performers at Covent Garden Theatre ‡ ' gives
us some information as to Gibson's merits as a player :—

> ' Were sterling sense, or excellence of heart,
> For fame's bright goal in Thespis bound to start ;
> Say, above Gibson who could think to rise.
> Or urge a nobler title to the prize ?
> But fate, perhaps, when Gibson first possest
> The strong conception, and the feeling breast,
> Suppos'd a voice was quite below his care,
> Or never once design'd him for a play'r—
> Yet though in parts of energy and fire,
> She ne'er permits him boldly to aspire ;

* ' Memoirs of Charles Lee Lewes,' (1805), Vol. II.
† *Vide op. cit.*, Vol. III, p. 617.   ‡ Book II.

And tho' that note's harsh, dissonance of jar
With quick-soul'd sense holds ever-living war;
Still there are times, when self-created farce
Subdues even Nature in her stern-ey'd course ;
And Gibson's mind too nervous for her laws,
Appeals to truth, and rises with applause—
Behold in Prim, what pleasantry we trace
Thro' all that sober, sanctified grimace ;
Where rebel flesh, with countenance demure,
Serenely hot and holily impure,
Betrays a sly concubinary flame,
And steals poor spirit into actual shame—
In *Old Rents* too, when Hearty, kindly wrong,
Thinks gath'ring grief must vanish at a song,
Then Gibson's face so tristfully is hung,
And holds such hum'rous combat with his tongue,
That ceaseless mirth will laugh herself to tears,
And quite fright the grating in her ears.'

The following curious anecdote of Gibson is recorded in
'The Monthly Pantheon,' for January, 1809. It is without date,
but it doubtless refers to his connexion with Covent Garden
Theatre. It begins by saying that Gibson was an extremely
inoffensive man, although remarkably intrepid when aroused.
Once the Hon. Mr. Fitzgerald, brother to a noble lord, hissed
him without reason, but on coming behind the scenes afterwards, apologised for his conduct by saying he had taken too
much drink. He subsequently repeated the offence, and was
well thrashed by Gibson for his impertinence.

David Erskine Baker in his ' Biographia Dramatica ' (1782),
speaking of Lacy Ryan, the Covent Garden actor, says :—
' Indeed all Mr. Ryan's connexions were such as served to show
how far he preferred the society of worthy men to that of more
fashionable characters. He is known to have been a great
walker ; and when he meditated a sally of unusual length, as
often as he could he would prevail on the late Mr. Gibson, of
Covent Garden Theatre, to be his companion. But much exercise not exactly suiting the disposition and rotundity of this
gentleman (who chose a book and his ease before a stock of
health purchased at the rate of such unmerciful agitation), he
was rarely to be tempted further than the outskirts of London.

Were it our task to describe Mr. Gibson as an actor, justice would compel us to allow that his mode of utterance (an habitual defect) threw every line he pronounced " into strong shudders and immortal agues." Yet we should likewise add, that he was never absurd or ridiculous in his deportment, unless when driven by the tasteless obstinacy of Mr. Rich into parts from which no man however skilful, could escape with reputation. On this account his performance of Aper in the tragedy of *Dioclesian*, would have forced a laugh from the tortured regicide expiring on a wheel. But—*cur inficiatus honora Arcuerim fama ?*

'In a few characters of age and simplicity, he was at once natural and affecting. We must likewise add that his understanding was sound, his reading extensive ; and what should outweigh all other eulogiums, his temper was benevolent, and his integrity without blemish. He died in the year 1771, during one of his annual excursions to Liverpool, where he had long been the decent manager of a summer theatre, first raised into consequence by himself, and licensed at his own personal solicitation.'

The acting of Gibson and Ridout was greatly esteemed by Liverpool playgoers, as the following anecdote shows : On one occasion two local critics went to see the great little David Garrick perform. Upon their return they were asked what they thought of him. ' Oh !' said they, ' Garrick is well enough ; but he is nothing to Gibson and Ridout.'

Messrs. Gibson and Ridout's management was much commended. Gibson, who was the principal manager, saw that the company preserved great decorum. A good paymaster himself, he took care that all debts incurred by the company should be regularly discharged. There were, however, several things which did not meet with the approval of local playgoers. For instance, the doors were opened as early as five o'clock so that on nights when a large audience were expected, play-goers had two hours to wait before the play began. There were seldom more than two new plays, or two new farces produced during the season. An unknown old play was seldom revived, and those that were acted were chiefly stock plays. Actors of superior merit received no particular encouragement either in the matter of salaries or benefits.

The most advantageous season for the benefit performances was about August, when the town was full of visitors for the bathing season.   Dice were thrown by the players in order to determine the precedence of the benefits.   Preference was always shown for a ' bespeak ' on a Monday night, in lieu of any other evening.

In plays where the characters should have been dressed in old English habits only the principal characters were properly garbed.   Richard III was given fitting attire, but Henry VI, Richmond, etc., wore soiled and threadbare dresses of the early eighteenth century ; while modern garments were worn by the actresses.*

The names of those who appeared on this stage between 1749 and 1756 I have never been able to discover.   Liverpool's second newspaper, 'Williamson's Advertiser' was not published until Friday, May 28, 1756, and so far as I am aware there are no playbills of that period in existence.†

In the first number of ' Williamson's Advertiser,' May 28, 1756, the following advertisement (constituting the earliest known local theatrical announcement) appears :—

' By Comedians from the Theatres Royal in London, at the Theatre in Liverpool.   During the months of June, July, and August next, will be perform'd variety of the best Plays.'

N.B.—The days of acting will be Mondays, Wednesdays, and Fridays.'

The ' Theatres Royal in London ' were the patent houses to which Royal Letters Patent had been granted.   At that time no theatre in this country could use the title ' Royal,' except the Theatres Royal, Drury Lane, and Covent Garden, London.   That explains why no title is given to the theatre in the advertisement just quoted.   Even the street in which it was situated is not mentioned.

What the attraction was for the opening performance of the season on Wednesday, June 2, 1756, there is nothing to show.   The following plays, however, were advertised in 'Williamson's Advertiser' to be given on Friday, June 4, and on Monday, June 7, 1756 :—

---

* Holt and Gregson MSS.

† ' The Liverpool Courant,' published in 1712, was the first local newspaper.   I have never been able to see a copy.   The earliest Liverpool newspaper in the British Museum is ' Williamson's Advertiser,' for September 19, 1766.

' By Comedians from the Theatres Royal, in London,
At the Theatre in Liverpool,
This present FRIDAY, JUNE 4th, will be acted, A Comedy call'd
THE CONSTANT COUPLE
or A Trip to the Jubilee,

With a Farce call'd
THE VIRGIN UNMASKED.

And on MONDAY, JUNE 7th, will be acted, A Tragedy call'd
THE LONDON MERCHANT
or The History of George Barnwell
With a Farce (never perform'd there before), call'd
THE CHEATS OF SCAPIN

Pit, Two Shillings.   Gallery, One Shilling
To begin exactly at Seven o'clock.
N.B.—The days of acting are Mondays, Wednesdays, and
Fridays.'

The earliest local playbill that I have been able to discover
is in the Athenæum Library, Church Street. It was probably
printed to do duty as a ' poster,' as it is of a larger size than
any I have seen of about the same period.   Although the
year is not given in the bill this defect is remedied by the
announcement in 'Williamson's Advertiser' for June 4, 1756,
where the same plays are advertised for performance.
The playbill (a reduced *fac-simile* of which is shown)
states :—' Nor any Servants to be admitted into the gallery
without Paying.'   Down to the year 1759 the galleries in
the London and provincial theatres were free to the servants
of those who had taken places in the boxes.   Free admission for servants was an old custom dating back as far as
the time of the Restoration.   A survival of the practice of
sending servants to keep places is found at the present day
in paying boys and youths a few pence for keeping positions
for their patrons in waiting queues outside our theatres.*

* The queue system in Liverpool was inaugurated at the Royal Court Theatre, in
the autumn of 1895.

On the first production of *High Life Below Stairs*, in 1759, the whole race of the domestic gentry were in a ferment of rage at what they conceived would be their ruin ; and from the upper gallery to which they were admitted *gratis* came hisses and groans, and even handfuls of halfpence were flung on the stage at Philip, my Lord Duke, Sir Harry and others. This tumult was continued for a few nights, but ultimately it turned out a good thing for all theatres, for it gave Garrick, as manager, a fair occasion to close the gallery against the servants, and ever after to make all pay who entered it.'*

The ancient custom of adding *Vivat Rex* and *Vivant Rex et Regina* to the playbills, and other theatrical advertisements, originated in the following manner :—

In Shakespeare's time it was customary for the actors to kneel down on the stage, and pray for their patrons ; and in the public theatres for the King and Queen. This prayer sometimes made part of the epilogue ; as, for instance, in the epilogue to *King Henry IV*, Part II. It is also referred to in the old play entitled *The New Custom*—' Preserve our noble Queen Elizabeth, and her councell all ' ; and in Middleton's *A Mad World My Masters*—' This shows like kneeling after the play; I praying for my Lord Owemuch and his good Countess, our honourable lady and mistress.'

The practice of having *Vivat Rex* or *Vivant Rex et Regina* on old playbills seems to have died out about the close of the reign of William IV, as on later nineteenth century bills it is conspicuous by its absence. Although it is only a conjecture of mine, I may here state that when praying on the stage after a performance was abandoned, and the *Vivat Rex* or *Vivant Rex et Regina* in after years disappeared from the playbills, both these two old customs survived in the playing of the National Anthem in our theatres and other places of entertainment as the means of dismissing an audience at the termination of a performance.

A Bold Stroke for a Husband, which had not been 'acted these three years,' and *The Anatomist* ; *or The Sham Doctor*, were played on Wednesday, June 9, 1756. Two nights later, *The Committee* ; *or, The Faithful Irishman*, and *The King and the Miller of Mansfield* were in the bill. The comedy of *Love*

* ' The Recollections of John O'Keeffe.'

for Love, with *The Comical Humours of Ben the Sailor,* and the farce of *The Cheats of Scapin* were submitted on Monday, June 14. On Friday following, the company gave Shakespeare's *Much Ado About Nothing,* and *The Devil to Pay ; or, the Wives Metamorphosed.* On June 21, *The Rehearsal* and the farce of *The Lottery* were played, and four nights later, *The Wonder* with *The Double Disappointment.* For June 28, the attractions were the farce of *Katharine and Petruchio,* and the tragedy of *Tamerlane,* which had ' not been performed these *six* years.' This is direct evidence that the theatre was in existence in 1750. On June 30, *Tunbridge Walks ; or, The Yeoman of Kent* was submitted. The second of July saw *As You Like It,* with Garrick's farce of *Lethe.* Three days later *Romeo and Juliet* with the farce (' performed but once '), *Katharine and Petruchio ; or, A Cure for a Scold,* 'taken from Shakespeare by David Garrick.' On July 7, *The Suspicious Husband* was given, and on the 9th, the comedy *The Man's Bewitched* was played for the first time. On July 12, *Hamlet* was performed, followed two nights later by *The Beaux' Stratagem.* The performances on July 16, were *The Committee ; or, the Faithful Irishman,* and *The Englishman in Paris.* July 19 witnessed *The Tragical History of King Richard III,* and two days later *Rule a Wife, and Have a Wife,* which was followed by a farce. On July 23 *The Mistake* was performed, and on the 26th, the tragedy of *Merope,* ' with a procession of a human sacrifice after the manner of the ancients.' On the 28th, the pantomime entitled *The Cheats of Harlequin* was brought out. On Friday, July 30, the performances of *Much Ado About Nothing,* and the farce called *The Apprentice* were in aid of the local public charities, the receipts ' to be disposed of by the magistrates.' It was also announced that on ' Monday next the company begin their benefits, and will continue acting them every Monday, Wednesday, and Friday to Monday, September 6, which will be the last day of their performing this season.'

The bill for August 6, 1756, consisted of *The Twin Rivals,* and *Miss in Her Teens.* These were supplemented by a burlesque cantata, entitled ' The Dust Cart,' given by Mr. Shuter, who also gave Mr. Hippisley's 'Drunken Man,' and Mr. Foote's ' Tea. '

Shuter was a great favourite with Liverpool playgoers. Of ' Facetious Ned '—as he was called—the following anecdote is told : On one occasion the absence of a popular actress excited considerable displeasure amongst the audience at our Drury Lane Theatre, they calling for ' Shuter ! Shuter ! Miss So and So ! Shuter ! ' Shuter at length came forward and facetiously declared that if they wanted to ' shoot her ' they must do it themselves.

The comedian's father was a chairman, and plied his calling in the purlieus of Covent Garden. Ned commenced life as a pot-boy, and was afterwards employed as a billiard-marker. In 1744, when a mere boy, he commenced as an actor at Richmond. In June, 1746, as Osric and the Third Witch he supported Garrick in *Hamlet* and *Macbeth* at Covent Garden. Garrick pronounced him the greatest comic genius he had ever seen. Shuter was the original exponent of Papillon in *The Liar*, Justice Woodcock, Druggett, Old Hardcastle, and Sir Anthony Absolute.

A friend once met Shuter in the street and said to him, ' Why, Ned, are you not ashamed to walk the streets with twenty holes in your stockings ? Why don't you get them darned ? ' ' No, my friend,' said Shuter, ' I am above it; and if you have the pride of a gentleman you will act like one, and walk rather with twenty holes than have one darned.' ' How do you make that out ? ' ' Why,' said Ned, ' a hole is the accident of the day, but a darn is *premeditated poverty*.'

Once when he was travelling to play here the stage-coach in which he was seated was ' held-up ' by a highwayman. The only other occupant of the coach was an old gentleman, who, in order to save his own money, pretended that he was asleep. The highwayman's request—' Money or your life,' being repeated, Shuter with a vacant expression on his face, and the ' Knight of the Road's ' pistol at his head, replied ' Money ! by gad, sir, they never trust me with any ; for my uncle here always pays for me, turnpikes, and all your honour!' Upon which the highwayman gave him a few curses for his stupidity, woke the old gentleman up with a smart slap on the face, and robbed him of every shilling in his pocket ; while Shuter, who did not lose a single farthing, pursued his journey, laughing heartily at his fellow traveller's discomfiture.*

* ' Theatrical Anecdotes.'

On August 20, 1756, Mr. White, one of the players at the Drury Lane Theatre, had for his benefit the tragedy of the *Earl of Essex*, and the farce of *The Englishman in Paris*. The performance concluded with an epilogue on ' Somebody to be spoken by Nobody.' For Monday, August 23, the bill comprised *Zara; or, Osman, the Emperor of the Turks*, 'with an occasional prologue by David Garrick, Esq., to be spoken by Mr. Palmer, in the character of a Drunken Sailor. And an epilogue (in character) addressed to the Society of Bucks in Liverpool, to be spoken by Miss Kennedy, and the farce of *The Mock Doctor*.' Mrs. Baker of the company had her ' bespeak ' on Friday, August 27, when Colley Cibber's comedy *The Refusal; or, The Ladies' Philosophy* and the farce *Duke and No Duke* were performed. ' The last night but one of the acting ' was for the benefit of Mr. Holtom and Mrs. Copen. This took place on Friday, September 3, and on the Monday following (September 6), the season terminated.

Having said good-bye to our comedians from the Theatres Royal in London for one whole year, let us briefly look at the lot of the poor strolling player.

Performances by itinerant companies took place during the eighteenth and early nineteenth centuries in and about well-known local hostelries* like the ' Angel ' in Dale Street, and in the great room, or ' Buck's Room '—as it was called—in the ' Golden Lion ' in Dale Street, where Samuel William Ryley (whose real name was Romney), of ' Itinerant ' fame performed, and where in the autumn of 1764 that celebrated theatrical worthy, Tate Wilkinson, gave two performances. The first took place on October 5, when £14 was taken, and the second, he tells us in his curious autobiography, three days later, when £16 was realised. The smallness of the receipts greatly displeased him. He had been informed that money, not grass, grew in the streets of Liverpool. Wilkinson, however, was a humorist by nature, and a great deal more of the humorist by art. The great David Garrick gave him his first engagement. Tate Wilkinson was born in 1736 and died in 1803. He had been a little too merry in his youth, and old age brought him great melancholy. In his ' mental wanderings,' says Leigh Hunt, ' he would interweave, for instance,

* ' It was the ancient Inn-yard, with its open area, its two or three tiers of galleries with rooms at the back, that was taken as a model for the first English Theatre.' ' The London Stage,' by H. Barton Baker, Vol. I, p. 2.

all at once the subject of a new engagement at his theatre, the rats, a veal pie, Garrick, Mrs. Siddons, Mrs. Tate, and the doctor.'

Although the poor strolling players cheered the drooping spirits of many, they were not respected by the populace. How could it be otherwise ? Repeated Acts of Parliament had dubbed them ' Rogues and Vagabonds,' and as such they were commonly treated. ' Take the linen from the line, the strolling players are here,' was once a familiar cry. Of course one must not confuse the strolling players with the actors who migrated from the London Theatres to some provincial town for a season.

It was about the 'fifties of the eighteenth century that George Farren visited Liverpool. Farren, according to Lee Lewes,* was not as popularly supposed, a Munster man, but a native of Dublin, and the son of a wine merchant. He was intended for his father's business, but was seized with hankerings after the stage. Lewes gives the impression that he made his *début* in Dublin, and then goes on to say :—' I beg leave to relate an anecdote, which has never yet been published, relative to his application to Mr. Gibson, the well-known and respected manager of a company of comedians many years ago at Liverpool. Mr. Farren's abilities as a performer not meeting with that encouragement in Dublin which he expected, he was resolved to take the first opportunity of quitting Ierne's metropolis, and try his fortune in England. Arriving at Liverpool, he applied to Mr. Gibson, then manager of the London company of Drury Lane, for a situation of even the lowest salary ; but this modest offer of his service did not produce the expected success. ' Our company, friend,' said Gibson, ' being formed and full ere we left London, cannot possibly admit of any addition. Thou hast told me friend, that thou hast never tried thy talents on the stage, and it is an unalterable maxim with me to reject all superfluities of any kind. I will not entertain more cats than will kill mice ; and therefore, as by thy own confession thou art not practiced in the business of an actor, the most prudent course for thee would be to push thyself into some other way of life, which may support thee better. Whatever thy vain hope may flatter thee with, expect not to keep up long the flashy appearance thou now

* ' Memoirs of Charles Lee Lewes,' Vol. II.

dost make, shouldst thou engage with any travelling company of comedians. But lest, peradventure, thou shouldst lack wherewithal to answer for a bed and a supper, I make thee a present of this half-crown ; thou dost look most pitifully lank young man, but this may, if properly used by thee, prevent thy growing thinner for a short space of time.' The exordium to this puritanical speech made poor Farren look blank , he thought proper, however, being in want of half-a-crown, to pocket the affront—and making his best bow to his monitor he went back to his lodging.' Gibson, as I have previously stated, had been a Quaker Lewes does not mention where Farren lodged Probably, it was at a small haberdasher's shop kept by a Miss Wright, who was the daughter of a Liverpool brewer, or publican. At any rate she married George Farren, and to them was born, about 1759, a daughter, Elizabeth, who in after years became the Countess of Derby. Elizabeth's elder sister, Margaret, became, in 1787, the wife of Thomas Knight, the celebrated comedian, who was afterwards one of the lessees of the Theatre Royal, Liverpool.

The month of June, 1757, saw the return of the comedians from the Theatres Royal in London to our playhouse in Drury Lane.

In 'Williamson's Liverpool Advertiser' for Friday, June 10, 1757, the following advertisement appears :

' By Comedians from the Theatres Royal in London,
At the Theatre in Drury Lane, Liverpool.
This present Friday, June 10, will be acted
A comedy, call'd
THE MISER.
To which will be added a Farce call'd
THE MOCK DOCTOR
with a dance call'd
THE ITALIAN PEASANTS
by
MR. GRANIER AND MRS. VERNON.

To begin exactly at Seven o'clock.
N.B.—The Company will act, every Monday, Wednesday, and Friday during the summer '

D

As this advertisement clearly mentions the locality in which the theatre was situated, the error committed by local historians in stating that it was not opened until 1759 is all the more glaring.

With no bills giving the cast of characters of the several plays performed, it is difficult to discover who appeared on old Drury's boards during this period. According to the advertisements in the local newspapers, the company during the summer of 1757 included Mr. and Mrs. Baker, Mr. Redman, Mr. Granier, Miss Cushing, and Mrs. Vernon.

During June, 1757, the players performed *The Suspicious Husband* and *The Lying Valet*, the tragedy of *Merope*, and (on Friday, June 24) *The Beggar's Opera*, followed by the farce *Miss in Her Teens*. *The Beggar's Opera* was announced as not having been acted these *four* years. This further shows that the Drury Lane playhouse was not a new theatre, while further proof is forthcoming in the advertisement for July 8, 1757, where *The Fair Penitent* is stated as not having been ' acted these *five* years.' The programme was also enriched by the dancing of Mr. Granier and Mrs. Vernon, and by a new pantomime entertainment (' never performed there '), entitled *The Jealous Farmer Outwitted*; or, *Harlequin Statue.*

July 15 saw the production of the *Merchant of Venice*, and the 18th of the month the new tragedy of *Douglas* (' never performed there '). On the 22nd, *Measure for Measure* was given for the first time, and three nights later *Love for Love* and *The Jealous Farmer Outwitted*. The last mentioned performance was in aid of local charities.

On August 11 was performed the once popular play of *The London Merchant ; or the History of George Barnwell*, followed by *Lethe*. The season terminated on September 5, 1757.

George Barnwell used to be played on Boxing-night in front of the Christmas pantomimes, by way, I suppose, of a great moral lesson to youthful patrons. Occasionally *Jane Shore* was given with the same object for the moral benefit of the female portion of the audience. Not so very long ago *Barnwell* used to be played every Shrove Tuesday at the Theatre Royal, Manchester, in front of the pantomime. When played at Covent Garden, Lillo's old tragedy was as much a panto-mime on Boxing-nights as the pantomime proper that followed. Of these ' Merry Moments ' Dibdin recalls that tragedies, comedies, and operas were doomed by the 'gods and goddesses' to suffer all the complicated combinations of ' Pray, ask that gentleman to sit down,' ' Take off your hat,' and the like. ' But the moment' says Dibdin, ' the curtain goes up (on the pantomime), if any unfortunate gentleman speaks a word they make no reply, but throw him over directly '

During June, 1758, the following plays were performed: *The Orphan*; *or, The Unhappy Marriage*, to which was added the farce, *The Mock Doctor*, with dancing between the play and farce , *Hamlet*, and *Miss in Her Teens*, with dancing between the play and farce ; *Love for Love* and *The Lying Valet* , and *The Merry Wives of Windsor*

During July, *Tancred and Sigismunda*, *Isabella* ; *or, The Fatal Marriage*, *The Conscious Lovers*, *As You Like It*, a new tragedy *Marianne* (written by Fenton), *Henry IV*, *The Mistake*; *or, The Wrangling Lovers*, and on the 24th instant, *The Beaux' Stratagem* for the benefit of the local charities. On August 4, Beaumont and Fletcher's *The Royal Merchant* ; *or, The Beggar's Bush* was played.   Seven nights later *Marianne* and a curiously entitled dance ' The Roast Beef of Old England ; or Antigallican,' were given for the benefit of Miss Hilliard   For the benefit of Mr. White on August 18, Congreve's *Way of the World*, and *The Sailor's Return* were performed. The characters in the latter play were undertaken by Mr Granier, Miss Hilliard, Mr. White, Mr. Holtom, Mr. Baker, and Miss Mullart   Later in the evening the audience were entertained by Mr. Hippisley's ' Drunken Man ' given by Mr Shuter, and the farce *Trick upon Trick* ; *or, The Vintner in the Suds*. For the benefit of Mr. Redman on August 25, *The Mourning Bride*, Hippisley's ' Drunken Man ' and ' The Cries of London ' by Mr. Shuter were given The season terminated on September 8, with *The Merchant of Venice*, and *The Devil to Pay*.

THE NEW DRURY LANE THEATRE.

During the time the theatre was closed from September 5, 1758, to June, 1759, the building was reconstructed   Proof of this is shown by the fact that when the house reopened in June 1759 it was called the New Theatre in Drury Lane.   Boxes were now added to the auditorium, and they were placed round the pit. Admission to the boxes cost three shillings. Charles Lee Lewes says* ' Here it was for the first time boxes were erected as a just partition for the better sort to withdraw from the near contact of drunken sailors and their female associates, who by paying two shillings, which many could and would, afford for the honour of mixing with their employers and their families.' That the gallery had also been altered is shown by the statement in the Holt and Gregson MSS. to the effect that ' before this season the gallery extended very far over the pit.'

The new theatre was described as ' a most beautiful and regular structure. The scenes entirely new and very elegant.'† The rent of the house was £65 per annum, the current expenses £10 per night, and the highest receipts on a single occasion £92.

I am unable to state with exactitude what was the opening attraction in the new theatre as there is only one copy of ' Williamson's Advertiser' in the Liverpool Free Library for the month of June, 1759, the issue for the 29th instant, when *The Stratagem*, and *The Anatomist* were played. Holt and Gregson state that the theatre was opened on June 22, 1760, ' with the comedy of *The Conscious Lovers* and the farce of *The Lying Valet*. The house was fitted up with boxes for the first time this year, price three shillings.' The year 1760 is a mistake for 1759, as the advertisements in ' Williamson's Advertiser ' show that the theatre had boxes for the first time in 1759.

During July the plays performed were : *The Orphan of China* (July 2) ; *The Mistake* (July 4) ; *The Rehearsal* and *The Lottery* (July 13) ; *Douglas* (July 16) ; *Tancred and Sigismunda* and *The Guardian* (July 20) ; *The Wonder* (July 25) ; *The Suspicious Husband*, ' The Cries of London,' and *Katharine and Petruchio* for the benefit of the public charities (July 27).

On August 3, 1759, the performance was under the patronage of the Society of Bucks, who for Mrs. Ward's benefit, desired Nicholas Rowe's tragedy of *Jane Shore*, dancing by Mr. and Mrs. Granier, *The Sailor's Return*, and the farce of *Lethe*.

---

* ' Memoirs,' Vol. I, p. 43.   † ' Liverpool Chronicle,' June 8, 1759.

Prior to the performance the Society of Bucks were ' requested to attend their Noble Grand at the Lodge Room, at six o'clock in proper Form, in order to proceed from thence to the Play.'* *Measure for Measure, The Sailor's Return,* and *The Jealous Farmer Outwitted* were played for Mrs. Vincent's benefit on August 10. For the benefit of Mr. Baker on August 17, *The Beggar's Opera* and the dance 'The Merry Peasants' by Mr. and Mrs. Granier were given. The performance on Friday, August 24, was for the benefit of Mr. William Gibson, when *Macbeth* was performed. At the end of the third act the dance of ' The Merry Peasants' was given by Mr. and Mrs. Granier. At the end of the fourth act Mr. Shuter entertained the audience with a new humorous piece called ' A Lick at the Town.' At the end of the play Mr. and Mrs. Granier danced ' The Swiss Revels,' and between the play and the farce Mr. Shuter treated the audience to ' A Dish of All Sorts.' This consisted of the following. ' First :—Observations of the bottle conjurer and Miss Canning. Second, A Medley Song. Third, A Dialogue upon himself, between an Old Man, a North Briton, and a Gentleman from Connaught. Fourth, The Liverpool Battle ; or, the History of Mr. Shuter and the Sow. To be sung by him as a cantata, with proper Accompaniments in Signora Gruntanilla's taste.' The performance concluded with an address to the ladies and gentlemen of Liverpool, after which the farce, entitled *The Contrivances* was played. Places for the boxes were obtainable from Mr. Gibson at Captain Briggs's in Drury Lane. On August 31, *As You Like It*, dances by Mr. and Mrs. Granier, *Pygmalion; or, the Statue Animated,* and an epilogue formed the attractions for the evening. The season concluded on September 7, upon which occasion Mrs. Baker took her benefit, the plays performed being *The Refusal* and *The Devil to Pay.*

The Holt and Gregson MSS. contain the following list of performers who appeared here during 1760 :—Messrs. Gibson and Ridout (managers), Holland, Shuter, Collins, Anderson, White, Cushing, Baker, Aikman, Holtom, Redman ; Mesdames Bennett, Baker, Dyer, Copen, and Miss Mullart. James Ward was the prompter.

* There is in the Liverpool Museum a tile with the arms and insignia of the Society of Bucks, and an enamel. There is also a silken badge, which is believed to have formerly belonged to the Society.

For June 6, 1760, *A Bold Stroke for a Wife*, and the farce, *The Honest Yorkshireman*, were submitted.   June 9, *The Miser*, with a farce and entertainments of dancing by Signor Maranesi and Signora Provensalla.   June 13, *Hamlet* and a farce, *The Virgin Unmasked*, with dancing by Signor Maranesi and Signora Provensalla.   June 16, the comedy of *The Conscious Lovers*, with a farce and dance called ' The Cow Keepers ' by Signor Grimaldi and Signora Provensalla.

Signor Grimaldi was the father of Joe Grimaldi, the prince of clowns.   Grimaldi *père* was originally a pantomime actor at the fairs in Italy and France.   At that time these fairs supplied the French theatres with some of the finest dancers. A writer in the 'London Chronicle' (1758) observes that 'Grimaldi is a man of great strength and agility ; he indeed treads the air.   If he has any fault, he is rather too comical.'

While in Liverpool the signor resided at Mrs. Davis's in the Old Churchyard, where he advertised his skill ' to draw teeth, or stumps, without giving the least uneasiness in the operation.'   He also offered to wait on those who wanted dental advice, or assistance.   There are not many instances of the union of the two professions of dentist and dancing-master : but the signor possessed ability in both.   In 1760, he was appointed dentist to Queen Charlotte, but he soon resigned his appointment, and commenced to give lessons in fencing and dancing.

' Boz ' says that the signor ' bore the reputation of being a very honest man, and a very charitable one, never turning a deaf ear to the entreaties of the distressed, but always willing, by every means in his power, to relieve the numerous reduced and wretched persons who applied to him for assistance.'*

The remainder of the month of June saw *As You Like It* and *The Lottery* (June 20), *The Orphan of China* (June 23), *Miss in Her Teens* and *The Committee* (June 25), performed. July 11 witnessed *The Siege of Damascus, High Life Below Stairs* and dances by Signor Maranesi and Signora Provensalla. On July 13, *The Rehearsal* and *The Lottery* were given, followed three days afterwards by the tragedy of *Douglas*.   July 18 saw *The Provoked Husband*, and July 25, *Venice Preserved* and *The Wonder*, with dancing and a pantomime.   For the benefit

---

* ' Memoirs of Joseph Grimaldi ' (1838), Vol. I, pp. 4-5.

of the public charities on July 27, *The Suspicious Husband,* the farce *Katharine and Petruchio,* and dancing were in the bill For the benefit of Mr. Gibson on August 1, *Tancred and Sigismunda, The Lying Valet,* dances by Signors Grimaldi and Maranesi, and Signora Provensalla, and ' The Cries of London ' by Mr Shuter were given.

Liverpool at that time was visited by Samuel Derrick, the Master of the Ceremonies at Bath Mr. Derrick, in his letters from Liverpool—or, as he styles it, ' Leverpoole '—to his patron the Earl of Cork, has left us an interesting pen-picture of Liverpool in 1760, and in one of them gives some noteworthy particulars of the playhouse in Drury Lane. The letter in which he refers to the theatre is dated August 2, 1760. ' The Liverpool playhouse, which is very neat,' he writes ' will hold about £80 Here a company of London performers exhibit during the summer season, and acquire a great deal of money. I saw several pieces really well done Holland, Shuter, and Mrs. Ward, who are at the head of the business, being very industrious, and careful to please, meet with great success, not more, however, than they deserve. The dances are admirably executed by Grimaldi, Maranesi, and Signora Provensalla. The scenes are prettily painted, the clothes very rich, and everything carried on with amazing propriety. They play three times a week , and behind the boxes there is a table spread, in the manner of a coffee-house, with tea, coffee, wines, cakes, fruit, and punch, where a woman attends to accommodate the company on very moderate terms, with such refreshment as they may prefer.'

Mr. Redman took a ' bespeak ' on August 22, when *Cleone; or, The Unhappy Wife,* was submitted. September 5 was for the benefit of Mr Collins, when the bill comprised *Isabella; or, The Fatal Marriage,* and dancing by Signors Grimaldi and Maranesi, and Signora Provensalla. The season terminated on September 8, 1760

During 1760, Mr. Ridout was unlucky enough to offend one of the magistrates It appears that the gentleman concerned wished to be shown the theatre, and he applied to Mr. Ridout The latter, however, did not know the magistrate, and he therefore refused him admission. In consequence of this the players were not permitted to perform here the following year

There are only a few details to be unearthed concerning
Ridout.   He spent most of his life at Covent Garden Theatre,
and was a useful tragic actor of the second or third order.   He
was the original Lord Randolph in *Douglas* in London,   on
March 14, 1757.   But the play had been previously performed
in Edinburgh   He created the part of Titus in Thomson's
Coriolanus at Covent Garden, on January 13, 1749.   His
wife was a pleasing actress.   After Lacy Ryan's death, Ridout
was the only man in whom Rich placed any confidence, and
he was always consulted in all matters of importance.   Consequently, he was bespattered with plenty of abuse, but that
he did not mind   Tate Wilkinson* used to ' take off ' Ridout,
but on the latter appealing to his good nature he promised not
to imitate him any more.   Macklin, however, used to say that
Wilkinson's happiest imitation was that of Ridout—that non-
entity Ridout, as he called him.   Early in 1761 ill-health
compelled Ridout to retire to Bath, where he died on May 28,
·1761   Rich never recovered the blow, and passed away some
few months later.

After Ridout's death Gibson became sole manager of
the Liverpool Drury Lane Theatre   In 1762 the players
were Messrs Gibson (manager), Holland, King, Collins, Anderson, White, Cushing, Fox, Castle, Holtom,   Redman , Mesdames Bennett, Ward, Dyer, Smith, Evans (née Miss Mullart),
and Miss Pope.   Signor Maranesi and Miss Baker were the
dancers who performed during, and after the plays

The Mrs. Bennett referred to above was Elizabeth Bennett
' This actress,' observes Genest,† ' is sometimes called Mrs.
and sometimes Miss.'   She was for many years the partner
of William Gibson's joys and sorrows ; in fact, until his decease.
She was a member of the London Drury Lane Theatre Company as far back as 1736, as on February 1 of that year she
played Margery in *The King and the Miller of Mansfield*   On
May 6, 1737, she portrayed Ann Bullen in *Henry VIII*, Quin
being the Wolsey.   On May 31, 1741, she, as the Duchess of
York, supported Garrick in *Richard III*.   In 1742 she performed Nerissa at Covent Garden to Macklin's Shylock and
Mrs. Clive's Portia.   In that year both Mr. Gibson and Mrs.
Bennett were members of the Covent Garden Company. When

* ' Memoirs.'   † ' Some Account of the English Stage,' Vol III, p 653

Garrick revived *King John*, on February 20, 1744, Mrs. Bennett was the Queen Elinor.

One of the players at the local Drury Lane Theatre in 1762 was Mr. King, who was walking one day with Woodward through the streets of Liverpool, when a chimney sweep and his boy came up. The boy stopped and stared at them ; and although the master called him several times to come along, he still stood staring, and at length exclaimed ' Why, they be players ! ' ' Hold your tongue, you dog, ' said the old sweep, ' you don't know what you may come to yourself ! '

In 1763, there came Messrs. Gibson (manager), Holland, King, Baddeley, White, Cushing, Baker, Wignel, Holtom, Redman ; Mesdames Bennett, Dyer, Smith, Evans ; and Misses Pope and Miller.   The dancers were Mr. Vincent and Mrs. Baker.   The company was the same in 1764-5.

The Mr. Baddeley mentioned above was Robert Baddeley, who was bred a cook, and worked in that capacity in the kitchen of Lord North.   He made his first essay on the stage at the Smock Alley Theatre, Dublin, in October, 1751.   His success in Dublin led to an engagement in London, where he made his first appearance at Drury Lane Theatre, on September 20, 1763, as Polonius.   This would be after he made his *début* at the Liverpool Drury Lane Theatre.   If poor Baddeley's memory is not kept green by means of the Twelfth Night cake-and-wine celebrations he will not be forgotten for two other reasons— he was the husband of that beautiful wanton, Sophia Baddeley, and he was the original Moses in *The School for Scandal*.

The performers during 1766 were Messrs. Gibson (manager), Bensley, Parsons, Dunstable, Anderson, Packer, Baker, Holtom, Johnson (prompter) ; Mesdames Bennett, Baker, Vincent, Parsons, Evans ; and Misses Flyn and Pope.   The dancers were Mr. Fishar and Mrs. Thompson.

In 1767 visits were paid by Messrs. Gibson (manager), Bensley, King, Parsons, Mattocks, Packer, Morris, Cushing, Wignell ;   Mesdames   Bennett, Mattocks, Didier, Dyer, Parsons, Evans ;   and Miss Pope.   The dancers were Mr. Fishar and Mrs. King (*née* Miss Baker).   Mr. Wild was again the prompter.

Until the engagement in 1767 of Mr. and Mrs. Mattocks no Green Room had been provided at the theatre. *   To

* So inadequate was the dressing-room accommodation that these artists had refused to come down on account of that deficiency.

remedy this defect an adjoining house was now taken and the parlour appropriated as a Green Room, while the other rooms were set apart for dressing-rooms for the principal players. A Mrs. Chevers, being a useful person, had the remainder of the house during the season, and the whole of it during the time the performers were away.*

In June, 1767, the plays submitted included :—*The Clandestine Marriage* and *The Virgin Unmasked* (June 12) ; *The Suspicious Husband* and *The Contrivances* (June 19) ; *The Double Falsehood* and *The Deuce is in Him* (June 26). During July, the following plays were performed :—*The English Merchant* (for the first time), ' as performed last season at the Theatre Royal, Drury Lane,' and *Polly Honeycomb* (July 3) ; *Love in a Village* (ballad opera), with music by Handel, Arne, etc. (July 10) ; *Romeo and Juliet* and *The Contrivances* (July 13) ; *The Maid of the Mill* (comic opera), ' music composed by the most celebrated masters ' (July 17) ; *The Busy Body* and *The Devil to Pay* (for the benefit of the public charities, July 22) ; *The English Merchant* and *Thomas and Sally; or, The Sailor's Return* (for the benefit of Mr. Packer, July 24) ; *The Beggar's Opera* and *Katharine and Petruchio* (for the benefit of Mrs. Bennett, July 31). For William Parsons' benefit on August 7, Wycherley's *Plain Dealer* was given. Parsons also recited a comic poem in praise of money. Thomas Davies says that ' Parsons was born a comic actor ; the tones of his voice, and the muscles of his face proclaim it ; his humour is genuine and pleasant ; nobody can forbear laughing either *with* or *at* him, whenever he opens his mouth.' *Hamlet*, with entertainments of dancing (August 14) ; *The London Merchant ; or, The True and Antient History of George Barnwell*, and *Harlequin's Invasion of Parnassus* ' in which will be given the exact representation of a Sea Engagement, Shipwreck, etc.' (August 21) ; *The Maid of the Mill* (for the benefit of Miss Pope, August 28) ; *Double Falsehood* and *Thomas and Sally* (for the benefit of Mr. Fishar, September 2) ; and *The Jealous Wife, The Contrivances*, and a general country dance (for the benefit of Mr. Gibson, September 4). This was the last night of the season.

The players during 1768 were :—Gibson (manager), Bensley, Palmer, Parsons, Packer, Morris, Cushing, Fox, Wignell,

* Holt and Gregson MSS.

Holtom, Wild (prompter).   Mesdames Bennett, Mattocks,
Didier, Williams, Parsons, Evans ; and Miss Pope.   The
dancers were Mr. Fishar, Mrs. Manesiere and Miss Besford.

The plays were :—*The Busy Body* ' with an epilogue in
the character of the Busy Body to be spoken by Mr. Palmer
(June 13) ; Farquhar's *Recruiting Officer* (dances by Mr. Fishar
—principal dancer of the Theatre Royal, Covent Garden—
and Mrs. Mattocks (June 17) ; *The Countess of Salisbury* (new
tragedy, June 24) ; *False Delicacy* and *The Lyar* by Samuel
Foote (July 8) ; *The Provoked Husband* and *The Citizen* (July
15) ; *The Clandestine Marriage* (for the benefit of Mrs. Bennett,
July 29) ; *The Double Falsehood* (for the benefit of Miss Pope)
(August 5) ; *Lionel and Clarissa*, dances and *The Lyar* (August
12). On August 19 *Love in a Village*, Mr. Palmer's comic para-
phrase on Shakespeare's ' Seven Ages,' and the farce *The
Deuce is in Him* were given for the benefit of James Wild,
the prompter, who was afterwards prompter at the Theatre
Royal, Liverpool.   On August 26, Mr. Mattocks had for his
benefit *The Beggar's Opera* and *The Honest Yorkshireman*.
For the benefit of Mr. Packer, *The Way to Keep Him* and
The Old Maid were performed on September 2.   The season
terminated on September 5, 1768.

According to ' Williamson's Liverpool Advertiser' for December 9, 1768, there was in the street adjoining Drury Lane—
Squire's Garden (now Chorley Street)—the Theatre Coffee
House.   The name suggests that it was an establishment
frequented by the players and their associates.   In all probability it was the first theatrical hostelry in Liverpool.   It
was either in one of the rooms of the coffee-house, or in the
yard of the establishment that the Venetian Company of Performers (from Sadler's Wells) gave specimens of their quality
from December, 1768, to about the end of January, 1769.

In the journal just mentioned the advertisement says that
' Several new performances never exhibited in this town '
were to be given, together with ' great variety of entertainments
viz. :—Signor Calino will dance on the tight-rope with a pair
of shackles at his feet ; also several droll and diverting tricks
by M. de Monkeyro.'   A Miss Wilkinson was also announced
to appear.   This lady was apparently a performer of much
versatility, as she not only engaged to sing several favourite
airs and play upon the musical glasses, but also to ' put herself

into full swing upon the wire, and at the same time play upon the tabor and pipe.'   Other attractions consisted of ' lofty tumbling by Master Nevey, Signor Calino, and others ' ; Signor Bassinini was to perform the Italian table trick ; and Signor Georgi was to dance a horn-pipe.   ' To which will be added a good pantomime entertainment, called *The Novelty*. To conclude with a comic dance.'

Meanwhile Mr. Gibson had been busy concentrating his energies on the organisation of a new theatre more worthy of the town.

Accordingly he drew up and presented a petition to the Corporation of Liverpool, praying them to support him in his application to Parliament for a theatre to be erected in Liverpool, to which Royal Letters Patent would be granted.   The Corporation agreed to grant his request.   The sum and substance of these proceedings is found in the following entry in the Corporation Records :—

December 7, 1768.   Matthew Stronge, Mayor.
' It is ordered that the Mayor, Magistrates and Council of this Corporation agree to Mr. Gibson's petition for erecting a Playhouse in Liverpoole, upon the same terms, conditions and agreement as was entered into with the Magistracy of the City of Norwich in the like case, and that Mr. Gibson be desired to send Mr. Mayor copys of all Acts necessary to be done previous to obtaining the Act of Parliament, and that the Lord Chamberlain be prayed to grant the same Licence and no other, as was granted to Norwich, and all proceedings to be done at Mr. Gibson's expence.   And to acquaint him that the Magistracy will not have the present house licensed, as its in a very dangerous place for company to resort to on account of the narrow streets and avenues leading thereto.'

In 1769 the performers at the Drury Lane Theatre were Messrs. Gibson (manager), Bensley, Packer, Palmer, Morris, Cushing, Fox, Wild, Keen, Holtom ; Mesdames Bennett, Mattocks, Didier, Williams, Parsons and Evans.   The dancers were Mr. Fishar, Signor Maranesi, and Miss Besford.

In 1769 the plays presented included :—*Lionel and Clarissa* and *The King and the Miller of Mansfield* (June 9) ; the new tragedy of *Cyrus* and *Miss in Her Teens* (June 16) ; *Hamlet* and *The Padlock* (June 23) ; *The School for Rakes* (new comedy) ' as it was performed with universal applause last winter at the Theatre Royal, Drury Lane, London,' and the farce *The Intriguing Chambermaid* (June 30) ; *The Provoked Husband* and *The Padlock* (July 7) ; *Cymbeline* and *The Virgin Unmasked* (July 14) ; *Cymbeline* and *The Padlock* (July 21) ; *The School for Rakes* and *The Padlock* (for the benefit of Mr. Keen and Mrs. Parsons, July 28) ; *The Countess of Salisbury, The Englishman in Paris*, and a minuet by Mr. Fishar and Mrs. Mattocks, for the benefit of Mr. Cushing (August 4) ; *The Miser* and the Italian pantomime dance ' The Raree Show,' by Mr. Fishar, Signor Maranesi, Master Blurton and Miss Besford, with *The Padlock* (for the benefit of Mr. Morris, August 11) ; *Love Makes a Man*, the comic dance, ' The Lamplighter,' and *The Padlock* (for the benefit of Mr. Parsons, August 18). September 8, 1769, was the last night of performing for the season.

Some delay must have arisen in granting Mr. Gibson the support he solicited from the Corporation of Liverpool in his appeal to Parliament for a Theatre Royal by Letters Patent, as there is the following entry in the Corporation Records for August 29, 1769 :—' It is ordered that this Council will petition the Parliament the next session for an Act to enable his Majesty to grant his Letters Patent to Mr. William Gibson, comedian, his executors, administrators and assigns, for the term of twenty-one years, to build a theatre in Liverpoole on condition that the said Mr. Gibson do pay all expences attending the obtaining such Act and Letters Patent, and shall also build the said theatre at his expence on such piece of ground as shall be agreeable to the Mayor and Magistrates of this town.'

This was succeeded by the following order, dated September 6, 1769 :—' It is ordered that before Mr. Mayor, the Magistrates of this town or the Council do petition Parliament for building a new theatre in this town and Letters Patent to be granted to Mr. Gibson according to the order of the last Council. That the said Mr. Gibson do give in to the Council his proposals, forms, and prices that he and his Company will during such Letters Patent perform in the said Theatre at and upon—to be signed by him and left with Council, and that the Town Clerk give Mr. Earle or Mr. Gibson a copy of these orders.'

It was not, however, until November 9, 1769, that the petition to Parliament was graced by the Common Seal of the Corporation, as the following reference shows :—' It is ordered that the petition of the Mayor and Council of this Borough and Corporation now read to this Council to the Honourable the Commons of Great Britain in Parliament assembled, for obtaining an Act to enable His Majesty to Grant his Letters Patent to Mr. William Gibson, his executors, and administrators for the term of 21 years, to build a new Theatre in Liverpoole, and to perform plays, etc., therein during the Term, be passed under the Common seal by Mr. Mayor and Bailiffs, and be presented to Parliament at the now ensuing sessions, according to the Terms and conditions in a late order of Council made for such purpose.'

The petition was passed by the House of Commons, but the House of Lords rejected it.   This, however, did not dishearten the town, and the Corporation on December 5, 1770, resolved to make a second effort.   This time they sent up no fewer than three petitions, all of which passed the Corporation Seal on January 7, 1771.   The petitions were transmitted to Mr. Gibson, to be respectively presented according to their superscriptions.   One was addressed to the House of Commons, one to the House of Lords, and one to the Lord Chamberlain. The petitions had the desired effect, and the bill passed both houses.   The following is a copy of the Act of Parliament :—

' Anno Regni

GEORGII III.

Regis

Magnæ Britanniæ, Franciæ & Hiberniæ,

Undecimo.

At the Parliament begun and holden at Westminster, the Tenth Day of May, Anno Domini 1768, in the Eighth Year of the Reign of our Sovereign Lord, George the Third, by the Grace of God, of Great Britain, France and Ireland, King, Defender of the Faith, &c.

Cap. XVI.

An Act to enable his Majesty to licence a Playhouse in the Town of Liverpoole, in the County Palatine of Lancaster. Whereas a licenced Playhouse in the Town of Liverpoole, in the County Palatine of Lancaster, would be of Convenience to the said Town ; May it therefore please Your Majesty, that it may be enacted ; and be it enacted by the King's most Excellent Majesty, by and with the Advice and Consent of the Lords Spiritual and Temporal, and Commons, in this present Parliament assembled, and by the Authority of the same, That so much of an Act of Parliament, made in the Tenth Year of His late Majesty's Reign, intituled, An Act to explain and amend so much of an Act made in the Twelfth Year of the Reign of Queen *Anne*, intituled, *An Act for reducing the Laws relating to Rogues, Vagabonds, Sturdy Beggars, and Vagrants, into One Act of Parliament ; and for the more effectual punishing such Rogues, Vagabonds, Sturdy Beggars, and Vagrants, and sending them whither they ought to be sent*, as relates to common Players of Interludes ; whereby all Persons are discharged to represent any Entertainment of the Stage whatever, in virtue of Letters Patent from His Majesty, or by Licence of the Lord Chamberlain of His Majesty's Household for the Time being, except within the Liberties of Westminster, or where His Majesty is residing for the Time being, be, and the same is hereby repealed, with respect to the said Town of Liverpoole · And that it shall and may be lawful for His Majesty, His Heirs, and Successors, to grant Letters Patent for establishing a Theatre or Playhouse within the said Town of Liverpoole , which shall be intitled to all the Privileges, and subjected to all the Regulations, to which any Theatre or Playhouse in Great Britain is intitled and subjected.'*

The site chosen for the erection of the Theatre Royal by Letters Patent was on the north side of the present Williamson Square, which takes its name from the worthy citizen, who, about the middle of the eighteenth century, first laid it out. So countrified was this district in 1769, that in that year there were advertised in 'Williamson's Liverpool Advertiser' 'Two fields, or closes, of land to be sold, near to Peter's Church, known by the name of Williamson's Fields.' In 1725, Frog Lane (now Whitechapel), was entirely unbuilt upon. At that time there was nothing but marshy ground thereabouts ; and apparently in that state it so remained until 1764, in which year the Williamson family proposed to sell

* I am informed by the Lord Chamberlain that this Act of Parliament has not been repealed

the land now occupied by the square to the Corporation for a market. The Corporation offered to take the proposal into consideration if the Williamsons would ' fill up the swamp ' in the land adjoining Frog Lane. At any rate the land upon which the Theatre Royal and the adjoining house in Murray Street (now Brythen Street) were built, was Corporation leasehold, and held from August 2, 1770, for a term of three lives—those of William Gibson, John Brownell, and Gerard Potter.

The Royal Letters Patent passed the Great Seal on April 30, 1771, ' unto William Gibson, of Liverpool, gentleman, for a term of twenty-one years from Midsummer next, to establish a Theatre, and to form, entertain, govern, privilege, and keep a Company of Comedians for His Majesty's Service in the Town of Liverpool.'

The cost of erecting the Theatre Royal by Letters Patent was estimated at about £6,000, which was raised in shares of £200 each, bearing 5 per cent. interest,* and entitling the holder to a silver free admittance ticket.† All the money necessary for the venture was subscribed in less than an hour after the list had been opened, and on June 3, 1771, the foundation stone was laid by the Mayor, Mr. John Sparling, ' who was attended by a great number of gentlemen.'‡

In 1771 the house in Drury Lane was styled the Theatre Royal, and the company were known as His Majesty's Comedians. This designation was only applied to those players who performed at the patent theatres. It was a distinct honour, and, at that time, was much sought after. During the season His Majesty's Comedians performed on Mondays, Wednesdays, and Fridays. The players were :—Messrs. Reddish, Palmer, Parsons, Packer, Morris, Cushing, Davies, Fox, Webb, Keen, Holtom, Wild ; Mesdames Bennett, W. Barry, Hopkins, Lee, Pink, Reddish, Davies, Parsons, and Evans. Mr. and Mrs. Ferreri, Signor Maranesi, and Miss Besford were the dancers.

* In 1797 one share in the theatre was sold for £260. In 1835 the Corporation paid £600 for a share. On May 18, 1881, the value of two shares was assessed at £1,586 13s. 4d., at whch sum the Corporation became the purchasers. Three years later one share cost them £793 6s. 8d.

† Subsequently ivory and copper tickets were substituted for some of the tickets. On all the tokens there was engraved the name of the theatre, with a representation of the Liver, while on the other side appeared the name of the proprietor. Similar free admission tickets were afterwards issued at the Amphitheatre, in Great Charlotte Street. Several of the silver tickets of both theatres are still in existence.

‡ Holt and Gregson MSS.

Most of the players engaged were from the Theatre Royal, Drury Lane, London.   Tom Davies, who subsequently kept a bookshop in the metropolis, and was honoured with the friendship of Dr. Johnson, lives in memory as Garrick's first and worst biographer, and as the author of ' Dramatic Miscellanies.' His pretty wife has been commemorated in ' The Rosciad.' Mrs. William Barry was a sister-in-law of the famous Spranger Barry.   She made her *début* on the Dublin stage as Miss Osborne, and subsequently married the treasurer of Crow Street Theatre.*

It will be noticed that William Gibson's name does not figure among the list of performers who appeared at the Drury Lane Theatre in 1771.   Sad to relate he was lying seriously ill at his residence in Everton.   A spirit of insubordination then broke out among the players.   Led by Samuel Reddish, William Parsons, and Palmer, they revived, not stock dramas but old plays, in direct opposition to Mr. Gibson's wishes. For instance, Reddish would have *The Gamester* for his benefit and played it in defiance of the manager.   Moore's play until it was performed at Drury Lane, London, for Reddish's benefit on March 16, 1771, had not been seen there for fifteen years. Reddish rather fancied the part of Beverley, and, as Palmer had acted Stukely, and Mrs. Reddish had portrayed Charlotte with him in London, the play was brought out, as I have stated at the local Drury Lane.   After this Reddish was informed that his services would not be required after the end of the season.†

Reddish, who died in York Lunatic Asylum, in 1785, married Mrs. George Canning.   Genest, however, hints a doubt of the marriage by stating that ' Mrs. Canning had at one time such a friendship for Mr. Reddish, that she assumed his name.'‡   Bell, in his ' Life of George Canning,' declares that her marriage ' rests on an authority which properly closes all discussion on the subject.'   Mrs. Canning was the mother of the famous statesman and orator, the Right Hon. George Canning, who represented Liverpool in Parliament from 1812 to 1823.   Canning Place and Canning Street are named after him.

* Some account of her will be found in a little work called ' Theatrical Biography ; or Memoirs of the Principal Performers of the Three Theatres Royal,' published in London in 1772.
† Holt and Gregson MSS.
‡ ' Some Account of the English Stage,' Vol. V, p. 475.

In 1771 Liverpool suffered a great loss in the death of Mr. Gibson.   He died at his residence in Everton, on August 21, and was interred on August 26, in Walton Churchyard, where stands a monument to his memory.   On one side of the tomb, which is close to John Palmer's grave, a white marble medallion was inserted bearing an inscription said to have been written by David Garrick.   The lines on the tomb cannot now be deciphered owing to the ravages of the weather. They are, however, preserved in the Holt and Gregson MSS., and I am therefore able to give a copy :—' To the memory of William Gibson, late patentee of the Theatre Royal in Liverpool, who died August 21, 1771, aged 58.   If Judgment and Industry in his Profession, if a steady uprightness of Heart, if an Invariable Attachment to Truth, Honour, and Friendship, desire the praises of Mankind, no one ever had a more just title to them than he whose remains are here interr'd.

> A Wit's a feather, and a chief's a rod
> An honest Man the Noblest Work of God.'

David Erskine Baker, in his ' Biographia Dramatica,' says ' That the worth of the deceased might have entitled him to the lasting honour which an epitaph by Doctor Johnson would certainly have conferred.'   Gibson is feelingly referred to in the prologue written by George Colman, the elder, and spoken at the opening of the Royal. ' Gibson's loss,' says J. Winston,* ' was much lamented, and he was an example of benevolence but rarely met, as he left a donation of a considerable amount to the indigent of the town.'   This latter statement is incorrect, as also are the statements of Genest,. and other stage historians, that he left his money to the Covent Garden Fund.   His will, dated June 12, 1771, now in the Chester Probate Registry, shows that he bequeathed all his ' bills, bonds, public funds, scenes, cloaths (sic), and the patent for playing in Liverpool, to his dear and best beloved friend, Mrs. Elizabeth Bennett, formerly of Drury Lane,' whom he appointed sole executrix.   The testator's will, which is apparently in his own handwriting, describes him as ' of Covent Garden, London, but now belonging to the

* ' The Theatric Tourist ' (1805), p. 50.

Theatre Royal, of Liverpool.' According to Baker's ' Biographia Dramatica ' Gibson's fortune amounted to ' upwards of eight thousand pounds.'

On August 23, 1771, the company at the Drury Lane Theatre appeared in *Othello* and *Like Master Like Man*. In the cast were Messrs. Palmer, Parsons, Reddish, Davies, Packer, Cushing, Webb, Keen, Morris, Mrs. Hopkins, and Mrs. Lee, the last of whom played Desdemona. The performance was for the benefit of Mrs. Lee, and a prologue was spoken by her daughter, a child of five. The season terminated early in September.

During the autumn of 1771 the celebrated actor-author Charles Macklin, was seen here in the characters of Shylock, Sir Archy, Lovegold, etc. Kirkman* says that he played ' with his accustomed ability at Leeds and Liverpool to very crowded houses,' and afterwards set sail for Dublin, where he arrived on November 11, 1771.

The Drury Lane Theatre remained standing many years after the Theatre Royal by Letters Patent in Williamson Square had been built. Performances were occasionally given at the former house, as it is recorded that on October 13, 1774, the masque of *Alexander's Feast* was played there. Another performance took place on October 23, 1775, when *The Revenge* and *Miss in Her Teens* were given in aid of a distressed family. A footnote to the advertisement states ' that great care has been taken to have the house thoroughly aired.' On November 23, 1775, representations of *Henry IV* and the farce of *The Toy Shop* were given in aid of the Infirmary (opened March 15, 1749), which then stood on the site now occupied by St. George's Hall. On another occasion, after 1776, a benefit performance was accorded a Mr. Leverton, a mathematical and optical instrument maker, of Pool Lane (now South Castle Street), but the performers were principally amateurs.

Brooke says that the Drury Lane Theatre ' was purchased in 1788, along with other property from Mrs. Chapman, and pulled down, and part of its site forms a portion of the site of Brunswick Street.'† As a matter of fact only part of the theatre was demolished, and the remaining portion converted

---

* ' Memoirs of the Life of Charles Macklin ' (1799), Vol. II, p. 46.
† Brooke's ' Liverpool,' p. 85.

into a warehouse,* which was used by the Corporation as an
engine-house.† According to the eighth edition of 'The
Stranger in Liverpool' (1825), what remained of the old
theatre was still used as a warehouse. The next edition of 'The
Stranger in Liverpool' (1829), records 'that the remains
were only *lately* taken down.' Therefore, we may take it
that somewhere between 1825 and 1829 the theatre ceased to
exist.

THE THEATRE ROYAL.

One hundred and thirty-six years ago, when the Theatre
Royal in Williamson Square was first erected, Liverpool presented a vastly different aspect from the Liverpool of 1908.
Pleasant landscapes, fruitful gardens, and picturesque wind-
mills dotted here and there on hill sides, could be found within
a mile of the Town Hall. But the town itself was ill-paved,
ill-drained, and ill-lighted.

As late as 1775 there was only one letter carrier for all
Liverpool, and the mails had to be brought into the town on
horse-back. Goods were conveyed on pack-horses, and in
waggons in which many of the inhabitants, and not merely
those in the humblest rank of society, used to ride when taking
a journey. There were few stage-coaches. The higher and
middle classes who did not keep carriages, invariably travelled
on horse-back, or in post-chaises. The roads, such as they
were, presented serious risks to travellers, being infested by
highwaymen of the Jack Sheppard and Dick Turpin type.
Oil lamps, tallow candles, and rushlights were the sole domestic
illuminants. Matches had not come into use, and in their
stead the flint and steel must often have tried the temper of
the most patient.

The bankers, merchants, and others of the upper and
middle classes were dressed in satin small clothes, silk

---

* The Holt and Gregson MSS., record : ' Part of the old house is cut away in making
the opening from Castle Street to George's Dock, now Brunswick Street. What remains
standing is converted into a warehouse.'

† On January 23, 1798, there was sold at the ' Golden Lion,' in Dale Street, sundry free-
hold properties formerly belonging to Charles William, first Earl of Sefton. One of the
properties was ' part of the Old Playhouse, now used as an Engine House, in the occupation
of the Corporation, of the yearly rent of £3.' (*Vide* ' Property Sales in Liverpool and
District,' 1798—1906).

stockings, and cocked hats and ruffles. Their coats, waist-coats (the latter very elaborately worked), and breeches, were oftentimes all of one colour, the prevailing hues being of a light or snuff colour. White stocks at the throat were invariably worn ; and the young men, and not a few of the middle-aged, wore their hair dressed with large curls on either side of the face with queues behind. Brown bob wigs, cauliflower wigs, and bush wigs seem to have been principally worn by middle-aged and elderly persons. Whether they wore their own hair or not, hair-powder, in the higher ranks was *de rigeur*, whilst canes and walking-sticks with large gold or silver heads were in general use.

The ladies powdered their hair, which, in those days, was worn very high ; and with their large hooped dresses wore very high-heeled shoes. Many of them carried large green fans to mitigate the heat of old Sol's rays. Such were some of the conditions of life in Liverpool when the Theatre Royal was built.

After Mr. Gibson's death, Mrs. Bennett, to whom the former had bequeathed the Royal Letters Patent for playing in Liverpool, granted the use of the theatre for fourteen years to Messrs. Joseph Younger and George Mattocks at a yearly rent of £140. The grant, which I have seen, bears date March 18, 1772, provided, among other covenants, 'that the said Joseph Younger and George Mattocks, their heirs, executors, administrators, or assigns shall not, nor shall either or any of them during the said term of fourteen years employ Samuel Reddish of the Theatre Royal, Drury Lane, London, Comed-ian, or permit, or suffer him to be employed in acting, repre-senting, or in any quality whatever in and about the theatre or playhouse to be opened or made use of by virtue of the said Letters Patent.'* It was also agreed that Mrs. Bennett, or her nominee, was to be admitted into the theatre free of charge to witness the performances.

Joseph Younger, one of the lessees, was a very capable actor, despite a persistent lisp. He had been prompter at Covent Garden Theatre during Rich's management. Rich, who never could remember names, used to call him ' Young-more.' The other lessee, George Mattocks, made his first

---

* This was occasioned by Reddish's conduct the previous year at the Drury Lane Theatre, Liverpool.

appearance in Liverpool at the Drury Lane Theatre in 1767. Both he and his wife were always favourites with the local playgoing public.

The new theatre was a large and handsome building, elegantly finished both internally and externally, and having admirable acoustic properties.   The front was of brick, in a line with the houses on either side, and it was surmounted by an artistic pediment in which was depicted a graceful and spirited carving of the Royal Arms.   In the middle of the *façade* was a large door led up to by stone steps.   This was the principal entrance.   Facing this the lobby leading to the boxes was situated, and on one side there was a passage which led to the pit, and on the other to the gallery.   The boxes were 3s. 6d., the pit 2s. 6d., and the gallery 1s.   Sir William Chambers was the architect.   Candles and lamps were the only illuminants, gas not being introduced until early in the nineteenth century.

'There was a peculiarity about the gallery,' says Brooke,[*] 'which is worth notice ; it was by no means as distant from the stage, or as much elevated from the ground as the present gallery,[†] and was one of the best situations in the house for hearing and seeing the performances ; the height of the front of the gallery was much the same as that of the present upper boxes ; it was frequented by persons of a higher grade of society than such as are now[‡] seen in the pit of a Liverpool theatre, and they were accustomed to sit on the left side of the gallery when looking towards the stage, whilst the lower classes, by a kind of tacit arrangement, seldom interfered with them, but took their seats on the right of it, and in the wings, which extended over a part of the upper side boxes.'

The back wall of the theatre at that time abutted on one of the walks of an extensive rope works, the site of which is now covered by St. John's Market.   In after years it became a matter for great regret that the rope-walk at the back of the theatre had not been taken in when the theatre was built so that the stage of the Royal could have been made much deeper than it was.   The opportunity, however, was lost, for soon afterwards the rope-walk became a narrow street (Charles Street), and so it remains to the present day.

[*] 'Liverpool During the Last Quarter of the Eighteenth Century,' pp. 275-6.
[†] The theatre opened in 1803.
[‡] 1853.

On Friday evening, June 5, 1772, the Royal was opened with great *éclat*. All the *élite* of the town were present on this very auspicious occasion, and the initial performance was a great success. The opening prologue was written by George Colman, the elder, and spoken by Mr. Younger. It was as follows :—

'Wherever Commerce spreads her swelling sail
Letters and arts attend the prosperous gale.
When Cæsar first these regions did explore,
And northward his triumphant eagle bore,
Rude were Britannia's sons, a hardy race
Their faith idolatry, their life the chase.
But soon as traffic fix'd her social reign,
Join'd pole to pole, and nations to the main,
Each art and science follow'd in her train.
Augusta then her pomp at large display'd,
The seat of majesty, the mart of trade.
The British Muse unveil'd her awful mien,
And Shakespeare, Fletcher, Jonson grac'd the scene.

Long too has Mersey roll'd her golden tide,
And seen proud vessels in her harbour ride ;
Oft on her banks the Muse's sons would roam,
And wish'd to settle there a certain home ;
Condemn'd alas ! to hawk unlicens'd bays,
Contraband mummeries, and unlicens'd plays.
Your fostering care at length reliev'd their woes,
Under your auspices this *Staple* rose.
Hence made free merchants of the letter'd world,
Boldly advent'ring forth with sails unfurl'd,
To Greece and Rome, Spain, Italy, and France,
We trade for play and opera, song and dance.

Peace to his shade, who first pursu'd the plan !
You lov'd the actor, for you lov'd the man.*
True to himself, to all mankind a friend,
By honest means he gain'd an honest end.
You, like patrons, who his merits knew,
Prompt to applaud, and to reward them too,
Crown'd his last moments with his wish obtain'd
A Royal Charter by your bounty gain'd.'†

* William Gibson. † Troughton's 'Liverpool,' pp. 148-9.

Then followed the tragedy of *Mahomet* and the farce *The Deuce is in Him*.   Although the names of the performers were first published in the local newspapers about this time,* I have, however, never been able to obtain a copy of the bill for the opening performance, therefore, I am unable to say who took part in it.   Genest says that in the tragedy Wroughton played Zaphna and Mrs. Mattocks the part of Palmira, while in the after piece Quick performed Prattle.†

In addition to Colman's another prologue was written for the occasion by Dr. Aikin, but it arrived too late to be of service.   It merits, however, a place in these Annals :—

' Where Mersey's stream long winding o'er the plain,
Pours his full tribute to the circling main,
A band of fishers chose their humble seat ;
Content'd labour bless'd their fair retreat :
Inur'd to hardship, patient, bold, and rude,
They braved the billows for precarious food :
Their straggling huts were rang'd along the shore,
Their nets and little boats their only store.

At length fair Commerce found the chosen place,
And smil'd approving on th' industrious race
Lo ! and she waves her hand, what wonders rise,
Stupendous buildings strike th' astonished eyes :
The hollow'd rock receives the briny tide,
And the huge ships secure from Neptune ride ;
With busy toil the crowd'd streets resound.
And wealth, and arts, and plenty spread around.

The Muses next a willing visit paid ;
They came to Pleasure's and to Virtue's aid ;
A graceful ease and polish to impart,
Refine the taste, and humanise the heart.
Their fair attempts obtain'd a kind applause,
And brightest forms appeared to grace their cause,
In whom each charming lesson shone confest
The polish'd manners, and the feeling breast.

* Holt and Gregson MSS.
† Vol. V, p. 338.

This night the Muse's messenger I come
To bid you welcome to their new-rais'd dome :
Well pleas'd the stately building they survey,
And here their annual summer visit pay ;
Where art, where knowledge reigns, they love the soil
And the free spirit of commercial toil ;
Where the quick sense of graceful, just, and fit
Awakes the chastened smile of decent wit ;
Where soft urbanity the breast inspires
And soothing pity lights her social fires.
O kindly cherish still their generous arts
And show their noblest praises in your hearts.'*

At first it was the rule to keep the Royal open only during
the summer months, commencing when the two London
patent theatres, Drury Lane and Covent Garden, closed, and
concluding when the two metropolitan theatres were about
to reopen for the winter season.

The company consisted of London performers, all of
whom had to pledge themselves under heavy penalties to remain for the whole of the Liverpool dramatic season. This
arrangement at first was a source of considerable monetary
gain to the management of the Royal, but it afterwards proved
both troublesome and expensive, inasmuch as the London
theatres became uncertain in their periods of opening and
closing.   Consequently, the players had to leave Liverpool
hurriedly, or, on the other hand, they were unable to arrive
here in time to open the season.

The performers who appeared during the first season
were:—Messrs. Younger, Mattocks, Palmer, Wroughton, Quick,
Packer, Davies, Baker, Thomson, Keen, Holtom, Wild,
(prompter) ;   Mesdames Mattocks, Baker, Hopkins, Davies,
Kniveton, Claggot, Evans, and Miss Miller.   The dancers
were Messrs. Vincent, Bolton, Vidini, and Miss Besford.†

The theatre had not long been opened when two accidents
happened, the first caused considerable alarm, and, unfortunately, resulted in loss of life, but the second was not of a very
serious nature.

* Troughton's ' History of Liverpool,' p. 391.
† Holt and Gregson MSS.

One night during the performance a house in Williamson Square took fire, and a false alarm of ' fire ' was raised in the theatre.   The actors did their best to reassure the audience that there was no danger, and the musicians were commanded to play in order to quieten the fears of those who had rushed for the doors.   Fortunately many remained seated, but, sad to relate, one man anxious to get down the gallery stairs was killed and several injured.   Holt and Gregson * say that the accident took place on August 24, 1772.   In the ' Annals ' in ' Gore's Directory,' August 29, 1772, is the date given.   Although there are no newspapers to guide one as to which date is correct, I am inclined to believe that the accident took place during June or July.   This inference is based on a date (July 25, 1772), appended to the verses written by Dr. Houlston on the second accident which took place during the performance of the burletta of *Midas*.

During the progress of *Midas* representatives of the gods and goddesses had to ascend in a chariot, singing the while the chorus of ' Jove in his Chair.'   Having reached the celestial regions the platform on which they stood parted in the middle, and several of the performers tumbled down upon the stage. The accident was occasioned by the carpenter having neglected to fasten the bolt which secured the platform.   The following is a copy of the verses penned by Dr. Houlston :—

> ' A terrible tale we have to rehearse,
> And to lessen its terrors we'll tell it in verse,
> The jingle is meant the sad tale to adorn,
> But not to convert your just pity to scorn ;
> Yet some droll misfortune is apt to bewitch
> As we laugh at our friends who fall in a ditch.
> But shunned be the man and detested the heart
> Which never at other's misfortune can smart,
> For generous pity of virtue's a part.
> We protest then once more that we mean no offence,
> Altho' we may smile at another's expence.
> You all of you know how in the polish'd age
> What noble improvements we made to our stage ;

* Holt and Gregson MSS.

How better'd in elegance bulk and design,
To show all our neighbours how fast we refine
To grace our new playhouse the manager chooses
To introduce to us Apollo, the Muses,
Jove, Juno, Cupid, old Midas and Pan,
To please us and fleece us as much as they can,
Behold these celestial troops in array
How glorious the view, but alack; what dismay !
As soon as the Deities got out of sight
An accident happened threw all in a fright,
The prompters, the fiddlers, the pit, and the boxes,
The gallery gentry, the sailors and doxies.
The platform, heaven, Oh ! wondrous to tell,
To the burden unequal most suddenly fell ;
The gods for awhile had suspended their care,
And no wonder they heavily dropped through the air :
Jove's orders was out when the storm soon arose,
And both gods and goddesses fell on their nose,
Juno being in the air for a time in full view,
But with the celestials no need ; tys new.

Some long-winded poets here hardly would fail
To wear out your patience, and lighten the tale
On such a disastrous subject to dwell,
And to pun on the fall of their godships to hell—
But I, more indulgent prefer to recall
The various disasters attending the fall !
How the fates so presumptuous old Jove dar'd dethrone,
Whilst fame spread abroad he had broken his backbone.
Apollo it happened had taken his leave ;
But that arch rascal, Cupid the danger would brave
And by his wings aided in safety departed
To render our *beaux* and our *belles* tender-hearted :
How quickly the demi-gods, Muses and Graces
Totter'd after great Jove, and fell on their faces.
But who can describe the confusion and noise
Which spread through the house at the fall of the skies,
And what's more agonising, not one of our sparks
Car'd on that occasion, for catching of larks,

An outcry, which ' fire ' made folks run for their lives,*
Some flew in a hurry forgetting their wives ;
How praiseworthy then would the medical tribe,
Have leapt on the stage to give help and prescribe ;
Forgetting themselves for the general good
They stain'd for the first time the stage with true blood,
Æculapius came in, and their good heads were mended,
And thus was the rare tragi-comedy ended.'

T. H., July 25, 1772.†

On September 14, 1772, the proprietors of the theatre granted Mrs. Elizabeth Bennett a lease of the house for twenty years at a yearly rental of £281.   According to the lease,‡ which I have seen, the following gentlemen constituted the proprietors : Messrs. John Sparling, William Gregson, John Tarleton, Matthew Stronge, Ralph Earle, Thomas Case, Thomas Rumbold, James Bridge, Thomas Earle, Thomas Smyth, Thomas Staniforth, Thomas Hodgson the elder, George Case, John Brown, Gill Slater, William Earle, Edward Brock, Thomas Hodgson the younger, William Farrington, and William Boats.   All the foregoing were merchants.   Then there were :—Messrs. John Lyon, surgeon, Lloyd Baxendale, up-holder, John Tarleton, mercer, Thomas Maddock, clerk, Robert Richmond, William Wilson, Francis Gildart, Ralph Williamson, and John Brownell, gentlemen ; and James Wrigley, inn-keeper.§ Afterwards Mrs. Bennett entered into a new agreement with Messrs. Younger and Mattocks, and for the due performance of the conditions of the lease George Colman, Jonathan Garton, and Joseph Redmond of Covent Garden Theatre, entered into a bond for £6,000.
    The earliest Royal playbill I have been able to discover, that for the reopening on June 4, 1773, just twelve months after the theatre was first opened,‖ is here given :—

---

* This I think refers to the false alarm of ' Fire ' during June or July, 1772.
† Holt and Gregson MSS.
‡ This lease is the earliest document I have seen in which the proprietors' names are mentioned.
§ Wrigley was the only one who could not write his name.   He was proprietor of the ' Golden Lion ' in Dale Street.
‖ The earliest Liverpool playbill in the British Museum Library is that of the Theatre Royal for June 5, 1773.

By their Majesties Servants.
THEATRE ROYAL, LIVERPOOL.
This present FRIDAY, JUNE 4th, 1773
Will be Performed
THE BEGGAR'S OPERA.

Macheath	by Mr. Mattocks
Peachum	by Mr. Quick
Lockit	by Mr. Thompson
Filch	by Mr. Holtom
Mat o' the Mint	by Mr. Baker
Lucy	by Mrs. Baker
Mrs. Peachum	by Mrs. Barrington
Jenny Diver	by Miss Day
Polly	by Mrs. Mattocks

To conclude with a Country Dance by the Characters of the Opera.

In Act 3d.
A Hornpipe by Miss Twist.
To which will be added a Farce called
THE CONTRIVANCES.

Rovewell	by Mr. Mattocks
Argus	by Mr. Quick
Hearty	by Mr. Thompson
Robin	by Mr. Baker
Betty	by Miss Day
Arethusa	by Mrs. Baker

The days of playing will be Mondays, Wednesdays, Fridays, and Saturdays.

Boxes 3s. 6d. Pit 2s. 6d. Gallery 1s.

The doors to be opened at half-past five. To begin exactly at Seven.

Tickets and places for the Boxes to be taken at the Stage Door of the Theatre.

No person can be admitted behind the scenes.
Vivant Rex et Regina.

Mrs. George Mattocks, wife of the co-lessee of the Royal, belonged to Covent Garden Theatre. Mrs. Mattocks's father and mother were both on the stage, the former being manager of the Goodman's Fields Theatre. Our Mrs. Mattocks (*née* Isabella Hallam) was a very good low comedy actress, and a capable performer in other lines.   Ryan in his ' Table Talk' mentions that 'Mrs. Mattocks was as much celebrated for the taste and elegance of her dress as for her histrionic talents.   The various dresses of Mrs. Mattocks after they had passed the ordeal of the female critics in the theatre, and been there displayed to the admiration of the town, were frequently sent for by the principal ladies of Liverpool, and other towns in the country, who adopted and spread the fashion.'

Roach* says that ' though for a while they (Mr. and Mrs. Mattocks) lived happy, frailties on both sides occasioned a separation.'   George Mattocks died in 1804.   Mrs. Mattocks survived her husband many years.   She bestowed a good marriage portion on her daughter, and on retiring from the stage had £6,000 in the stocks left for herself.   As she lived in Kensington, London, and it was inconvenient for her to receive her own dividends, she gave her son-in-law, a barrister named Hewson, a power of attorney.   This man proved wholly unfaithful to the trust for he died greatly in debt. Upon going to the bank to receive her expected dividends Mrs. Mattocks found to her great consternation that her son-in-law had sold the securities, and spent the money.   She had no suspicion of the fraud until too late, as the dividends had been paid to her with strict regularity.   She died June 25, 1826.

In 'Williamson's Advertiser' for July 30, 1773, Mr. Barry, the treasurer of the theatre, advertised for a quantity of sper-maçeti candles.   Amongst the poorer brethren of the sons of Thespis candle-ends were not ' unconsidered trifles' but were in fact a source of emolument.   In Cape Everard's 'Memoirs'† there occurs this passage : ' I remember,' says Mr. King, 'that when I had been a short time on the stage, I performed one night King Richard, gave two comic songs, played in an inter-lude, danced a horn-pipe, spoke a prologue, afterwards harlequin in a sharing company ;   and after all this fatigue, my share came to *three-pence and two pieces of candle !* '

Candles are mentioned in some of the Theatre Royal accounts as forming an additional part of the receipts. The theatre staff included one or more attendants to go round

---

* ' Memoirs of the Green Room' (1796), p. 58.   † P. 62.

and snuff the candles at intervals.   These worthies were invariably tall and thin, and were known by the name of 'Tallow Jack.'   I may mention that I have spoken with those who remembered attendants on the stages of the local Royal and Amphitheatre being greeted with cries of ' Tallow Jack ! ' This epithet was bandied about even after gas had been introduced.

When Mrs. George Farren (*née* Wright, of Liverpool) was left a widow with four children, and in poor circumstances, she applied for an engagement to Whiteley of Chester, but he having no vacancy recommended her to Younger of the Royal. A favourable report of Kitty Farren (the elder daughter) induced that gentleman to engage the whole family.   In 1774 Elizabeth (Betsy) Farren made her *début* at the Royal at the age of 15 as Rosetta in *Love in a Village.*   ' But such was the poverty of her wardrobe,' says a writer in ' Walker's Hibernian Magazine,' for July, 1794, ' that the ladies of the company, it is remembered, were obliged to subscribe each a proportion of apparel before she could be properly equipped.   So much may great merit and superior talents be depressed by poverty. She next performed Lady Townly, and pleased Mr. Younger so well that he procured credit with his tradesmen for what cloaths any of the family stood in need of.'

After remaining at the Royal some three years gaining experience, and winning approbation for her performances, especially for her Lady Townly, she was introduced by Mr. Younger to George Colman, and made her *début* in London at the Haymarket, on June 9, 1777, in the part of Miss Hardcastle.

There was recently sold at Sotheby's an autograph letter from Garrick to Colman, in which the former says : ' I like your piece and that other most promising piece, Miss Farren— 'tis a shame that she is not fixed in London.   I will venture my life that I could teach her a capital part in comedy, aye and tragedy too, that should drive half our actresses mad. She is much too fine stuff to be worn and soiled at Manchester and Liverpool.'   After her London *début* she was engaged for Covent Garden, which theatre in a little while she left to become a member of Old Drury, where she performed a considerable time as a first tragic actress and became successor to Mrs. Abington in comedy.

Miss Farren moved in the best society ; and long before she withdrew from the stage it was said of her that when ' One certain event should happen, a Countess's coronet would fall on her brow.' This contingency was the death of the Countess of Derby.   It was through an introduction of the Duchess of Leinster that Miss Farren first became acquainted with Edward, the twelfth Earl of Derby, who was himself a clever amateur actor.   A platonic affection between the two soon ripened into something more lasting.   In her ' Diary of a Lady of Quality,' Miss Wynne recalls ' the circumstance of seeing Lord Derby leaving his private box to creep to her behind the screen, and, of course, we all looked with impatience for the discovery, hoping the screen would fall a little too soon, and show to the audience Lord Derby as well as Lady Teazle.'

On April 8, 1797, Miss Farren, in the part of Lady Teazle, took her farewell leave of the stage, and on the 1st of May following she was married to the Earl of Derby.   Three children were born of this union, but only one survived, Mary, born in 1801, who, in 1821, married the Earl of Wilton, eight years before her mother's death, which took place at Knowsley on April 23, 1829.   The Earl of Derby survived her some five years.

On May 1, 1774, permission was granted by the Corporation to change the names of the leaseholders of the theatre on payment of one hundred pounds fine, ' or to change the lives of John Brownell and Gerard Potter only, paying two guineas fine, at the election of the said proprietors to be made and signed to Mr. Mayor in a month.'*

The proprietors of the theatre petitioned against this, and claimed an abatement of the fine laid on them.   In their petition they set forth ' that they had laid out near six thousand pounds in building the said house, and that they had lost in a life† therein within a year after the finishing the same building, and thereby greatly improving the Corporation Estate.' To this the Corporation made answer that they would do ' what hath been done in many similar instances to encourage the improvement of said Corporation Estate, to mitigate the said fine of one hundred pounds to twenty guineas, and that they have the said lease granted accordingly, and with this abatement of the said price.'‡

---

* Corporation Records.   ♭ † William Gibson.   ‡ Corporation Records.

On April 25, 1775, the oratorio of *The Messiah* was performed, and on the following evening the oratorio of *Samson*.
On the twenty-seventh a sacred oratorio, ' never performed
in this country,' called *Jephtha* was given, and on the following
night Dryden's Ode, set to music by Dr. Wainwright, was submitted.   The performers, who were selected from different
parts of the country, included Messrs. Brown, Saville,
and Spence ; Mesdames Barthelomon, Weichsell, and
Miss Radcliffe.

According to J. Winston, author of ' The Theatric Tourist,' Garrick performed in Liverpool in Ben Jonson's comedy,
Every Man in His Humour.   No date is mentioned.   It
must, however, have been prior to June 10, 1776, when Garrick
took his farewell of the stage.   Winston says that ' the piece
was highly patronised,' not so on its revival a few years afterwards.   ' They (the Liverpool folk) said it was unworthy of
representation.'*

On June 26, 1775, Charles Macklin enacted Shylock, and
on June 30, Richard III.   Mrs. Barrington appeared as the
Duchess of York.   On July 7, Macklin acted Macbeth for
his benefit.

On August 25, *The Rivals* was produced at the Royal,
Larry Clinch being the Captain Absolute, and Moody the Sir
Lucius O'Trigger.   This comedy of Sheridan's was first produced in the January of that year, the original Sir Lucius
being an actor named Lee, who died in 1781.   Lee, however,
had not made genteel Irish comedy parts a speciality, and in
consequence the piece was not a success until Clinch took over
the part.   Clinch so well satisfied the audience that Sheridan
requested him not long after to create the Irish part of Lieutenant O'Connor in *St. Patrick's Day.*

Moody was also a celebrated actor of Hibernian parts.
His real name was Cochrane, and he was born in Cork, where
he was apprenticed to his father, who was a hairdresser.
Moody was the original Captain O'Cutter in Colman's *Jealous
Wife* ; but his greatest stage triumph was as Major O'Flaherty
in *The West Indian.*

During his engagement at the Royal in the summer of
1775 Moody received a letter from David Garrick in which
Roscius asked, ' Have you ever heard of a Mrs. Siddons who

* P. 53.

is strolling about somewhere near you ? '   The Mrs. Siddons
referred to was the eldest daughter of Mr. and Mrs. Roger
Kemble, two itinerant players, and was born in Brecon, on
June 13, 1755.   Sarah Kemble's first audience hissed her
as too young to be listened to ; but she won their approval
by the clever manner in which she recited a fable.   A similar
occurrence (to be noted later on) happened to her in after
years at the Liverpool Royal.

Sarah Kemble was in her nineteenth year when, on November 6, 1773, she became the wife of Mr. Siddons, a poor
player, and an ex-apprentice from Birmingham.   Parental
displeasure at the union caused Mr. and Mrs. Siddons to
depart from Mr. Roger Kemble's company and join that of
Messrs. Chamberlain and Crump.   These two managers were
commonly known by the names of ' Fox and Bruin.'   S. W.
Ryley, in his 'Itinerant,' describes Chamberlain as being sly
and cunning, and Crump as having a blunt, morose and brutish
character.   At Cheltenham Mrs. Siddons's playing excited
universal admiration ; and Lord Ailesbury mentioned her to
Garrick.   Lord Dungarvon's daughter, the Honourable Miss
Boyle, looked after her wardrobe, lent her many of her own
dresses, and helped to make others with her own hands.   On
one occasion Mrs. Siddons had to appear on the stage in a male
disguise ; but the necessary habiliments not being forthcoming
she was compelled to accept the loan of a coat from a gentleman who sat in one of the boxes, while he stood at the wings,
with a petticoat thrown over his shoulders, waiting to receive
his property.

On December 29, 1775, she made at Drury Lane Theatre
her first appearance on the metropolitan boards.   *The Merchant of Venice* was billed for that evening, the part of Portia
' by a young lady,' and Shylock by Mr. King.   After playing
a variety of parts with not very great success, Mrs. Siddons
terminated her London engagement in the June of 1776.

Although Lee Lewes states that Mrs. Siddons was sojour-
ning in Liverpool with her two children about November,
1775, I have never been able to ascertain when she first played
here.   At any rate she performed a number of parts during
the winter season of 1776.

Boaden, in his ' Memoirs of Mrs. Inchbald,'* tells us that in the early part of October, 1776, Mrs. Inchbald first met Mrs. Siddons in Liverpool, thus beginning a friendship that extended through all the changes of their fortunes for five-and-forty years.   On the twenty-seventh of the month West Digges (who was the son of Elizabeth, sister to the first Earl of Delaware, and Thomas Digges of Chilham Castle, Kent) arrived to act Cato and a round of other prominent characters.

Mr. and Mrs. Siddons and Mr. and Mrs. Inchbald terminated their engagement with Messrs. Younger and Mattocks in December, and, on the seventeenth of the month, they took, at eight o'clock in the morning, a post-chaise for Manchester.   On the way the vehicle was upset, but luckily none of the occupants were hurt.   They ultimately arrived at their destination at six o'clock in the evening.

In 1776, William Thomas Lewis, who in 1803 became one of the lessees of the theatre, made his first appearance on these boards.   During his engagement he played Oakly, Orestes, Pierre, George Hargrave in *The Runaway*, Leon, Kitely, Lord Falconbridge in *The English Merchant*, and Arnold in *Edward, The Black Prince*.   Mr. Lewis also acted as manager that year for Messrs. Younger and Mattocks.

It was about 1776 that Joseph Munden made his first appearance here.   He was then about eighteen years of age, having been born in Brooks Street, London, in 1758.   He became ' stage-struck ' at an early age, and joined a band of strollers.   A performer (probably Shuter) with whom he had scraped acquaintance, was engaged for the Royal, Liverpool, and with him Munden set out from the metropolis in the hope of obtaining some employment in the theatre.   His hopes were not realised ; and he found himself in a strange town, quite destitute ; his friend, however, kindly provided him with food.   Eventually Munden, being a skilful penman, obtained a situation in the Town Clerk's office.

In the ' Memoirs of Munden ' there is a footnote† in which it is stated by the editor, the comedian's son, that 'the late Mr. Pope presented me with the cash-book of this office (the Town Clerk's), which had somehow fallen into his hands. Munden's salary is there entered at ten shillings and sixpence

* Vol. I, p. 69.   † P. 9.

a week ; it does not seem to have been suffered to remain long in arrear.' According to Oxberry's ' Memoir of Munden,'* he also obtained employment as a copyist at the theatre, ' to which was added the honour of walking in procession, bearing banners, carrying links, and other little matters of that agreeable description ; and for these dramatic efforts, he received the handsome remuneration of one shilling per night.'

Of Munden, ' Elia ' wrote:—' I have seen this gifted actor in Sir Christopher Curry, in Old Dornton, diffuse a glow of sentiment which has made the pulse of a crowded theatre beat like that of one man. . . . . I have seen some faint approaches to this sort of excellence in other players. But in the grand grotesque of farce, Munden stands out as single and unaccompanied as Hogarth. Hogarth, strange to tell, had no followers. The school of Munden began, and must end, with himself.'

About this time, 1776, and onwards, a series of tiles were printed in Liverpool with the portraits of famous actors and actresses in character. The prints are similar to those in ' Bell's British Theatre.' Some of the printed tiles are in the Liverpool Museum. The art of printing on earthenware from copper plates was invented about 1756, by a Liverpool man, Mr. Sadler, who, in partnership with Guy Green, carried on business at 14 and 16 Harrington Street, Liverpool. Mr. Sadler's discovery was accidentally made by seeing his children stick pictures on broken pieces of pottery. The following theatrical tiles were manufactured in Liverpool :— Mrs. Abington as Estifania (*Rule a Wife and Have a Wife*); Mrs. Barry as Sir Harry Wildair, and Athanais (*Theodosius* ; or, *The Force of Love*) ; Mr. Bensley as Mahomet (*Mahomet, The Impostor*) ; Mrs. Bulkley as Angelina (*Love Makes a Man* ; or, *The Fop's Fortune*) ; Mrs. Cibber as Monimia (*The Orphan* ; or, *The Unhappy Marriage*) ; Mr. Foote as Fondlewife (*The Old Batchelor*) ; Mr. Garrick as Abel Drugger (*The Alchemist*), Sir John Brute (*The Provoked Wife*), and Don John (*The Chances*) ; Mrs. Hartley as Lady Jane Grey, and as Imoinda (*Oroonoko*) ; Miss P. Hopkins as Lavinia (*Titus Andronicus*) ; Mr. King as Lissardo (*The Wonder : a Woman Keeps a Secret*) ; Lee Lewes as Harlequin (*Harlequin's Invasion*), and as Sir Peter Teazle (*The School for Scandal*) ; W.T. Lewis as Hippolitus

* ' Dramatic Biography ' (1825), Vol. II, p. 71.

(*Phædra and Hippolitus*), and as Douglas (*Douglas*) ; Mrs. Lessingham as Ophelia (*Hamlet*) ; Mr. Macklin as Sir Gilbert Wrangle (*The Refusal; or, The Ladies' Philosophy*), and as Shylock (*The Merchant of Venice*) ; Mrs. Mattocks as Princess Katherine (*Henry V*) ; Mr. Moody as Teague (*The Committee*), and as Simon (*Harlequin's Invasion*) ; Mr. Smith as Lord Townly (*The Provoked Husband; or, a Journey to London*) ; Mr. Shuter as Lovegold (*The Miser*) ; Mrs. Ward as Rodogune (*The Royal Convert*) ; Mr. Woodward as Razor (*The Upholsterer*), and as Petruchio (*The Taming of the Shrew*) ; Mrs. Wrighton as Peggy (*The Gentle Shepherd*) ; Mr. Wroughton as Barnwell (*The London Merchant; or, the History of George Barnwell*) ; Mrs. Yates as Lady Townly (*The Provoked Husband*), and as Jane Shore ; and Miss Younge as Zara (*The Mourning Bride*).

In 1777, Mr. and Mrs. Siddons and her brother, John Philip Kemble, were engaged at the Royal. This was Mr. Kemble's first appearance on the Liverpool stage, and his *début* was made on Friday evening, June 27, as the Earl of Somerset in the tragedy of *Sir Thomas Overbury*. He also spoke the prologue.

John Kemble (who was born at Prescot, February 1, 1757) made his first appearance on the stage at Wolverhampton, January 8, 1776. When eight years old he was sent by his father, Roger Kemble, to Douai, with the intention of qualifying for the priesthood. The prospects of a restricted mode of life induced him to quit Douai before he had attained the age of twenty. On arriving in England he was coolly received by his father, and seeing that his room was preferable to his company, he hastened to join Chamberlain and Crump's company at Wolverhampton, and he made his *début* there in the character of Theodosius in Lee's tragedy so called. His first effort was not very successful, but his second; Bajazet in *Tamerlane*, met with more approval.

The salary of a provincial actor at that time was very meagre ; and in this respect Kemble was no more fortunate than his brethren, albeit regarded as a rising performer. On one occasion his pecuniary resources were so low that it is related that he could not even pay his laundress the sum of fifteen pence, nor obtain credit for that amount ; she, consequently, refused to deliver him his one and only shirt, which he badly needed to dress for his part, Ventidius in *All for Love*. The result was that he was reduced to the necessity of shifting an odd ruffle from one wrist to the other, alternately, during the performance, concealing the temporarily bared wrist in his coat to prevent the audience noticing the deficiency.

Kemble, at length, released himself from the managerial authority of Chamberlain and Crump, but, previous to leaving them, he chalked the following couplet upon the theatrical barn-door :—

> ' I fly to shun impending ruin,
> And leave the Fox to fight with Bruin.'

He then strolled about the country with a man named Carleton, practising various schemes and experiments in order to raise the necessaries of life.   After undergoing a variety of mortifying experiences and enduring all sorts of contumely and neglect, we next hear of him at Worcester, where he was arrested for debt.   From durance vile he was released by his sister, Mrs. Siddons, and by her introduced to Mr. Younger.

On August 25, 1777, *Falstaff's Wedding*, Dr. Kenrick's sequel to *The Merry Wives of Windsor*, was performed, with Wilson as the Fat Knight.   The play was originally produced at Drury Lane, London, on April 12, 1766.

On Wednesday, December 3, 1777, Mrs. Siddons played Hamlet for the third time on any stage ; Miss Farren was Ophelia ; J. P. Kemble, Laertes ; Mr. Younger, Ghost ; Mr. Siddons, Horatio.   It was the occasion of Mrs. Siddons's benefit, which she took with Barry, the treasurer of the theatre. In an article by W. Moy Thomas on ' Lady Hamlets,' in 'The Graphic,'* he says that she dressed the character in ' a black fringed cloak draped about her like a lady's shawl,' and that the general effect was that of a ' burly, ill-formed man.'

' I played Hamlet in Liverpool ' she wrote to her friend, Mrs. Inchbald, 'to nearly a hundred pounds, and I wish I had taken it myself, but fear of charges, which you know are most tremendous, persuaded me to take part of a benefit with Barry, for which I have since been much blamed ; but he, I believe,

---

* June 17, 1899.

was very much satisfied ; and indeed so am I. Strange resolutions are formed in a theatrical ministry ; one of them I think very prudent (this little rogue Harry* is chattering to such a degree I scarce know what I am about), but to proceed : our managers have determined to employ no more exotics ; they have found that Miss Younge's late visit to us (which you must have heard of) has rather hurt than done them service; so that Liverpool must from this time forth be content with such homely fare as we small folk can furnish to its delicate sense.'† Miss Younge's first appearance in Liverpool was made at this theatre on Monday, July 14, 1777. She was a *protégé* of Garrick's, and was excellent in both comedy and tragedy.

From the first it was the invariable custom at the Theatre Royal to have only London performers. An effort had previously been made by the lessees, Messrs. Younger and Mattocks, to have, in imitation of Tate Wilkinson, a company consisting of only provincial performers ; but an outcry of such gravity was raised against the threatened innovation that the lessees very wisely desisted from putting into force their intended scheme.

On several occasions they had, however, introduced with gratifying success several provincial performers like Mrs. Siddons and Miss Farren. Although they possessed no metropolitan reputation these two budding geniuses became great favourites with the Liverpool public, and their popularity probably emboldened the lessees to try and establish a company of unseasoned performers.

Their intended innovation for the dramatic season of 1778 soon leaked out, and, in consequence, they were threatened by the townsmen with all manner of pains and penalties if they persisted in their scheme. This time, however, the lessees were not to be intimidated by any threats, and, accordingly they engaged a company (consisting principally of country performers, amongst whom were Mr. and Mrs. Siddons, and J. P. Kemble) for the opening on June 15, 1778.

The eventful night arrived. Ominous signs of disorder and discontent very early prevailed. To quieten the audience and, if possible, to prevent a riot, Mr. Younger, before the play

* Henry Siddons, born October 4, 1774.
† Boaden's ' Memoirs of Mrs. Inchbald,' Vol. II, p. 363.

began, advanced in front of the curtain.   ' In vain,' wrote
J. P. Kemble in a letter (dated June 18, 1778) to Mrs.
Inchbald, who was then at Leeds, ' did he attempt to ora-
torize ;   the remorseless villains threw up their hats, hissed,
kicked, stamped, bawled, did everything to prevent him being
heard.   After two or three fruitless entrances, and saluted
with volleys of potatoes and broken bottles, he thought proper
to depute Mr. Siddons as his advocate, who entered bearing
a board, large enough to secure his person, inscribed with
Mr. Younger's petition to be heard.   The rogues would hear
nothing, and Siddons may thank his wooden protector that
his bones are whole.   Mrs. Siddons entered next P.S., and
Mrs. Kniveton O.P.—*mais aussi infortunées—hé bien !—
Madame Kniveton a la mauvaise fortune de tomber dans une
convulsion sur les plancs* : the wretches laughed, and would
willingly have sent a peal of shouts after her into the
next world loud enough to have burst the gates of her destination.   They next extinguished all the lights round the
house ; then jumped upon the stage ; brushed every lamp out
with their hats ; took back their money ; left the theatre and
determined themselves to repeat this till they have another
company . . . . I had almost forgotten to tell you that
every wall in the town is covered with verse and prose expressive
of the contempt they hold us in.'*

Kemble is reported to have asked the local public ' Shall
I tell you what you are like ?   You are like Captain Driver
in *Oroonoko*.'   The tragedy of *Oroonoko* was at that time
prohibited from the local stage as reflecting too much on the
conduct of those Liverpool merchants who were engaged in
the Slave Trade.   After this engagement, ' Black Jack,'
as George Frederick Cooke termed the peerless Kemble, did
not perform again in Liverpool until 1784.

On June 26, 1778, *The School for Scandal* was played by
' particular permission of the author.'   August 21 saw John
Henderson as Richard III ; and on the following night,
Lee Lewes appeared as Harlequin in *The Birth and Adventures
of Harlequin*.   Henderson, from all accounts, was a fine actor ;
' his Hamlet and his Falstaff,' says Rogers, ' were equally good.'
Boaden states that Lee Lewes was ' a comedian of the

* Boaden's ' Memoirs of Mrs. Inchbald,' Vol. I, pp. 91-3.

Woodward class, and, like him, an excellent ground harlequin.' Lewes was born in 1740, and died in 1803.

The company for the summer season of 1779 included Mrs. Siddons, Mrs. Ward, Mrs. Baddeley ; Messrs. Lee Lewes, Kniveton, Quick, Booth, Siddons, and Hollingsworth. Hollingsworth made, when a boy, his first appearance on the stage at this theatre, Mr. Younger being sponsor. His line was low comedy. He was also considered an excellent clown in pantomime. After having performed at York, Edinburgh, Manchester, etc., he joined the Drury Lane company. Hollingsworth played at the Liverpool Royal for many years. He must have died at an advanced age, for when Miss O'Neill appeared in 1815 at the local Theatre Royal, he supported her in *The Fatal Marriage*.

On one occasion when Hollingsworth was playing at the Royal, he, during an interval, went to have a look at the audience through a favourite peep-hole in the curtain. A mischievous fellow in the gallery noticed the actor surveying the house, and with considerable force threw a knife at him, happily, however, missing his mark.*

Disturbances at the Royal on the part of the audience had, for some considerable time, been a source of great anxiety to the lessees, Messrs. Younger and Mattocks. In 1779 they applied to the Court of King's Bench for leave to file a criminal information against several respectable townsmen who were supposed to be in the habit of frequenting the theatre in order to create a disturbance. The action, however, was discontinued on payment of costs. At the same time the Court was informed, ' that the defendants wished to meet the plaintiffs in issue, in order to evince the propriety of their conduct, and to maintain the exercise of their judgment, to approve or disapprove individually, during the representation of theatrical performances ; but as they are not influenced by personal or by hostile motives towards Mr. Younger, they had directed their solicitor to return Messrs. Younger and Mattocks their costs, after the discontinuance of the action.'†

During 1779 the bills of the play contained the announcement that ' Those ladies and gentlemen who have taken places are requested to send their servants by six o'clock to keep them.'

* ' The Theatric Tourist ' (1805), p. 51.
† ' Gore's General Advertiser,' June 2, 1779.

There is no mention that the servants would be afterwards admitted into the gallery without payment.

On the occasion of Mr. Aldridge's benefit on August 25, 1779, there was introduced the grand pantomimical dance, entitled ' The Liverpool Prize ; or, Who's Afraid ? ' with a view of the arrival of the ' Mentor ' and her prize, the ' Carnatic.'

August 28, 1780, witnessed the production of a new interlude, entitled *Derby Wakes*, in the course of which there was exhibited a representation of bull-baiting.   This piece was founded on the wakes, which, for many years, used to be held at West Derby, Liverpool.   In addition to other forms of amusement, the cruel sport of bull-baiting was freely indulged in.

Apropos of these wakes, Brooke tells the following story in his ' Liverpool '*: ' On one occasion, a party of sailors went to West Derby and brought the bull to Liverpool, resolved to conclude the frolic by showing him the play, and actually dragged him by means of ropes tied to his horns into the theatre, and introduced his head into one of the centre boxes ; and then, as he had seen (to use their own expression) the play, they led him out.   There was no great difficulty in getting him in or out, because the principal entrance door was in the middle of the front of the theatre, with an ascent from Williamson Square, of only two or three steps, and was exactly opposite the centre boxes.'   Mr. Brooke's father was in the theatre at the time this occurrence took place, but he could not recollect the date.   In Troughton's ' Liverpool,'† the date is given as 1783.

The elder Farren played here during the season of 1781. On June 5, he appeared as Charles Surface in *The School for Scandal*.   On July 28 of the same year was performed *Harlequin Freemason*, ' to conclude with a procession of the Grand Masters from the Creation to the present time.'   On the occasion of Mrs. Mattocks' benefit on September 5, 1781, it was announced that the theatre would be ' illuminated with wax.' Two days later Mrs. Kniveton had her ' bespeak ' when, by desire of the Earl of Derby, *The Generous Impostor* was performed.

* P. 267.   † P. 98.

One of the members of the company in 1782 was an erratic comedian named Tony Le Brun, who was no less remarkable for his singular simplicity than his extreme fondness for angling. Of Tony it is recorded that when he was a member of the company at the Royal, ' he laid one evening several lines in a stream near the town, in hopes of procuring an excellent dinner for the next day. In the course of the night, a theatrical wag belonging to the same company went to the place, drew up his hooks, and on some of them fixed *red herrings*, and on others *sparrows*, carefully placing them again in the former situation. Early in the morning, Tony went with a friend, to secure his expected prize, and drew up the red herrings ; upon which he said, ' Before God ! here are herrings ! and, upon my faith, *ready pickled* too ! ' Proceeding further, he drew the sparrows on shore : after examining them attentively, he exclaimed, ' God bless my soul ! this is indeed very surprising ! I don't wonder at catching the *red herrings*, because they were in their own element, but I really never before thought that birds lived in *water* ! I should as soon have expected to have shot *fish* in the *air* ! But I will take care and not be disappointed a second time, by laying my lines here for *fresh fish*.'*

For the benefit of William Farren on August 28, 1782, *The East Indian*, ' a new comedy as it is now performing at the Theatre Royal in the Haymarket with universal applause,' was submitted. The representation was ' by permission of the author and manager of the Theatre Royal, Haymarket,' and it was also announced ' that the comedy cannot on any account be performed after that evening, as the manuscript, which is kindly lent him for that night only, must be returned to London the day after the performance.' The principal characters were undertaken by Messrs. Henderson, Farren, Thompson, Suett, Phillimore, Hollingsworth, Quick, Mrs. Kniveton, and Mrs. Mattocks. The season's receipts amounted to £3,000.

The theatre re-opened on June 9, 1783. In the company were Mrs. Siddons and Messrs. Henderson and Farren. This was Mrs. Siddons's first appearance here since 1779, and the first time that she and Henderson had played together: ' Williamson's Advertiser ' says that ' the theatre was

* Oxberry's ' Dramatic Biography,' (1825), p. 261.

extremely crowded. Large sums were offered for seats, but
there were none to be had.' Mrs. Siddons afterwards sailed
for Dublin, where she was engaged for the summer season.

December 13 of that year was a Freemason's night. The
performance was for the benefit of Mr. and Mrs. Stephen
Kemble. The stage was fitted up in representation of a
Mason's Lodge. The ceremony opened with the Master and
Brethren singing ' Hail, Masonry Divine,' after which an
epilogue was given by Sister Kemble, who was dressed in the
character of a Freemason's wife, with the apron, jewels, etc.,
of a Master Mason. An ode in honour of Masonry was
delivered by Brother Kemble, who sat as Master of the
Lodge. The function concluded with ' When Earth's Foundation First Was Laid.' There was also performed a musical
entertainment, written by Mrs. Kemble, entitled *The Elope-
ment; or, The Liverpool Welcome.* The performance was
by desire of the Ancient and Honourable Fraternity of Free
and Accepted Freemasons, who, prior to the representation,
walked in procession from the St. George's Coffee House in
Castle Street to the theatre.

John Philip Kemble was here during the summer of 1784.
' By this agreement a copy of which I have seen,' writes
Fitzgerald, ' he was to perform in all plays, farces, operas,
and pantomimes, and all for the modest sum of ten shillings
a night, and a benefit which was to be subjected to the
thirty-five pounds' deduction, the charges of the house.'[*]

' The provincial engagements of Mr. Kemble,' says Boaden, ' produced for him frequent mortification, and little of
either profit or fame, with the exception of Manchester and
Liverpool, in both of these towns he left a favourable impression, which has constantly been kept up by summer engagements.'[†] During his engagement at the Royal in 1784, he
played Hamlet, Jaques, Leontes, Prospero, Malvolio, Don
Felix, and Beverley.

On September 4, 1784, Joseph Younger, one of the lessees
of the theatre passed over to the majority. He was 52 years
of age when he died, and the interment took place on September 7, in Sefton Churchyard.[‡] The grave, which is situated

* ' Lives of the Kembles,' Vol. I, p. 178-9.
† ' Memoirs of the Life of John Philip Kemble,' Vol. I, p. 20.
‡ Boaden, in his ' Memoirs of The Life of John Philip Kemble,' erroneously states
that Younger died on September 3, 1784, in his 50th year.

in a secluded corner by the western wall of the church, is covered by a plain flat stone, the cost of which was defrayed by Mr. Forres and a few others.

Boaden says that Younger was an indifferent actor ; yet he had good judgment and an extensive knowledge of the stage. ' To show,' he writes, ' the fluctuation of popular favour, it may be well to record that, about seven years before Mr. Younger's death, he found himself at Mattocks's theatre in Birmingham, opposed to Henderson, who was at Yates's in the same town. The play was *Lear* at both houses ; and thus curiously contrasted in the principal characters :—

"Lear . . . . . HENDERSON against Younger
Cordelia . . . . The SIDDONS and Mrs. Mattocks!!"

' The great talents played to about half the nightly charges and the house of their surprising rivals literally overflowed.'*

Younger had rich relations, and it is stated that he formed expectations which were not realised. At his death he was indebted to the elder Colman in the sum of £1,200, and to Garton, the treasurer of Covent Garden Theatre, he owed as much as £5,000. Boaden says that Garton had as security a mortgage upon the Liverpool and Manchester theatres. In respect to the Liverpool theatre the probability is that Garton had only a lien on the lease. After Younger's death Mattocks became sole lessee of the Liverpool Theatre Royal.

George Frederick Cooke visited Liverpool (apparently, for the first time) in the autumn of 1784, after having acted at Manchester. He played Sciolto (*The Fair Penitent*), Bellarius (*Cymbeline*), Claudio (*Much Ado About Nothing*), Friar Tuck (*Robin Hood*), etc. Cooke was born in 1756, and his first regular attempt as an actor was made at Brentford in 1776. Of him it was truly observed that he did not play many parts well, but that he played those he did play well better than anyone else.

On September 11, 1785, charming Mrs. Abington (the original Lady Teazle) made her first appearance on this stage, in playing Charlotte in *The Hypocrite*. Mrs. Abington was born in 1731 and died in the year of Waterloo. Of her

*'Memoirs of The Life of John Philip Kemble,' Vol. I, p. 200.

Davies writes :—' Her person is formed with great elegance, her address is graceful, her looks animated and expressive.' Dr. Johnson was solicited by Mrs. Abington to attend her benefit. He went.   Boswell's inquisitiveness broke out.   Good nature might have kept him quiet.   ' Why, sir, did you go to Mrs. Abington's benefit ?   Did you see ? '   ' No sir.'   ' Did you hear ? '   ' No, sir.'   ' Why then did you go ? '   ' Because, sir, she is a favourite with the public ;   and when the public care a thousandth part for you that it does for her, I will go to your benefit too.'

The veteran actor, Charles Macklin, commenced a short engagement at the Theatre Royal, on October 7, 1785, opening as Sir Archy MacSarcasm in *Love à la Mode*.   He also performed Shylock, ' the Jew that Shakespeare drew,' on October 14, and Sir Pertinax MacSycophant in *The Way of the World* three nights later.

Prior to fulfilling this engagement Macklin had been asked by Mattocks if he knew of any young man capable of playing Gentlemen Fops and Tragedy in Liverpool and Manchester. A very likely young actor named Macready (afterwards father of William Charles Macready) presented himself to Mr. Macklin while the latter was performing at the Smock Alley Theatre, Dublin.   In a letter dated August 18, 1785, preserved in the British Museum, Macklin wrote to Macready, who was then at Waterford, acquainting him of Mr. Mattocks' wants, and pointing out ' that it might be a step towards his being introduced to Covent Garden Theatre.'   Macready was introduced by Macklin to Mattocks, and by him engaged.   In the course of the winter he played the Duke of Suffolk (*Lady Jane Grey*), Harry Stukely (*All the World's a Stage*), Stephano (*The Tempest*), Trueman (*George Barnwell*), Altamont (*The Fair Penitent*), and Pylades (*The Distrest Mother*).   Macklin was as good as his word in procuring Macready a London engagement, and the young actor duly appeared at Covent Garden on September 18, 1796.

On Thursday, September 14, 1786, Mrs. Jordan, the celebrated actress, played Hippolita in *She Wou'd and She Wou'd Not*, and the Romp in the farce of that name.

Mrs. Jordan was born in 1762, at Waterford, and was the natural daughter of a Captain Bland, her mother being one of

the olive branches of a poor Welsh clergyman. Dorothy
Bland commenced her stage career in Dublin as Miss Francis,
afterwards migrating to Tate Wilkinson, where she assumed
the name of Jordan, as the eccentric York manager had spoken
of her flight across the channel as ' Crossing Jordan.' Dorothy
soon reached the top rungs of the histrionic ladder of fame, both
in comedy and tragedy, but ' Thalia's favourite child ' soon
found that ' laughing agreed with her better than crying,' and
so abandoned the buskin. Her connection with the Duke of
Clarence is well known. By him she had several children.
Finally, unbefriended and in sad distress, she withdrew to St.
Cloud, in France, where she died on July 31, 1816. When
the Duke became King William IV, he ennobled all their children, raising the eldest to the rank of Earl of Munster.*

Of Mrs. Jordan, Hazlitt penned the following eulogy :—
' It was not as an actress, but as herself that she charmed
everyone. Nature had formed her in her most prodigal
humour ; and when nature is in the humour to make a woman
all that is delightful, she does it most effectually. Her face,
her tones, her manner, were irresistible ; her smile had the
effect of sunshine, and her laugh did one good to hear it ; her
voice was eloquence itself—it seemed as if her heart were
always in her mouth. She was all gaiety, openness and good
nature ; she rioted in her fine animal spirits, and gave more
pleasure than other actresses because she had the greatest
spirit of enjoyment in herself.'

It is recorded that on one occasion when Mrs. Jordan
came to the Royal to perform she felt ill and languid ; ' but in
a quarter of an hour, her very nature seemed to undergo a
metamorphosis ; the sudden change in her manner appeared
almost miraculous. She walked spiritedly across the stage
two or three times, as if to measure its extent ; and the moment her foot touched the boards her spirit seemed to be re-
generated. She cheered up, hummed an air, stepped light
and quick, and every symptom of depression vanished.'†

On December 13, 1786, Captain Ash played Captain
Macheath in *The Beggar's Opera*, for the first time

* In the autumn of 1902, a house of history in histrionics was pulled down at the corner
of Birkett Street and Richmond Row, Liverpool. About half-a-century ago its tenant
was a daughter of Mrs. Jordan, the famous actress. A son of Mrs. Jordan also resided for
some years in one of the houses on the right-hand side of Gradwell Street, coming from
Hanover Street.
† ' The Stage and The Players,' by John Diprose, p. 61.

locally. 'In the first act,' says Winston 'he wore a morning dress ; a full dress in the second ; and a suit of black in the last ; he had a clean shirt for every act—an instance of cleanliness only to be exceeded by that of a brother captain who washed his money. This process, for which the Green Room was allotted to him, detained the audience between the acts a good half-hour.'*

I may mention here that in emulation of the Covent Garden and Drury Lane Funds for the relief of old actors, an attempt was made in 1786 by a Mr. Williamson to establish, in connexion with the Royal, a Liverpool Theatrical Fund.† Winston states that this fund proved a failure.

Another fund was inaugurated on August 29, 1818. It was called the Liverpool and Manchester Theatrical Fund, and was established to afford permanent assistance to such actors and actresses as age, infirmity, or accident should render incapable of pursuing their profession. It was supported by weekly subscriptions from the members of the companies engaged at the Liverpool and Manchester Theatres, and by occasional donations from merchants and others. It was agreed at the beginning that no claim should be recognised for the first seven years, so that a substantial sum might accumulate. The scheme was inaugurated at the King's Arms, Castle Street. Mr. John Wright presided. The Mayor, Mr. Thomas Case, and Messrs. John Banks and John M. Vandenhoff were also present. Miss O'Neill subscribed twenty guineas to the fund.

In 1819, the patrons of the Liverpool Theatrical Fund included the Right Hon. George Canning and Mr. Thomas Earle ; Mr. Thomas Case was the president ; Messrs. Thomas Knight, Thomas Lewis, and John Banks of the local Royal, were the trustees ; and Mr. Banks was the treasurer. In 1819 the annual dinner was held at the King's Arms. Previously the inn was known as the Liverpool Arms. The site is now occupied by the branch Bank of England. Macready in his ' Reminiscences '‡ (mentions that on his arrival in Liverpool for the summer dramatic season of 1820 he was present at the annual dinner given in aid of the Liverpool and Manchester

* ' The Theatric Tourist' (1805), p. 52.
† At that time this was the only fund out of London, Bath excepted, the Theatre Royal, Norwich, Fund not being established until January 21, 1791.
‡ Edited by Sir Frederick Pollock, Bart., Vol. I, p. 218.

Theatrical Fund, at which the Mayor, Sir John Tobin, Knt., was present. ' To this,' says Macready, ' as to all other provincial theatrical charities, I subscribed my £10 ; but I should have acted more wisely in keeping my money in my pocket. A very considerable sum was accumulated in course of a few years, which was unjustly, and dishonestly, in my opinion, as a manifest diversion from the purpose of the endowment, divided amongst the few remaining members of the fund. If no legitimate claimants for relief were left, it ought to have been transferred to some other similar charity, or the different contributions returned to their subscribers.' When the fund ceased to exist I cannot say definitely. At any rate a Liverpool Theatrical Fund was in existence in 1830-1, as it is referred to in ' The Picture of Liverpool.'

Mr. Mattocks remained sole lessee of the Royal until 1786, in which year he retired from the management financially ruined. On December 21, 1786, the Privy Seal Bill was signed, and a few days later a new patent was granted to George Case, one of the trustees for the proprietors of the theatre. The licence granted to Mr. Case was for fifteen years, and to date from midsummer, 1792, when the patent granted for twenty-one years in 1771 to William Gibson expired. The patent was renewed by Mr. Case in 1807 for twenty-one years, and again in 1828 for a further period of twenty-one years.

In 1786 Francis Aickin was manager for the proprietors, and a Mr. Johnson the following year. Aickin was born in Dublin, and was brought up to his father's trade, which was that of a weaver. Emulating his brother James's example he became a strolling player, choosing the character of George Barnwell in the tragedy of that name for his first appearance. After playing various other parts he became associated with the Smock Alley Theatre, Dublin. On May 17, 1765, he made his first appearance at Drury Lane in the part of Dick in *The Confederacy*. On June 12, 1786, he made his first appearance at the Theatre Royal, Liverpool, as Evander in *The Grecian Daughter*. Aickin acquired considerable fame at Drury Lane, where he remained until about the close of 1773-4. Afterwards he went over to Covent Garden. For a time he left the stage and having married an Irish lady of good family, he turned hosier in York Street, Covent Garden, where he was patronised by both royalty and nobility. On the death of his

G

wife he closed his shop, and set out for Liverpool to take up the management of the Royal.   At first his venture was not a great success, but it afterwards must have proved of considerable gain to him as, until the beginning of the nineteenth century, he was associated in a managerial capacity with the destinies of the Liverpool Theatre.

At one period of his career Aickin was associated with John Jackson in the management of the Edinburgh Theatre. Tyrants in tragedy and serious parts in comedy were Francis Aickin's *forte*.   It was owing to his impassioned delivery of tragedy parts that he won the nick-name of ' Tyrant Aickin ' —' a character in private life no man was more the reverse, either in temper or the duties of friendship.' Genest* gives a list of upwards of eighty characters which Francis Aickin had appeared in.   We are told he was of pleasing appearance and declaimed both sonorously and distinctly.

On January 1, 1789, Aickin and John Philip Kemble obtained a seven years' lease of the theatre. ' I heard at the time,' says Boaden, ' that the consideration they were to give was £1,200 down and a rent of £350 per annum.'†

Boaden further states that ' Mr. Kemble opened (June 15, 1789) the theatre with an address by M. P. Andrews, which said or seemed to say, some trash like the following :—

> " For me, the new-made monarch, fix'd by fate
> To sway the sceptre of this mimic state,
> May the reign prosper, as desert shall seem."

' A new-made monarch, fix'd by fate,' to ' prosper as desert shall seem,' writes Boaden, ' is a combination of nonsense so exquisite that it wanted only a proper mouth, like Liston's, to give it utterance.' The plays submitted were *The Impostor* and *The Waterman*.

Mrs. Charles Mathews records (without date) an amusing story of an actor named Holland who played at the Royal during one of John Kemble's visits.

Charles Holland was a very anxious actor, and on one occasion he played Horatio to Kemble's Hamlet. He was very nervous, and though he got on well in the earlier scenes of the tragedy, feverish anxiety made him have recourse to a little false courage. He therefore sent a little boy, a hanger-on of the carpenters, to the tavern next door for a glass of cold brandy-and-water. Away rushed the boy, and returned with a huge tumbler filled to the brim. Mr. Holland drained the glass to the very dregs, and in doing so noticed a dark red sediment at the bottom of the glass. He had barely asked what filthy stuff had been mixed with the brandy-and-water when his ' cue ' was given. While on the stage he noticed the landlady of the tavern standing at the wings with several of the performers, who seemed listening to some awful tale of woe she was unfolding. From time to time she looked anxiously towards Mr. Holland, and made as if to approach him. He, however, motioned her ' to a more removed ground.' At last the scene was concluded, and Mr. Holland asked her ' What's the matter, my good woman ? ' Thus addressed she only cried the more, and with hands and eyes uplifted in supplication begged his forgiveness. ' Forgiveness for what ? ' queried Holland. ' Oh, sir ! Oh, sir ! oh, Mr. Holland, you are a dead man ; you are *poisoned*,' she replied. ' Poisoned ? ' cried Holland, ' Oh, yes, sir, you are indeed ! I didn't know what I had done, till you sent back the tumbler. Oh, sir ! red arsenic, kept to poison the rats ; didn't see what glass I took off the shelf, your boy was in such a hurry, only one candle in the bar—didn't notice anything was in it— oh, that unlucky tumbler ! '

Poor Holland did not know what to do. Everyone seemed paralysed with fear ; but they assisted Mr. Holland to a chair for he felt his sufferings of mind increasing every moment. Kemble seeing the commotion asked what was the matter. Holland told him that he was poisoned. ' Well, well,' said the tragedian (patting him on the back), 'never mind, my good fellow, you can play the rest of your part, I dare say, if you are poisoned—the tragedy can't finish without you.' ' It will finish *with* me, Mr. Kemble,' exclaimed the unhappy man.

However, Holland braced himself up to go through the remainder of the play, and at the conclusion, the rat-destroying hostess again appeared before him. This time her face bore a joyful expression, and she deposed to the effect that Mr. Holland had not taken the deadly potion after all, as her husband had found the identical tumbler containing it. The

little errand-boy was questioned, and it was elicited that in
hastening for the brandy-and-water he snatched, as he passed,
a tumbler from the shelf of the property-room, without looking
whether it was clean, or not. This glass, the property man
explained, had had some rose-pink prepared in it the evening
before for Macbeth.*

During the summer season of 1789 Miss Romanzini played
at the Royal, and became a favourite, both as an actress and a
concert singer. About this period she married Mr. Bland,
brother to Mrs. Jordan.†

For the months of November and December, 1789, the
Royal was rented by Stephen Kemble, who opened on November 4, with *The School for Scandal* and *The Virgin Unmasked*.
The performers engaged were from the Theatres Royal in
London, Dublin and Bath. During the month several com-
plaints were received as to the coldness of the theatre. Mr.
Kemble thereupon made it known ' that he had placed a large
stove in the middle of the pit, and two others in the upper and
under box lobbies, which, he is informed, will make the house
warm and comfortable.'

Stephen Kemble was a very corpulent man, one able to
play Falstaff ' without stuffing.' He married a very beautiful
and clever woman, Miss Satchell, the daughter of a musical
instrument maker. It was to this lady that the poet Burns
addressed the following lines, on seeing her in the character of
Yarico, at Dumfries, on October 21, 1794 :—

' Kemble, thou curest my unbelief of Moses and his rod ;
At Yarico's sweet notes of grief,
The rock with tears had flow'd.'

Mrs. Siddons was here in November, 1789, and on the
twenty-third of the month she played Alicia in *Jane Shore* for
the first time in Liverpool. On December 30 following,
Stephen Kemble took a benefit. One of the plays for the
occasion was a new one-act piece, entitled *The Genius of
Liverpool*, written by Mr. Harpley.

The principal performers during the dramatic season of
1790 were Messrs. Stephen Kemble, Barrymore, Aickin, Suett,

---

* ' Anecdotes of Actors,' p. 47.   † *Vide* Gilliland's ' Dramatic Mirror.'

Dignum, Miss Romanzini ; and Mesdames Billington, Kemble, Mattocks, Hopkins, and Ward.

The following year (1791), the dramatic season was inaugurated on June 20. *Love Makes a Man* was the opening attraction, and the company included Mesdames Billington, Ward, Mountain, and Quick ; Messrs. Aickin, Quick, Ward, Dignum, Whitfield, Pope, Fox, and Munden.

For the musical festival week of 1791, the theatre was let to Messrs. Ward and Banks, who gave Thomas Dibdin his first and long-coveted engagement at a Theatre Royal. Dibdin tells us that ' Mrs. Billington sang at the theatre, as well as the oratorios ; and the managers who had engaged the theatre only during the festival had reason to be well pleased with their adventure, although on one particular night, there were so few people in the theatre, that their money was returned, and the house dismissed. I had heard of, but never witnessed, a similar occurrence in inferior theatres ; and did not imagine it could have happened in such a town as Liverpool.'*

Thomas Dibdin was a son of Charles Dibdin, the celebrated dramatist and writer of nautical songs. Charles Dibdin gave his popular entertainments on more than one occasion in the ' Golden Lion,' Dale Street. ' Tom ' Dibdin was also a very successful dramatist. His god-fathers were David Garrick and Francis Aickin. Mr. E. R. Dibdin, the popular curator of the Walker Art Gallery, is ' Tom ' Dibdin's only surviving grand-nephew.

Thomas Dibdin was engaged by Mr. Aickin for the 1792 season at the Royal. At his first interview with Aickin, Dibdin ventured to inform him that he was spiritually related to him, as he (Aickin) had answered for him at the font. Aickin's answer in his gentlemanly half-Irish accent was, ' Shiver me, sir, I remember the ceremony, but upon my honour, I did not recollect you ; ' ' which ' adds Dibdin, ' was by no means astonishing considering we had never met since the said ceremony had taken place.'

The 1791 season terminated on September 7, on which occasion Mr. Betterton took a benefit. The house was very crowded, paying patrons being congregated on the stage as well as round the ventilator in the ceiling over the pit. The

* ' The Reminiscences of Thomas Dibdin ' (1837), pp. 110-111.

receipts amounted to £231 17s., besides gold tickets. *
Betterton was the father of the famous Mrs. Glover.

On December 31, 1792, the trustees, on behalf of the proprietors of the theatre, granted a seven years' lease to Mr.
Aickin at a yearly rental of £350, to date from the expiration
of Aickin and John Philip Kemble's lease on January 1, 1796.
This lease, which I have seen, was doubtless solicited by
Mr. Aickin in order that he might recoup himself for the
money he had expended in raising the roof of the theatre,
erecting a new gallery, and building a new colonnade over the
principal entrance in Williamson Square.

Messrs. Caulfield and Farley played in the masque of
Comus, on August 5, 1793.   October 5 of the same year saw
Mr. Aickin as Jaques and Mrs. Siddons as Rosalind (with song,
' The Echo ').   On November 11, Mrs. Crouch and Michael
Kelly appeared in *The Maid of the Mill*, and on November 22,
Mr. Kemble performed in *Henry V*.

The theatre re-opened on June 23, 1794, upon which occasion
Henry Siddons, junior, made, as Young Dornton in *The Road to
Ruin*, his first appearance on the local stage.   During the
season Munden, Betterton, Incledon, and Bannister, junior,
performed.   On August 18, O'Keeffe's one-act piece, *Peeping
Tom*, was revived, Miss Valois being the Lady Godiva.   In
addition to other plays Messrs. Siddons and Holland had for
their benefit on October 3, a one-act piece, entitled *The Liverpool Prize; or, An Offering to Britannia*, in which there was ' a
grand procession of all the nations of the world, the Genius of
Liverpool in a Triumphant Car, attended by Loyalty, Peace,
Commerce, and Plenty.' ·

The season of 1795 saw Messrs. Munden, Incledon, Lee
Lewes, and Bannister, junior.   On August 31, the town was
regaled with a lady Hamlet in the person of Mrs. Powell.
During the season, a Miss Sylvester performed a variety of
respectable parts.   She was the daughter of a Mr. John Silvester
Hay, a surgeon.   She first appeared at Richmond in 1792, and
afterwards spent almost a year in Scotland.   Mr. Aickin engaged
her for the Royal with a promise of every encouragement to
render her happy and popular, but according to Gilliland's
' Dramatic Mirror,' the lessee did not keep his word, and she

---

* Holt and Gregson MSS.

returned to London before the end of the season.   Not long afterwards she married John Litchfield, a literary man, who was an intimate friend of Charles Mathews.   Many of Litchfield's letters are given in ' The Life and Correspondence of Charles Mathews,' by Mrs. Mathews.   ' Mrs. Litchfield,' says Genest, ' had great judgment, and one of the finest voices that was ever heard.'*

The unruliness of a certain section of the frequenters of the Royal had long been proverbial ; in fact, so atrocious was their conduct, that the editor of ' Gore's Advertiser ' felt constrained to publish the following in the interests of the theatre in his issue for September 24, 1795 :—' We cannot help expressing our astonishment that no steps are taken to curb the disorderly proceedings which every night take place in the Gallery, but particularly in the *side slips*, from which the people in the Pit are pelted during the whole of the performance, and their lives put in danger by drunken fellows traversing round on the outside of the iron rails. A man repeatedly attempted last night, to throw one of the chandeliers into the Pit, and was suffered singly to continue to brave and insult the whole house.   As long as these slips remain a part of the Gallery, a play will never be heard in this House, nor will the audience in the Pit or Upper Boxes have any comfort: several Boxes were evacuated last night in consequence of the streams which descended from above, and some of the company in the Pit had their cloths soiled in the same abominable manner.'

On June 10, 1796, Harriot Mellon (afterwards the Duchess of St. Albans) arrived in Liverpool with her step-father and mother, and took lodgings at a hosier's.   On the 22nd she made her first appearance at the Theatre Royal, where she was destined to become a great favourite. ' Her engagement,' says her biographer, Mrs. Cornwell Baron-Wilson,† ' was for the season at two pounds per week, and half a clear benefit, which were thought very handsome terms.   She improved exceedingly here ; and as she had understudied many principal characters whilst in town, she had now an opportunity of essaying her powers in their representation. . . . . Young, and with a quick ear, she had caught the tones of some of the original performers, but who had not been seen in plays

* Vol. VIII, p. 19.   † ' Memoirs of Miss Mellon,' Vol. I, p. 174.

presented for the first time at Liverpool; she had, therefore, the place of the London favourite ; and it occurred more than once, that when the originals subsequently acted the parts in the country, they were deemed copiers or borrowers from Miss Mellon.'　　On August 17, she took her half-benefit, played Sabina Rosni in *First Love*, spoke an address and epilogue, appeared as Polly in *Polly Honeycomb*, and the Page in *Follies of a Day*, in which she introduced two songs.　The half-benefit realised for her £130, and she obtained about £25 more by her engagement.　While here, Miss Mellon was introduced to Mrs. Siddons, with whom she became a great favourite.

The following amusing incident occurred during one of Miss Mellon's early visits to the Theatre Royal : 'When I was a poor girl,' she used to recount, 'working very hard for my thirty shillings a week, I went down to Liverpool during the holidays, where I was always kindly received, and derived the greatest advantage from all my benefits.　I was to perform in a new piece, something like those pretty little affecting dramas they get up now at the minor theatres ; and in my character I represented a poor, friendless, orphan girl, reduced to the most wretched poverty.　A heartless tradesman persecutes the sad heroine for a heavy debt, owing to him by her family, and insists on putting her in prison, unless someone will be bail for her.　The girl replies, '' Then I have no hope—I have not a friend in the world.''　'' What, will no one go bail for you, to save you from prison ? '' asked the stern creditor.　'' I have told you I have not a friend on earth,'' was my reply.　But just as I was uttering the words, my eyes were attracted by the movements of a sailor in the upper gallery, who, springing over the railings, was letting himself down from one tier to another, until he finally reached the pit ; he bounded clear over the orchestra and footlights, and placed himself beside me in a moment, before I could believe the evidence of my senses.

'" Yes, you shall have *one* friend at least, my poor young woman," said he, with the greatest expression of feeling in his honest, sun-burnt countenance.　" I will go bail for you to any amount.　And as for *you* (turning to the frightened actor), if you don't bear a hand and shift your moorings, you lubber, it will be the worse for you when I come athwart your bows."

'Every creature in the house rose ; the uproar was perfectly indescribable : peals of laughter, screams of terror, cheers from his tawny mess-mates in the gallery ; preparatory scrapings of violins from the orchestra ; and, amidst the universal din, there stood the unconscious cause of it, sheltering me, "the poor, distressed, young woman," and breathing defiance and destruction against my mimic persecutor. It was impossible to resume the play, so the orchestra played "God save the King," while the curtain dropped over the scene, including the chivalric sailor. He was only persuaded to relinquish his care of me by the illusion being still maintained behind the scenes ; the manager pretending to be an old friend of mine, unexpectedly arrived to rescue me from all difficulties with a profusion of theatrical bank notes. To these the generous sailor would fain have added his own hardly-earned gains ; which being gratefully declined by such a newly-made heiress as myself, he made his best sea-bow to all on the stage, shook hands heartily with me and the manager, and then quietly went home, under care of some of the party.'*

Cork in an Uproar was the title of a spectacle presented here on March 13, 1797, by Astley's equestrian and dramatic company. The piece was founded on the late invasion of the French at Bantry Bay. An invasion was also expected at various seaports in England. The Liverpool merchants resolved to defend the town to the utmost. They accordingly practised gunnery at the fort, until they could work, serve, and manage the guns as well as the most proficient.

On June 12, of 1797, Mrs. Siddons appeared in *Jane Shore*. The house was crowded, and the ' galleryites ' seeing the principal merchants with their families present, thought it a delightful opportunity of indulging their wit respecting the ' soldiering.' Accordingly, they formed two bands, one on each side of the gallery, and kept up a cross-dialogue of impertinence, about ' charging guns with brown sugar ' and cocoa-nuts,' and ' small arms with cinnamon-powder and nutmegs,' from the commencement of the play until its very end.

* ' Memoirs of Miss Mellon,' Vol. I, pp. 201-3.

Mrs. Siddons saw that it was useless to act, and went through the performance in dumb show.*

Astley and his company were here the following year (1798). It was advertised that the profits of the performance on March 8, would be applied by Mr. Astley ' in aid of the Bank Subscription for the defence of this country; for which, also, his personal actual service on horse-back will be devoted in any part of the three kingdoms, whenever it may be necessary to oppose the enemy.'

After an absence of five years John Philip Kemble made a welcome reappearance here on June 8, 1798, as Zanga in *The Revenge.* The same evening also saw Mr. and Mrs. John Emery perform in *Rosina.* Emery possessed those qualities which indicate the first-rate artist—pathos and humour. ' Never since Emery's death,' says Donaldson, ' has Dandie Dinmont (*Guy Mannering*), Tyke (*The School of Reform*), and Giles (*The Miller's Man*), been brought out in such bold and original relief.' Once when playing in *The School of Reform* a quaint retort was heard in the scene where Tyke finds the old man, whose purse he has taken, to be his father, and exclaims, ' What! rob my own feyther! ' ' Yes, you vaga-bond,' said a sailor in the pit, unable to contain himself any longer at Tyke's duplicity, ' you'd rob a church! '

I now come to a very melancholy incident—the death of John Palmer on Thursday, August 2, 1798. How he came by his death, and if it occurred just after he uttered those mem-orable words in *The Stranger*, ' There is another and a better world,' has long been a debatable question.

Miss Mellon, who, according to her biographer, was to have appeared in the after-piece, *The Deserter*, on the evening of August 2, 1798, when the performance was suddenly and tragically closed, knew the particulars of the sad fatality.† In her ' Memoirs '‡ it is stated that ' Mr. Aickin prevailed on him (Palmer) to perform The Stranger on July 12,§ and the representation was so fine that, by general desire, he was in-duced to repeat it. While rehearsing on the morning of performance, he received an express, relating the sudden death

* ' Memoirs of Miss Mellon,' Vol. I, p. 197.
† Although Miss Mellon was at that time a member of the Theatre Royal company her name does not appear on the playbill for August 2, 1798.
‡ Vol. I, pp. 217-9.
§ This is a mistake for July 26.

of his son, a youth universally beloved, and of great promise in point of talent.

' The play, of course, was deferred, for the wretched father was carried almost senseless from the theatre. It was the general opinion that, after an interval of some days, he ought to be roused from his apathy, and perhaps nothing could excite an actor like professional exertion. Therefore he was urged to reappear, and the broken-spirited man made but little resistance.

' He arrived at the theatre tolerably calm in the evening, but was silent, as if afraid to trust himself in conversation ; whilst respect for his misfortunes threw a solemnity over the generally gay party in the Green Room.

' He went through the play almost mechanically, until the fourth act, when the Stranger has to refer to his children. He was dreadfully agitated; the audience feeling too deeply even to encourage him ; finally, in uttering the well-known words, " *There is another and a better world*," he expired— a case, if ever there was one, of *a broken heart*. It will be noticed that Miss Mellon's biographer states that it was in the *fourth* act Palmer expired. According to my printed copy of the play the lines mentioned do not occur in that act but only in the first and third acts.

' Billinge's Liverpool Advertiser,' for August 6, 1798— four days after Palmer's death—states : ' Mr. Palmer, whilst he was performing the character of the Stranger, in the play of that name, suddenly fell down dead upon the stage in the full view of the audience. Medical assistance was immediately administered, but it was of no avail, every spark of life was totally extinguished. Mr. Palmer is generally believed to have fallen a sacrifice to the poignancy of his affliction by the loss of a darling son, of whose death he received intelligence only a few days since. In the course of the performance his frame was observed to be agitated with a general tremor, and his eyes to overflow with tears. In the fourth act of the play the Stranger relates his woes to his friend Baron Steinfort. In this stage of the performance Mr. Palmer's manner was amazingly impressive, his agitation visibly increased, and at the mention of his wife and children, he staggered, and fell backward a lifeless corpse upon the stage. He has left eight orphan children to bewail his loss.'

'Gore's General Advertiser,' for August 9, 1798—seven days after Palmer's death—says: ' In the fourth act Baron Steinfort obtains an interview with the Stranger, whom he discovers to be his old friend.   He prevails upon him to relate the cause of his seclusion from the world—In this relation the feelings of Mr. Palmer were visibly much agitated, and at the moment he mentioned his wife and children, he fell life- less on the stage. . . . . One consolation is left for us, which he so emphatically expressed in the play just before his death, "There is another and a better world."'

Last words of a tragic nature are, however, always viewed with suspicion.   The truth of the matter seems to be that the fourth act had been reached, and that Palmer having replied to Baron Steinfort's question as to the whereabouts of his children, but when asked, ' But why did you not keep your children with you ?' They would have amused you in many a weary hour,' the recollection of his own recent loss was too much for him ; he turned and tottered, and then fell on the stage, dying in a few minutes.   A fit of apoplexy, doubtless, occasioned his death, but professional men differed as to the cause of it ; some asserted that his constitution must have been prone to apoplexy, and that his life would have been so terminated at all events ; while others affirmed the fit to have been occasioned by the effort of the moment.   Doctors Mitchell and Corry gave it as their opinion that he died of a broken heart.

Hamerton,* Callan, and Mara conveyed the lifeless body from the stage into the Green Room.   'Medical assistance was immediately procured ; his veins were opened, but they yielded not a single drop of blood ; and every other means of resuscit- ation was had recourse to without effect.'†   Mr. Aickin being too much overcome with grief to announce the melancholy event to the audience, Incledon came forward, and mustered up sufficient resolution to communicate the dreadful circumstance. The house was instantly evacuated in mournful silence.   Out- side in Williamson Square the audience formed themselves into groups and discussed the fatal occurrence until a late hour

* Hamerton was a good Irish comedian. He was born in Dublin on June 28, 1759. In 1780 he was at the Royal, Liverpool, under Younger and Mattocks. They wanted him as an apprentice, but he refused, and went on salary for two years. Then he returned to Dublin. In 1796 he was again at the Liverpool Theatre under Aickin. In 1798 he was in Dublin when the theatres closed on account of the Rebellion, so he went to Liverpoo for the summer. *Vide* Memoir in ' The Dublin Theatrical Observer,' December 29, 1821
   † ' The Gentleman's Magazine, August, 1798.

next morning.   Out of respect to the memory of the deceased the theatre remained closed for the remainder of the week.

The funeral took place on Monday, August 6, and was conducted with great ceremony.   Mutes on horseback (as was the custom in those days) preceded the hearse.   Then came Messrs. Aickin, Holman, Whitfield, Incledon, Mattocks, and Wild.   The chief mourners were Mr. Hurst (as the oldest acquaintance) and a Mr. Stephens, cousin to the deceased. Then came Major Potts, Captain Snow, Captain Kennedy, Messrs. Hamerton, Farley, Tomkins, Toms, Emery, Demaria (the painter), Clinch, Hollingsworth, and the other members of the Theatre Royal company.   The *cortège* set out for Walton at eight o'clock in the morning, and reached the church at half-past nine.   Prayers having been read over the body, it was committed to a grave seven feet deep, dug in the rock.

On the coffin-plate there was simply inscribed, ' Mr. John Palmer, aged 53.'   ' He was, however,' states the ' Gentleman's Magazine,'* ' three or four years older, but there was no person in Liverpool who correctly knew his age.   A stone is to be placed at the head of the grave with the following inscription, being the very words he had just spoken in the character of *The Stranger*.   ' There is another and a better world.'   This, I may mention, was never done, as a recent visit there plainly revealed.   The grave (in which another interment has since taken place) is surmounted by a plain, flat stone, part of which is broken right across.   Palmer's name is simply inscribed at the foot of the stone.   The grave I may add, is situated in the western portion of Walton Churchyard.

' As an actor,' observes the ' Gentleman's Magazine,' for August, 1798, ' his death is a great loss to the stage, and therefore to the public.   His figure and manner gave import- ance to many characters, which, in other hands, would have passed unnoticed.   In delivering a prologue, and in the grace- ful and insinuating way in which he impressed an occasional address, he was unequalled.   A more general performer since the days, and during the latter part of the days, of the inimit- able Garrick, the stage has not boasted, and, in the peculiar

* August, 1798.

province in which his talents were adopted, he not only stood
without a competitor, but possessed very great excellence.'

On August 13, 1798, a benefit performance was given at
the Royal in aid of Palmer's children, who in a few months
had lost father, mother, brother, and uncle.   The receipts
amounted to £450, including a donation of £50 from the
Countess of Derby.*   A monody written for the occasion by
Roscoe, the celebrated poet and historian, was delivered by
Mr. Holman.   The following is a copy :—

'Ye airy sprites, who oft as fancy calls,
Sport 'midst the precincts of these haunted walls ;
Light forms, that float in mirth's tumultuous throng,
And frolic, dance, and revelry, and song,
Fold your gay wings, repress your wonted fire,
And from your fav'rite feats a while retire.
—And thou, whose powers sublimer thoughts impart,
Queen of the springs that move the human heart,
With change alternate, at whose magic call,
The swelling tides of passion rise or fall ;
Thou too withdraw—for 'midst thy lov'd abode,
With step more stern, a mightier power has trod.
—Here, on this spot, to every eye confest,
Inrob'd with terrors, stood the kingly guest.
—Here, on this spot, Death wav'd th' unerring dart,
And struck his noblest prize—An Honest Heart !
What wond'rous links the human feelings bind ;
How strong the secret sympathies of mind !
As fancy's pictur'd forms around us move,
We hope, or fear, rejoice, detest, or love :
Nor heaves the sigh for selfish woes alone,
Congenial sorrows mingle with our own ;
Hence, as the poet's raptur'd eyeballs roll,
The fond delirium seizes all his soul ;
And, whilst his pulse concordant measures keeps,
He smiles in transport, or in anguish weeps.

* The 'Monthly Mirror' for July, 1799, states ' that on account of Palmer expiring
in the last act of *The Stranger*, the manager stopt the whole of the salaries, though he
pocketed the receipts of the night, and those also of the next night ; and refused to give
up their salaries to the executors, which he stopped from the performers, by their desire,
for that purpose, on the night he advertised to give a *free* benefit, for the late Mr. Palmer's
distressed family.   It is reported, the stipulation for Palmer's performance was a night
free of all expence whatever, so the manager *gained* half a week's expences, by only
playing three nights instead of four.'

—But, ah ! lamented shade ! not thine to know
The anguish only of imagin'd woe ;
Destin'd o'er life's substantial ills to mourn,
And fond parental ties untimely torn :
Then, whilst thy bosom, labouring with its grief,
From fabled sorrows sought a short relief,
The fancied woes, too true to nature's tone,
Burst the slight barrier, and became thy own,
In mingl'd tides the swelling passions ran,
Absorb'd the actor, and o'erwhelm'd the man !
Martyr of sympathy, more sadly true,
Than ever fancy feign'd, or poet drew !
Say, why by Heav'n's acknowledg'd hand imprest,
Such keen sensations actuate all the breast ?
Why throbs the heart for joys that long have fled ?
Why lingers hope around the silent dead ?
Why spurns the spirit its incumb'ring clay,
And longs to soar to happier realms away ?
Does Heaven unjust the fond desire instil,
To add to mortal woes another ill ?
Is there thro' all the intellectual frame,
No kindred mind that prompts the nightly dream ?
Or in lone musings of rememb'rance sweet,
Inspires the secret wish—once more to meet ?
—There is—for not by more determin'd laws
The sympathetic steel the magnet draws,
Than the freed spirit acts with strong controul
On its responsive sympathies of soul ;
And tells in characters of truth unfurl'd,
—*There is another, and a better world.*
Yet, whilst we sorrowing tread this earthly ball,
For human woes a human tear may fall.
—Blest be that tear—who gives it, doubly blest,
That heals with balm the orphan's wounded breast ;
Not all that breathes in morning's genial dew,
Revives the parent plant where once it grew,
Yet may those dews with timely nurture aid
The infant flow'rets drooping in the shade ;
Whilst long experienc'd worth, and manners mild
A father's merits—still protect his child.'*

* 'Gore's General Advertiser,' August 16, 1798.

For some time after Palmer's death a place in the Green Room where the body was laid after being conveyed from the stage was known as ' John Palmer's corner.' It is curious to learn that after his death performers of the Stranger purposely omitted those memorable words in the utterance of which he is commonly supposed to have breathed his last.

A paragraph in ' Gore's Advertiser ' for Thursday, September 20, 1798, says : ' A young man (whose name we understand is Green) appeared for the first time in public last night at our theatre, in the part of Young Norval. He was received with great applause, and acquitted himself in a manner highly creditable.' The player referred to was Charles Mayne Young, one of the brightest ornaments of the English stage.

Napoleon's threatened invasion of England in 1798 was responsible for the production at the Royal on September 12 of a one-act musical piece, called *The Raft*; *or, Both Sides of the Water*, ' with a representation of a French raft.'

About December, 1798, Samuel William Ryley, of ' Itinerant ' fame, was in negotiation with Mr. Aickin to take the theatre for a period of five weeks at a rental of £150, for which he was to have the use of the wardrobe, books, and music. One hundred pounds were to be paid down ; but at that time Ryley did not possess one hundred pence. Singularly and luckily enough, however, a casual acquaintance agreed to become his bond. Consequently the theatre passed temporarily into Ryley's hands, and was opened on December 17, 1798, with the following company : Messrs. Grant, Valiant, St. Leger, Meadows, Austin, Cowley, Quinn, Blandford, Pierson, Smith, Kennedy, King, Stanton, and Briscoe. Mesdames Ryley, Kennedy, St. Leger, Brown, King, Grant, Freeman, Meadows, and Miss Meadows. The theatre was opened under the patronage of Lord Milsington to seventy-five pounds.

That Ryley looked after the comfort of his patrons is shown by the playbill for December 26, which records that ' This theatre is well-aired by Stoves in different parts of the House,' and on December 31, ' Six additional Stoves have been procured, in which good Fires will be constantly kept up, in the Box-lobbies, and other parts of the House during the performance.'

' During the season,' says Ryley in his ' Itinerant,'* ' I received a variety of whimsical applications from theatrical candidates, amongst the rest, a lady waited upon me whose hair was silver'd by the hand of time, and whose mouth display'd evident marks of decay.   She had fixed her mind upon the stage as affording a *pleasant, easy*, and *genteel* livelihood— a *certain* resource against the calamities of *indigence*—and had not the *smallest* doubt of *success*, particularly in *sentimental young ladies*.   .   .   .   .

' I endeavoured with all the eloquence I was master of to paint in true colors the *real* life of a player.   That it was pleasant in some respects, I readily allowed, as it afforded a greater opportunity of seeing and knowing the world than probably any other profession ;   the *easy* life of an actor, I denied in *toto* ; a more laborious employment, a greater mental drudgery than that experienced by itinerant performers, I asserted could not well be imagined, where the intellect is, or ought to be in constant exercise : the generality of the world see them go through their parts on the stage, with perfect ease, and apparent pleasure, without giving a thought to the labor, the study, the intense application necessary to imprint not only the words on the memory, but the character on the mind.

' My candour was not much relish'd by this vain old woman, who I have no doubt, called both my judgment and politeness in question, but I invariably discouraged applications of the kind, even where appearances held forth a probability of success.

' One young man express'd an ardent desire to make his appearance as a pantomimic clown ; this was so uncommon an attachment that I agreed to give him a trial.   On his *début* two circumstances occur'd which I beg leave to relate.   A public nuisance in the shape of a box-lobby lounger chose to disturb the audience with repeated interruptions from the balcony box over the stage door ; in one of the pantomimic pursuits this young adventurer, with astonishing activity, ran up the wainscot, gave the coxcomb a neat slap on the cheek, and was down again in a moment amidst thundering applause. But before the pantomime was half finish'd, he fell down a trap

* First edition, Vol. III, pp. 357-8.

and broke his collar-bone, which for that night put an end to
his mimic career.   This young man is now well-known by
the name of Bradbury, as the principal clown at the Royal
Circus.'*

Mr. Ryley tells how he was introduced to that worthy
Dr. Samuel Solomon.† 'One evening a glass bottle was wan-
tonly thrown from the gallery, by which a lady in the pit received considerable personal injury, and caused great alarm
through the whole house.   I immediately offered a reward
of five guineas for the apprehension of the offender, and
Doctor Solomon, who happened to be in the stage box, in the
most handsome manner promised to double that sum, at the
same time painting the atrocity of the action, and the guilt
of those who endeavoured to screen so atrocious an offender.
This had the desired effect, the culprit was apprehended,
tried at the Quarter Sessions, and sentenced to two years
imprisonment.'

At the conclusion of the season Ryley found himself a
gainer by £350.   The major part of his best performers were
engaged by Mr. Aickin for the summer season at the Theatre
Royal.

The following account of the Liverpool Theatre from a
local correspondent, appears in the 'Monthly Mirror,' for
July, 1799 :—' I have more pleasure in looking into your
mirror, than from any reflection I see in my own, or the
veluti in speculum placed in the proscenium of our theatre
as a motto ; for when the curtain rises, nothing is to be
seen but nature disfigured by art, and character disguised
in tarnished tatters of the penurious manager's wardrobe.
The women provide (out of their slender salaries) suitable
dresses, and some few of the men.   The ' Phœnix ' paper used
to give just *critiques* on public exhibitions ; but now, like the
rest of the papers, it has degenerated to be the vehicle of
managerial puffs.

' The theatre opened the 3rd of June, with a company
much above mediocrity.   The only strangers to the London
stage, I believe, are a Mr. Grant, and a Mr. and Mrs. Ledger ;
the former is by very few excelled in any line of acting, and

* This was Robert Bradbury, who afterwards became Grimaldi's great rival.   During
the period Ryley had the Theatre Royal, Bradbury played clown in *Harlequin in the
Moon* on January 9, 1799, and sixteen days later clown in *Harlequin Sailor.*
† His name is perpetuated locally in Solomon Street.

is of so accommodating a disposition, that he would undertake any subordinate part, rather than that a play should not be got up.

' Mrs. Ledger is a very fine woman, has an expressive countenance, and a good voice, without art, trick, or mimicry. Mrs. Chapman, from Covent Garden, was welcomed here with unbounded applause. She is as much respected for her deportment in private life, as for her professional abilities ; yet these ladies, with the merit of Mrs. Ward, Mr. Young, etc., with the reinforcement of the Murrays and Knight,* could not bring a tolerable house, till *Lover's Vows* was performed, which seems extraordinary, for Mr. Ryley last winter, with a very inferior company, and hacknied plays, had very good houses, and some overflowing, though the weather was uncommonly severe ; which indicates that the summer manager is no favourite, and that good order is much wanted in the front of the house. The wardrobe is shockingly bad, the scenes want painting, and are seldom appropriate to the country where the scene is laid.'

During this summer some of the patrons of the theatre made themselves very obnoxious. Mr. Aickin stated on his playbills that he had determined ' to prosecute to the extremity of the law, every person who throws anything from the gallery, or in the avenues of the theatre.' He also offered a reward ' for the apprehension of anyone who may in future so offend.'

These warnings, however, did not have very much effect, as one evening late in August, some scoundrel threw a quart bottle on the stage. It is needless to point out the possible danger to life of such a missile. At the foot of his playbills (August 30), Mr. Aickin announced that ' Two guineas will be paid on the apprehension of the person who threw the bottle on the stage last night.'

During the season Messrs. Young, Johnstone, Bannister, junr., Murray, and Misses Mellon and Leake appeared here. On August 26, Miss Mellon took her benefit, spoke an address, and played for the first time Lady Contest in *The Wedding Day*. The receipts amounted to £269 8s. 6d. Miss Mellon lodged at that time with a Mrs. Woodells, 13 School Lane.

---

* On June 17, 1799, ' little ' Knight, the comedian, made his first appearance on **this** stage. He played Young Rapid in *A Cure for the Heartache*, and Tag in *The Spoiled Child.*

A one-act musical piece, entitled *The Maid of Liverpool ; or, The Royal Tar*, was brought forward on October 11. The principal characters were sustained by Messrs. Young and Emery, and Mesdames Emery and Second.

The state of the Liverpool Theatre, and the character of the contemporary audience, are thus described in the ' Monthly Mirror ' for October, 1799 :—

' Our manager is accused of a degree of parsimony, little consistent either with his duty as a caterer for the public, or with his own interest.   The theatre is in a shameful condition ; the box-lobbies disgracefully filthy ; the almost subterranean avenues to the pit are choaked with " a foul and pestilent congregation of vapours " ; the coverings of the seats miserably old and tattered ; and the house is throughout so detestably dirty, neglected and forlorn, that the audiences are necessarily thinner than if they were accommodated in a tolerably decent manner.   The scenery and decorations, are also, in general, old, broken, weather-beaten, begrimed with oil, etc.   As a proof of the disgusting state of the house, suffice it to mention, that, at the late festival of music held here, which attracted a great concourse of fashionable company, a *ridotto*-ball was intended to have been given at the theatre ; but, upon inspection by the committee, the place was found so uncomfortably dirty, damp, and noisome, the floor of the stage so worn and uneven, that it was judged impossible to cleanse the Augean stable so as to render it fit for the accommodation of the company, whence the design was given up and the ball was held in the rooms of the Athenæum.

' Again, the manager is reported to be extremely hard in his dealings with performers ; scarcely even solicitous to secure a tolerable company, he is not thought to aim at anything extraordinary or brilliant.   This I apprehend to be the reason why Mrs. Siddons, who has performed at many a petty town in the vicinity, Mr. Kemble, Mr. Holman, etc., have not condescended to visit Liverpool this season.

' But our greatest grievance remains to be told, and is, perhaps, the cause of every other—for according to the audiences so will be the entertainment.   More turbulent, indecent, and tasteless audiences, than have been met with here, have seldom, I believe, assembled within the precincts of any theatre, amphitheatre, barn, booth, or stable.   .   .   .   .   .

' The gallery is composed chiefly of drunken sailors and their doxies, who come to the playhouse, evidently and professedly, for no other purpose than to drink gin and crack nuts, or some other similar diversion, which purpose is promoted by the sale of strong liquors, wine, ale, etc., in that part of the house.

' The pit, too, is often the scene of riot and confusion, of boxing, and of scolding matches, of brandy-drinking, and of beer-tippling, and those honest people who come to see and hear the play, are forced to sit intermingled with Jack Tars, who are, properly speaking, nor more sober, but rather less drunk, than their mess-mates in the gallery.

' In the upper side boxes, assemble all the frail sisterhood of Cyprian notoriety ; and there, the more dashing merchants' clerks, who pay their evening devoirs to venal beauty, are loud and licentious, in order to prove their gentility ; and insulting to the unfortunate females, who, notwithstanding their infamy and vice, are still women, in order to prove their manhood and humanity. In the upper front boxes, indeed, the *best* company is generally met with, because it consists of the *middle*-classes, but those seats are not very desirable, from their distance from the stage, and the noise in the house which usually confines the entertainment of that part of the audience to the mere pantomime of the play.

' In the lower boxes we have sometimes a display of elegance and fashion which is pleasing and interesting, yet the uncontrolled anarchy of the rest of the house, encourages the idle and noisy, even here, to indulge in equally offensive laughter and uproar.'

On July 11, 1800, *The Fair Penitent* was performed. The play had ' not been acted these years,' and the part of Calista was performed by ' a young lady, being her first appearance on any stage.' The lady referred to was Miss Lavinia Walstein, a niece, it is said, of Kotzebue, the famous German dramatist.

Miss Walstein's *début* was very successful. She afterwards played Cora (*Pizarro*), Mrs. Beverley (*The Gamester*), Miranda (*The Tempest*), Angela (*The Castle Spectre*), and Jane Shore. In fact, for several years she remained a great favourite with local and other audiences. Her manner was always studious and reserved. ' Off the stage,' says Mr. W. J. Lawrence in

an interesting article on Miss Walstein in the ' Dublin Evening
Herald ' for September 15, 1905, ' she seldom seemed happy,
save when she was with her mother.   The two were inseparable.   In Ireland she was known as " the Hibernian Siddons,"
until her star was bedimmed by the advent of the beautiful
Miss O'Neill.'   Poverty afterwards overtook her, and in January, 1833, she breathed her last in dingy lodgings in the
Great City on the Thames.   On January 31, an inquest was
held on her body, which had been taken to a neighbouring
hospital for dissection.   The house-surgeon of the hospital
said that rigid inquiries had been made as to the deceased
being Miss Walstein, an erstwhile actress, in view of the remarkable circumstances of the case.   And he assured the
jury (his evidence being corroborated by the assistant-
surgeon), that the body was that of a man !   At this juncture
a woman in the court screamed and fell into a faint.   After
she had recovered she went into the witness box, and, amidst
a torrent of invective which she showered upon the heads of
the two surgeons, stated that she had formerly been Miss
Walstein's devoted companion, sleeping or waking, at bed
and board.   Latterly, however, she had lost all trace of her
poor, dear friend.   She also declared that the house-surgeon's
evidence was a pack of lies, with more to the same purpose.
The usual verdict having been recorded in such cases, I drop
the veil upon one of the strangest life histories in the annals of
the stage.

Frederick Reynolds' comedy, *Management*, was played on
August 4, 1800.   Mr. Bannister impersonated Mist, the Manager.   The following lines in the comedy are worth noting :—

' My country playhouse, ere I came to town,
Almost knocked up, has been in lots knocked down.
A sturdy farmer bought the walls—what then ?
What was a barn will be a barn again ;
Corn on the stage, not mummers, will be seen,
And oats be *thrashed*, where actors should have been.'

The ' Monthly Mirror ' for August, 1800, mentions that
' The parsimony of the manager is still the subject of general
complaint.   The following is an extract from one of our letters

on the subject :—'' The manager would have shewn more gratitude for the liberality he has experienced in this town if he
had lighted up the stage properly, and the front of the house
with wax, instead of lavishing colours in confused paintings
on the proscenium and boxes.   Last season, over the drop
curtain was the motto *Veluti in speculum*, which appeared to
have been painted on one of the athwart seats of a ferry-boat,
and fastened up by a wooden pin at each end.   They have
now attempted something like a mirror for the ground, and
the words seem as if written on a dirty looking-glass with the
end of a tallow candle.   *Speed the Plough* has brought crowded
houses ; but a number of the spectators came away with their
clothes terribly besmeared with the tallow that dropped from
the lustres, and their stomachs disordered by the stench of
the train oil in the foot-lights.   Wretched parsimony ! the
difference between lighting the front with 130 tallow and the
same number of wax candles, would only be about twelve
shillings.'' '   Apparently the directors of the theatre took the
hint, as the ' Mirror ' for the following October records the
fact that the house was ' illuminated with wax.'

Encouraged by his previous managerial success at the
Theatre Royal, S. W. Ryley arranged with Mr. Aickin to
rent the theatre from December, 1800, to February, 1801.
The company Ryley got together under his banner included
Messrs. Macready, the elder, Harley, Fullerton, Austin,
Emery, Lee, Battye, Patterson, Waylett, Montague Talbot,
Roberts, Wilkinson, Welch, Spragg ; Mesdames Beaumont,
Burton, Coats, Emery, Sinnet, Battye, Patterson ;   and
Misses Cornellies and Crowshaw.   Mrs. Stephen Kemble
came on a starring engagement for a fortnight, for which she
was paid 150 guineas   The season, however, was unpro-
ductive, but notwithstanding this, Ryley determined to try
again, and engaged with Aickin to rent the theatre from
December, 1801, to March, 1802.

On August 10, 1801, Mr. Wild, the prompter of the theatre
died, aged fifty-two.   He was quite a young man when he
first acted as prompter at the local Drury Lane Theatre.
For several seasons he was prompter at the Covent Garden
Theatre.   Early in life he had the misfortune to sustain a
compound fracture to one of his legs.   The fracture was of
a remarkable nature, and a metropolitan surgeon jocosely

told him that if he did not bequeath the limb to them they would certainly have his body.   This so alarmed Mr. Wild that he always expressed a desire to be buried in Liverpool, and for this purpose wished he might die there.   He was buried in Walton Churchyard, close to where John Palmer lies.

In a letter published in ' Gore's General Advertiser ' for November 19, 1801, a correspondent complained of the ' old-fashioned, inconvenient, square-shaped theatre, which was everywhere giving away to the elegant circular form.'   He also expressed the wish that it might ' be found practicable to have the comfort of a saloon to the boxes, and other conveniences about the entrances and passages of which this house is now so destitute.'   This letter voiced the opinion of many as to the desirability of having a new and more commodious theatre in the town.   During the season 37 benefits took place, and the amount realised was £4,986.

S. W. Ryley commenced his third managerial season at the Royal in December, 1801.   In order to obviate as far as he could the deficiency of first-rate actors he engaged dancers of superior eminence.   To St. Pierre and Madame St. Amand he paid ten pounds per week.   Dubois and his family had eleven pounds a week. Dubois himself was a good pantomimist, but the performances of the family ' proved not to be worth a shilling.'   Richer, the rope-dancer, was engaged for a fortnight at a salary of one hundred guineas.*   The regular company were Messrs. Chalmers, Crisp, Bannerman, Hurst, Vandeleur, Knox, Fothergill, Ratcliffe, Leonard, Skerrett, Fowler, Kelly ;   Mesdames Kennedy, Crisp, Vandeleur, Barry, Ratcliffe, Skerrett, and Miss Brown.   ' In addition to these,' says Ryley in his ' Itinerant,'† ' I engaged John Woodruffe Clarke, on whom I solely depended as a second and support to Mr. Pope ; he was advertised for Iago on the first night, but five days previous to the opening, I received a letter dated Birmingham, intimating "he was thus far on his road, but detained for want of cash, and depended upon me sending him five pounds" . . . . . To make short of the story, he acknowledged the receipt of my answer and pledged himself to attend the first rehearsal, but from that day to this, I have

---

* Richer subsequently married the widow of a clergyman who had died extremely rich. They were living in great style at Cheltenham when Grimaldi visited them in 1817. *Vide* Boz's ' Memoirs of Grimaldi,' first edition, Vol. II, p. 147

† Vol. III, p. 379-91.

never heard from John Woodruffe Clarke, whose non-atten-
dance threw our little state into dreadful confusion, and but
for the indefatigable exertions of a Mr. Bannerman, who
studied the part of Iago in a few hours, and other characters
of equal importance, from one play-night to the other, we
must prematurely have closed the theatre, or properly
speaking, never have open'd it at all.'

' The receipts,' he continues, 'were confined to fourteen,
sixteen, and eighteen pounds, out of which ten were due to
Mr. and Mrs. Pope, and independent of them, the nightly
expences were never less than forty pounds . . . . Mr. Quick
now join'd us, and as he was only to have a clear benefit, the
risque was trifling, but all would not do; every struggle
proved useless . . . . To add to the pecuniary misery which
multiplied daily, I was under the necessity of supporting a
comic line in the drama, ill according with my unhappy state
of mind; to assume a face of mirth, and cause a laugh in others,
whilst my breast was torn in anguish; to support a character
in *A Cure for the Heartache* when my own was nearly bursting
with grief, were efforts greatly beyond my powers of mind,
and had a visible effect upon my health.   For ten weeks, in
hopes of better times, I struggled against the stream, accu-
mulating nothing but distress; to add to this, at the beginning of the season, flatter'd with the apparent certainty of
success, I had taken a house, and furnish'd it on credit; this,
with losses of various kinds, placed me nearly £800 in debt,
without any probable means of liquidation; £300 of this
was due to Mr. Aickin for rent . . . . As I sat brooding over
my unfortunate situation, in the foreground of which appear'd
a distinct vision of Lancaster Castle . . . . I was interrupted by
a letter from Mr. Astley, junior, with an offer of bringing down
St. Clare, the celebrated foreigner, who had made so much
noise in London, by an optical deception, call'd Phantasmagoria.   As this was the reigning folly of the day, I closed
in an instant with his terms . . . . The evening was finally
fixed for the exhibition, when again the cup was dash'd to
pieces, ere it reached my lips.   Astley despatched a long letter
of mutual condolence (saying) " St. Clare had fallen through a
trap and dislocated his collar-bone." ' . . . .

As a matter of fact, St. Clare was an imaginary being,
as Ryley found out for himself on his arrival in London.

He saw the individual who called himself St. Clare, and for the payment of sixty guineas was initiated into the mysteries of the *magic lantern* ! ' The important secret was nothing more, except a slight improvement of a transparent medium placed between the audience and the apparatus, on which the figures were reflected.'   So far Ryley had done his best to keep faith with the local public, but a foreign name was indispensable to the success of the undertaking.

On his arrival back in Liverpool, after an absence of eight days, he repaired to the French prison,* in order to find an individual who would play the *rôle* of St. Clare.   Ryley says that he ' was fortunate enough to encounter a man whose discharge had been made out that day ; and though but a rough sailor, clad in the coarsest habiliments, when metamorphosed by a handsome suit of black, his hair dressed with a bag and *solitaire*, he might have passed for one of the *noblesse*. The very little English he was master of, rendered him still more valuable ; on that account I became his interpreter, and after leading him forward, previous to the exhibition, interrupted his attempt at apology (which I had previously taught him) by observing, that as the ingenious foreigner was not sufficiently master of our language to express himself to the satisfaction of the audience, I would, with their permission, become his substitute.'   The scheme worked well, and the Phantasmagoria brought in three hundred pounds.

On Monday, March 1, 1802, ' St. Clare ' took a benefit, when in addition to the tragedy of *Macbeth* and the pantomime *Harlequin's Restoration* the *bénéficiaire* announced that ' several spectres of living and dead characters will be brought forward.' These included : ' the late John Palmer, a well-known character in Liverpool ; Robespierre ; the Devil ; Mr. Cooke, a late well-known and much esteemed medical character in Manchester.' The season terminated with ' St. Clare's ' benefit, which brought £120, and Ryley found himself in a large well-furnished house, without any means of livelihood, and nearly £500 in debt.

The following entry appears in the Corporation Records for January 6, 1802 :—

* Probably the Tower in Water Street, which at that time was used for the incarceration of prisoners of war.

'The proprietors of the Liverpool Theatre Royal having signified their intention of enlarging and altering the same agreeable to the Plans, Sections, &c., now produced and hereby it appears to be necessary to permit them to extend their building somewhat further into Williamson Square than the present colonnade, but in no part to project more than four yards beyond the same.   Unanimously resolved, that in the opinion of this Council such alteration will be of public convenience and ornament, and that the proprietors be allowed as far as any authority from this Council may be necessary, to proceed upon such alterations without further loss of time.'

Early in May of 1802 it was advertised in the local press ' that the present lease of the premises would expire on January 1st next, and that the proprietors are ready to receive proposals from any person or persons inclined to treat for a new lease.   The theatre is intended to be new modelled and enlarged.'

William Thomas Lewis and Thomas Knight were selected by the proprietors out of many applicants.   Their lease was for 14 years at a yearly rental of £1,500.   ' Aickin offered £100 more than the new managers, but he was so disliked in Liverpool that the proprietors deemed it politic to end his *régime*.'*

June 11, 1802 saw Mrs. Billington and Messrs. Young, Munden, Powell, and Knight here.   July 19, Mr. and Mrs. Henry Siddons in *Venice Preserved*; and on September 27, the celebrated Mrs. Jordan came on a visit.   She was seen as Hippolita in *She Wou'd and She Wou'd Not*, Lady Contest in *The Wedding Day*, Lady Racket in *Three Weeks after Marriage*, Nell in *The Devil to Pay*, Lady Teazle, and Rosalind.   She also performed in *The Belle's Stratagem* and *The Country Girl*.

This year there were in all 36 benefits, and the total amount realised by them was £5,053.   Benefit receipts are generally a good gauge of an actor's popularity, and I, therefore, give a list of the sums realised by the principal performers: Mrs. Billington, £219 ; Mr. Kelly, £223 ; Mrs. Powell, £177 ; Mr. Knight, £197 ; Mr. Munden, £235 ; Mrs. Siddons, £215 ; Mr. Simmons, £206 ; Miss Sims, £213 ; Mrs. Ward, £172 ; Mr. Mattocks, £164 ; Mrs. Jordan, £240 ; Mr. S. W. Ryley,.

---

* ' The Monthly Mirror,' June, 1802.

£199; Miss Walstein, £240; Mr. Grant, £192; Mr. Rock, £182; and Mr. Hurst, £173.

For Mr. Hurst's benefit on November 12, a new tragedy, entitled *Idela*, written by Mr. Simeon, junr., of Liverpool, was produced. Nine days later Charles Mathews, the elder, performed Dan in *John Bull* to the Mary Thornberry of the beautiful Julia Ann Grimani, eldest daughter of Gaspar, second son of the Marquis Grimani, a member of one of the very noblest and proudest houses in Venice.

Wednesday, November 24, 1802, was the last night of the season, and of acting under this roof. The performance was for Mr. Young's benefit, and the plays presented were Boaden's *Voice of Nature*, *The Midnight Hour*, and the burletta of *Tom Thumb*. The receipts amounted to £241.

THE NEW THEATRE ROYAL.

The rebuilding of the theatre commenced in December, 1802, and the new house was ready for opening in June of the following year. The following is a copy of the bill for the inaugural performance :—

'NEW THEATRE ROYAL,
Will Open this present Monday, June 6th, 1803,
when
An Address, in Character,
written by T. Dibdin, Esq.
And to be Spoken by Mr. Knight.
After which their Majesties' Servants
will perform the Comedy of,

SPEED THE PLOUGH.

Sir Philip Blandford,......................Mr. Grant,
Farmer Ashfield,.........................Mr. Knight,
    (by Permission of the Proprietors of Covent-Garden Theatre)
Morrington,.............................Mr. Witton,
    (his third Appearance on a public stage)
Sir Abel Handy,........................Mr. Simmons,
    (by Permission of the Proprietors of Covent-Garden Theatre)
Bob Handy,.............................Mr. Young,

Henry,................................Mr. Howard,
(his second Appearance on a public stage)
Evergreen,......Mr. Ryley,   Gerald....Mr. Shaw,
Postillion,..Mr. Moreton,—Handy's Servant,..Mr. Howell,
Peter,......Mr. Woodward,
Miss Blandford,........................Mrs. Mountain,
(by Permission of the Proprietors of Drury Lane Theatre)
In which she will introduce the new Polaca Song and Bravura.
Lady Handy,...........................Mrs. Kennady,
Susan Ashfield,........................Miss Smith,
(from the Theatre Royal, Bath)
Diana Ashfield,........................Miss Biggs.
The Dance incidental to the Comedy, by Messrs. Simmons,
Young, Knight, Howard, Moreton, Howell, Woodward, &c.
Mrs. Mountain, Miss Biggs, Mrs. Grant, Mrs. Moreton,
Mrs. Shaw, &c.

To which will be added, a Musical Entertainment, called
NO SONG, NO SUPPER.

Robin,......Mr. Penley,   Dorothy,......Mrs. Chapman,
(his first Appearance on   (her first Appearance here these
this Stage)   three Years)
Crop,........Mr. Shaw,   Louisa,........Mrs. Mortimer,
Fredrick,....Mr. Byrne,   Nelly,.........Miss Sims,
(from the Theatre-Royal,   Margaretta,....Mrs.Mountain,
Dublin)   (who is engaged for a short
Endless,....Mr. Simmons,   time only).
Servant,....Mr. Woodward,

The Doors to be opened at Six, and the Curtain to rise precisely at Seven.

Tickets to be had at the Box-Office, Front of the Theatre, where Places for the Boxes may be taken from *Eleven* till *Three* o'clock.—Tickets also to be had of Egerton and William Smith, Navigation Shop, Pool Lane.

Nights of Performing will be Monday, Wednesday, Friday, and Saturday.

††† Miss Edmead from the Theatre Royal, Dublin, will make her first Appearance on Wednesday next.

☞ Mrs. Glover from the Theatre Royal, Drury Lane, will shortly make her Appearance in "The Jealous Wife."

Messrs. LEWIS & KNIGHT most respectfully submit to the Liberality and Candor of the Public, the justice of a small addition to the Prices of Admission :—the considerable Increase of weekly Disbursements, in consequence of rebuilding the Theatre ; the great expence of new Scenery, Decorations, Wardrobe, Furniture, additions to the Band, and the general Establishment, (so essentially necessary to render it worthy the Opulence and Spirit of the second Town of England) encourage the Managers to rely with confidence on the Support of a generous Public ;—and while they presume, that for elegance and Accommodation, and for the *true purposes* of a Theatre, that of Liverpool is not surpassed by any in the Kingdom ; they have the honour to assure the Town that in the Direction of it, no exertion shall be wanting to support its consequence, and to give general satisfaction. Boxes, 4s. 6d...Upper Boxes, 4s...Pit, 3s...Gallery, 1s. 6d.

N.B —These additions to the Prices will be again taken off when the Engagements of the Auxiliary Performers shall have ceased ; and during the Winter Season the House will continue open (under the same Direction) at the Old Prices.

Smiths, Printers, Pool Lane, Liverpool.'*

The front of the building was (as now) semi-circular, and of stone and was decorated with the King's arms, and several emblematical figures in bas relief.   The interior was commodiously arranged and tastefully ornamented, while the acoustic properties were admirable.   I cull the following account of the re-opening from the ' Monthly Mirror ' for July, 1803 :—' This truly elegant theatre opened on Monday, June 6, under the management of Messrs. Lewis and Knight.   We do not hesitate to pronounce it at once the most elegant, commodious, compact, and chastely proportioned building for the purpose of theatrical exhibition in the United Kingdom.   The shape of the interior is nearly that of a horse-shoe, the performance may be very wel seen, and the lowest whisper, if articulate, distinctly heard.   We could wish the proscenium had been less richly ornamented, for, however beautifully executed, it does not entirely harmonise with the light, elegant decorations of the other parts of the house.   The fronts of the boxes

* Reproduced by kind permission of the Committee of the Athenæum.

are painted with a sort of lattice work silvered, and medallions beautifully executed.   The supporters of the boxes are light, well-proportioned, cast-iron pillars, gilded.   There are four-and-twenty of the handsomest lustres we ever saw ;   twelve of which, somewhat larger than the others, are suspended at equal distances round the lower tier ;   eight round the second tier, and four above those, round the third or highest tier.

'The very limited time in which all this was effected (scarcely six months, and commenced in the depth of winter), reflects the highest credit upon the active spirit, skill, and perseverance of Mr. Foster, the architect, to whose taste and ability we are indebted for most of our well-built houses all over the town.   An address, written by Mr. T. Dibdin, comparing the theatre to a ship, and carrying on the figure with neat and appropriate allusions throughout, was delivered with much spirit by Mr. Knight, whose entrance was greeted with enthusiastic applause.'

The following is a copy of the address : —

'Well—our tackle's all ready, our hands are all stanch,
And a glorious sight, if you come to the lanch !
We've built, as you see, a snug, tight pleasure-boat,
And we hope that your honors will keep it afloat.
Each *cabin's* convenient, at least so we plann'd,
We've snug births *below*, and our *tops* are well mann'd ;
Our timbers are taught, all our canvass is new,
From London *first-rates* we've selected our crew.
And each on *this* deck comes, with free inclination,
To rise in the service, by your approbation,
At least we'll endeavour, in good or bad weather,
To keep all our passengers happy together ;
Tho' with other provisions you find your own table,
We'll keep you in *spirits* as long as we're able.
We've *artillery* too, care and folly to shoot,
And are arm'd, as these gentlemen tell you, *influte.* (*the
    Orchestra*).
We've great guns of tragedy, loaded so well,
If they do but go *off*, they'll be certain to *tell* ;
While with small shot of farce, and low comedy swivels,
We've sworn to burn, sink, and destroy the blue devils ;

But aim where we will, we shall ever desire,
From *your* hands a broadside to second our fire.
Should you ask with what freightage our vessel is stor'd,
What cargo, what riches, we carry on board ?
Look round, you'll see all Briton's value on earth,
True freedom, good nature, wit, beauty, and worth ;
With such lading as this, while our voyage we measure,
Our anchor is hope, and our compass—your pleasure.
    (*going, returns*).
Yet hold—ere I go, you may think it but right,
To know under what sort of colours we fight :
Our vessel is royal—the standard you view,
Which can ne'er be pull'd down—while supported by you.'*

' The scenes,' says the ' Monthly Mirror,'† chiefly painted by Whitmore, Walmsley, and Wilkins, together with the dresses, &c., are with such elegance and good taste displayed in the *tout ensemble.'* *Apropos* of the scenic artists, the two first mentioned had graduated in Ireland. Whitmore was a pupil of the celebrated Robert Carver, and succeeded him as scene painter at Covent Garden. He was in the height of his powers in 1803, so Liverpool at that period saw some good scenery.

At the advanced prices (boxes 4s. 6d. ; upper boxes 4s. ; pit 3s. ; and gallery 1s. 6d.), the house would hold nearly £400. The prices were lowered during the winter season. Messrs. Lewis and Knight's first season lasted for ten months.

The ' Monthly Mirror ' for August, 1803, says, ' *A Cure for the Heartache* introduced Mr. Emery to this audience, in the part of Frank Oatland ; and Mrs. Glover commenced her career in the part of *The Jealous Wife,* a character in which her reputation is deservedly so high. Mr. Lewis appeared first in Ranger. He has since played Benedick, Archer, Copper Captain, and Marplot. He appears in high health and spirits ; his reception was most flattering. Mr. Cooper, from Drury Lane, has played Richard twice, and Macbeth once, on his road to Dublin, with success. A prize bought in here (French), had on board nearly thirty gentlemen and ladies. The managers, humanely wishing to soften the rigours of captivity, politely offered them a free admission to the theatre,

---

* Troughton's ' Liverpool,' p. 325.   † July, 1803.

which they with joy accepted, and they nightly attend, escorted, in parties of ten or a dozen. It has been stated in some of the London papers that the managers have been obliged in consequence of the badness of the house, to call in the aid of Messrs. Fawcett and others ; but this is not the fact, they have sought for no additional attractions ; their engagements for the season were made some months ago. Mr. Fawcett opened July 18, in Goldfinch and Caleb Quotem ; he is to perform three weeks, and will be succeeded by Munden.'

On September 17, 1803, *The Man of the World* and *The Sultan* were played for the benefit of Lady Perrott, who pathetically announced that ' having no other emoluments for her performances and expenses from London entreats a generous public, ever ready to alleviate unmerited misfortune, to patronise the efforts of a mother, struggling for the support of a large orphan family, the two eldest having already come forward in the noble cause so dear to every British heart, the defence of their country. She appeals to the father and the fond mother for support—who can feel for her situation as to compel a woman, nobly born, to such painful efforts.' The performance realised only £60.

The Belle's Stratagem was presented on October 20, with Charles Mayne Young as Doricourt and Miss Grimani as Letitia Hardy. Apparently this was the first meeting of the two who were fated to become husband and wife. It was a sheer case of love at first sight.

Young had made considerable progress in the art of the stage since his *début* at the Royal in 1798 ; in fact, his proficiency was so great that for the last two years he had practically led the business of the stock company at the old theatre, and was doing the same in the new house.

The following extracts are from a letter, dated Liverpool, October 30, 1803, written by Charles Mathews to his friend John Litchfield :—' I opened on the 24th, in Pedrillo (*The Castle of Andalusia*), and Sir David Dunder (*Ways and Means*). My reception was the warmest, I think, I ever experienced. When I spoke behind the scenes in reply to Fernando's call, the audience applauded, which applause was kept up for some time after my entrance. This, of course, gave me confidence, and I played up, and hit them very hard. I introduced the song of the "Old Bachelors," which was uproariously encored.

I

Sir David was a good card : it has never been played, but by Bannister many years ago. It was very well received, and I repeated it three nights after. . . . .

' I find one line of Yorkshire worth a length of anything else. Emery was adored here ; never was anything like the favour in which he stood with the audience, so I am told. The Lancashire bears a strong resemblance to the Yorkshire dialect. Young advised me, notwithstanding this, to try them in that line, which I did, first in Young Testy ; and finding it likely to take, I played Robin Roughead, in which I hit them ; and have, in consequence, chosen Dan, in *John Bull*, which we play to-morrow night. Job Thornberry, Young ; Peregrine, Cooper ; Dennis, Hamerton (a good Irishman) ; Mary, Miss Grimani, who is a great favourite here. I have seen her in Mrs. Haller and Juliet, and like her much. She is a better actress than she appeared to be in London. I am much pleased with Young ; I think he is the best actor I have seen in the country. In Rolla, Romeo, and the Stranger, I have greatly admired him ; he is particularly happy in the latter. His appearance is fine ; and his face admirably suited to the expression of melancholy.

' The theatre is beautiful ; and holds, at 4s. 6d., 2s. 6d., and 1s. 6d., nearly £400. The prices are now lowered, and we play to houses of £90 or £100, which is thought to be bad ; the pit is usually well attended. They have little opinion of any actor who has not played in London. Young is the only exception ; he is a favourite, and is greatly respected in private ; he has better connections than any actor here, and visits the first people. I have found him a valuable acquaintance. There is one thing here which annoys me intolerably. The clerks decamp at the end of the play to devour veal pies, in consequence of which when the farce begins half the pit is deserted, and they come clattering in again with greasy mouths when the first act is nearly over. They are sometimes a dull audience, and I have not much respect (from report) of their judgment. I am told they accuse Munden of copying Simmons—*risum teneatis !* I have, however, not much reason to complain, and expect to be a favourite. The town I like ; the situation is beautiful. I have ridden seven miles on the sands ; the sea on one side, the town and harbour on the other. The opposite Cheshire coast and distant Welsh

mountains form altogether a most enchanting prospect. Prince
William is here, and will remain, it is supposed for the winter.
He has bespoken plays three times ; the boxes promise well,
by the by, for *John Bull* and *Love Laughs.*'*

While here, Mathews met with a very serious accident.
He had gone to a review, and at the first sound of fire the horse
upon which he was seated threw him with great violence upon
his head.   Prince William of Gloster, who knew Mathews,
immediately descended from his horse, and went to his assistance.   Mathews, who was unconscious, was quickly carried
home.   This accident produced a brief, but severe illness,
and set up a local complaint of a serious tendency, which distressed him ever afterwards, but of which he never openly
complained.

Charles Young and Miss Grimani were both friends of Mr.
and Mrs. Charles Mathews. The December of 1803 saw all four
in Liverpool, as they were engaged to perform at the Royal.
On December 26, *Paul and Virginia* was to have been
brought forward, but owing to an interesting event it was
postponed.   This was the birth to Mr. and Mrs. Mathews
of a son.   'I came into the world,' says the younger
Mathews,† 'with the pantomimes, in a laughing season, and
my first cry, if it could have been understood, was I have no
doubt: "Here we are!" The spot selected for my first
appearance was a nice little house in a nice little street, in
Liverpool, contiguous to the theatre where my father and
mother were at that time fulfilling their first provincial pantomime engagement after their first season in London.   It
was called then as now, Basnett Street.'

Albeit a number of players used to reside in Basnett
Street when they visited Liverpool, I am of the opinion that
the younger Mathews was in error when he said that he was
born in that thoroughfare.   Shortly after his birth his father
and mother advertised that they were to take a benefit at the
Royal on January 25, 1804. 'Gore's General Advertiser,' for
January 19, 1804, mentions that ' tickets could be had of
Mr. Mathews, Leigh Street,' and the playbills announced that
' tickets could be had of Mr. and Mrs. Mathews, No. 8, Leigh

* ' Memoirs of Charles Mathews, Comedian,' by Mrs. Mathews. Second edition, Vol. I,
pp. 419-421.
  † ' The Life of Charles James Mathews,' edited by Charles Dickens, Vol. I, p. 5.

Street, Basnett Street.'   It is rather unlikely that Mr. and
Mrs. Mathews would change their lodgings in the depth of
winter, when their son and heir was only a few weeks old.
The infant was not baptised in Liverpool, but at St. Helen's
Church, York, where in the month of March, 1803, his father
and mother had been married.   The child, according to the
baptismal register of St. Helen's, was christened there in May,
1804, and under the heading of ' Abode ' his parents are referred to as being ' on their way to London.'

'When Charles arrived,' according to his mother's account,
' he was the very smallest and funniest little thing that was
ever seen ; rarely smiled from the first, and seemed perfectly
easy and self-possessed.   I had been told to prepare for a
minute baby, and the clothes were, therefore, far below the
average size, but they were so ridiculously large, that they
hung upon him like a sack ; he was, therefore, wrapped in
wadding, and put into a basket by the fire, while his first out-
fit was prepared by cutting up one of his father's soft white
neckcloths, which was tacked together and snipped up the
edges in imitation of ruffles.   There he lay on his back in
perfect comfort, with both his tiny hands lifted up as high as
he could, the fingers incessantly wriggling as they peeped out
of the frilled cuffs.'*

Charles Mayne Young was the possessor of a Roman
proboscis, ' and ' says Mrs. Mathews, ' I was constantly jesting
with him about the said nose.   When an interesting prospect
was open to me, he said, one day : " Take care !   I warn you,
if you set your mind on this nose of mine, that baby will be
born with a hook." '

When little Charles was born, ' there, exactly in the right
place, was the most absurd little protuberance, not bigger
than a good-sized pea, and certainly not deserving the name
of nose.   Miss Grimani remarked upon this, and when I told
her there was a good story upon that subject, she left me in great
delight to play a trick upon Charles Young.   In reply to his
question, " How's Narny ?" (Mrs. Mathews), she gravely said :
"She is going on very well, but she has the most ridiculous
little baby, and, only fancy, with a Roman nose !"   "Don't
tell me so !" roared out Young, who went into fits of laughter,

* ' The Life of Charles James Mathews,' Vol. I. p. 8-9.

danced round the room, and told Miss Grimani of the warnings he had given the mother ; and said he should insist upon seeing it.   When he was allowed, after much preparation, to see the child, and discovered the hoax that had been played upon him, he made such a noise in the room that he was turned out bodily by the nurse.'*

The principal benefit receipts during the 1803 season were as follows :—Mr. Fawcett, £245 ; Mr. Munden, £235 ; Mrs. Glover, £330 ; and Mr. Emery, £300.   In the after season, the prices having been reduced, Mr. Young, £162 and £290 ; Miss Grimani, £207 ; and Mr. Mathews, £238.   Altogether there were 36 benefits, the total amount of which came to £5,604.

On Wednesday, October 10, 1804, William Henry West Betty, the ' Young Roscius,' made his first appearance in Liverpool.   He was then in his fourteenth year, and on his opening night played Young Norval in *Douglas*.   He also performed during his visit Hamlet, Frederick (*Lover's Vows*), Richard III, Romeo, Osman (*Zara*), and Rolla (*Pizarro*). Here he completely eclipsed his brilliant and unprecedented successes at other places in the Kingdom. ' When the box office opened in a morning,' says Merritt,† ' the pressure to secure places was so excessive, that many gentlemen had their clothes torn to pieces; their hats and shoes carried away in the crowd, and themselves, sometimes, severely bruised, and almost suffocated in the attempt.   There is reason to believe, that if the theatre had been twice as large, it would have been equally thronged.   The terms of his engagement were so liberal, that he received from the managers, for his share of the profits of fifteen nights, the enormous sum of fifteen hundred and twenty pounds ; as appears from Mr. Betty's receipt in Mr. Knight's possession.' Just after Betty's visit *Guilty, or Not Guilty* was played to only £20.‡

In 1804 it was found expedient to reduce the salaries of the company.   The highest salary was £2 per week.   The management had then two sets of articles, one for the summer and the other for the winter engagements.   They still played only four nights in the week, with the exception of the race

* ' The Life of Charles James Mathews, Vol. 1. p. 10.
† ' Memoirs of the Life of William Henry West Betty,' by J. Merritt (Liverpool, 1804), second edition, p. 48.
‡ ' The Theatric Tourist ' (1805), p. 53.

week when six performances were given.   The charges for the
use of the house for the summer benefits amounted to sixty
guineas, and for the winter fifty-five guineas.

On March 9, 1805, Charles Young and Miss Grimani were
married at St. Anne's Church, Richmond, Liverpool.   The
wedding would have taken place before but for the lady's
anxiety to see her mother established with her eldest son, and
her younger brother and sister placed at school.

Soon after their honeymoon the newly-married pair
accepted an engagement for twelve months at the Manchester
Theatre Royal.   In days when their services were not required at the theatre, they indulged much in short country
excursions.   On one of these happy occasions the two stayed
at Prestwich, and after an hour's walk through the meadows,
they came to the village church.

While Young passed the time in looking at the dates and
ages on the tombstones, his wife stood still, musing with
rivetted gaze on a solitary weeping birch, situated near the
centre of the Churchyard. ' One can fancy it,' writes the Rev.
Julian Charles Young in the memoir of his father, Charles
Mayne Young,* ' pensively drooping its tresses over some little
grassy mound, as if in pity for its tiny tenant.   The husband,
seeing his wife mute and absorbed, asked her what she was
looking at, and of what she was thinking.

" I was thinking—that I should like to exact a favour of
you—a conditional one."

" What is it, darling ? "

" You know I'm hoping soon to be a mother ! (a pause).
If it should be God's will I die in giving life to my babe, promise me, Charles, you will lay me beneath that sweet tree."

' Distressed to find her thoughts running in such a channel,
he gently chid her, and begged her to banish such morbid
apprehension from her mind.   Alas ! the shadow of the coming
event must have passed over her spirit at that time ; for a few
brief weeks saw her lying in the very cemetery she had lately
visited, and under the tree of her own choice.'

May 27, 1805, witnessed the return of the ' Young Roscius,'
when he played Young Norval in *Douglas*.   The other characters were undertaken by Smith, Wheatley (from Plymouth,

* ' Memoir of Charles Mayne Young ' (1871), p. 22.

his first appearance here), Grant, Mrs. Wrench (from Bath), and Mrs. Fagan (from Weymouth). The after-piece was *No Song, No Supper*. Robin by Brown (from Warwick, first appearance here); Margaretta, Miss Stephens.   May 29, *Barbarossa* and *Catherine* and *Petruchio*. Catherine, Mrs. Young ; Petruchio, Wheatley.   May 30, Betty as Hamlet ; Ophelia, Mrs. Young. The after-piece was *The Padlock*. May 31, Master Betty as Frederick in *Lover's Vows*.   Count Cassel, Knight, his first appearance this season.   Also *The Man of Quality* (a poor alteration of *The Relapse*). Miss Hoyden, Mrs. Johnson (from Drury Lane, her first appearance here) ; Lord Foppington, Mr. H. Lewis. June 3, young Betty as Earl Osmond in *The Castle Spectre* (for the first time on any stage).   June 5, *Romeo and Juliet*. Romeo, Betty ; Juliet, Mrs. Young ; Mercutio, Young.   Afterpiece *The Quaker*.   June 6, Betty as Zanga in *The Revenge*. This was announced as his first appearance in the character, but a bill in Mr. A. Hunter's collection, which formerly belonged to the Betty family, shows he played the part at Londonderry on April 23, 1804.   June 10, Betty as Orestes in *The Distrest Mother* (first appearance in that character), Hermione, Mrs. Young.   June 14, Betty in name part of Henry Brooke's tragedy, *Gustavus Vasa*, his first appearance in the *rôle*, and the first local production of the play.   The play was written in 1739, but its performance was then prohibited by the Lord Chamberlain.

Bannister, Emery, Fawcett, and Miss Mellon were also here about this time.   On Monday, October 14, the celebrated Miss Mudie (seven years old) appeared as Widow Cheerly (*The Soldier's Daughter*, and Roxalana (*The Sultan*).

On July 14, 1806 Robert William Elliston made his first appearance in Liverpool on this stage.   He played Duke Aranza in *The Honeymoon*. During this visit he was also seen as Octavian in *The Mountaineers*, and Felix in *The Hunter of the Alps*.   This noted player was always a favourite in Liverpool, both on and off the stage.   When the Royal was to let in 1802, he offered to take it, and his uncle agreed to become security for the rent for two years—namely, £3,000— but nothing came of it*.   The reader will learn with interest that a grand-daughter of Elliston now resides in Canning Street in our city.

* Raymond's 'Life and Enterprises of Robert William Elliston' (1857), p. 77.

On July 24, 1806, Mrs. Galindo, from the Theatre Royal, Dublin, made her *début* in Liverpool as Elvira in *Pizarro*. This was the actress who subsequently brought a vile and utterly unsubstantiated charge against Mrs. Siddons. She accused the great tragedienne of improper intimacy with her husband.

George Frederick Cooke commenced an engagement on Monday, August 18, 1806, when he played Richard III. Ten nights later the tragedy was again performed, ' when Mr. Cooke was so overcome with the beauty of Lady Anne (Miss S. Norton), that in recovering himself from his kneeling pastime he made a false step and lost his equilibrium. We are sorry to add that '' Richard was not himself again ; '' and that Mr. Archer (King Henry) was obliged to finish the character.'* One can see from the foregoing that poor George Frederick was drunk. Perhaps it was at this time (if ever) that Cooke made that caustic rejoinder about the Liverpool bricks all being cemented by negro blood. The story is set forth in Mrs. Mathews' ' Anecdotes of Actors.'†

' Cooke had appeared upon the stage one night while under the influence of the demon—*drink*. He was, as in most places, an immense favourite with the Liverpool audience, who fully appreciated his vast powers and were entirely disposed to regard the failings of the man as venial and accidental, while his intrinsic qualities were solid and positive ; indulgence, therefore, to his *one occasional* infirmity was willingly shown. But there are limits, unhappily, to human charity, and on the evening alluded to, Cooke's *dark hour* o'ershadowed his professional and private excellencies ; he was, in fact, incapable of proceeding in his performance with bearable propriety, and public favour was suddenly obscured by public resentment elicited by his disgusting state, and manifested at length by indications of a pretty general and expressive nature, which, dimmed as Cooke's perceptions were by his situation, and the " potations pottle deep " which he had swallowed, proved comprehensive enough to his practiced experience, and stepping forward to the stage lamps, with his powerful brow contracted with disdain, he addressed his reprovers in the following pithy sentence :—

" What ! do you hiss me ?—hiss George Frederick Cooke ? —you contemptible money-getters ! you shall never again

* Liverpool chit chat in ' The Dublin Evening Post,' September 6, 1806.
† Pp. 98-9.

have the *honour* of hissing me ! Farewell ! I banish *you* ! "
And concentrating into one vast heap all the malice of his
offended feelings, he added, after a pause of intense meaning,
" *There is not a brick in your d———— town, but what is cemented
by the blood of a negro* ! "

'This shameful address was suffered without notice and
the utterer of it was allowed to retire without further mani-
festation of resentment—a moderation speaking volumes in
proof of the good sense and good temper of the Liverpool
public.'

In Hawkins' ' Life of Edmund Kean,' it is stated that
Kean used to relate, from his own personal knowledge, the
following anecdote : ' When George Frederick Cooke was
playing in Liverpool the managers found great difficulty
in keeping him sober ; but, after repeated transgressions,
he solemnly promised not to offend again during his stay.
In the evening of the day upon which the promise was made,
Cooke was not to be found when wanted for Sir Pertinax
MacSycophant ; the audience grew impatient, the manager
stormed, and all was in " most admired disorder." After a
long search the manager discovered him at a pot-house near
the theatre, where he was drinking with great composure and
perseverance out of a very *small* glass. " Oh, Mr. Cooke,"
exclaimed the irritated manager, "you have again broken your
solemn promise ; did you not tell me you would give over
drinking ? "   Cooke surveyed the manager with the most
provoking coolness, and said, "I certainly did make such a
promise but you cannot expect a man to reform all at once.
I have given over drinking *in a great measure*," and the incorrigible player held up the *small* glass to the manager's nose.'

Apropos of the dictum that actors to put forth their best
efforts must be stimulated by applause, Mr. Bram Stoker in
his ' Personal Reminiscences of Henry Irving '* tells a story
of Cooke coming down to the front and saying to our townsmen,
' If you don't applaud I can't act.' If half the stories told
of Cooke's escapades and audacities in Liverpool are true, the
wonder to me is that he ever escaped from the town with his
life.

Cooke was announced to make his re-appearance as
Richard III, on August 24, 1807, but in consequence of his

* Vol. I., p. 74.

non-arrival Mr. Grant had to perform the part. C. M. Young commenced an engagement on May 2, 1808, and Mr. and Mrs. Henry Siddons* appeared during the following June and July. Then came Elliston for a few nights. George Frederick Cooke visited the theatre on September 12.

During the season of 1808, Miss Mary Catherine Bolton, the singer, appeared in Liverpool. Here her youth, beauty, and musical talents made her very popular. Her return visits were equally successful. In 1813 she married Edward, Lord Thurlow, a poet of some distinction, and nephew to the first Lord Thurlow. She died of consumption in 1830.†

June of the following year (1809), witnessed Cooke as Richard III and as Kitely (*Every Man in His Humour*). Commencing July 10, Mrs. Siddons played for a few nights. Dowton, Emery, and Mr. and Mrs. Henry Siddons followed. On September 18, Mrs. Jordan made her first appearance here these seven years. She played Peggy (*The Country Girl*), Miss Hoyden (*A Trip to Scarborough*), Widow Belmour (*The Way to Keep Him*), and Nell (*The Devil to Pay*).

On October 18 a new ballet was presented, entitled ' All Alive at Liverpool ; or, the Wapping Landlady.'

On May 14, 1810, the theatre opened‡ for the season under the most inauspicious circumstances, as rioting broke out with the first performance and continued for a week. The cause of the disturbance was the question of Half-Price, and as the lessees, Messrs. Lewis and Knight, would not give way, a certain number of play-goers took it into their heads to adopt coercive measures. The rioters not only disturbed the performances by using flappers, horns, whistles, and other cacophonous instruments, but they broke all the windows in the theatre, and smashed a large pier-glass, besides doing other damage. Ultimately the Riot Act had to be read, after which the mob dispersed.

The riots were doubtless occasioned by those in the previous year at Covent Garden Theatre, although they were not[7] precisely of the same order. In London resistance was

---

* Mrs. Henry Siddons's father, Charles Murray, was educated for a doctor, and became a surgeon's mate in the Navy, but resigned, and having gained some applause by a private performance at Liverpool, made his intention known to Mr. Younger, the manager of the Theatre Royal, of going on the stage. Apparently, Murray made a public appearance in Liverpool. Younger gave him an introduction to Tate Wilkinson, under whom, at York, he made his professional *début* in 1775.
† *Vide* ' Our Actresses,' Vol. I, p. 158.
‡ The plays were *Pizarro* and *The Benevolent Tar*.

made to the adoption of a new measure, while here in Liverpool, the attempt to compel the adoption of a new measure was resisted.   Local play-goers, however, undoubtedly laboured under an old-standing grievance, inasmuch as the question of Half-Price had frequently been brought before the lessees of the theatre without avail.   It was pointed out to them that to charge full-price for admission was an inequitable tax upon those whose business avocations only enabled them to see half the performance ;   and that a certain section of the community was thus deprived of the rational amusement of the theatre.

To this the lessees made answer that the one shilling gallery (which held 1,200 persons) usually contained half the components of the audience.   In the London theatres it was common for the boxes to be wholly taken, so that often persons were obliged to wait for weeks before they could be accommodated.   The Half-Price in the metropolis served chiefly to fill the lobbies.   At the Royal, Liverpool, it seldom happened (except on benefit nights) that a *sixth* part of the boxes was taken previous to the commencement of the performance. The full price for admission to the upper boxes (more accommodating than most others, and with a capacity for nearly 400 persons), only exceeded by sixpence the Half-Price to the same part in London.

The principal rioters, Abraham Lemon, clerk to Lionel Lemon, timber merchant, Thomas Turner, gentleman, John Robinson Molyneaux, broker, Charles Rowlandson, attorney, Matthew Carter, merchant's clerk, and Barton Wilson, coachmaker's apprentice, were indicted for conspiracy and riot. Several of the defendants were young, Barton Wilson was only twenty, and John Robinson Molyneaux, twenty-one.   At the Lancaster Assizes, held in September, 1810, before Mr. Baron Graham and a special jury, they were all found guilty of rioting, but not of conspiracy.   Sentence was deferred until the Michaelmas sitting of the Court of King's Bench.   Abraham Lemon was found to be ' eminently culpable, his crime being increased in an uncommon degree by having published a most violent and improper paper by way of vindication.'   Charles Rowlandson, as an attorney, was severely censured for being a party to riotous proceedings. On November 26, the rioters were sentenced by Mr. Justice Grose to the following terms of imprisonment:—Abraham Lemon and Charles Rowlandson to be confined for twelve months in the Castle of Lancaster; John Robinson Molyneaux and Thomas Turner for three months; and Barton Wilson and Matthew Carter for two months all in the Castle of Lancaster.

The appearance of Mrs. Edwin here on June 25, 1810, as Widow Cheerly in *The Soldier's Daughter* marked her *début* on the local stage.   On September 4, *The Road to Ruin* was performed for Munden's benefit.   Munden sang a new comic song expressly written for the occasion by J. Pocock (author of *Hit or Miss, Twenty Years Ago*, etc.), entitled 'All Alive at Liverpool.'   The music and words were afterwards published by Messrs. Hime and Son, of Castle and Church Streets, Liverpool.   As the ditty presents an interesting view of the old town, I feel constrained to give it *in extenso* :—

'Being rather flush of Cash
I resolv'd to cut a dash
So I pack'd up all my Riches,
Coats, Pantaloons, and Breeches
And to Liverpool, e'gad
I set off with Mam and Dad
To see all the Lions in the Town O!
All so prime—nick'd the time
Tumbl'd in—Broke my Shin
Together cram'd—squeez'd and jam'd
Off we dash—What a splash
Father bawl'd—Mother squall'd
Hey down, oh, down derry, derry down
To see all the Lions in the Town O!

Then thro' the Streets we range
And we see the Grand Exchange
Where Britannia's looking down
So delighted on the Town
And they say if once their Siller
Shou'd raise up her Nelson's Pillar
She'd turn round and drop a Tear to his Mem'ry O!

There you'll see—frank and free ⁊
Trade and Commerce—not gone from us
Merchants Trading—Bills of Lading
Sugar, Cotton—Fairly gotten
Spite of Boney—Bags of Money !
      Hey down, etc.
Oh Liverpool's a wonderful town O !

Then the Papers wou'd you see 'em
You must visit the Athenæum
See the Docks in fine condition
And go to the Exhibition
Then on Turtle would you dine
With a glass of good old Wine
You'll get the very best in the Globe O !
Calipash—cut and slash
Calipee—then you'll see
Green Fat—all that
Lemon juice—white spruce
Good for Lunch—cold Punch !
      Hey down etc.
Oh Liverpool's a wonderful town O !

But what most made me stare
Was to see the Washing Fair
Where the Lads are all so witty
And the Girls are all so Pretty
For in spite of wind and weather
They jump'd in Pell Mell together
And said that they had Physic in the Water O !
Together yok'd—ladies douk'd
Water dashing—kicking, splashing,
Indeed its true—Buff and Blue
Men and Women—all a swimming
Cheek by jowl—upon my soul !
      Hey down etc,
Oh Liverpool's a wonderful town O !

For further merriment
To the Play-House next I went
'Twas Joe Munden's Benefit
So I squeezed into the Pit
And there so long he sung out
I thought he'd wear his tongue out
And 'twas all about the Liverpool Lions O !
Lyceum reading—Turtle Feeding
Tea and Coffee—Cakes and Toffee
Nelson's story—Briton's Glory
House a thumper—quite a Bumper
'Till at last—the Joke was past
   With hey down etc.
Success to the Town and its Trade O ! '

When Sir Sidney Smith visited the Royal, this verse was substituted for the fifth verse as originally sung :

' For further merriment
To the Play-House next I went
And there I saw a crowd
Applauding long and loud
They kicked up such a clatter
Says I, pray, what's the matter ?
And they said 'twas for the Hero of Acre O !
Who banged so hearty—Bonaparte
King approves him—Country loves him
Sidney's story—Briton's glory
Then let the rays—of honour blaze
For ever be on—Cœur de Lion.
   Hey down etc.
And all such Heroes as these are.'

On January 13, 1811, William Thomas Lewis, one of the lessees of the theatre, died at his residence in Westbourne Place, London.   Lewis is supposed to have been born at Ormskirk, about 1748.*   He was of Welsh descent, and was the son of William Lewis, linen draper, of Tower Hill, London, who quitted

* There is no entry in the Ormskirk Parish Church register of William Thomas Lewis's baptism there between 1743 and 1753. The house in which he was supposed to have been born is now converted into a shop, and numbered 23, Aughton Street.

trade for the stage.   Of 'Gentleman' Lewis it is recorded that 'he blended the gracefulness of Barry with the energy of Garrick, and superadded to these acquirements his own unceasing activity and amazing rapidity of utterance and motion.'* 'Billy Lewis,' says Cooke in his 'Memoirs,' 'was the model for making everyone do his duty by kindness and good treatment.'   Therefore, the sobriquet of 'Gentleman' Lewis was not bestowed without reason.   Among his best parts may be reckoned Belcour, Petruchio, Young Norval, Ranger, Sir Charles Racket, Millamour, Mercutio, Percy, Marplot, Copper Captain, Atall, Rover, Squire Groom, Lackland, Faddle, Vapid, Goldfinch, Tippy, Tom Shuffleton, and Diddler.

In 1811, Messrs. Elrington, Johnstone, Emery, Munden, Mathews, Edwin, and Dowton were here.   Dowton gave (July 1) his celebrated performance of Dr. Cantwell in *The Hypocrite*.   On July 8, John Philip Kemble played Hamlet. Power and Mrs. Stirling and Mr. and Mrs. John Tayleure appeared in *The Peasant Boy* and *The Bee Hive* on September 9.

Mr. and Mrs. Tayleure (*née* Grant) were married in Liverpool.   The former, who was a very clever man, was facetiously called by his waggish companions, 'Six feet two inches of melancholy.'   His friends never could understand how a very tall person could be a *low* comedian.   Mrs. Tayleure was the daughter of an actor.   She and her husband afterwards went to London, but the 'Lancashire Liston' did not set the Thames on fire. Perhaps the metropolis did not, or *would* not, understand his humour.   'They have been prudent in pecuniary matters,' writes Mrs. Cornwell Baron-Wilson,† 'and are independent of the world and their profession ;   although the lady fills an engagement when a comfortable and sure salaried one offers : and the gentleman is in business, and has on view, and on sale, one of the most extensive private collections of curious old prints, perhaps, in the world.   He makes it his profit as well as his hobby ;   for in his museum, on the east front of St. Martin's Church, he has upwards of 50,000 old and scarce matters connected with the arts and the drama.'

On November 14, 1811, and the two following nights, Italian operas were given for the first time on the stage of the Royal.   In consequence of their success the opera company gave another performance on November 30.

* 'Records of a Stage Veteran.'   † *Vide* 'Our Actresses,' Vol. II, p. 306.

Jack Bannister performed on May 18, 1812, and July witnessed John Kemble in *Cato* (July 6), *Julius Cæsar* (July 13), and *Macbeth* (July 20). On August 24, Liston played Somno in *The Sleep Walker*. June 28, 1813, saw Munden as Sir Anthony Absolute in *The Rivals* and Crack in *The Turnpike Gate*. On September 6 Charles Kemble played here for the first time. He performed Hamlet to Mrs. Howard Payne's Ophelia, and was also seen later as Shylock and Macbeth. Mrs. Charles Kemble also appeared.

In the spring of 1814 the house was beautified throughout. The re-opening night was May 16, when *Pizarro* was presented, and Messrs. Vandenhoff and Bass made their first appearance upon this stage, the former playing Rolla. John M. Vandenhoff was educated at Stonyhurst College, where his bent for the stage was awakened by a performance of *Oroonoko* in the large play-room, or Truck-house, as it was styled from the ancient game of Truck being played in it. Vandenhoff was born in 1790, and died in 1861. He was of Dutch origin. One of his ancestors came over to England with William of Orange, and was by that Prince allowed to use armorial bearings, with the crest, a mailed hand and sword, and the motto ' En Avant.' On May 11, 1808, Vandenhoff made his first appearance on the stage at the Salisbury Theatre, as Osmond in *The Castle Spectre*. After an apprenticeship of seven or eight years in various provincial theatres he joined the stock company at the Royal, Liverpool, in 1814. Afterwards he was engaged to lead the business at £3 per week. This was ultimately increased to £5—an Irishman's rise, as the extra money was in reality, Mrs. Vandenhoff's salary.* In Liverpool he became the idol of all classes, and during a long acquaintance with the local public he secured their affectionate regard to such an extent that little children were taught to remember him in their prayers and say ' Pray, God, bless my father and mother, sister and brother, and—Mr. Vandenhoff ! '†

On Friday, September 15, 1815, the great Edmund Kean played here for the first time, opening in *Richard III*. During his fortnight's engagement he also played Shylock, Othello,

---

* Vandenhoff afterwards held a proprietor's share in the theatre. This was sold to the Liverpool Corporation on May 14, 1881, for £396 13s.
† George Vandenhoff's ' Leaves from an Actor's Note Book ' (1860), p. 31.

and Richard II. While the last mentioned play was being performed, on Monday, September 25, a false alarm of fire was given, and in the rush for the doors a young woman in the gallery named Mary Edge was unfortunately trampled to death. Sad to relate she had only been a few hours in the town. At the inquest it was stated that a Mr. G. . . . (the name was suppressed in the published reports), accompanied by a Mr. Harrison, came to the theatre dressed in woman's clothes. They were about to be turned out when Mr. G. . . . . called out loudly, ' O Ireland, Ireland, Ireland ! ' This, curiously enough, was taken to be a cry of fire ! Kean deposed that he had known Mr. G. . . . . since 1814 ; and that he was brother-in-law to Major-General Ross. After a verdict of ' accidental death ' had been returned, the managers of the theatre presented the relatives of the deceased with twenty pounds.

On July 12, 1816, John Kemble took his farewell of the Liverpool public in playing Coriolanus. After the fall of the curtain he came on and said good-bye in the following graceful manner :—' Ladies and gentlemen, I have to-night appeared before you for the last time, and cannot take my leave without expressing my high sense of the liberal support that I have always received from you, for which I feel the strongest sentiments of '—(here Mr. Kemble's emotion interrupted his speech, and he and the audience appeared equally affected. Mr. Kemble then proceeded). ' The play we have been acting this night brings to my mind a circumstance which I shall ever remember with pleasure, that occurred to me in an age of years since. It was on this stage that I first adapted this play of Shakespeare's for representation, and the success which it met with in the fostering smile of your approbation encouraged me to persevere in my profession and determined me to pursue an industrious and methodical study of my art. I mention this, perhaps, more on account of others than myself, to remind you that the best method of securing to yourselves a good stage is to support with your approbation and encouragement, the efforts of inexperienced talent. Ladies and gentlemen, I wish you all a very good night, and every prosperity and happiness to this town.'*

* ' Liverpool Mercury,' July 19, 1816.

K

'An Amurath, an Amurath succeeds!' No sooner had the stately John Philip Kemble said farewell when Liverpool was honoured by a return visit from Edmund Kean. Next came the beautiful Miss O'Neill, who charmed all hearts on September 9, as Belvidera in *Venice Preserved*.

Miss O'Neill was in society what she was on the stage— gentle, pleasing, and interesting. Mrs. Piozzi, Dr. Johnson's friend, said that she was 'a charming creature'; and Walter Donaldson thought her to be ' the only actress with that genuine feeling that is capable of melting her audience to tears. In her hand the handkerchief is not hoisted as the only signal of distress. Her pauses are always judicious and impressive ; her attitudes appropriate and effective, either in regard to ease or dignity. Her figure is of the finest mould, her features beautiful, yet full of expression, displaying at once purity of mind, and loveliness of countenance. Her demeanour is graceful and modest, her voice melody itself in all its tones.'*

Miss O'Neill was about twenty-five years of age when she played at the Royal in 1816. She afterwards retired from the stage, and on December 18, 1819, married William Wrixon Beecher, who on the death of his uncle succeeded to a very ancient baronetcy, his wife thus becoming Lady Beecher. It is pretty generally known that she and her father suggested the Fotheringay and Captain Costigan to Thackeray. 'Miss O'Neill's father,' says Charles Mathews, 'was the manager of a small strolling company in Ireland. He was an eccentric of the first water. If any member of his company disappointed him, O'Neill had one speech—"Confusion burst his skull, a blackguard! What will I do ? Here, give me a greatcoat, and I'll double his part with my own." The greatcoat was the universal panacea, whatever the general costume of the play might be. If the Ghost in *Hamlet* complained to Mr. O'Neill of the lack of armour in the wardrobe, the manager would shrug up his shoulders and after a pause exclaim, " Oh, bother ! sure if ye'll put on a greatcoat ye'll do very well." Matters of much greater moment he met with the same indifference. Once proceeding by a barge along a small river, the captain and O'Neill quarrelled, and in the scuffle O'Neill was knocked overboard.

* ' Fifty years of Green Room Gossip.'

He swam to shore, and called out, "Confusion burst your soul! I suppose you thought I couldn't swim." A knot of novices once joined Mr. O'Neill, and having played some time without receiving their pay, they resolved to take proceedings against him. He met the charge with a counter-claim against them for a considerable sum due to him by them for spoiling all the plays and farces they appeared in. To avoid the *exposé* they abandoned the claim.'

On May 26, 1817, Junius Brutus Booth, the tragedian, commenced an engagement of nine nights in *Richard III*. Mrs. Glover was the Lady Anne. Messrs. Harley and Liston were here in June and July.

On July 17, 1817, the Royal was leased by the trustees on behalf of the proprietors of the theatre, for a term of nine years to Messrs. Thomas Knight, Thomas Denison Lewis (son of W. T. Lewis), and John Banks. Besides providing for the use of the theatre, the scenery, and properties (all of which are specifically enumerated), and the dwelling house in Brythen Street, at a yearly rental of £1,700 (payable quarterly), the agreement stipulated that the lessees should ' not permit, nor suffer, the present prices of admission into the theatre to be increased, or reduced, without such consent as aforesaid ; nor permit, nor suffer, any spirituous liquors to be sold in any part of the said theatre ; nor suffer any performers or others to lodge, or sleep in the audience part of the said theatre ; nor suffer any fruit, or other articles of refreshment to be sold in the audience part of the theatre during the time of any performance.'

On July 30, 1817, Joe Grimaldi made his first appearance here.* He was engaged for three weeks at a salary of £12 per week, with half a clear benefit, or the whole house for £40, the latter of which he chose. 'As the night fixed upon for his benefit (which was the last of his engagement) drew nigh,' mentions 'Boz' in his 'Memoirs of Grimaldi,'† 'he began anxiously to deliberate whether he should speculate in the " whole house" or not. He had no friends or acquaintances in Liverpool to assist him, but, on the other hand, he had made a tremendous

---

* 'Boz,' in his 'Memoirs of Grimaldi,' says, that Grimaldi played one night in Liverpool in 1808. He may have done so, but not at the Royal, as his visit to the patent theatre on July 30, 1817, is stated on the bills to have been his *first appearance on this stage.*

† Vol. I, pp. 138-41.

hit ; so, not being able to decide himself, he called in the aid
of his friends, Emery, Blanchard, and Jack Johnstone, who
chanced to be there at the time, and requested their
advice how he should proceed.   With one accord they advised
him to venture upon taking the house, which he, adopting their
advice, forthwith did, paying down his £40, however, with
many doubts as to the result.   He lost no time in making
out his bill, and getting it printed.   The play was *The Rivals*,
in which he acted Acres, and the after-piece the pantomime of
Harlequin's Olio, in which his son was to appear as Flipflap,
a kind of attendant upon Harlequin, and he as a clown.   Several days elapsed, but nothing betokening a good benefit
presented itself, and Grimaldi began to suspect it would turn
out a complete failure.   On the morning of the very day he
had sold only fourteen tickets, and walked to the theatre with
rather downcast spirits.   At the box door he met Mr. Banks,
one of the managers, who addressed with him, " Well, Joe, a
precious benefit you will have ! "
    ' " So I expect, " he answered with a sigh.
    ' " Have you looked at the box-book ? " inquired the man-
ager, with a slight degree of surprise in his manner.
    ' " No," said Grimaldi ; " I really am afraid to do so."
    ' " Afraid ! " echoed the manager ; " upon my word, Mr.
Grimaldi, I don't know what you would have, or what you are
afraid of.   Every seat in the boxes is taken ; and if there had
been more, they would have been let."
    'Hastening to the box-office, Grimaldi found that this good
news was perfectly correct.   His benefit, which took place
on August 20, produced the greatest receipts ever known in
that theatre : the sum taken was £328 14s., being £1 more
than was received at Miss O'Neill's benefit (who was a wonderful favourite in the town), and beating John Emery's by £5.
He cleared upwards of £280, by following the advice of his
friends ; upon the strength of which they all dined together
next day, and made very merry.'
    Conway, the abnormally tall tragedian, made his first
appearance in Liverpool in performing Hamlet on October 6.
    Before the re-opening night on May 18, 1818, the
theatre was redecorated, and a splendid new gas chandelier
upon the most approved principles hung from the ceiling of
the auditorium.   The principal performers were Messrs.

Vandenhoff and Bass.   On June 15, Miss Waldron was seen here for the first time.   She played Ninette in *The Young Hussar*.   Seven days later Mrs. Alsop (from Drury Lane) made, as Donna Violante in *The Wonder*, her first appearance here.   Mrs. Alsop was the natural daughter of the famous Mrs. Jordan by the *in*famous Richard Daly, the libertine manager of the Dublin Theatre, who was responsible for her mother's downfall.   The daughter inherited some of her father's vices, and a few of her mother's talents.   Mrs. Alsop eventually went to America, where she committed suicide on June 2, 1821.

Mathews played on July 13, 1818, after an absence of seven years.   Grimaldi paid his second visit to the Royal on July 27.   He was again engaged for three weeks, and his profits amounted to £327.   During his visit he resided at 9, Williamson Square.   On August 19, he took a benefit when his scapegrace son also performed.

For several years both father and son played together in various pantomimes ; and it was thought that before young Joe there was a brilliant future.   This, however, was soon dissipated, as he embarked upon vicious courses, and through a blow on the head received in some brawl, became a wild and furious savage.   He was frequently attacked with dreadful fits of epilepsy, and often committed actions which nothing but lunacy could prompt.   In 1828 he had a decided attack of insanity, and was confined in a strait waistcoat in his father's house for some time.   From engagements at Drury Lane, Sadler's Wells, the Pavilion, and the Surrey Theatres in turn, he was dismissed, finally falling into the lowest state of wretchedness and poverty.   His dress had fallen to rags, his feet were thrust into two worn-out slippers, his face pale with disease, and squalid with dirt and want, and he was steeped in degradation.   His unhappy life came to a final close in a public-house in Pitt Street, off the Tottenham Court Road.

On May 31, 1819, Mrs. Alsop commenced a fortnight's engagement.   During the autumn, Edmund Kean returned for a fortnight.   He was followed by Miss O'Neill.

On February 4, 1820, Thomas Knight, one of the lessees, died suddenly at his residence, the Manor House, Woore. Knight was an admirable actor and a worthy man.   His great parts were Jacob Gawkey, Plethora, Count Cassel, and Farmer

Ashfield. There is a portrait of him in the Garrick Club, by Zoffany, as Roger in *The Ghost*. In the same collection are portraits of him by De Wilde and Wageman. Tate Wilkinson says he retired from the stage on being left a fortune by his uncle, but did not live long to enjoy his *otium cum dignitate*.

Hamlet was played by Charles Mayne Young on May 29, 1820. He had not been seen on this stage for four years, and was engaged for a fortnight. Others then here were Messrs. Dowton, Emery, and Blanchard; Mrs. Bunn, Miss M. Tree, Mrs. Glover, and Mrs. Bartley.

Mrs. Bartley was born in Liverpool on October 23, 1785. Her mother, Mrs. Williams (an Irish lady), was apparently acting here at that period. Miss Williams subsequently took the name of her step-father, Smith, by which she was known until her marriage with George Bartley in the summer of 1814. Both were then members of the company at the Royal. She was Bartley's second wife. They afterwards went to America.*

The great Macready performed here for the first time on September 11. He was engaged for a fortnight, and during his visit he appeared as Macbeth, Othello, and Richard III. Edmund Kean followed. On the last night of Kean's engagement (October 6), he played Othello. On the fall of the curtain he was loudly called for, and on making his appearance was received with universal cheering. When the enthusiasm had subsided he said: 'Ladies and gentlemen,—I do assure you, most sincerely, that I can scarcely find words in which to express myself in answer to this very flattering and unexpected mark of your approbation and attention. I beg you, however, to accept of my warmest thanks.

' Whenever I have had the honour of appearing before a Liverpool audience, I have always been most anxious to exert myself to the utmost of my humble abilities. I hope, therefore, that, if ever I have failed in my endeavours, you will attribute my deficiencies to a want of talent, and not of assiduity.

' But I should not fully do justice to my feelings, if I did not remark, most respectfully, *that in this town I have not experienced that warmth of approbation, and that alacrity of attention, with which I have been honoured in other large cities and towns of the three kingdoms.* To those, however, to whom my

---

* 'Our Actresses,' Vol. I, p. 139.

exertions have been acceptable, I am deeply grateful ; and to those, in whose opinions I have not been so successful, I wish greater gratification and instruction from other and superior actors.

'As an Englishman strongly attached to, and proud of, my country, I look forward with anxiety to that period when I shall revisit these shores ; but, as a professor, I beg leave, very respectfully, to bid you farewell.'

Upon this curious effusion the ' Liverpool Mercury '* offered the following observations :—'A considerable part of the audience warmly applauded the speech, while many persons withheld any expression upon it.   There is no doubt, that the Liverpool audience is the most sparing of that encouragement which arises from judicious but liberal applause, of any in the kingdom.   There is a coldness in our theatrical manners, which, whether proper or not, is oppressive to all performers who have experienced the warmth of more indulgent audiences.   Kemble, and many others, remarked it : nay, more recently, Mr. Macready privately complained of it depressing his spirits, making him fear that he was not at all approved.   If, therefore, Mr. Kean had alluded to it on behalf of the profession generally, it would have done great credit to his spirit and his candour ; but he certainly has offended many friends of the drama, by speaking exclusively of himself, when it is well-known that he has been, next to Miss O'Neill, more praised and applauded than any of the recent candidates for public favour.'

'For this hit,' writes Hawkins in his ' Life of Edmund Kean,' ' he (Kean) did not go unpunished. Two hours later he was celebrating his last night, previous to his departure, with some choice associates, when he intimated his intention to erect a monument to Cooke as soon as he arrived in New York. A suggestion was started that an appropriate line or two should be furnished for an epitaph ; and one of the company present, wishing to "serve him out" for his rebuke of the unimpressionable audience, immediately wrote something on a piece of paper and passed it to him with a smile. Kean read out :—

" Beneath this stone lies Cooke interred,
And with him Shakespeare's Dick the Third."

* October 13, 1820.

"*Dum lego, assentior*," was the tragedian's happy reply. On October 11, Kean was *en route* for America, per the 'Matilda,' where he arrived after a quick passage of twenty-eight days.   This was his first transatlantic trip.

On May 29, 1821, there was published, for the first time, 'The Liverpool Theatrical Investigator.'   This publication focussed a revealing search-light on things theatrical, which had apparently fallen into a parlous state in Liverpool with the death of Knight.   The third number of the publication* states that 'the Managers had not been at much trouble in beautifying, or even *cleaning*, the theatre ; and by this we are perhaps given to understand, that they are resolved to persevere in a system of the most rigid economy ; or, at least, to avoid any very profuse, or lavish expenditure. . . . .' The stage properties are described as ' the veriest apologies we ever saw . . . . the masks appeared to be pieces of perforated brown paper.   As to the Scenery, excepting an old wreck or two painted by some artists of celebrity, it is wretched in the extreme. . . . The machinery is equally bad. . . . Nor is it a little strange, that in the town of Liverpool we have not even a sufficient number of performers ; and on this account, one person is frequently made to personate two characters in the same piece.   We should not wonder at such a circumstance occurring in a barn ; but what apology can we make for such a thing being reduced to a matter of course in a Royal Theatre ? ' The ' Investigator ' also comments very severely on the management in admitting the ' frail fair ' into the theatre.   'There is,' it says, ' scarcely a part of the house where a tradesman can take his wife and family, without being in their vicinity— the pit in particular, which ought, of all other places, to be kept free from them, is the constant and favourite place of their resort.'

The issue for June 16, 1821, refers to the dresses as having been selected, ' for the most part, from the purlieus of Monmouth Street, or Rag Fair ; and after having undergone the operation of the patent renovator are brought out with a pompous announcement of " new dresses."   In the issue for June 26, we are informed that ' the orchestra consists of 5 violins ; 2 tenors ; 2 horns ; 2 oboes ; 2 violoncellos ; 1 double

* May 31, 1821.

bass : total 14. . . . . Any persons unacquainted with managerial shifts would wonder how, with this band, anything like harmony could be produced, there being in the list, neither flutes, clarionets, trumpets, or drums ; but we must inform them that as the managers make their fourth and fifth-rate actors play many parts in the same play ; so also are their musicians forced to perform on different instruments. . . . . For these laborious services, they receive only from one guinea to thirty shillings per week, with the exception of their very able leader, who receives, we believe, fifty shillings. . . . There are, however, some of the musicians in the orchestra, who would scarcely be tolerated to play jigs in a country pot-house.'

The ' Investigator ' for July 17, 1821, observes that ' the theatre pays no government taxes ; nor is it assessed at more than two-thirds of the rack-rent for the poor rates ; admitting therefore that it pays all parish taxes, the amount will scarcely reach £400 per annum.   The length of the season is generally more, but never less, than six months ; the theatre must therefore be open twenty-six weeks at least ; consequently, the rent and taxes (£2,100) which is stated at " about £100 per week " amounts to no more than £80 and a fraction per week.' . . . . There are, we believe, sixteen male performers, who are paid from twenty shillings to fifty shillings per week (fifty shillings is the very highest salary !), their salaries, therefore, taken at the utmost, cannot amount to more than £28 per week.   Ten female performers, say £15 per week.   Musicians, or rather mostly apologies for musicians, £19 10s., per week.   Twelve door-keepers, money takers, etc., whose salaries (box book-keeper into the bargain) will not average more than 16s. per week, £9 12s.   Scene shifters and scene *daubers*, £6 per week.   Lighting, £8 per week.   Printing and advertising, £8 per week. . . . . Now, allowing £25 18s. per week for the supernumeraries, and incidental expenses, the weekly expense will amount to £200, or £40 per night.

' The London performers, are generally engaged for a fortnight ; and to use a managerial expression, " share after the expenses " ; we will suppose, therefore, in order to put the matter in a clear point of view, that, at one of these benefits, there shall be £170 in the house :—60 guineas, in the first place, will be deducted for what are called the *expenses*, to which may be added a number of items, for extra *properties*, etc., which will, on an average, increase the amount to £70—there still remains £100 which is divided between the Managers and the Star, the latter paying for the extra printing, advertising, etc., out of his fifty ; while the managers pocket altogether £120.   Now, if only one benefit took place each week, and the receipts of the other four nights amounted, in the whole, to only £80 (£20 per night) it is clear the management could not lose.   But, judging from former seasons, more than one Star-Benefit occurs weekly, the stock houses have also averaged much more than £20 per night : take, then, into consideration the *native* performers' benefits for the last five weeks of the season, which average to the management more than £60 per night, and some tolerable idea may be formed of the manner in which ample fortunes have been made, with little trouble and less genius.'

In 1821 the London theatres, which used to close in June, were kept open two months longer, consequently, the Liverpool managers were deprived of the services of several metropolitan performers.   Vandenhoff was not here this year to lead the business of the stock company, and his place was taken by James Salter.   The managers also had the services of Harley, Emery, Miss Clara Fisher, Mrs. Faucit, Mrs. Davison, Mrs. Bunn, and Mrs. Glover.

On Tuesday, July 10, 1821, James Wallack* appeared as Rolla in *Pizarro*.   ' This gentleman,' says the ' Liverpool Theatrical Investigator,' ' visits us as a star, but not, we conceive, of the first magnitude : at all events, his lustre is not sufficiently refulgent to throw even provincial brightness into the shade.'   Ten days later Wallack was to have performed Lord Hastings in Rowe's tragedy of *Jane Shore*, but an apology had to be made for his non-appearance.   Shortness of notice was alleged to be the cause of his absence.   Be this as it may, Wallack when he ought to have been at the theatre was engaged with Edmund Kean in the utmost conviviality at the Star and Garter, in Paradise Street.   Commenting on this the ' Investigator ' observes : ' How far

---

* James Wallack, who was born in London in 1790, was the son of William Wallack, a comic singer and comedian. In 1817, James Wallack married the daughter of Jack Johnstone, the Irish comedian.   Lester Wallack was the son of James Wallack.   The latter's sister, Elizabeth, married a Mr. Pincott, and became the mother of Mrs. Alfred Wigan.

Mr. Wallack can reconcile such conduct with his imperious duty to the public, we know not ; but we cannot help regarding the circumstance altogether as one of the grossest insults that was ever offered to the town of Liverpool.'

On July 27, 1821, Mrs. Glover played Hamlet for her benefit, and made a very obese young prince. The following lines appeared in the ' Theatrical Investigator ' for July 24 :—

' So Friday next is Mrs. Glover's night,
The part of Hamlet, too, by Mrs. Glover—
Query.—Is this a managerial spight ?
For other motive I cannot discover ;—
Unless she means to shew that passions' rage
Cannot be well express'd, unless 'tis felt :
Giving one bright example to the stage—
" Oh ! that this too—too solid flesh would melt." '

Mrs. Glover on the occasion referred to above was supported by a fat Ghost in the person of Mr. McGibbon. The ' Investigator,' for the day following the performance, says ' that if Mr. McGibbon's Ghost was not awfully appalling, and indescribably terrific, it was at least ponderously weighty : it moved like a well-rounded mass of sluggish matter, and was altogether as remote from the purpose, and as ridiculous as the Hamlet of Mrs. Glover.'   Three days later the following verses were published in the same journal.—

' The managers, their wisdom to evince,
And show how much thereof they have to boast ;
Cast Hamlet—Mrs. Glover, as the Prince
And sixteen-stone McGibbon for the Ghost.

' When he (the Ghost), talk'd of the sulphurous flames,
To which at " morning dawn " he must retire ;
Some ladies near me—I'll not mention names—
Said—" all the fat will then be in the fire ! "

' And when he vanished, leaving Ham alone,
The silence shew'd how little we had lost ;
The laugh—that followed his latest groan—
How glad we were he had given up the ghost.'

Mrs. Glover, in the following June, played Hamlet at the Lyceum in London. Edmund Kean was in one of the stage boxes, and at the end of the first act came behind the scenes and shook her, not by one, but by both hands, exclaiming 'Excellent, excellent!' 'Away, you flatterer!' replied Mrs. Glover, 'you come in mockery to scorn and scoff at our solemnity!'

On August 13, 'Jack' Johnstone the famous Irish comedian, played Dennis Brulgruddery in *John Bull*. This was announced to be his farewell visit to Liverpool, but he had been taking similar farewells for some time. The 'Investigator' said that Mr. Johnstone had been a great actor, but 'his day is gone by, and for his own fair fame, he ought to have retired long ago.'

William Farren came on August 20, when he played Sir Peter Teazle in *The School for Scandal*. His appearance did not give the 'Investigator' an impressive idea of an elderly gentleman of the old school, or of Sheridan's Sir Peter Teazle. 'In fact, there appeared nothing of the gentleman throughout. . . . . His acting from beginning to end was rather a caricature than the genuine sterling character as drawn by the author.' Praise, however, was given to the majority of his other impersonations.

On September 3, Macready appeared as Virginius. 'Mr. Macready is, undoubtedly, a very respectable, though we cannot call him a great actor,' wrote the critic of the 'Investigator.' Four days later Macready was seen in Banim's fine tragedy of *Damon and Pythias*, then performed in Liverpool for the first time. The eminent tragedian's Damon, was described as 'a good, but not a great performance.' *The Comedy of Errors* was presented on October 16, but the performance was described as 'superlatively contemptible.' 'Yet, after all,' continued the 'Investigator,' 'there was one redeeming delight—the sweet, the melting warbling of Miss Stephens,' who played Adriana. In 1838 this charming vocalist married the fifth Earl of Essex.

The theatre re-opened on June 3, 1822, with *Coriolanus*. According to the 'Investigator,' the seats were newly covered, the house was repainted, and the *tout ensemble* was altogether different to what it was the year before. There was some new scenery, and some of the old scenery had been

repainted; while the prices of admission had been lowered to:—
boxes, 4s.; upper boxes, 3s. 6d.; pit, 2s.; and gallery, 1s.

To the great satisfaction of many patrons, Vandenhoff
was re-engaged for leading business in place of James Salter.
When Salter was engaged he was informed that Vandenhoff
would not return to the theatre.   In February, 1822, Vandenhoff received a letter from Mr. T. D. Lewis, in which he was
asked to resume his former place at the theatre.   And this he
agreed to do.   Consequently, Salter, although he had given
satisfaction, was dismissed.

On the re-opening night the theatre was in an uproar
owing to the audience being divided into two factions—the
Vandenhoff Guelphs and the Salter Ghibelines.   Placards
were exhibited by the friends of Salter inscribed 'Salter
for ever,' etc., and Vandenhoff's adherents had placards
in their hands of a similar description.   Vandenhoff was loudly
cheered on making his appearance on the stage, and Salter
showed himself to his partisans from one of the upper lower
boxes.   Much the same thing happened on the second night,
when the partisans of the two actors attended in strong force,
but the excitement slowly simmered down, and in a little while
peace and harmony were restored.

Charles Young paid a welcome return visit on July 1.
Others here during the summer were Blanchard, Harley,
Knight, W. Farren, Dowton, Miss Smithson, and Mrs. Faucit.

Miss Smithson charmed local audiences with her Mrs.
Haller and Miss Dorillon.   Here her talents procured her
many friends, notably Mr. Arthur Heywood, the banker.
She eventually went to Paris, and married Berlioz the composer.

On September 17, Mrs. Davison* took her benefit in *The
Suspicious Husband* and *The Miller and His Men*.   Elliston
was to have appeared as Ranger in the former play, but before
the curtain went up Bass came forward and announced his
non-arrival.   He offered the audience their money back, but
everybody applauded and stopped.   The part of Ranger was
read by Browne.   Subsequently the 'Liverpool Advertiser'
published a letter from Elliston to Mrs. Davison, dated
London, Saturday, September 25, 1822, saying she had full

* Mrs. Davison was formerly Miss Duncan.   See memoir of her in 'Our Actresses,'
Vol. I, p. 167.

authority to announce his appearance for her benefit, but
that he was prevented from coming by the business of Drury
Lane preparatory to his opening there.   The gross receipts
of Mrs. Davison's benefit amounted to £224 3s.   'It is a
well ascertained fact,' says the 'Liverpool Theatrical Investigator,' 'that the real nightly expenses of the Liverpool
Theatre amount to a few shillings less than three-and-twenty
pounds, yet Mrs. Davison was charged in the first instance,
fifty-five pounds to which a number of extra charges were
added.   These included :—" Ale, rosin, and toe (*sic*) 1s. 6d.,
one full set of fireworks for mill, 10s., and six men for stage,
and five men for mill and bugle horn, 12s.—total £1 3s. 6d." '
The total expenses amounted to a trifle less than £70.

Commencing October 22, that phenomenal success, *Tom
and Jerry* was played for a fortnight.   This play formed the
subject of a debate by the Liverpool Literary Society in the
Large Room of the York Hotel, Williamson Square, on November 26, Mr. S. W. Ryley being in the chair.   On December 6,
Vandenhoff was accorded a benefit.   He played Damon
in *Damon and Pythias*, and in the after-piece of *Winning a
Husband*, Miss Rock (a local favourite), portrayed seven
different characters.   The benefit brought Vandenhoff a clear
£100.

Diddear made his first appearance here on May 26, 1823,
and on June 2, the youthful Clara Fisher performed Richard
III.   A little later she played Young Norval.

On August 8, 1825, Maria Foote made her first appearance on this stage, when she played Letitia Hardy in *The
Belle's Stratagem*.   She was born in 1798, and died on December 27, 1867.   Her charms and histrionic powers were
celebrated by painters and song writers.   Theodore Hook
wrote—

> 'If all the world I were to lose,
> I'd heed it not a farden,
> If only there was left to me
> One *Foote* of Covent Garden.'

On her retirement from the stage it was pertinently asked
'Will she no more cling so tenderly about Virginus, the living
image of all that is daughterly and gentle ?   Shall we not see
her again bend silently before the accusations of Guido, like

a fair flower stooping beneath the rough blast, with which contention would be vain ?   Is comedy entirely to lose the most delicate and graceful of its hand-maidens, and tragedy the loveliest of its sufferers ? . . . . In return for those images of pure and innocent beauty with which she has enriched our imaginations, we wish her all the good which should attend one of nature's choicest favourites.'   Miss Foote retired from the stage in 1831 preparatory to her marriage with Charles, the fourth Earl of Harrington.

July 5, 1823, saw Charles Mathews for the first time in England in a burlesque on *Othello*.   Yates was the Iago. Mathews had played the Moor in this travesty in America. Others here this season were Mrs. Faucit, Dowton, Elliston, and Macready.   On October 10, Macready played Hamlet for the first time in Liverpool.

On June 21, 1824, Charles Kemble commenced a fort-night's engagement.

On August 22, 1825, Kean commenced a short engage-ment in *Richard III*.   He also played Sir Giles Overreach, Othello, and Macbeth.   Prior to his departure for America he took a farewell benefit on August 26, when he appeared as Gloster (*Richard III*), and Baron Willinghurst (*Of Age To-Morrow*).   ' On this occasion,' writes Hawkins in his ' Life of Edmund Kean,' ' he played the crook-back tyrant with unusual brilliance and earnestness ; and in the farce he seemed so full of animation that had it not been for the touching fare-well which he pronounced at the close of the performance, the audience might have gone away with a belief that he had been in excellent spirits.'   At the conclusion of the perform-ance he said :—' I should be lost to every feeling of sensibility if I did not most respectfully thank you for this expression of kindness.   At this moment when I am about to leave my country perhaps for ever—(loud cries of No ! No !)—such an exhibition of your feelings is of particular value to me. Driven as I am from England by the machinations of scoun-drels, by a combination of ruffians who seemed determined to destroy me, I receive on the eve of my departure, the highest gratification from what I now see.   No absence, no contumely, no sorrow,—none of the numerous indignities to which professional men, in all countries are obliged to submit— will ever efface from my mind the gratitude I feel to my countrymen.'* The allusions were, of course, to the persecution he had undergone after the Cox trial.

One of the rules of the theatre in 1825 was that if any person refused to act a penalty of £5 was incurred.   Another rule was that for each night's absence, from sickness or any other cause, the fine would be £5, but if a performer sent a doctor's certificate of illness, he only lost his salary during the period of such illness, but was expected to give notice when he would be able to play again.

On Monday, May 29, 1826, Messrs. Raymond and Hammond made their *début* on this stage.†   The former was from the Theatre Royal, Glasgow, and the latter from the Theatres Royal, York and Hull.   Raymond played Frank Hardy in *Paul Pry*, and Hammond Figaro in *The Barber of Seville*. These gentlemen afterwards figured prominently in Liverpool as managers.   Messrs. Macready, C. Kemble, Dowton, Liston, Harley, Paul Bedford, Mathews, Yates, and Mackay; and Miss Foote and Miss F. H. Kelly were also here during the season. During the first week in October a clever Dublin boy, Master Burke, played Doctor Pangloss in *The Heir at Law*, and Doctor O'Toole in *The Irish Tutor*.   The following month Ducrow and his celebrated stud of horses performed.

The season of 1827 was notable for visits from Edmund Kean, Charles Kemble, Maria Foote, Maria Tree and Mrs. Waylett.   A series of Italian operas was presented in November.   Charles Kean made his first appearance here on June 24, 1828, when he played Frederick in *Lover's Vows*. July saw Miss Foote, and Charles Mayne Young on these boards.   In August there were visits from John Pritt Harley, Paul Bedford, and Miss Stephens.   In September, Mackay —the celebrated Scottish comedian—appeared in his favourite character of Baillie Nichol Jarvie in *Rob Roy*.   On September 29, Madame Vestris made her *début* in Liverpool.   She was engaged for eleven nights.   A French company of comedians followed.   On December 22, a benefit performance was given for Elton.

* 'Billinge's Advertiser,' August 30, 1825.
† In 1829 Messrs. Raymond and Hammond opened the Liver Theatre, in Church Street. In 1836 they dissolved partnership, and Mr. Hammond opened the Strand Theatre, London, in conjunction with his brother-in-law, Douglas Jerrold. Three years later Hammond was tempted to take Drury Lane Theatre, but the venture proved unsuccessful.

The 'Liverpool Mercury' of June 5, 1829, says: ' A new regulation has been adopted at the box-keeper's office of our theatre of which the public cannot fail to approve. On taking places in the boxes a slip of paper is given to the party, containing the date when the places were taken, the name of the parties, the number of places, and the number of the box. This arrangement is well calculated to put an end to those clamorous altercations and appeals to the box-keeper, by which an audience is often annoyed, whilst the first act of the play is proceeding.'

In August, 1829, Edmund Kean was here. ' The house was crowded each evening of his performance ; and we believe on no former occasion did his acting ever receive more cordial marks of approbation.'* Kean was succeeded by Miss Foote, who commenced a ten nights' engagement on August 10. On September 12, Madame Malibran-Garcia made her first appearance in Liverpool. Braham followed. Macready played in October, and in the following month the Italian Opera company (which included Signor de Begnis), paid a welcome return visit. In 1829 the theatres were in a bad way all over the country, and no star made any money, except at Edinburgh, Liverpool, and Dublin.†

On June 16, 1830, Miss Huddart (afterwards Mrs. Warner), made her first appearance on the local stage. She played Belvidera to Vandenhoff's Pierre in *Venice Preserved*. The new opera of *Masaniello* was played at the Royal, for the first time in Liverpool, on July 5, 1830. The scenery was by William Beverley. The principal dancers were Madame Celine Céleste (Mrs. Elliot), and her sister Mademoiselle Constance from the Academie Royale de Musique, Paris. This was Madame Céleste's English *début*. Her first appearance on the English stage in a dramatic *rôle* was made here on July 22, when she and her sister took a benefit. On that occasion Céleste, who at that time did not speak English, appeared in the non-speaking parts of Julio, the deaf and dumb boy in *Deaf and Dumb* ; or, *The Orphan Protected*, and of Julietta, the dumb girl in *The Dumb Girl of Genoa* ; or, *The Bandit Merchant*.‡

* ' The Freeman's Journal ' (Dublin), August 13, 1829.
† ' The Freeman's Journal.'
‡ Pascoe erroneously states in his ' Dramatic List ' that Céleste first appeared on the English stage in 1830, at Liverpool, as Fenella in *Masaniello*. As a matter of fact that part was played by Miss Huddart.

L

Miss Ellen Tree and her future husband, Charles Kean, came in July, 1830.   August 2, brought Madame Vestris, and fourteen days later Fanny Kemble made her first appearance here.   She was accompanied by her father, the gifted Charles Kemble.   In October Charles Mayne Young took his farewell of the Liverpool public.   On his last night (October 29), he performed the title character in *Rienzi ; or, Rome in the Fourteenth Century.*

For the re-opening night on May 30, 1831, it was announced that ' the large centre chandelier had been removed, and an improved plan of lighting the house had been adopted, by placing twelve new superb chandeliers round the boxes.'

Miss Turpin performed during June as Virginia (*Paul and Virginia*), and Elvira (*Masaniello*).   She was the daughter of two performers favourably known at the Royal, who, on their retirement from the stage, kept a small tavern in Liverpool, near the theatre.   They gave their daughter a good musical education, and she having a natural gift for the stage joined the profession.   She was for several seasons at the Haymarket, London, and at Covent Garden, and ultimately became Mrs. Henry Wallack.*

On July 8, Mr. Keeley and Mr. Wallack played in *The Rivals.*   Madame Vestris and Charles James Mathews were also here in the same month.   Ellar and Paulo, both celebrated pantomimists, commenced a week's engagement on September 5.

Tom Ellar died April 8, 1842, aged 62.   Previous to his death he must have fallen upon evil days, as Thackeray, in 1840, wrote : ' Tom, who comes bounding home from school, has the doctor's account in his trunk, and his father goes to sleep at the pantomime to which he takes him.   *Pater infelix,* you too, have laughed at clown, and the magic wand of spangled harlequin ; what delightful enchantment did it wave round you in the golden days " when George the Third was king ? " But our clown lies in his grave ; and our harlequin Ellar, prince of many of our enchanted islands, was he not at Bow Street the other day, in his dirty, faded, tattered motley— seized as a law-breaker for acting at a penny theatre, after having well-nigh starved in the streets, where nobody would

* ' Our Actresses,' Vol. II, p. 308.

listen to his old guitar ?   No one gave a shilling to bless him :
not one of us who owe him so much ! '

Commencing January 9, 1832, Paganini gave the first of
three concerts.   Wallack was here in June for ten nights,
previous to his departure for America.   On June 18, Mr.
Chippendale played in *The Brigand*, and on July 16, Fanny
and Charles Kemble came.   On Monday, September 17, a
new farce written by Lieutenant John Shipp (Superintendent
of the Liverpool Night Police), entitled *The Birth Day ; or,
Hide and Seek*, was brought out.*   On October 1, the Italian
Opera company began its season.   *Il Don Giovanni* was
performed on the 8th, for the first time in Liverpool.

July 22, 1833, witnessed the first appearance here of Mrs.
Nisbett, ' of the laugh.'   She was engaged for a fortnight.
Mrs. Nisbett, whose maiden name was Louisa Mordaunt, was
born April 1, 1812.   She first appeared at Drury Lane as the
Widow Cheerly in *The Soldier's Daughter* on October 16, 1829.
On October 15, 1844, she married Sir William Boothby, who
died April 21, 1846.   Her first marriage had taken place
when she was only nineteen years of age ; her husband,
Captain John Alexander Nisbett, of the Life Guards, died
shortly after as the result of an accident.

On August 15, 1833, Taglioni appeared.   She was here
for six nights.   On September 23, Charles Kean came, and on
the last day of the month Sheridan Knowles commenced an
engagement.   Knowles remained a fortnight, and played
in *Virginius, As You Like It* (Rosalind, Miss Ellen Tree), and
The Wife.   October 25, Charles Kean essayed Hamlet for the
first time at this theatre.   Braham played in *The Devil's
Bridge* on December 2.   He was also seen in *Artaxerxes, Der
Freischutz, Guy Mannering, Love in a Village*, and *The Beggar's
Opera*.   A fortnight later a new play, written by a Liverpool
gentleman, entitled *Captain Ross, the Hero of the Arctic
Regions*, was produced.   This year the rental of the theatre
was reduced to £1,300, and the lessees were given another
seven years' lease.

During 1834 visits were paid by the Italian Opera company, Wallack, Macready, Charles Kean, Miss Ellen Tree,

* In 1829, Lieut. Shipp, who had had an extraordinary military career, published
his ' Memoirs ' in three volumes.

Sheridan Knowles, W. Farren, Madame Céleste* Madame Vestris, and Charles Mathews. In 1835 there came Madame Vestris, Charles Kean, Charles Kemble, Dowton, Ellen Tree, Harley, Sheridan Knowles, Mackay, Cooper, and Sinclair.

In 1836 performances were given by the Italian Opera company, Mr. and Mrs. Yates, Madame Vestris, Charles Mathews, Miss Helen Faucit, Mr. Brough, and Mr. Keeley.

Of Keeley the following anecdote is told :—' One mid-summer day Keeley was standing at the stage door of the Royal, when a heavy shower of rain fell, and forgetting their discipline, a flock of ducks disobeyed their driver and waddled into a pool of water that had been formed opposite the door. Having lost control of them the driver shouted to Keeley, ' Oi say, me little man, would ye be afther spakin' to thim ducks for me ? ' Keeley, who was a born comedian, saw the fun of the situation, and immediately replied, ' Oi will, me man.' Thereupon he knelt down in the rain, and with a droll expression of face held up his forefinger, and thus addressed the ducks in tones of rebuke—' My little fellows, you are enjoying yourselves, but why don't you do what your master tells you ? ' Two drakes looked at him with an impudent toss of the bill and a stare, and boldly cried ' Quack, quack.' Keeley retaining his mock gravity rejoined—' Yes, you may cry '' Quack, quack,'' but if you only knew what lovely weather it is for green peas you would cry ''Quack, quack,'' in another way.' †

On October 7, 1836, Charles Kean played in *Hamlet*, which was followed by the drama, *Gustavus III ; or, The Masked Ball*. According to the London custom visitors to the lower boxes were admitted on the stage in the last act to join in the masked ball, or as spectators in the galleries erected on the stage. On December 26, Edwin Forrest made his first appearance on this stage. He played in *Othello, King Lear, Damon and Pythias, and Virginius*.

On the occasion of the re-opening of the theatre on March 27, 1837, Basil Baker and Harriet Faucit were members of the company. Miss Faucit was the elder sister of Helen Faucit, who became Lady Theodore Martin. Miss Faucit

* It was about this time Céleste first commenced acting speaking parts in her quaint broken English. On October 1, 1834, she sailed from Liverpool for New York.
† ' Liverpool Mercury,' August 19, 1890.

married Mr. W. H. Bland in Liverpool, and in 1845 went with him to America, where she died two year later.

J. B. Buckstone and Mrs. Fitzwilliam made their first appearance here on May 29. Others here during the season were Mathews and Vestris, Sheridan Knowles, and the two Bedfords, Henry and Paul.

April 16, 1838, witnessed the first performance in Liverpool of the *Lady of Lyons*. Helen Faucit played Pauline. On November 19 Henry Betty, son of the ' Young Roscius,' performed.

Van Amburgh and his performing animals were here on April 29, 1839. On May 14, Thomas Horsfield was fined £3 and costs, or in default, to undergo six weeks' imprisonment, for throwing a stone ginger beer bottle from the gallery on to the head of a gentleman named Closs, who was seated in the pit. Vestris and Mathews visited the theatre in June. July 17 saw Taglioni. She was engaged for three nights. On August 5, James R. Anderson, the tragedian, made in *Romeo and Juliet* his first appearance on these boards. On November 11, George Vandenhoff (son of John Vandenhoff) made his *début* on this stage. He played Leon in Beaumont and Fletcher's *Rule a Wife and Have a Wife*, the part in which he made his first appearance in London.

Vandenhoff *fils* was brought up to the law, and prior to taking to the stage in 1839, had been the solicitor to the Trustees of the Mersey Docks. He tells us in his interesting volume* that he played for five nights during his first engagement at the Royal, and received £211.

An amusing incident happened to him when here. He was blessed with a luxuriant crop of light, curly, hair, but in his æsthetic determination to have his stage wigs set as closely and naturally as possible, he sacrificed his locks to the razor, and wore during the day a *toupée*. In Julian St. Pierre he wore a wig which fitted his shaven crown like wax. To aid the effect of St. Pierre's entrance and discovery in the fifth act, he enveloped himself in an ample disguise-cloak, and covered his head with a large black sombrero. The hat was quite new, and was very stiff and tight to the head. When he confronted the Duke, and threw off his cloak and hat in order

---

* ' Leaves from an Actor's Note Book' (1860), p. 37.

to reveal himself, the hat brought off the wig with it, and there he stood with a crown as bald as a billiard ball. The house remained silent, in fact, not a soul laughed, or testified in any way to the ludicrousness of the mischance.

A correspondent wrote to the ' Liverpool Mercury ' of December 6, and suggested that it would be very convenient if the manager of the theatre would furnish rails or backs to the seats in the pit.

George Vandenhoff played Hamlet on February 27, 1840. *Love* was performed on March 23, with Ellen Tree as the Countess Epperstein. This play had been played the month previous (February 28) ' by royal command ' at Covent Garden. Mr. T. D. Lewis severed his connection as lessee of the theatre on November 13. On the same evening Ellen Tree appeared as Pauline in *The Lady of Lyons* for the first time in any theatre. Charles Kean portrayed Claude Melnotte.

The Royal re-opened on February 15, 1841, under the direction of Mr. Robert Clarke, who had previously been acting manager of the theatre. George Vandenhoff commenced an engagement on the first of March. Vandenhoff received £15 per week and a clear half-benefit, which brought in £90. On March 19, Elton played Hamlet. Elton (whose real name was Elt), was lost in the ' Pegasus ' on the passage from Leith to Hull, July 18, 1843. He was an intelligent and thoroughly conscientious actor.

In June and July, 1841, George Vandenhoff appeared with his father and sister in *Romeo and Juliet,* ' *As You Like It, Ion, The Wife, Love, The Hunchback,* and *The Bridals of Messina.* Their joint engagement created considerable interest, and drew good houses. ' My father,' writes George Vandenhoff, ' I was sorry to see, was very ill at ease in playing with me, and I felt no less *gene* with him. He could not get over his feeling of disappointment at my having adopted the stage as a profession : this affected his acting, and I saw that it did : it was continually betraying itself, and destroying his abstraction, and his self-identification with his character, for the night. My sister was aware of this too ; and, of course, she was unpleasantly acted on by her consciousness of it. In fact, it threw us all off our balance ; and we were very uncomfortable all round. The audience, of course, knew nothing of these " secret stings" : to them, the affair was a delight, and to us, in their eyes, a triumph. They applauded, and called us, night after night, regarding us as the happiest, most united, mutually-contented family party ever seen upon any stage.'*

July 12, 1841, saw Mrs. Nisbett and her beautiful sister Jane Mordaunt here. Seven days later, a series of German operas were given. Madame Vestris, Charles Mathews, and Frank Mathews were also here in July. Then came the Italian Opera Company, Ellen Tree, J. R. Anderson, and Mr. and Mrs. Keeley.

On January 12, 1842, the theatre, scenery, and properties, and the dwelling-house adjoining were leased to Messrs. J. H. Anderson and W. J. Hammond, for a term of six years at a yearly rental of £1,500, payable half-yearly. Messrs. Anderson and Hammond opened the theatre on January 31, when G. V. Brooke played Hamlet to Julia Bennett's Ophelia. Brooke was at that time leading actor at the Royal. He was then in full possession of his noble voice, and other great natural gifts. Julia Bennett was in the fresh bloom of youthful beauty, almost girlish in appearance, and the *beau idéal* of feminine softness and delicacy.

On March 28, 1842, *A Midsummer Night's Dream* was performed for the first time in Liverpool.

In 1842-3, the great fight between the respective managements of the Theatre Royal and the Liver Theatre took place. The Royal, be it noted, was the only theatre sanctioned by law, and duly licensed by a special Act of Parliament for the representation of dramatic performances in Liverpool. All other establishments were only open on sufferance. The Liver, in 1842, was under the sole management of Mr. Richard Malone Raymond, who in conjunction with Mr. W. J. Hammond had had the theatre for several years. In 1836 Messrs. Raymond and Hammond dissolved partnership, and while the former still retained the Liver, Mr. Hammond joined forces with Mr. J. H. Anderson.

The Act of Parliament referred to above specifically stated ' that stage representations shall not be suffered to take place within eight miles of any patent or licensed theatre.' Therefore, in having permitted dramatic representations to take place in his theatre Mr. Raymond had clearly violated

* ' Leaves from an Actor's Note Book,' p. 119.

the rights and privileges of the patent theatre, and these as we have seen, had only been obtained by the expenditure of considerable time and money. According to Messrs. Hammond and Anderson, Raymond introduced ' established pieces with new names, and at length barefacedly represented the legiti- mate drama, acted too, by the manager of, and actors from, a Royal Patent Theatre of London, evidently for the purpose of braving the feelings of those whose existence depends upon the success of the same speculation in which they have en- tered, and setting at defiance the enactments which from time to time have been made for the protection of Patent or Licensed Theatres.' The penalty for producing, or acting in, the legi- timate drama in unlicensed theatres was £50 nightly.

Subsequently, sworn information was laid against Mr. Raymond and he was heavily fined. This case, was primarily, the cause of the passing of ' The Act for Regulating Theatres ' (1843), whereby the patent theatres lost all their ancient pri- vileges, save that of being exempt from a yearly renewal of license to act; and the legitimate drama could be performed in any licensed theatre.*

In the latter part of 1842 the theatre was under the sole management of Mr. W. J. Hammond. Vandenhoff *fils* tells us that ' in his (Hammond's) hands the Royal lost its high prestige as the school in which artists were formed for the London arena, to which, "in its high and palmy days," it was the stepping stone. But its glories were passed, it had fallen from its high estate. From being next in rank to the metropolis, and where, as " I have heard my father tell," John Kemble was wont to say, a tragedy was as well done as in London, it had, in 1842, sunk to the level of a mere country theatre. And this fact of the decay of the Liverpool Theatre Royal was most significant of the general decline of the drama in England, which has been going on with a *facilis descensus Averni* ever since.'†

The eventful year of 1842 came to a close with a visit from Mr. and Mrs. Charles Kean (*née* Ellen Tree).‡ The two had

---

* See also my account of the Liver Theatre.
† ' Leaves from an Actor's Note Book,' p. 120.
‡ When at the Royal, Manchester, in 1842, Kean was paid by Anderson and Hammond £20 per night, and given a ' put up ' benefit, while Miss Tree received £10 per night, and a clear half benefit. The terms given to them in Liverpool were probably the same. The foregoing particulars are culled from a cash account of the Theatre Royal, Man- chester, during the season 1841-2.

only just been married. Kean had previously been a suitor
for the hand of Miss Coutts, afterwards the Baroness Burdett-
Coutts.   In Dublin one day, where he and Ellen Tree were
acting, he suddenly entered her rooms and abruptly exclaimed, ' Elled (he never could pronounce the ' n '), if you
care to marry me, it must be to-morrow, or never.'   It is said
that he was smarting under the flat rejection he had just received
from Miss Coutts.   Miss Tree, however, had long been in
love with him, and they were married privately on January
29, 1842.   By a curious coincidence they appeared together
the same evening in *The Honeymoon.*

On January 20, 1843, William Hoskins, from the Park
Theatre, New York, made his first appearance here in
playing Othello.   Hoskins afterwards went to Sadler's Wells
under Phelps.   In the ' Life of Samuel Phelps,' he is
spoken of, I think erroneously, as a light comedian.   In 1855 at
the Wells he played Buckingham in *King Henry VIII*, and Rob
Roy, in neither case a *rôle* that would fall to a light comedian's
share.   It was Hoskins who first instructed the late Sir Henry
Irving in the art of the stage.   These lessons were given at
eight o'clock in the morning, so as not to interfere with Irving's
duties in the counting-house of the Messrs. Thacker, India Merchants, of Newgate Street.   Hoskins was attracted by the young
fellow's enthusiasm and conscientious spirit, and introduced
him to Phelps, who in his blunt, good-natured way advised
the stripling to have nothing to do with the stage, as it was a
very bad profession.   Irving at that time was about seventeen years of age.   In the latter part of 1855, Hoskins emigrated
to Australia, and endeavoured to persuade his beloved pupil
to accompany him.   It was a toss-up, but *la mère* Irving
objected—happily for the future of the English stage.

On Monday, July 24, 1843, the Theatre Royal was opened
by a committee of gentlemen for the benefit of W. J. Hammond.   Subsequently the theatre remained closed until Tuesday, December 26, when it was opened by Benjamin Webster
and Madame Céleste.   The initial attractions were *St. Mary's
Eve, The Happy Man,* and *The World of Dreams; or, The Man
in the Moon.*

' The theatre,' says the local correspondent of ' Oxberry's
Weekly Budget,'* ' has been entirely repainted and renovated

* December 25, 1843.

throughout, under the superintendence of Mr. G. Morris and
Mr. Ireland, of the Theatre Royal, Haymarket.   The medallion
paintings, descriptive of the history of a ship, from the pencil
of Mr. G. Morris.   For the comfort of visitors, the seats
of the boxes re-stuffed, and pit, have been covered in damask.
We regret, however, to add that the spirited lessees have thought
proper to reduce the prices, which are now as follows :—Dress
Boxes, 3s. ; Upper Boxes, 2s. ; Pit, 1s. ; Gallery, 6d. ; all the
evening.   This is another knell to the drama, and we fear
a decidedly impolitic step on the part of Webster and his fair
partner.   Hitherto the Theatre Royal, Liverpool, has had
the unpopular distinction of being more opposed to the ex-
tension of the drama, than any house in England, through its
determined hostility to minor theatres, and it would now seem
as if that spirit of opposition, instead of emulation, was meant
to be carried on, even after the legalization of the minors, by
the recent statute.   The successful proprietor of the Theatre
Royal, Haymarket, had a right to rely upon the influence of
his name and well-known excellent system of management,
without having recourse to prices lower than many of our
London minors, and which must operate unfavourably upon
the interests of other houses.   We think the step decidedly
calculated to produce unpopularity, and venture to predict
that in a very little time the old prices will be restored.' This
prophecy proved to be sound.

On January 8, 1844, J. B. Buckstone and Mrs. Fitzwilliam
performed in a new drama, entitled *Josephine ; or, The Fortune
of War*.   Afterwards T. P. Cooke played his famous part of
William in *Black-Eyed Susan*.   July 25, saw the first local
performance of *The Bohemian Girl*.   Mr. and Mrs. Charles
Kean were here in November.

On May 13, 1844, the following singular announcement
appeared in the playbills—' Madame Céleste and Mr. Webster deem it due to themselves to state to the Liverpool Public
that the gross misrepresentations of a silly-bilious critic, in a
certain weekly (query weakly) newspaper, induced them to
cut the Editor and friend off the Free List—and to withdraw
the advertisements, hence the violence of the remarks, which
will give a tolerable notion of the independence of its opinions
in this as in other matters.   The only papers that have the
entrée and the advertisements, and the respectability and

circulation of which are undoubted, are the " Mail," " Chronicle," " Mercury," " Albion," " Standard," " Advertiser," " Times," and " Courier." '

' A great sensation,' says the local correspondent of ' Oxberry's Weekly Budget,'* ' has been made by Professor Risley and his son, who made their appearance on Monday week with the Vandenhoffs.' The Risleys were clever acrobats. Madame Vestris and Charles Mathews were here in March.

This year the townsfolk and the authorities of the Theatre Royal got at loggerheads over the quality of the entertainments submitted. It was complained that the fare presented was mostly of the blue-and-red-fire school. Another grievance—tell it not in Gath !—was the ugliness of the actresses. The fact of the matter was that Benjamin Webster had disappointed the Liverpool public. He opened with a company seldom equalled in the provinces, and held out a hope that the Williamson Square Theatre would become a second Haymarket. Gradually he drew off the cream of his forces to London, and endeavoured to foist upon his patrons a number of inferior performers. This affront was resented by our townspeople, and the consequence was ' empty benches.' Mr. Webster's two theatres demanded his constant care and personal attendance, but the polka epidemic (inaugurated by Jullien) having broken out, he was tempted to neglect his duties, and went dancing about the country with Madame Céleste.

The late James Carr of Norton Street in this city used to recount that during the Webster-Céleste *régime,* a pantomime was produced, but the first night audience, would not have the clown ' at any price.' A substitute had to be found, and Webster bethought him of Holloway's Sans Pareil Theatre in Great Charlotte Street. Going there he asked the proprietor for the loan of a clown. Old Holloway, flattered by the lessee of the Royal coming to his wooden building, granted the request forthwith. ' But,' said Webster, ' what will you do for a clown ? ' ' Oh ! ' replied Holloway, ' all my company can work in that line.' John Wood was the clown who went from the Sans Pareil to the Royal. He was a success, and

* February 12, 1844.

when he received his first week's salary he was astonished at the margin between it and the Holloway remuneration.

Towards the end of 1845 the theatre came under the direction of Mr. Mercer H. Simpson, whose son was for long lessee of the Theatre Royal, Birmingham. Vestris and Mathews were here in February, 1846. April 13 brought Creswick and Helen Faucit as Romeo and Juliet. On the same evening Henry Farren (son of the second William Farren), made his first appearance in Liverpool as Nicholas Flam in the piece of that name. Clever Emmeline Montague was a member of the company this season. Here she made the acquaintance of her future husband, Henry Compton, a very popular comedian. Edward Compton the well-known actor is their son.

During the Simpson *régime* James R. Anderson, the tragedian, came on a visit. In ' An Actor's Life,'* he tells us that he ' made arrangements with Mr. Simpson to play four weeks at the Theatre Royal, Liverpool, he having agreed to produce *Alexander the Great*, with new scenery, dresses, and decorations. I now added *The Robbers* to my repertory, and sent Mr. Simpson the MS. and parts, together with sketches of scenes and costume. Monday, February 16, opened at Liverpool in *Hamlet*, it being found impossible to bring out *Alexander* for another week. This was a great drawback to the receipts, as the play had been announced during the past month, and the old ones were worn threadbare. I ran through the week with *Hamlet*, *Lady of Lyons*, *The Stranger*, and *Othello*, to poor houses. And no wonder, for the company of actors was wretched, myself included.

' Monday, February 23, *Alexander the Great* brought a crowded house, and went off with great enthusiasm. Mr. Simpson put the tragedy before the public with great splendour. The adjuncts were admirable. Beautiful and elaborate scenery was painted by Mr. William Gordon. A magnificent triumphal car, drawn by twelve Amazonian warriors clad in glittering armour, made an imposing entrance for the hero, shining in a suit of burnished gold, helmet, cuirass, and greaves, furnished by that great artificer, M. Granger, of Paris. The applause was loud and long ; but I nearly came

* Pp. 138-9.

to grief in the moment of my triumph.   I had arranged to descend from the car without turning my back on the audience, and selected four strong soldiers to form a platform with their Greek shields to bear me down to the footlights : the moment they felt my weight, one staggered, another collapsed, and as I imagined they were all going to drop, I leaped to the ground, " accoutred as I was," when down they went like ninepins in a skittle alley, amidst shouts of laughter.   When the fun was over, and the warriors had picked themselves up and joined the ranks, the public gave me two rounds of applause.   Friday, March 13, was a good Friday for me—a red-letter day.   The result of my fraternisation and labouring with *The Robbers* was this night crowned with success.   After many rehearsals much toil and anxiety, the play was produced for my benefit, and met with a glorious reception.   Nothing could have been more satisfactory, for it was acted to a crowded house with general approbation, and as Charles de Moor, I added another string to my bow.'   *The Robbers* was Anderson's own version of Schiller's play.

James Rodgers, who afterwards managed the Liver Theatre in Church Street, once stated to an interviewer,* that the company engaged by Mr. Simpson at the Liverpool Royal was one such as would be hard to get together nowadays, and included more than one young actor who has since made his mark.   Tom Swinburne was there, and Tom Mead (subsequently of Irving's company) was just commencing his long and successful career.   Creswick and John Coleman, and Nye Chart, were also of the company, and during the season I played also with such distinguished actors as Vandenhoff and his daughter, Miss Vandenhoff, a great actress, and Miss Fanny Kemble, who played Julia in *The Hunchback* as I have never since seen it played.   At the termination of the season the theatre closed, and the great company disbanded.   Some of them asked me to take a theatre, so as to keep part of the company together, and I consented.   I was barely 23 years old then, but I commenced my managerial career by engaging the theatre at Newcastle-under-Lyme.   During part of the season G. V. Brooke came to star with me, as did Miss Cushman, and I was successful.

* ' The Birmingham Daily Mail,' January 26, 1886.

' When the lease of the Liver, Liverpool, expired I arranged with Mr. Simpson to open the old Theatre Royal there with him for a fortnight.   Mr. Simpson's object was to introduce Buckstone and Mrs. Fitzwilliam in the new farce *Box and Cox** which had just made a great sensation in London, and in which Buckstone had been specially commanded to perform at Windsor.   The two had previously been playing with Charles Mathews at the Lyceum.   *Box and Cox* was a very great success in Liverpool, and this circumstance is interesting for the reason that its success caused the very first introduction of the travelling company system which has since revolutionized the English theatre.   I took the company *en bloc* to the old Queen's Theatre, Manchester, and we played there with the greatest success, and then we began an extensive tour with *Box and Cox* and *The Green Bushes*.   This, as far as I know, was the very first occasion in England of a complete company travelling from town to town with the same piece.'

Later on Rodgers managed theatres in the Isle of Man, at Hanley, Coventry, Worcester, Shrewsbury, and in several Lancashire towns.   In 1866 he bought the Prince of Wales in Birmingham and remained there until his death.   He was a sound comedian.   His *début* on the stage was made *circa* 1843.

Apropos of Rodgers's reference to Fanny Kemble's performance of Julia in *The Hunchback* on March 4, 1847, this was the occasion of her first appearance on the Liverpool stage since her marriage to Pierce Butler, a southern planter, in 1834.   John Coleman, as Rodgers states, was at that time a member of the company at the Royal, where he had the honour to form Fanny Kemble's acquaintance.

'' At that period,' says Coleman,† ' the showman's art had not invaded the profession of a gentleman ; advance agents, press wire-pullers, and so-called acting managers were not in existence.   Hence it came to pass that Miss Kemble walked upon the Liverpool stage (where we awaited her arrival with anxiety and curiosity) alone and unattended. We had expected to see a Tragedy Queen.   We saw instead a quiet, unassuming lady of middle age and middle height, simply attired in a black silk dress.   Her pale, classic features

* First produced at the Lyceum, London, November 1, 1847.
† ' The Theatre ' Magazine, March, 1893.

were irradiated by a pair of dark, lustrous eyes, which wore
an eerie expression—imperious one moment, pleading the
next—and which showed forth in vivid contrast to the glory
of her abundant hair, even then slightly streaked with grey
at the temples.   As we simultaneously bared our heads to the
last of the Kembles, she responded to the recognition in one
comprehensive and gracious courtesy, then, introducing herself *sans ceremonie* to the stage manager, commenced the
rehearsal.

' On the occasion of Miss Kemble's reappearance at Liverpool she was assisted by Creswick, then in his zenith, as Master
Walter, Robert Roxby as Modus, Nye Chart as Fathom, and
a stripling then in his teens, who shall be nameless here, was
her lover, Sir Thomas Clifford, while Miss Kathleen Fitzwilliam
was the Helen.   The play being at that period a "stock" one,
only one rehearsal was required.   We were all so perfect in
the text and "business" that the "star" scarcely called anyone
back.   She gave no indications of tragic fire in the morning,
but old Salter, who had often seen her act at Covent Garden,
muttered, "Wait till you see her at night!"   When Master
Walter spoke the tag—

"Thou know'st thy peace by finding out its bane,
And ne'er will act from reckless impulse more,"

she said, "A vastly pretty excuse for trying to break this poor
woman's heart!" then with another sweeping curtsey and a
silvery laugh she bade us "Good morning!"'

During her visit Fanny Kemble appeared as Mariana
(*The Wife*), Juliana (*The Honeymoon*), Lady Macbeth, Mrs.
Beverley, Mrs. Haller, and Queen Katharine.

On March 5 she played Lady Teazle.   During the performance a somewhat amusing incident occurred.   ' Lady
Teazle,' says Coleman, ' was at the wing on the O.P. side
waiting for her cue to go on in the third act.   It will be remembered that in this situation her ladyship usually makes
her entrance humming an air of the period.   I had contrived
to engross her attention by asking her to explain whether Sir
Thomas Clifford was really ruined when he presents himself
as Lord Rochdale's secretary, or whether he was merely "making believe."   She replied that "Even then she did not know.

She had asked the author the question, but that he himself
was not quite sure, that at her father's request Knowles had
interpolated a line in the last scene to the effect "There has
been masquing here," and that consequently she was under the
impression that—.   At this moment the call boy sang out,
"Stage waiting, ma'am." With a laugh she caught up her train
and swept on the stage singing—

> " Oh ! Hi ! Ho ! the boatmen row—
> Going down the Ohio ! "

This happened to be the most popular negro melody of the
day, and despite its absurd incongruity it made the hit of the
evening.   Roar followed roar till I thought the house would
have come down about our ears.'

On May 3, 1847, the theatre opened under the management of Mr. Henry Coleman, with Robert Roxby as the stage
manager.   The leading man of the stock company was T. B.
Sullivan, who, subsequently, reached the highest eminence
as Barry Sullivan.   His salary in 1847 was £5 per week.
The other members of the stock company at that period were
Messrs. Artaud, Mortimer, Fitzroy, Willis, Suter, J. W. Benson, James Lunt, W. S. Branson, Mrs. Seyton, Miss Treble,
Miss Murray, and Miss K. Love.

Barry Sullivan made his first appearance at the Royal
on May 3, 1847, as Sir Edward Mortimer in *The Iron Chest*—
a part he had never studied, and moreover, greatly disliked.
But he did his best with the character, and, as he afterwards
remarked, ' if he had selected the part himself he could not
have made a bigger success.'   The ' Mercury,' of the following day said : ' The acting of Mr. Sullivan as Sir Edward
Mortimer, and of Mr. Fitzroy as Adam Winterton, was
deservedly appreciated.'

Of Sullivan's performance John Coleman, who had
joined Copeland's company at the Amphitheatre, writes :
' While I was occupied with rehearsal he (Sullivan) came to
renew our acquaintance, and to borrow an indispensable
" property," or, to be precise, to borrow a pair of black silk
tights for Sir Edward Mortimer in *The Iron Chest*, in which
gloomy play he was about to open.   By-the-way, those same
tights that very season did duty to introduce Robert Brough

to the stage as Lampedo in *The Honeymoon*, after which in-auspicious event—for poor Bob did not set the Mersey on fire—they went the way of all—tights.   They passed from my gaze and I saw them no more.

' The gallery was a shilling in those days, and thither I went with a friend to give the new tragedian "a hand." Sir Edward Mortimer was no more suited to Sullivan than it was to John Kemble.   Latterly, it has been the fashion to decry Barry Sullivan as being stilted, formal, and old-fashioned, but, as I have shown already, in Glasgow he had been pro-nounced a walking gentleman actor of tragedy, and unques-tionably his style was too modern and too natural for this mouthing, supersensitive, hypochondriac.   Of late years I have seen little of Sullivan's acting, but when I knew him at his best, he was vigorous, vivacious, and versatile.   His Charles Surface, Young Rapid, Petruchio, Benedick, and Falconbridge were hard to beat ; and his Long Tom Coffin, William in *Black-Eyed Susan*, Rory O'More, Myles-na-Coppa-leen, and Shaun-the-Post were performances of unapproach-able excellence. '

' The second performance in Liverpool was Jaffier in *Venice Preserved* (May 4).   There was a miserable house, and the good old tragedian who played Pierre was wretchedly imperfect, while the beautiful, but unfortunate woman who played Belvidera was worse ; but Sullivan was a tower of strength in his knowledge of the text, and pulled the play through to a successful termination.   From that moment I felt convinced he only needed time and opportunity to make his way—the world itself comes round to him who knows how to wait, and at length it came round to him.'*

My friend, Mr. W. J. Lawrence, in his interesting biogra-phical sketch of Barry Sullivan, says : ' When the manage-ment of the Theatre Royal passed into the hands of Mr. W. R. Copeland, who also presided over the fortunes of the Amphi-theatre, Sullivan transferred his services to that sterling man-ager.   Acting principally at the Amphitheatre his reputation and popularity in Liverpool grew apace ; so much so that Cope-land before his death made him promise that whenever he revisited his old friends he would never play at any other house

* ' The Theatre,' June, 1891.

M

so long as it remained in the hands of his family. The tragedian religiously kept his word, making his last appearance at the Amphitheatre, prior to its reconstruction, on November 15, 1880, when he sustained the character of Hamlet to Miss Maud Brennan's Ophelia.   To his credit be it said, he never forgot the kindness of those early Liverpool friends, who, by dint of liberal encouragement, helped him on the way to fame and fortune.'

A story of Barry Sullivan and Henry Irving appeared in the ' Pall Mall Gazette ' the day following the former's death, which took place at Brighton on May 3, 1891.   Irving is reported to have told Sullivan that once when the latter was playing in Liverpool, Irving made his *début* at the same theatre and carried a banner !   Irving in a letter* to Mr. Lawrence, characterised the story as ' a silly one.'   The only occasion upon which they acted together was at Edinburgh in 1857, when Irving played Gaston to Sullivan's Richelieu.

On July 28, a benefit performance was given in aid of Leigh Hunt.   The following excerpt from a criticism of the performances is taken from the ' Mercury,' of the Friday following :—' We now come to the principal " lions " of the evening, Charles Dickens and Douglas Jerrold, the former personating the redoubtable Captain Bobadil and the latter Master Stephen, a country gull.   Never was greater enthusiasm evinced by any audience within the walls of this theatre than that which attended the clever acting of these distinguished men.   Rounds of applause greeted them every time they came on the stage, and they seemed deeply sensible of the good feeling manifested towards them.   Bobadil, the valorous, boasting soldier—yet, when put to the test, the basest of all imaginable cowards, was well personated by " Boz " ; he looked the character to perfection, and went through the many parts assigned to him with an ease that would lead one to believe him an "old stager."   Nor was Jerrold, as Master Stephen, in any way behind Bobadil. The wit and sarcasm of his various writings seemed as if it were concerted in the little foppish, self-satisfied country simpleton. . . . . This visit of Charles Dickens and the other distinguished amateurs is in every way memorable.

* Dated May 22, 1891.

All, together with Mrs. Dickens and the other ladies of the party, were entertained by Mr. Richard V. Yates, who gave a brilliant *soirée* on the occasion, to a large and fashionable assemblage at his residence in the Dingle.' The performance realised £480.

On August 16 the divine Rachel made her first appearance in Liverpool and remained for three nights. She played Camille in the tragedy *Les Horaces.* On September 6, Jenny Lind made her first appearance here, and was heard to advantage as Amina in *La Sonnambula.* She created quite a *furore*, and a hundred and one articles were named after her, down to voice lozenges.

Charming Anna Thillon was seen at the Royal for three nights, commencing March 14, 1848. Sims Reeves was here on June 26, it being the occasion of the first concert given by the Roscoe Club. On December 22, a benefit performance was given in aid of the widow and family of W. J. Hammond. On February 19, 1849, Mr. Fred Lloyds, who for upwards of 30 years had been prompter and stage director, took a farewell benefit.

On September 7, 1849, Mr. Thomas Denison Lewis, formerly lessee of the Royal, died in Paris. He was the last surviving son of William Thomas and Henrietta A. Lewis. He was buried in the family vault in Christ Church, Hunter Street, Liverpool, where there is a marble tablet to his memory, recording that he was ' devotedly affectionate in the relations of son and brother, constant and true in his friendships, munificent, yet discriminating, in his charities, respected by a large circle of acquaintances, and esteemed by all who knew him. This marble was erected by a beloved sister, who " sorrows not without hope." '

Thomas Denison Lewis was well known in Liverpool, where his stiff gait, prim walk, and elegance of attire, which was always in the pink of perfection, earned for him the sobriquet of ' Dandy Lewis.' His gait and mannerisms, were not, however, the result of pride, or of any desire to be *outré*, but of sad necessity. He suffered from a spinal complaint, which required him to wear a tight band round his chest and loins to keep him erect, and at no time could he turn his head without turning the whole of his body. ' But the Liverpudlians '

says W. G. Herdman,* ' either did not know this, or paid no
attention to it.   He was ridiculed in caricatures, lampooned
on the stage, particularly at the Liver Theatre, and otherwise
sneered at by ignorant, uneducated people, who did not know
that within this walking automaton existed a man of most
amiable disposition, beloved by all who had to do business
with him ; of generous nature and kind manners, he was liberal
to all whom he employed, and preserved sufficient pride to
take no notice of a public who did not understand or appreciate
him.'

' Dandy ' Lewis, his two sisters, and their friend Tom
Tarleton were inseparable.   ' To see,' continues Herdman,
' their carriage and pair turn out of Birchfield (Islington), with
the Misses Lewis at one side with their white lap-dogs dressed
in blue and scarlet ribbons, and Tom Tarleton on the opposite
side, was a pretty sight.   To the best of our recollection
Mr. Lewis never rode, perhaps his complaint prevented him ;
we always saw him walk.   He lived at one time at the house
by the theatre.   Then in a large house in Soho Street, subsequently at Chadwick Mount, Kirkdale.'   Mr. Lewis bequeathed £10,000 to the charities of the town.

In 1850 the management was assumed by Mr. W. R.
Copeland, who is still well remembered by many of the older
playgoing brotherhood.   He was manager of the Amphitheatre when he entered upon control of the Royal, and the
proprietors of the latter, thinking that he might set one house
against the other, bound him down by agreement to keep the
Royal open six months out of the twelve.†

On Tuesday, February 19, 1850, Macready took his fare-
well of the Liverpool public.   He performed Wolsey (*Henry
VIII*), and Lord Townly (*The Provoked Husband*).   The
Pyne and Harrison Opera Company were here during June,
and Professor J. H. Anderson, ' the wizard of the North,' in
November.   The pantomime at Christmas was of local inter-
est.   It was entitled *Harlequin and the Child of Hale ; or, The
King of the Red Noses and the Liver Queen*.   The celebrated
Harry Boleno was clown.

---

* ' Pictorial Relics of Ancient Liverpool,' Vol. II, p. 11.
† In 1851 Mr. W. R. Copeland, the manager of the theatre, opened the Strand Theatre,
London.   He called the theatre ' Punch's Play-house,' but a couple of seasons were
sufficient for him.

Apropos of the visit of the Pyne and Harrison Company, an amusing anecdote is told of a ' super ' at the Royal named Paddy Quinn. *Maritana* was being played, and Paddy impersonated one of the soldiers of the guard that cluster round Don Cæsar de Bazan in the second act of the opera. When the soldiers turned to go off, Paddy loitered in the rear, and Eugene Corri, the stage manager, lowered the curtain and closed him out, greatly to the delight of the audience, and the discomfiture of poor Paddy. In a terrible rage he rushed off, and told Louisa Pyne, William Harrison, and others that for the insult offered him they would be all thrown out next morning into the street without their salaries!

During the Tuesdays and Thursdays of January and February, 1851, the performances commenced with the pantomime, *Harlequin and the Child of Hale.* This was in order to give those living on the Cheshire side of the river an opportunity of witnessing it, as the boats ceased running between 10 and 11 o'clock. The plays which followed included *Jane Shore* and *The Gamester*, in which Barry Sullivan performed. G. V. Brooke, and Helen Faucit were also here during that year.

On June 7, 1852, Miss Vandenhoff's new play, *Woman's Heart*, was produced. In this, Mr. and Miss Vandenhoff performed, as did also Barry Sullivan. The 1852-3 pantomime was founded on one of Roby's ' Traditions of Lancashire,' and was entitled, *Three Legs, King of Man ; or, Harlequin Lord Stanlie and the Eagle and Child.*

The bright particular stars during 1853 were Charles Mathews, Mrs. Fitzwilliam,* Buckstone, Henry Compton, Mrs. Stirling, William Farren, Robson, G. V. Brooke, Helen Faucit, Charlotte Cushman, and Barry Sullivan. The pantomime produced at Christmas was founded on one of Mr. Roscoe's poems. It was styled, *The Butterfly's Ball and the Grasshopper's Feast ; or, Harlequin and the Genius of Spring.*

On November 9, 1854, Mr. and Miss Vandenhoff appeared in the lyrical tragedy *Antigone.* Other performers at that period were Mathews, Mrs. Keeley, Miss Woolgar, and Charlotte Cushman. May 28 and 29, 1855, saw Madame Alboni in *La Sonnambula* and *La Cenerentola.* Céleste and Webster appeared on August 27. They were followed by the

* Mr. W. R. Copeland's sister.

annual visit of the Italian Opera Company, with Mario and Grisi as the stars. *Harlequin Steam ; or, the Old Swan and the Knotty Ash*, was the Christmas attraction.

On February 11, 1856, Barry Sullivan commenced an engagement at the Royal. During his visit *Macbeth* was produced in a style of unexampled splendour and completeness, and enjoyed an unbroken run of three weeks. On May 19, Madame Constanti (a native of Liverpool), came with her company and gave a series of operatic performances.

Sir William Don—a Scotch baronet—appeared on July 28. James R. Anderson tells us in ' An Actor's Life,'* that Sir William Don ' was seven feet and something more ; he was the tallest man I have seen upon the stage.' '' Billy '' was a prince of good fellows, high-spirited, full of fun, and a perfect gentleman with a University education. ' He married an actress named Saunders, and made her " my lady " but the match was an unhappy one, and the pair soon parted.' Sir William Don held a captain's commission in the Fifth Dragoon Guards, and within three years managed to run through an estate worth about £85,000. After he left the army he decided to turn player, having previously won some fame as an amateur actor. He journeyed to New York, and, in 1850, made there, in *The Jacobite*, his first appearance on the professional stage. Irving acted with Don in Edinburgh in 1857. Irving was then an obscure actor, commencing his stage career at a salary of thirty shillings a week. After experiencing great vicissitude, Sir William Don, impoverished and neglected, died at Hobart Town, Tasmania, on March 19, 1862, aged 36. His wife, Lady Emilia Don (*née* Emily Saunders), returned to England, and on several occasions acted at Liverpool. She died September 20, 1875.

The great theatrical event of 1856 in Liverpool was the first appearance of Madame Ristori on July 18 as Medea. Three days later she was seen in *Rosamunda*. Her visit created great enthusiasm. In September Webster and Madame Céleste produced the pantomime of *Jack and the Beanstalk ; or, Harlequin and Mother Goose at Home Again*. In this, Madame Céleste played Jack (afterwards Harlequin). *La Traviata* was performed for the first time locally on

* P. 222.

October 21, when the youthful prima donna, Mdlle. Piccolomini, made her first appearance here.   Barry Sullivan and Mr. and Mrs. Keeley paid visits in December.

In January, 1857, was published an interesting volume called ' The Liverpool Year Book for 1856.'   It was ably compiled and edited by Messrs. Lee and Nightingale.   ' Liverpool,' says the work referred to, ' is now the most musical and theatrical town in Great Britain, after London, and while Manchester has but two theatres and two concert-rooms, no musical society, and no resident artistes worthy of special mention, with the exception of Herr Hallé and Mr. Seymour, the Liverpool public support four theatres and half-a-dozen of the finest concert-rooms in the world—while our Philharmonic and Festival Choral Societies give oratorios and miscellaneous musical performances, often superior, in many respects, to anything heard in the metropolis.   In no town in the kingdom have the working classes such admirable and cheap musical recreations as in Liverpool, and here were originated those Saturday Evening Concerts, which have been imitated in the metropolis, and other large towns, though nowhere with the success which has attended those in this busy money-making "modern Tyre." '   May not the present veracious chronicler interpolate a sigh for ' the good old times ' that once belonged to Liverpool ?

Madame Grisi, Madame Gassier, and other noted vocalists were here with the Italian Opera Company on February 10, 1857.   On August 10, Ristori commenced a three nights' engagement.   Charlotte Cushman and Madame Céleste followed.

On October 29, 1858, John Vandenhoff took his farewell of the stage in playing Brutus in *Julius Cæsar*, and Cardinal Wolsey in the third act of *Henry VIII*.   In the latter selection Henry Neville enacted Cromwell, and he it was who led this last representative of the once famous Kemble school of acting from the boards which he had so long adorned.

On Wednesday evening, November 3, 1858, the performance was under the distinguished patronage of Field Marshal Lord Combermere, Sir Robert Gerard, the officers of the Masonic Grand Lodge, and the Masters and Brethren of West Lancashire.   The occasion was a complimentary benefit to Malone Raymond on his retirement from the stage.   Mr. Raymond appeared in his favourite character of Sir Lucius

O'Trigger, and Mr. W. J. Hammond, out of compliment to the partner of his late father, performed Bob Acres.* Thus the names of Raymond and Hammond figured once again on the bills of the Theatre Royal. On that night many an old play-goer visited the theatre in remembrance of times gone by.

Commencing April 25, 1859, Anna Bishop and her opera company were here for five nights. During the following month Mr. and Mrs. Barney Williams appeared. Mdlle. Titiens came with the Italian Opera Company on November 14.

On August 3, 1859, the patent first granted to the theatre in 1771, and allowed to lapse in 1849, was renewed for a period of twenty-one years to Mr. W. R. Copeland. The Privy Seal Bill was dated May 4, 1860, and the patent would bear date some few days later. Mr. Copeland was the last holder of the patent, which expired on August 3, 1880. The grant of Letters Patent has now lost most of its value.

In the drama of *Paris and Pleasure*, produced by Madame Céleste on April 23, 1860, she impersonated no fewer than eight *rôles*. In the company with her were Miss Kate Saville, Miss Hudspeth, and John Rouse.

On August 20, 1860, the Zouaves made their first appearance in Liverpool. They were the original founders of the theatre at Inkerman, where they performed under the enemy's fire. The battles in which they played a sterner *rôle* were : Alma, Balaclava, Inkerman, and Malakoff (Sebastopol). There were no actresses in the organisation.

The company from the Theatre Royal, Manchester, com-menced an engagement on October 2. One of their number was a young player who made his first appearance in Liverpool as Faust in the play of *Faust and Marguerite*, and afterwards became celebrated throughout the world as Henry Irving. The 'Daily Times' of October 3, spoke of his im-personation in the following terms :—' Mr. H. Irving was rather too tall to permit of his successfuly realising the pop-ular idea of a learned doctor, and there was not the least, of an alchymist—which we certainly think there ought to have been—about his appearance. He offered a very truthful picture of a " spooney " youth who was ready to die, and

* Mr. Hammond, who only died recently, carried on business as a brewer for many years at 168, Brownlow Hill.

something more, for the object of his passion, but the portrait failed to recall the original ; and the consequence was that when he " went below " much more of our pity followed him than the author intended he should receive.'

The Italian Opera Company came on September 2, 1861, and with them Adelina Patti, who then made her second appearance out of London.   She performed Amina (*La Sonnambula*), Lucia (*Lucia di Lammermoor*), Violetta (*La Traviata*), and Zerlina (*Don Giovanni*).   Mdlle. Titiens performed with the company in the following month.   The conductor was Signor Arditi.   On November 7, Madame Grisi commenced the first of her ' farewell ' performances in Liverpool, making her final curtsey on the 15th inst.

Blondin was here on March 10, 1862.   May 5, the Pyne and Harrison Company ;   October 20, Charles Mathews ; and November 14, the Italian Opera Company including Mdlle. Titiens.   On December 26, the pantomime *Harlequin and the Three Bears ; or, Little Golden Hair and the Fairies*, was produced, and a new act-drop, from the brush of Charles Brew, was then shown for the first time.

In ' The Porcupine,' for November 1, 1862, there appeared an article, entitled ' Reform Your Theatres.'   ' We have in Liverpool,' says the journal, ' four theatres and a circus, and we appeal to everyone who has visited some of the theatres in Paris, Brussels, Berlin, New York, and even Melbourne, if the wretched buildings in this great town are not a disgrace to us, and totally unsuited to the purposes for which they are used.

' What can be worse than the *locales* of the Theatre Royal and the Royal Amphitheatre ?   Every sense is offended as the visitor approaches them.   The stenches from market refuse and close, dank, reeking streets are even dangerous to health, while the sights and sounds are so offensive that hundreds of ladies are denied the pleasures of theatrical entertainments in consequence of the certainty of having their eyes and ears polluted in a manner which will be well understood by mere allusion.   The same may be said of the Adelphi Theatre, which few respectable ladies will visit, let the attractions be what they may.   Next, as to unfitness.   What can be shabbier, meaner, or more unsuitable for a large public building than the entrances to our two principal theatres ?   They are

narrow, dirty, and badly lighted.   There is no proper provision for the care of external articles of clothing—no decent
foyer, or refreshment saloon ;   nothing in fact, but narrow,
cheerless, ill-lit lobbies, paltry rooms, and draughty staircases.
As to the interior accommodation, the idea that it is requisite
to sit at ease to thoroughly appreciate a performance seems
to be as little understood by theatrical managers as by clergy-
men and churchwardens.   At the Theatre Royal, the chairs
in the dress-circle are hard and far too small, and the sitting-
room in other parts of the house as beggarly and comfortless
as possible.   At the Amphitheatre matters are even worse,
and the dress and side boxes more particularly, human ingenuity could not invent anything more miserably deficient in
every quality a comfortable seat ought to have.   Then, again,
the ventilation is wretched.   In summer the ardent playgoer
is parboiled, and the only relief is a *tic-doloreaux*-giving blast
of cold air ;   while in winter, the gusts of icy air from both
stage and lobbies is enough to freeze even a Polar bear. Behind the curtain matters are even worse.   The stages, both
above and below, are encumbered with useless, antiquated
old machinery ;   the dressing-rooms are the veriest dog-holes ;
while the whole place—dangerous from absence of light—is per-
vaded by noisome smells, which, in the Theatre Royal must
be injurious to health.   That the musicians—whose wretched
fate it is to sit in the orchestras—are ever free from colds and
rheumatism speaks wonders for the acclimatizing powers of
human nature.'

On January 24, 1863, *A Loan of a Lover* was played, the
part of Gertrude ' by a young lady, her first appearance on
any stage.' The young lady referred to was Miss Alice Dodd.
April 27 was the first night locally of Balfe's new opera, *The
Armourer of Nantes*.   It was interpreted by the Pyne and
Harrison Company, which included Mr. and Mrs. Aynsley Cook,
who appeared as Fabio Fabiani and Dame Bertha.

In ' The Porcupine,' for May 23, 1863, it was stated that
Mr. Copeland's playbills ' are even worse than they were some
thirty years ago.—That is to say, they are larger, dirtier, and
more incorrect.   In fact, not to " put too fine point on it,"
they are positively disgraceful to any respectable establishment.' What was asked for was ' a small, clean, neatly-printed
octavo ' in lieu of ' the yard of flimsy, daubed over with filthy,

oily ink.' The bills were printed by Mr. Copeland himself, and it was pointed out that in all the London theatres, and at most of the respectable theatres in the provinces, the managers had long since discarded the old style of playbill.

Mr. Copeland acted on the advice given, and early in the following month issued a free programme, called ' The Curtain.' This was published every morning and distributed gratuitously in the Theatre Royal and Amphitheatre. ' The Porcupine,' for June 13, 1863, says : ' It is very pleasant to have a neat little playbill which does not stain one's gloves, and the one which has been distributed out at the Amphitheatre proves that a desirable degree of neatness and cleanliness is perfectly compatible with a high degree of economy.'

On July 15, 17, and 18 (*matinée*), Madame Ristori graced these boards as Medea, Lady Macbeth, and Maria Sturda. Two nights later Mr. Copeland inaugurated a summer season of English Opera, under the direction of Mr. Henry Corri. On November 6, G. V. Brooke took a farewell benefit, prior to his proposed departure for Australia by the ' Blanche Moore.'* J. L. Toole, W. S. Branson, Paul Bedford, J. D. Stoyle, and Marie Sydney appeared on the occasion.   On December 15, Holcroft's comedy *The Road to Ruin* was performed by the Liverpool Press Guards, assisted by the Literary and Dramatic Society.   It is worthy of note that the part of Old Dornton was played by Mr. J. C. Bigham, now one of His Majesty's judges of the High Court.

In *Donna Diana*, presented on February 22, 1864, Mr. Hermann Vezin and his wife (formerly Mrs. Charles Young) played.   This being the Tercentenary year of Shakespeare's anniversary, special performances of the bard's plays were given.   On April 22, the Mayor, Mr. Charles Barned Mozley,† caused all the theatres and other places of amusement in Liverpool to be thrown open to the working-classes free of charge.   *Much Ado About Nothing* was submitted at the Royal, and Miss Kate Saville portrayed Beatrice.   A grand fancy dress ball was also given in St. George's Hall.   *As You Like It* was presented on our poet's supposed birth (and actual death) day with Kate Saville as the Rosalind.   The ensuing

* He never went.   See R. M. Sillard's ' Barry Sullivan and his Contemporaries,' Vol. II, p. 79.
† He was the principal of Barned's Bank, 9, Lord Street, Liverpool.

week saw *Romeo and Juliet* and *The Merchant of Venice* performed.   Representations of the bard's plays were also given at
the Prince of Wales, Adelphi, Amphi,' and Colosseum Theatres.
Mrs. Swanborough's vaudeville and burlesque company commenced an engagement on June 27.   The company included
Marie Wilton (now Lady Bancroft), Maria Simpson, David
James, Thomas Thorne, and George Honey.   Frank Musgrave
was the musical director.   It was during this visit that Marie
Wilton first met her future husband, S. B. Bancroft, who
was at that time a member of the stock company at the Prince
of Wales' Theatre.

One night Mrs. Swanborough's company played the burlesque of *Orpheus*.   A big handicap had been run that day,
and the winner was a horse called ' Black Deer.'   ' In the
evening,' says Mrs. Bancroft in ' On and Off the Stage,'*
' George Honey, who was playing Black King Pluto introduced
an unexpected joke in my scene with him.   " Saucy boy !
You've been to the races, it is clear."   I was taken by surprise ;
but soon recovered, and replied, " Yes, and was a winner, too,
you *Black Dear*."   The audience at once recognised the introduction, and received it with much laughter and applause.
Mr. Honey, seeing that I had the best of it, added " Oh, so I
thought ; well, long may you *reign*, *dear*."   This, being done
on the spur of the moment, was more successful than if it had
been pre-arranged.'

Fechter performed on September 25, 1865, as did also
John Ryder and Carlotta Leclerq.   The plays were *Hamlet*
and *Ruy Blas*.   The Christmas pantomime was *King Salmon*,
preceded by *Somebody Else*.   In the company were Mrs.
Burkinshaw, Charles Dornton, and J. L. Warner.   Mr. Burkinshaw (afterwards of Colquitt Street), was the stage manager
of the theatre.

On January 26, 1866, Miss Millicent Palmer had a benefit,
when she performed Pauline to Charles Calvert's Claude in
The Lady of Lyons.   The celebrated Joe Jefferson portrayed
Rip Van Winkle on May 14.   He was supported by Mrs.
Billington (who was specially engaged), and Charles Vanden-
hoff.

On July 9, the American Slave Serenaders (' the only
combination of genuine darkies in the world '), paid their first

* Sixth edition, p. 53.

visit to Liverpool.   The company was under the direction
of Sam Hague, and by his name the minstrels were afterwards
known.   Towards the end of 1866, the theatre came under
the management of Mr. H. J. Byron, as did also the Amphitheatre and Alexandra.   His first Royal pantomime, which was
from his own witty pen, was entitled *Little Dick Whittington,
Thrice Lord Mayor of London ; or, Harlequin Hot Pot and The
Fairies of the Elfin Grot.*

Miss Madge Robertson (now Mrs. Kendal), made her first
appearance here on February 18, 1867, as Madame de Fon-
tanges in *Plot and Passion.*   According to custom all the
theatres were closed during Passion Week.   On April 1, Mr.
(now Sir) F. C. Burnand performed Captain Crosstree in his
own burlesque of *Black-Eyed Susan.*   Rosina Ranoe (Mrs..
Burnand), played William, and Edward Saker figured as
Dame Hatley.

On May 29, 1867, Mr. W. R. Copeland died.   The ' Liverpool Daily Post,'* said ' that at the interment in Smithdown
Road Cemetery there were some present who had grown up
as little children under the fostering care of the deceased ;
there were others who had only known him a short time, but
not too short a time to learn his worth ; there were others who
had travelled long distances to be present, and managers who
had been pitted against him in the battle of life—from one
and all the expression was unanimous, that the earth had never
closed over a kinder or a more considerate friend and master
than William Robert Copeland.'

Offenbach's *Grand Duchess* was performed on April 27,
1868, with a cast comprising Mrs. Howard Paul, and Messrs.
W. Harrison, Frank Mathews, and J. D. Stoyle. Henry Leslie
now directed the destinies of the theatre.   Commencing July
20, Buckstone's Haymarket Company were seen in a
series of old English comedies.   The company included
Messrs. W. H. Chippendale, Henry Howe, Walter Gordon,
W. H. Kendal, Henry Compton, Mrs. Fitzwilliam, and Mrs.
Chippendale.   On August 31, Miss Bateman performed Leah.
The company included the late F. A. Scudamore, who made
his appearance—his first here, by the way—as Hermann.
Mr. Scudamore afterwards acquired considerable reputation
as a dramatist.   Alfred Dampier and Miss Eliza Rudd were
also in the cast.

* June 3, 1867.

In 1869 the Royal was under the management of Mr. E. D. Davies of the Theatre Royal, Newcastle-on-Tyne.   In March, 1869, Miss Bateman was here with Mr. T. W. Swinbourne and Miss Virginia Francis.   Commencing April 5, Charles Dickens gave a series of farewell readings.   On the last night, April 9, he was heard in ' Sikes and Nancy ' and ' The Christmas Carol.'   On May 12, Fred Maccabe was ' benefitted ' by the Liverpool Literary and Dramatic Society.   Among those who took part in the performance were Messrs. William and Robert Crompton.   May 17, saw Fechter and Miss Carlotta Leclerq here in *Hamlet* and *Black and White*.   J. B. Buckstone and his company came on July 12.   In the company were Madge Robertson, Mr. and Mrs. Chippendale, Mrs. Fitzwilliam, Henry Compton, and W. H. Kendal.   At Christmas the pantomime was entitled *The Queen Bee ; or, Harlequin Prince Golden Land, Jack Frost, and the Lazy Drones of the Enchanted Valley*.

In 1870 Mr. J. Pitney Weston succeeded Mr. Davies as manager of the theatre.   On February 6, 1870, Henry Loraine came on a visit.   Charles Dillon began an engagement on November 19.   He was supported by Miss Kate Saville and Miss Romer.   On January 9, 1871, Mr. J. Pitney Weston appeared as Hamlet.   The tragedy was followed by the pantomime *Blue Beard*.   Mr. Edward Garcia commenced his management of the theatre on February 4, 1871, with Mr. C. H. Reynolds as his acting manager.   The opening bill comprised *The Way of the World* and *The Peepshow Man*.

On August 21, 1871, the house was opened as the Theatre Royal Palace of Varieties, under the direction of Mr. Harry de Frece.   Madame Colonna and her troupe of dancers were here during the year.   The close of 1871 saw the building styled the Theatre Royal and Opera House.   Later it became again the Theatre Royal.   Madame Colonna and her troupe of dancers visited the theatre in February 1872, and returned again the following year.   A new farce from the pen of Maurice de Frece, entitled *Is Brown at Home ?* was produced on February 24, 1873.   Messrs. T. F. Doyle, Alfred Hemming, and W. Walton were among the performers who appeared here during the year.   In 1874, Mr. Isaac de Frece, Mr. Harry de Frece's brother, was the lessee.

On June 16, 1876, the late Alexes Leighton played Romeo for her benefit. It was either Miss Leighton's father or uncle who handed to Barry Sullivan the presentation sword subscribed for him by a number of Liverpool gentlemen. Mr. Robert Crompton was the speech-maker.

On November 6, 1876, W. H. Pennington (who had seen active service in the Crimea, and had taken part in the famous Balaclava charge), commenced an engagement. For his benefit on November 17, he played Hamlet, and was honoured by the presence and patronage of Mr. and Mrs. William Ewart Gladstone. Mr. Gladstone afterwards wrote to Pennington and congratulated him upon his interpretation of the *rôle*. He spoke of it as ' your admirable conception and performance of the great and unsurpassed part of Hamlet.' In Morley's ' Life of Gladstone,'* the following extract from the great statesman's private diary is given :—' Went to Liverpool to see Pennington in *Hamlet*. It was really excellent.'

On February 19, 1877, a drama, entitled *The Leprechaun ; or, The Lovers of Tara Vale*, was produced for the first time on any stage. The author was Mr. John Levey, who was for some years associated with the Theatre Royal. Mr. Levey, who carries on business in Brownlow Hill in this city, is father of Mr. J. Langley Levey, the well-known journalist. Another first production took place on March 12, when *St. Leger ; or, Sporting Life* was submitted.

On October 20, 1879, the Royal opened under the management of Henry Loraine. The opening attraction was *D.T. ; or, Lost by Drink*. By January 17, 1880, the theatre was under the lesseeship of Mr. John C. Chute.

Mr. Chute commenced his management with a new drama, entitled *Connemara ; or, The Wild West*, but soon found that the theatre was in bad odour with the local public. ' The house,' he tells me, ' was dirty, and the scenery faded. My only success was *Connemara*, which I afterwards successfully toured.' Mr. Chute, who was the last theatrical lessee of the theatre, managed the house for about three months.

After Mr. Chute left, the Royal was without a tenant for several years. Fate had overtaken it, and it was *eheu !* to be a theatre no longer. The patent granted to Mr. Copeland

* Vol. II, p. 558.

for twenty-one years from 1859 expired on August 3, 1880, and was not renewed.   On December 19, 1881, the Clerk to the local Magistrates informed the Lord Chamberlain that ' the Corporation of this city is in treaty for the purchase of the theatre for public improvements.'

At a special sessions held in the autumn of 1882 the following rules for the regulation of the local theatres were unanimously adopted by the licensing bench of magistrates : (1) ' That no theatre shall be open for the performance of stage plays during Passion Week, or on any occasion when the magistrates, for the preservation of the peace, may signify their desire in writing, to the manager or other person, having at the time the care and management of such theatre, that the same should not be opened.   (2) That there shall be no performance of any stage plays in any theatre on Sunday, Christmas Day, Ash Wednesday, Good Friday, or any day appointed for a national feast.   (3) That the several theatres shall be closed not later than twelve o'clock every night during the week, except on Saturday night, when the same shall be closed at eleven o'clock.'   These rules placed all the Liverpool Theatres on the same footing as to closing during Passion Week.   Once all the theatres had to close during this period, but the prohibition was afterwards struck out of the conditions of licensing, in so far as it related to the theatres licensed by the Lord Chamberlain or the local magistrates, but not to the Theatres Royal by Letters Patent, which had to observe the rule according to the terms of the patent.   This rule was really a survival of an ancient custom whereby all the theatres were compulsorily closed during Lent.

The revival in 1882 of the order as to the closing of the theatres in Liverpool during the whole of Passion Week, created quite a storm of indignation among our townsmen, and the rule was rescinded almost as soon as it was passed. The Good Friday observance was, of course, still retained, and also the Ash Wednesday prohibition.   The latter prohibition was ultimately rescinded in 1886 by the Lord Chamberlain, owing to the well-organised agitation of John Hollingshead.

In 1884 the shapely interior of the Theatre Royal was altered to adapt it to the requirements of a circus, and as such the house was opened by Mr. Alfred Eugene Godolphin Cooke on November 24, of that year.   Although Mr. Cooke went to

considerable expense in altering the theatre, the experiment
was not successful. In August, 1885, the Royal was put up
for sale by auction, when the highest bid was £7,000. Verily,
the old place had indeed fallen on evil days, when it had
to go a-begging for a purchaser. What would former managers have said if they could have revisited the shades of
their former glories and realised the insignificant value placed
upon the historic site ? *Sic transit gloria theatri !*

The Liverpool Corporation subsequently purchased the
building for £23,000. The purchase included, of course, the
house in Brythen Street, wherein ' Gentleman ' Lewis and
his son, ' Dandy ' Lewis used to reside, and where, subsequently, W. R. Copeland lived for a time, but which had long
ceased to be used as a dwelling-house. Afterwards a limited
company acquired the theatre and transformed it into a
cold storage, which it still remains. Of the old theatre there
still remains the noble *façade* in Williamson Square to
remind us of the glories of the past.

THE OLYMPIC CIRCUS

AND

ADELPHI THEATRE.

The first recorded visit to Liverpool of the celebrated
equestrian performer, Philip Astley, is to be found in ' Williamson's Liverpool Advertiser,' for February 12, 1773, which
states that recently Mr. Astley and his pupils from London
had exhibited their wonderful feats of horsemanship to
upwards of 20,000 of the inhabitants of Liverpool ' in a large
field near Mr. Roscoe's* bowling-green, Mount Pleasant.'

Philip Astley was born in 1742 and died in 1814. He and
his son were both remarkably handsome, the father being a
veritable giant, but of perfect symmetry. Old Astley used
to talk of a ' Krockadile wat stopped Halexander's harmy,
and when cut hopen, had a man in harmour in his hintellects.'
' Pestiferous,' he always substituted for ' pusillanimous,' and
he was wont to observe that he should be a ruined man, for
his horses ate most ' vociferously.'

---

* Father of William Roscoe, the celebrated poet and historian.

N

The wife of Astley senior was a minor actress of much merit. 'She had such luxuriant hair that when she stood upright it covered her from head to foot like a veil.   She was very proud of these flaxen locks ; and a slight accident by fire having befallen them, she resolved ever after to play in a wig. She used, therefore, to wind this immense quantity of hair around her head, and put over it a capacious *caxon*.   The consequence was that her head looked about the same proportion to the rest of her figure as a whale's skull does to its body.   As she played most of the heroines, the reader may judge of the effect.'*

Though Astley and his company doubtless made frequent return visits to Liverpool in the interim, I can find no trace of subsequent visits here until early in January, 1788, when the equestrians performed for some time in the Royal Tent in Vernon Street, off Dale Street.† The performances consisted of dancing, tumbling, and vaulting, and musical entertainments by educated horses. The announcement in ' Williamson's Advertiser,' says that ' these equestrian amusements are honoured by His Majesty's Royal Letters Patent.'   The company included Astley, junr., Master Crossman, and Signor Garcia.   A note is added to the advertisement in which it is stated that the materials of the Royal Tent would shortly be put up for auction.   Astley and his troupe afterwards appeared at the Theatre Royal in 1789, and again in 1790.

Brooke in his ' Liverpool '‡ states that ' there was not any Amphitheatre or Circus in Liverpool, in 1775, nor for many years afterwards.   A Circus, in Christian Street, for the exhibition of equestrian performances, was, however, in existence at least as early as the year 1795, because both the circus and the street of that name leading to it, are laid down in the Map of Liverpool of that date, published in "Aikin's Description of the Country from Thirty to Forty miles round Manchester."   It is now§ the Adelphi Theatre.'

The Christian Street Circus was first opened in 1789.   On May 4, 1789, the following   advertisement   appeared   in ' Williamson's Liverpool Advertiser': ' Circus, Repository and Livery Stables. Mr. T. Tinkler having given the Public the outline of his intended Plan, at the time he engaged to

* ' Records of a Veteran.'   ‡ P. 88.
† ' Williamson's Advertiser.'   § 1853.

take the capital Livery Stables, then building in the vicinity of St. Anne Street, begs leave to inform the Ladies and Gentlemen of Liverpool, and its Neighbourhood, that they are now finished, and open for the reception and complete accommodation of Forty Horses. The Riding School cannot, however, be completed before the 1st of June, owing to the covered Ride for the convenience of learning and of taking exercise under, not being yet finished ; but Mr. T. will make it as commodious as possible . . . . ' The Riding School or Circus, was, however, not completed until November, 1789, as on November 30 of the same year it was announced in ' Williamson's Liverpool Advertiser ' that ' Mr. Tinkler begs leave to inform those Ladies and Gentlemen who wish to ride for exercise in the Circus, that the School is now compleated, and a fire will be constantly kept, with every other accomodation to render it agreeable and pleasant . . . . ' Although the first advertisement quoted speaks of the Circus as being ' in the vicinity of St. Anne Street,' without naming the street, this defect is remedied in a plan of Liverpool, published by John Gore on August 12, 1790, whereon the Circus in Christian Street is clearly indicated.

Old Astley was at the Theatre Royal in the March of 1793, and in March, 1794, he opened at the Circus in Christian Street, where an advertisement in ' Billinge's Advertiser,' tells us that the ' great and wonderful company will exhibit their wonderful exercises.' Young Astley was at the Royal towards the close of March, 1794. It was probably owing to Old Astley having appeared at the Circus in Christian Street that Aickin and he quarrelled, as on June 3, 1795, the patentee gave the great equestrian notice to quit the Royal, which he had rented from him for eight seasons at one hundred pounds per annum. In the following month Philip Astley caused the subjoined advertisement to be issued in the local papers :—

' Proposals for building an Amphitheatre in the town of Liverpool.

' Mr. Astley having, for a series of years, rented from Mr. Aickin, the Theatre, and that gentleman having given Mr. Astley a certain notice to quit the same, he is under the necessity of immediately building an Amphitheatre, for the following purposes :—Music, Dancing, Pantomimes, Equestrian, and other Exercises, Pieces of Mechanism, and Scenic Representations ;

for which purpose the sum of Five Thousand Pounds will be wanted to complete the same.   It is, therefore, proposed to build an Amphitheatre by subscription, by way of Tontine, viz.:—one hundred subscribers at fifty pounds each, to have a free admission ticket, on the same plan as the Theatre. The building to be held in trust by six of the subscribers, by way of security. Mr. Astley to keep the same in substantial repair, and pay every encumbrance.

'It is intended the Amphitheatre shall be open twice a year, viz.: November and December, also July and August, and to continue three or more days in each week.

'Further particulars will be made known on Mr. Astley's arrival in Liverpool.   In the meanwhile, such ladies and gentlemen as are inclinable to subscribe, either for themselves or families, are humbly requested to send their address immediately to Mr. Astley, Westminster Bridge, London.

N.B.—'When the subscription is complete, Mr. Astley will undertake to have the building ready in four months.'*

Sir James Picton tells us in his 'Memorials'† that Astley's appeal for the erection of an Amphitheatre ' was responded to and the building was erected within six months.' This, I think, is an error, as according to ' Gore's General Advertiser,' Philip Astley and his company commenced an engagement at the Theatre Royal, on March 16, 1796, the great equestrian, apparently, having made up his quarrel with Aickin. If he had had a circus of his own in Liverpool he would, doubtless, have appeared there and not at the patent theatre. Furthermore, the Astleys appeared at the Royal in the March of the four succeeding years (1797-1800).   Therefore, I think, we may take it that Astley's appeal was *not* successful, and, that the Christian Street Circus still pursued the even tenor of its way.

Towards the end of April, 1799, performances were announced to be given in a circus called the ' New Olympic,' at the bottom of Shaw's Brow, now William Brown Street. The performers included Ducrow and Davis of equestrian celebrity. The advertisement in ' Billinge's Advertiser ' tells us that ' Mr. Davis will attend the Circus every day to instruct ladies and gentlemen in the polite art of riding and managing their horses.   The company will perform every evening, except Saturday, as they are engaged to exhibit their uncommon exercises on Whitsun Monday in London.'   The circus had boxes, pit, and gallery.

In the following year Mr. Davis opened the Circus in Christian Street.   The building had been altered somewhat, boxes having been introduced.   The performances, which commenced on February 21, 1803, were ' by permission of the Worshipful the Mayor,' and embraced horsemanship, tight-rope dancing, vaulting at full speed, equestrian exercises, and the precocious ponies.   *The Taylor's Journey to Brentford* was also given. During his stay Mr. Davis announced that he would ' take scholars to instruct them in the polite art of riding, and properly to manage a horse.'   On March 14, the last five nights were announced, but on March 21, the paper states that ' the Mayor has permitted the Circus to remain open a few days longer.' On Monday, April 23, 1804, the Circus was re-opened under the joint management of Messrs. Parker, Smith, Crossman, and Davis.   Vaulting, slack wire and rope performances, followed by a new pantomime dance, ' Dermot and Kathleen,' were given.   On May 3, it was advertised that ' this place of entertainment is (at a very great expense), newly fitted up in a genteel and elegant stile.'*

During the last week of the company's stay Signora Belinda was advertised to ' stand on her head on the pillar of a chair, also, on one side of a ladder, which is fixed upright on a table, and while in that position, will unscrew the staves, and the ladder will fall to pieces, leaving her on the remaining part, she will likewise stand on her head on the point of a spear, which has never been attempted by any female performer but herself, and will go through the same surprising balances on a candle-stick.'   The entertainment was to conclude with displays in fireworks, ' The Town and Trade of Liverpool,' ' Peace and Plenty,'   and ' God save the King.'

On April 1, 1805, the Christian Street place of entertainment was opened as the Olympic Circus.   Our local historians say it was opened under that name in 1803, but this is decidedly inaccurate.

The following account of the opening performance is culled from ' Gore's Advertiser ' of April 4, 1805 :—

* ' Gore's Advertiser.'

' On Monday night last the Public were gratified by the opening of the Olympic Circus, in Christian Street, with the best set of entertainments we remember to have seen in Liverpool.   The powers of some of the actors in this new store of mirth and wonder are well-known.   Smith, Crossman, and Mrs. Parker are, as they always have been, the theme of admiration in everything they do ; their exertions are of a very superior cast to those of any of their contemporaries.   Mrs. Parker seems to have taken a dip into Medea's kettle by way of antidote, for she is absolutely more agile and fascinating than ever, and Mr. Merriman in the hands of so intelligent a humorist, and so excellent an equestrian as Crossman, is rescued from all the usual vulgarity and nonsense of uneducated professors.   The neatness and effect of the infantile feats of Master Davis were loudly and universally manifold ; and, indeed the whole arrangements of novelty, variety and whim, equestrian and pedestrian, met with the most unbounded applause and promises to be the favourite lounge as long as it shall continue here.'

The season terminated on May 25, when Mr. Davis took a benefit.   The performance was ' by command of Prince William Frederick of Gloucester,' who at that time was military commander of the district.

The Olympic Circus had a good reputation for a long time, and prospered exceedingly well.   In addition to feats of horsemanship, equestrian dramas and spectacles were given with good effect.   In those days many celebrated riders, gymnasts, and clowns took part in the performances.

On January 27, 1806, Joe Grimaldi's great rival, Robert Bradbury, took a benefit at the Olympic.   Bradbury, it is stated, wore on his person, nine strong ' pads' in order to go through some extraordinary feats.*

Towards the end of 1806 the Olympic Circus was under the direction of Mr. Banks of the Theatre Royal.   Early in December, D'Egville's new *ballet d'action* ' The Visit of my Grandmother ;   or, Little Red Riding Hood,' was given. D'Egville, Woodward, and Johannot were among those who appeared at that time.

* For further details concerning this first of knock-about clowns, see my account of the Theatre Royal.

Early in January, 1807, there were feats of horsemanship and tight-rope dancing by Master Ducrow, and a new panto-mime was given called *The Magic Star*, in which D'Égville played clown.   On March 30 following, Mr. Banks took his benefit, when a new comic ballet, entitled ' The Folly Fair ; or, The Humours of Low Hill ' was submitted.   Mr. Ducrow, ' the Flemish Hercules,' was also announced to ' balance nine persons on his hands and knees.'   Two pantomimes were played, *Robinson Crusoe* and *The Golden Dream ; or, The Miser*. In the course of the latter there was exhibited a balloon twelve feet high, which ascended with two persons in a golden car.

The Olympic re-opened early in December for the season of 1807-8, with Mr. Banks still as manager.   On December 10, ' Dickie ' Usher, the celebrated clown made his first appear-ance here.   Usher it was, who once on the occasion of his benefit at one of the London theatres in order to attract the attention of the public to his ' bespeak,' obtained a large washing-tub to which he harnessed a couple of geese, and seated in this frail barque, he braved the waters of old Father Thames.   Needless to say his feat drew a great concourse of people.   Unfortunately, owing to the crowding and jostling on the river's banks, several people fell into the water and were drowned.

About this time (1808), the advertisements state that ' The entrances to every part of the house are now in Christian Street.'   Previously, one or more of the entrances had been in Springfield Street.   Friday night, April 8, 1808, concluded the season, when Mr. Banks took his benefit.   Afterwards the Circus was altered and greatly improved.   ' Billinge's Ad-vertiser ' for December 5, 1808, contains the following : ' In addition to the many numerous public buildings lately erected in this town, for the various purposes of utility and amuse-ment, we have much satisfaction in announcing to the public, that this favourite place of resort has lately been enlarged, improved, and ornamented in so great a degree as almost to entitle it to the appellation of a new edifice.   The old roof having been examined by Mr. Foster, he was clearly of opinion that it was incapable of such a repair as would render it safe. This report determined the proprietors to new model the whole, and give every possible accommodation to those who frequent this place of amusement, which the situation of the building admits of.   The walls have accordingly been raised sufficiently high to admit a second tier of boxes, so constructed as completely to command a view of the riding area and stage. These are called the upper boxes, and are ascended by an easy flight of wide and very commodious stairs which lead to a handsome ante-room or lounge.   The present roof is constructed on the newest and most scientific principles of carpentry, and done in a most firm manner with strong oak king posts, double principle rafters, and hammer beams, which give every truss a double bearing on the wall.   The whole is securely framed and iron bolted together so as to give all the strength and accommodation requisite for the use of machinery, etc., to which it may be applied.   The wood columns which supported the boxes have been taken away, and others of neat cast iron introduced in their place, in order more effectually to support the new boxes.   The Circus now forms three complete tiers or stories for spectators.   The lower one, which is level with the ground floor, is to be called the gallery ; the second, the boxes ; and the third, the upper boxes.   The principal girders which support the floors of these boxes rest on a strong double curb, to which, and through the boundary wall, they are secured by strong iron screw bolts.   The frontispiece has been ornamented with real pilasters, capitals and bases (they were before only painted) ; new stage doors* decorated with architraves and entablatures, and from the front of the proscenium rises a bold cove which joins the new ceiling and which is to be elegantly painted in fresco.   The whole of the house is to be new painted and lined in an elegant manner, and we believe it is the intention of the manager, Mr. Banks, to open it early in this month.   The whole of the alterations have been made from the design of Mr. John Foster, architect, and executed by Mr. Joseph Spencer, the contractor, who has completed the whole in a most firm and substantial manner ; the building does him the greatest credit, and he deserves high praise for his taste as an artist.   We feel pleasure in saying

---

* Stage or proscenium doors are still to be seen in the present building. *Apropos* of this I may refer to an article in ' Anglia ' (June, 1903), by Mr. W. J. Lawrence, entitled ' A Forgotten Stage Conventionality,' in which it is stated that proscenium doors were peculiar to the English theatre, and had no Continental prototypes.   They were manifestly a survival of the Elizabethan theatre.   It is also reasonable to presume that their oblique position was borrowed from the same source.   For further information on the subject, see an article by Mr. William Archer on the Fortune Theatre, which appeared in the ' Tribune ' for October 12, 1907, and was reprinted in the ' Shakespeare Jahrbuch ' of Berlin for 1908.

that, for the elegance and accommodation, the Liverpool Circus is not surpassed, if equalled, by any in the kingdom.'

From 1809 to 1812 the destinies of the Olympic remained in the hands of Mr. Banks, ' by permission of the Worshipful the Mayor.'   On November 28, 1813, the Circus was opened by Messrs. Astley, Davis, and Parker as the New Olympic Circus. ' Dickie' Usher was the equestrian clown, Ridgway the pantomimic 'Joey,' and Blanchard the pantaloon. On February 13, 1814, the pantomime *Take Warning ; or, Harlequin in Scotland* was presented.   During this ' a mechanical harlequin made a flight from the stage round the dome of the Circus, and returned to the stage.'   The season terminated on March 25, 1814. On December 9, 1816, Il Diavolo Antonio, the rope-dancer, made his first appearance in Liverpool.   He was here again in 1821, when he was assaulted by J. B. Booth, the tragedian.*   To avoid the consequence of his act, Booth fled from England, accompanied by his wife, and sailed for the West Indies.   The vessel in which he embarked called at Madeira, and there he changed his mind, for instead of continuing his journey, he took passage on a schooner bound for Norfolk, Virginia, where he arrived in the month of August, 1821. These were causes which preluded the foundation of the Booth family in the United States.

In 1817, Ducrow, Usher,† and one of the Flexmores were here.   In 1820, Mr. Stebbing performed, and quickly became a great favourite.   I have in my possession a coloured print of Stebbing in his favourite character of Molly Maloney in *The Battle of Waterloo.*   Stebbing had a well-fitted-up hostelry in Upper Dawson Street, which he called the 'Molly Maloney.'‡

On Monday, December 11, 1820, Walter Donaldson played Brunoff in *The Boor's Hut ; or, Russian Perfidy.* Donaldson was the author of an interesting volume, entitled ' Fifty Years of Green Room Gossip,' in which he gives§ some notable particulars of old theatrical life in Liverpool.

* Father of Edwin Booth.
† In 1821 Usher opened a circus in the old tennis court in Hanover Street (near the Excise office), and for so doing was fined £50 by the authorities. He afterwards reopened the circus under ' Royal Authority,' but with very indifferent success.
‡ In 1839 there was published a pamphlet, entitled ' The Remarkable Adventures of Reuben Rambler, Gentle : near the Theatre Royal, Liverpool.'   The pamphlet, a copy of which is in the Liverpool Free Library, is nothing but a glorification of Stebbing's hostelry, the ' Molly Maloney.'
§ Chapter VI.

'Having performed,' he writes, 'under the direction of the managers of the Theatre Royal, Liverpool, Messrs. Banks and Lewis, I am cognisant of the working of the old system, when patents were respected. It is true, patents were a monopoly; but it was a monopoly in a good cause, as it preserved the legitimate drama in all its bearings. Now, in regard to Liverpool, no proprietor of a booth, no equestrian troupe could enter the town; and as this restriction was the means of keeping public attention on the Theatre Royal, the legitimate and classic works of the stage were year after year presented by an efficient and educated set of artists, more likely to elevate and advance society than the light and trifling performances of the present day that may be regarded more in the light of amusements than carrying out Shakespeare's idea of "holding the mirror up to nature." The managers of Liverpool—Banks and Lewis—were men of note in society; the former had been for years a respected tragedian, and the latter a son of the never-equalled comedian, Lewis of Covent Garden. Those men legislated in Liverpool for the legitimate and illegitimate drama. In the summer the Theatre Royal was the temple for tragedy, and in the winter the Olympic Theatre in Christian Street was the arena for equestrian exercises, melodramas, ballets, and pantomimes. In this amphitheatre, in 1820, I made my bow as a vocalist, and gained some popularity by Blewitt's splendid melody of " Katty O'Lynch." Here I met with two Italian ladies—the M'lles. Ferzis—celebrated on the rope—not in the Blondin style; those aerial flights were never then attempted, save and except by the famous Madame Saqui.

' Diavolo Antonio, a Portuguese slack-wire performer, was much noticed in Liverpool, both in his public capacity and in private circles.

' Although Liverpool at that time could not boast of half the population of the present time, yet the pure and legitimate drama flourished. But when the door of the temple of the immortal bard was left open, and one adventurer after another rushed into the town, the Theatre Royal—the scene of the triumphs of the Kembles, Keans, O'Neills, and Vandenhoffs—was totally neglected, and extravanganza became the rage. A futile attempt in the way of opposition, made by an old servant, induced the respective managers,

Banks and Lewis, to give up the Olympic Circus ; and finally they retired from the town altogether, tired and disgusted with the ingratitude of those whose tastes they had fostered and encouraged.   Lewis—called " Dandy " Lewis—died some years ago, after his withdrawal from management, and left £15,000 to the National Gallery, on condition that Sir Thomas Lawrence's (?) portrait of his father as the Marquis in the *petite* comedy of *The Midnight Hour* should be hung up among the other pictures.[*]

' The breaking up of the establishment in Christian Street was keenly felt by all who came under the management of such characters as Banks and Lewis ; and no one parted from these honourable and respected men with greater regret than the writer of these Recollections.'

In December, 1821, Mr. Banks engaged Mr. John Cooke and his equestrian company for the season, which terminated at the end of March, 1822.

In 1823, the Olympic was known as Cooke's Olympic Circus. The clowns were Usher and Bradbury. Cooke and his dramatic and equestrian companies appeared at the Olympic during the winter of 1824, and in the early part of 1825. He had, also, engaged to perform there at Christmas, 1825, but when he arrived in November to make preparations for the ensuing season, he found that, through the bursting of a sewer the ' ride ' of the Circus was immersed in water. Cooke immediately employed a surveyor to see what was wrong, and the latter reported that the building was unsafe.   Thus situated, Cooke determined to erect a new Olympic Circus [†] upon an excellent foundation, ' which,' he says in an advertisement in ' Billinge's Advertiser ' for Tuesday, December 27, 1825, ' I will take care shall be firmly and substantially built, and which will be ready in three weeks, when it will be opened with a superior company of stage and ring performers, and my well-known unrivalled stud of horses.'

In his address to the public he further tells us that the Olympic in Christian Street was first let to him by the lessees of the Royal at a moderate fair rent.   ' I exerted myself in the production of pieces,' he says, ' which I thought were calculated to give satisfaction, and that my efforts were regarded

---

[*] The picture referred to was by Sir Martin Archer Shee.
[†] Afterwards known as the Royal Amphitheatre, Great Charlotte Street.

in a favourable light, is evident from the unprecedented success which followed, and which so liberally rewarded them. Yet, strange as it may appear, my success was viewed with envious jealousy by those who ought to have entertained very different feelings ; my progress was thwarted by a succession of petty, contemptible vexations, of which words will convey but a feeble idea ; and I was ultimately compelled to pay a very considerable advance of rent, or abandon the service of those by whom I had been so generously and warmly supported.   Still the kind encouragement of the Liverpool public enabled me to meet an unprecedented increase of rent, and I continued to prosper ; and, although numerous obstacles were vexatiously thrown in my way, I persevered, and should have continued to persevere, had not what appeared to me an insurmountable obstacle presented itself.'   This 'insurmountable obstacle' was the flooding of the arena already referred to.

After Cooke left the Christian Street Circus a committee of management was appointed, and under its direction the building, which was newly named the Royal Olympic Circus, was considerably strengthened and improved, while the audience part was newly painted and decorated.   Arrangements were entered into with Andrew Ducrow to re-open the Olympic, which he did on Monday, December 26, 1825.

On February 3, 1826, *Harlequin and The Three Wishes* was performed.   The scenery was by Clarkson Stanfield.   On March 13, Ducrow and his company presented the melodrama, *Guy Fawkes*.   In this, those clever performers Mr. and Mrs. Gomersal played.   Messrs. Henderson and Sloman were also in the bill.   The latter gentleman was announced to sing ' Love and the Treadmill,' and ' Billy White and Peggy Green ; or, The Ghost of a Sheep's Head.'

Mr. Scott was one of the succeeding managers of the Olympic.   Apparently from an old salary list in my possession, he had another circus in Liverpool besides the Olympic under his control.   This other building was known as the Pavilion.   The salaries given by Mr. Scott at both circuses ranged from £1 10s. to £3 weekly, though on the production of extra novelties, or the provision of particular talent, these terms were extended to ten guineas per week, and even more.

The capabilities of the Royal Amphitheatre, and the energetic way in which the management was conducted soon told on the fortunes of the Olympic. In 1831 the latter building was rebuilt and redecorated, and the ring space was converted into a pit, with what had long been a *desideratum* in Liverpool theatres, backs to the seats. The partition between the pit and the orchestra was surmounted by iron spikes, in order to prevent riotous spectators from climbing on to the stage. This partition was in evidence right down to the time when the house ceased to be a theatre. Similar partitions were to be seen in other local theatres.

The theatre was christened the Queen's, and was opened on December 26, 1831, by Henry Beverley, the comedian, with *Harlequin Gulliver*, in which Beverley himself played clown. He was at that time lessee of the Queen's Theatre, Manchester, and he competed pretty closely with Messrs. Raymond and Hammond, who managed the Liver Theatre, in Church Street. The scenic artist of the Queen's was the manager's brother, William Roxby Beverley, who soon made a name for himself.*

Robert Roxby, the father of the Beverleys, had in his youth served as a midshipman in the Navy under Nelson, but tiring of a seafaring life had entered the dramatic profession, and assumed the name of Beverley.

During Henry Beverley's management not a few of the best-known players of the day trod his boards, notably Madame Céleste, who, on Monday, April 2, 1832, appeared as Matilde de Grammont in *The French Spy*. On the 26th of the same month she played in *Wizard Skiff ; or, The Tongueless Boy*, and in *The Dumb Brigand*. Céleste remained for about three months . In May, Mr. and Mrs. Leclerq were here. In that month, when *Life in London* was produced, Mr. Beverley played Jerry, and Jem Ward gave a taste of his pugilistic quality.

In the competition between Henry Beverley and the Liver managers the rivals reduced their prices—the admission to the gallery being cut down by both to sixpence. Beverley, however, soon found that he was losing money, and in a little while gave up the theatre. He was succeeded by a variety of different managers, one of whom was ' Dickie ' Usher.

* Within comparatively recent years some of William Beverley's beautiful scenery was still to be seen at the theatre.

Usher, after redecorating the house, re-opened the Queen's on December 28, 1835 with *Lodoiska ; or, A Tartar's Vengeance*, followed by a pantomime, entitled *The Woodman and His Ass ; or, Harlequin in Fairyland.* There were also equestrian performances in the arena.

Early in 1839, Master Stanislaus Calhaem, ' The Liverpool Young Roscius,' aged 5, made his appearance at the Queen's. On March 5, he played Albert in *William Tell.* This was followed by a series of *poses plastique*, in which Master Stanislaus was assisted by Mr. Gould. Then came a laughable interlude, entitled *The Little Hunchback ; or, The Modern Richard III.*, Master F. Calhaem appearing in the title-*rôle*. After the interlude, our young Roscius spoke Collins' ' Ode to the Passions,' accompanied with music, and illustrated by groupings. Afterwards Master F. Calhaem gave a comic song. The concluding performance of the evening was *Frankenstein ; or, The Man and The Monster*, in which Stanislaus Calhaem played Felix.

On Monday, April 29, 1839, Mr. Taylor, a celebrated professor of the art of legerdemain, opened the Queen's for a few weeks. An attractive item of the performance was the announcement that ' Mr. Taylor will borrow a gentleman's hat, in which he will cook a plum-pudding, large enough for 500 persons.'

The next managers were Messrs. Ridyard and Newton, the former of whom had been lessee of the Theatres Royal, Chester, and Newcastle, and a member of the Liver dramatic *corps*, while the latter had been a member of the stock company at the Amphitheatre. They opened the theatre with a well-mounted play called *The Wizard of the Waves*—the cast of which included the name of W. S. Branson—and on the first night the house was crowded at popular prices.

' An incident, or rather a couple of incidents, occurred ' says a writer in the ' Liverpool Courier' in dealing with the opening, ' which utterly damned the piece and spoiled the managers' prospects. In the most important of the sensational scenes, which form a principal attraction in the drama, representing a ship at sea, the mist (composed of gauze), became ignited by some means, and was speedily in flames, and there was no little excitement in the house, but the panic was allayed without much difficulty, and no harm resulted beyond the destruction of the

inflammable mist.   The other incident was the refusal of
the water to make waves—the men being in a striking humour
—and the consequence was a calm sea during the storm.
The spoiling of the best scene in the first play dimmed the
managerial prospects so much that the house was soon permitted to change hands.'

On July 10, 1842, the theatre opened under the management of Messrs. Hudspeth and J. L. Parkinson, two actors
from the Theatres Royal, London, Liverpool, and Bristol. The
initial attractions were *The Dream of Fate ; or, Sarah, The
Jewess,* and *Dominique, The Deserter ; or, The Gentleman in
Black.* Afterwards Mrs. Bickerstaff was lessee for a brief period.
The next tenant was Mr. W. J. Holloway, late of the Sans
Pareil in Great Charlotte Street, which theatre (according to
the Liverpool correspondent of ' Oxberry's Budget,'), ' had
just been pulled down to make improvements in the neighbourhood.'   This would be about the latter part of October,
1843.

Mr. Holloway opened the Christian Street playhouse
under the name of the Victoria.   The initial performance
took place on November 13, 1843, the attractions being *The
Venetian ; or, The Council of Ten,* and *Our Old House at Home.*
' The houses,' says Oxberry's correspondent, ' have been very
indifferent.   Mr. Holloway, the manager, has reduced his
prices.'

Under date December 4, 1843, the same correspondent
writes : ' Good houses now and then, but taking it on the
whole it is a failure.   *The Bohemians* is underlined to-night,
Mariner's Dream, and *Timour, the Tartar.'* Later on in the
same month he reports : ' Houses generally but poor.   The
entertainments are excellently got up, and reflect great credit
upon the stage manager, Mr. Hutchinson.'   At Christmas
the pantomime of *Mother Bunch* was produced.

' On Monday, January 22, 1844, *Othello* was performed with
Mr. Donald as the Moor and Mr. Edgar as Iago. Yankee Mellor
sung several of his admired comic songs : and there was dancing
by Mr. Summerland and Miss Sharpe.   The whole concluded
with the admired American burletta, written expressly for
Mr. Harper, entitled *The Virginian Mummy ;* Ginger Blue,
Mr. Harper ; Dr. Galen, Mr. Mellison ; Captain Rifle, Mr. Bel-
mont ; Charles, Mr. Latimer ; Mr. Patent, Mr. Gibbs ; Paddy

O'Leary, Mr. Lyons ; Schoolmaster, Mr. Simmonds ; Waiter, Mr. Summerland ; James, Mr. Burgess ; Lucy, Mrs. Letchford ; Susan, Mrs. Hutchinson.'

February 26, 1844, ' A Mr. Grierson has been playing during the last week in *Virginius, Pizarro,* and *Venice Preserved.* Messrs. Cony and Blanchard are still here.   Business excellent.'

March 12, 1844, ' Mr. H. Beverley and the Edwin family have been playing here to good houses.   Mr. and Mrs. Hutchinson took their benefit last night, and were rewarded with a bumper.'

March 20, 1844, ' Mr. and Mrs. Campbell's night, a piece was played under the name of *The Daughter of Erin,* said in the bills to be written by a gentleman of Liverpool.   It is published as *Mary O'More,* and is a disgrace to the stage. We wonder that such pieces are allowed to be brought out.'

April 23, 1844, ' The Shakesperean Society gave a performance at this theatre on Tuesday last.   *The Stranger, The Innkeeper's Bride,* and *The Irishman in London,* were the pieces chosen, the first-named piece was well played, considering that several of the members were inexperienced.'*

About 1846, a townsman, W. J. Hammond, who had been in partnership with Mr. Raymond at the Liver, and who had made an attempt to manage the local Theatre Royal, took the theatre under his care.   Down to this time the building had been outwardly a very plain-looking structure, with an ordinary brick front, while the interior had become dirty and dingy with time.   Mr. Hammond decided to revive the departed glories of the house.   Accordingly, he gutted the building, refitted and decorated the interior in a most beautiful manner, and put an ornamental face on the front wall, surmounting the whole with several statues, one of which was blown down in the 'sixties, and the others afterwards removed.   He re-opened the house as the new Theatre Royal Adelphi, on Easter Monday, April 13, 1846, when Charlotte and Susan Cushman appeared as Romeo and Juliet before a crowded house, though the prices had been increased, the charge for the best seats being 7s. 6d.   No bonnets were allowed in the boxes, there being a retiring-room for ladies. The prices of admission were afterwards considerably reduced.

* ' Oxberry's Budget.'

I may mention here that on March 9, 1848, Susan Cushman married Dr. James Sheridan Muspratt, brother to Mr. E. K. Muspratt, J.P., of Seaforth Hall, Seaforth, Liverpool. The latter gentleman informs me that he has in his possession a sketch of Charlotte and Susan Cushman in the respective characters of Romeo and Juliet.

Apropos of Susan Cushman's marriage with Dr. Muspratt, the following is quoted from the 'Theatrical Journal':—'In the United States, where Susan Cushman passed the first six years of her professional life, she was well-known as an artist of taste and judgment, and a highly-accomplished woman. Her first appearance was at the Park Theatre, New York, in April, 1837, as Laura Castelli, in Mr. E. Sargent's play, *The Genoese* ; and so immediate was her success, that she was, on the fourth night, cast for Desdemona, to the Othello of Mr. Vandenhoff, who was then starring in America. From New York she went to Philadelphia and played for some time with Mr. Ranger, now of the Haymarket Theatre, London. During her brief career she successively played the "juvenile tragedy" and "genteel" comedy business, as it is theatrically termed, to Mr. James Wallack, Mr. Forrest, and Mr. Macready; and was the representative in Philadelphia and New York, of the principal female parts of most of our recent dramas,—Grace Harkaway to her sister's Lady Gay Spanker, Pauline in *The Lady of Lyons*, Florentine in *Time Works Wonders*, Julie de Mortemar, Lady Alice Hawthorn, and Satan in Paris. The last of these characters had a remarkable triumph, and was played by her for many consecutive nights.

'In *The Happy Man*, and in most of poor Power's best pieces, that delightful comedian has often declared that he never had a more clever supporter than Miss Cushman, who displayed a racy humor and a love of fun seldom looked for among the Juliets and Desdemonas of the stage. The former character was not one of this lady's American parts (?), but since her arrival in England she has actually performed that one character of Juliet upwards of *two hundred nights*.'

At the distribution of the estate of Mr. James Muspratt, who died in 1886, a marble bust of Charlotte Cushman by her friend and biographer Miss Stebbins passed into the possession of Mr. James Liebig Muspratt, of Rhyl. Susan

O

Cushman died at Wavertree, Liverpool, on May 10, 1859, and was buried in Smithdown Road Cemetery.

Those who saw Susan Cushman's elder sister, Charlotte as Meg Merrilies and Lady Macbeth will never forget those two brilliant impersonations.   In a word, Miss Cushman's portrayals were founded upon intellectual ideas, and not upon conventionalisms.   She was also very successful in dissimilar *rôles* like Rosalind, Nancy Sikes (*Oliver Twist*), Hamlet, Lady Gay Spanker (*London Assurance*), Mrs. Haller (*The Stranger*), and Cardinal Wolsey in *Henry VIII*.   To the regret of two hemispheres she died on February 18, 1876.

On Friday, April 17, 1846, Miss Cushman took a benefit at the Adelphi, when she played Mrs. Haller to G. V. Brooke's Stranger.   The following week the Misses Cushman were seen in *Ion, The Lesson of the Heart*, and *Guy Mannering*. April 27 witnessed Madame Céleste as Miami in *The Green Bushes*.   For her benefit on May 8, Benjamin Webster played in *The Lioness of the North*, and *The Miseries of Human Life*. The month of June saw the Misses Cushman paying a return visit with G. V. Brooke.   On the occasion of Prince Albert's visit to Liverpool, July 30, 1846, an amusing farce was got up specially for the occasion, in which Hammond, James Browne, and other local favourites were to take part.   A couple of days previous to the performance, and during the rehearsal of the piece, for which special local scenery had been painted, Mr. Hammond received a communication from the Lord Chamberlain prohibiting the production in consequence of some allusions in it to royalty.   Mr. Hammond was in a difficulty, but in order that the expense in getting up the farce should not be thrown away, he rummaged through the theatre library and, with the aid of the author of the interdicted play, managed to localise the old farce, *John Street, Adelphi*, into *H.R.H.P.A.; or, The Royal Guest*.

The summer of 1846 saw Miss Romer, Mr. Borrani, and William Harrison and company in *Maritana, La Sonnambula, The Bohemian Girl, Fra Diavolo*, etc. Afterwards there came Edwin Forrest, the famous American tragedian, who appeared in a round of favourite parts.   He was then taking his farewell of the British stage.   Later on came charming Madame Anna Thillon, followed on Monday, September 7, by the celebrated danseuse, Mademoiselle Taglioni, who appeared with Monsieur

Silvain, and Madame Procter Giubelli in the ballets entitled
' La Sylphide,' and ' Nathalie.' Taglioni's engagement lasted
for three weeks. During the return visit of the Misses Cushman
in September and October, the lessee, Mr. Hammond, played
Touchstone to Charlotte Cushman's Rosalind   This was the
first time that Shakespeare's comedy was played in this theatre.
Susan Cushman was the Celia.   Mr. Hammond also supported
Miss Cushman in *Guy Mannering*   On December 11, General
Tom Thumb enacted Hop O' My Thumb in Albert Smith's
drama, entitled *Hop O' My Thumb ; or The Ogre and His
Seven League Boots.* On January 1 and 2, 1847, the General
took a couple of benefits, when he sang a Scotch song, danced
the Highland fling, and played in *Bombastes Furioso*, and *Hop
O' My Thumb*   The Misses Cushman followed, and on March
1, came Henry Farren, who performed Sir Charles Coldstream
in *Used Up*.   On May 14, George Vandenhoff played Hamlet
for three nights.

Monday, November 22, saw Batty's Equestrian Company
in *Mazeppa ; or, The Wild Horse of the Desert*. Towards the
end of that year, Mr. J. C. Cooke was the lessee of the
theatre.

On Friday evening, October 29, 1848, the bill comprised
Oliver Twist, Antony and Cleopatra, and *The Dancing Barber*.
Performances were given by Misses Fielding and Farrell,
Mrs. Campbell, and Messrs Edward Edwards, J. Gardner,
F. Young, and Charles Rice, the last of whom was also acting
and stage manager.

After Mr. J. C. Cooke left, the theatre was taken by Mr.
Henry Egerton, who commenced his sway in 1849. During
the Egerton *régime*, many persons who afterwards trod the
boards of greater theatres fretted and strutted their hour on
the Adelphi stage   The late Alice Marriott, the famous
tragedienne, may be said to have graduated on Mr. Egerton's
stage. Her husband, Robert Edgar, was at the same time
acting manager of the theatre.

During Mr. Edgar's sojourn a benefit performance was got
up for an actor named Harry Pearson.   Benefits or ' bespeaks'
in the old days of the ' Delly,' as this theatre was affectionately
called, were always of much importance, and the following
copy of a ' writ of summons ' (for the original of which I am
indebted to a talented pupil of Hermann Vezin), goes to

prove, I think, that over half a century ago our histrionic forebears were not afraid of using plenty of 'printer's ink':—

' Writ of Summons, Liverpool.
Printed at the University, Great Howard Street.

' Victoria, by the Grace of God, of the United Kingdom of Great Britain and Ireland, Queen, Defender of the Faith, to anybody who will serve me, of Brownlow Street, in the Borough of Liverpool, in the County of Lancaster, Greeting. We command you that within Eight Days after the service of this Writ on you, inclusive of the day of such service, you do make an appearance and enter the Theatre Royal Adelphi, of Liverpool, to do a good Action, at the suit of your Old Friend, Harry Pearson, who intends taking a Benefit on Tuesday, the 3rd of April, 1849.   And take Notice, that in default of your so doing, the said Harry Pearson will think it extremely unkind of you, as the Failure of the Benefit may cause his appearance at Lancaster, and they will proceed therein to Judgment and Execution.

' Witness, Robert Edgar, Acting Manager of the Adelphi Theatre, at Liverpool, the 24th day of March, in the year of Our Lord One Thousand Eight Hundred and Forty Nine.

' Mind ! try and strain a point, and come to the Adelphi Theatre on my Benefit Night, April the 3rd ; you shall have your value.'

The performance of the nautical drama, *Fifteen Years of a Seaman's Life*, on January 16, 1850, records the fact that representations were given by Miss Marriott, Ada Dyas, and W. S. Branson.   The drama was followed by the pantomime of *Queen Mab ; or, Harlequin and the Fairy of the Golden Pippin*, in which Miss Marriott appeared as Brillianta.   The titular part was performed by Miss Curryer, and Valentine Vousden* from the Theatre Royal, Sadler's Wells, played harlequin.

In February, 1852, the theatre was closed for a little while in order to remodel and redecorate the interior.   On March 3, Montague Smythson made his first appearance as Hamlet, Miss Marriott playing Ophelia.   April 5, saw produced a new local drama, entitled *The Bride of Everton ; or,*

* Afterwards a very popular monologue entertainer.

Liverpool in the Olden Time. The principal characters were undertaken by W. S. Branson, Montague Smythson, Charles Rice, and Ada Dyas. On the occasion of Mr. Egerton's benefit (December 17), Edmund Falconer, the dramatist, and Edward Weston (from Drury Lane Theatre) performed.

Tuesday evening, November 30, 1852, witnessed the first performance here of the romantic spectacle entitled *Jeanne d'Hatchette*, in which one hundred female warriors appeared. Louis XI was played by Mr. Branson, and Jacques de Villiers by Montague Smythson (always a favourite at this house), while the name part was sustained by that celebrated actress, Ada Dyas   Other popular performers here at that time were Mr W. H Dentith, and Mrs. Appleby.

The pantomime of *Cinderella , or, the Fairy of the Crystal Fountain*, produced at Christmas, 1854, had witty Walter Hildyard as clown and ' Bob ' Cousens as pantaloon. The pantomime was stated to be ' interspersed with hits, jokes, and jests of the past, the present, and to come, prophesying, typifying, and verifying old saws and modern instances ; replete with fun, frolic and folly with all, at all, and among all, having a Lancaster range from Liverpool to Sebastopol.'

The Sleeping Beauty , or, Harlequin, Prince of the Emerald Isle was the 1855-6 annual. This was amusingly described on the bills as ' an entirely new, old, ancient, modern, operatic, autocratic, quite dramatic, antoatic, quizzical, physical, mysical, fistical, omniferous, sqaliferous, puniferous, loquacious, pugnacious, queerfacious, rumantic, half-frantic, laughable, chaffable, quaffable, screaming, steaming, blowahead, New Comic Pantomime.' This elaborate description leaves Polonius quite behind in phrase-making. The pantomime was preceded by the drama entitled *The Round of Wrong*

In the production of *The Corsair ; or, The Bride of Abydos*, on February 2, 1857, Caroline Elton played Oneiza. She was also the Fairy Queen in the pantomime of *The Fairy of the Coral Grot; or, Harlequin Beauty and the Beast*, which followed. Mrs. Henry Bickerstaff played Beauty.

On Wednesday, April 6, 1859, Frederick Maccabe appeared here and gave his celebrated entertainment entitled ' Begone, Dull Care,' in which he sang ' The Shamrock,' ' The Bould Soger Boy,' and other ditties.   He also appeared as Paddy in the Irish farce entitled *Stand up, Dick , or, Paddy's*

Adventures with an Indian Princess.   The occasion was for
the benefit of Mr. J. Hogan.

On Monday, June 18, 1860, John Coleman appeared as
Hamlet, and on the 19th as Charles Von Moor in *The Robbers ;*
or, The Parricide's Doom, and as Dred in the play of that name.
He was supported by W. S. Branson, Fred Lloyd, Ada Dyas,
M. Henderson, and that fine emotional actress Mrs. W. H.
Dentith.   The serio-comic drama, *The Sailor of France*, was
also performed, but in this Mr. Coleman did not play.

The once well-known drama *Nick of the Woods ; or, The
Jibbenainosay*, was presented on September 17, 1860.   In
it, J. Proctor, the American tragedian, made his first appearance here.

August 17, 1861, witnessed the representation of *The
Corsican Brothers.*   T. H. Glenney (a fine actor), doubled
the parts of Fabian and Louis de Franchi.   It was at the
Adelphi that *The Corsican Brothers* was first played in Liverpool.

On Monday, July 21, 1862, a local drama entitled *Jane
of Liverpool ; or, The Licensed Victualler's Daughter* was
the *pièce de résistance.*   On the same evening another
'Young Roscius' appeared. This was Master William Lunt,
who played during the week Richard III, Hamlet, and other
characters.   It was about this time that our townsman
Mr. James Kiernan acted as call boy at the theatre, while
working during the day as a 'printer's devil' at Mr.
W. McCall's Printing Works in Cartwright Place, Byrom
Street.

In July the theatre came into the hands of William Scholes
Branson, who did much to raise the character of the house.
Mr. Branson had been a member of the celebrated Roxby-
Beverley company, a provincial school much sought after
by budding actors.   He first visited Liverpool about 1838, and
played at the local Royal when, on May 3, 1847, Barry Sullivan
made his first appearance in our town.   'Heavy leads' were
his *forte*, although he also appeared to advantage in comedy.
His Mr. Nicodemus in *The Spectre Bridegroom* was particularly
good, and so were his renderings of Whate (*The Ruby Ring*),
Lurcher (*The Bottle*), Ludovico (*Evadne*), and Bill Graham
(*The Hand of Cards*).

The Adelphi under Mr Branson's management became recognised as the home of spectacular drama   At Christmas excellent pantomimes were given, and on these occasions, as in Mr. Hammond's time, it was quite usual to see lines of carriages reaching as far as Islington.

On September 15, 1862, T H. Glenney and Henry Beverley appeared in *George Barrington, the Gentleman Pickpocket ; or, The Queen Witch and the Man of the Red Hand.* This drama was founded upon a story then running in ' Reynold's Miscellany.'

The Crown Prince ; or, the Buckle of Brilliants, was performed here by members of the 1st L.R V. and others on Thursday, December 4, 1862.   The occasion was Mr. J. W Gladman's complimentary benefit, which was under the patronage of Major Bousfield, Captain Steble, Lieutenant Anderton, Adjutant Holden, etc., etc.

In 1863, Wilson Barrett made his first appearance on the local stage, just three months after making, at Halifax, his professional *début*   At the commencement of his career here, Barrett played ' utility ' parts for a small weekly sum —a trifle of twenty shillings or thereabouts.   Mr. Branson took a liking to this earnest young actor, who was still in his teens, and determined to promote him at the first available opportunity.   This presented itself owing to the inability of one of the players of the company to sustain Hardress Cregan in *The Colleen Bawn,* for which he had been cast.   Mr. Barrett was given the part—his first of importance—and he played it very successfully.

Henry Loraine gave an excellent performance of Macbeth here on Thursday evening, October 30, 1863   He was supported by W. S. Branson, Henry Beverley, George Revill, Walter Crosby, and others.

On April 22, 1864, Mr. Branson revived *A Winter's Tale* in order to commemorate Shakespeare's Tercentenary.   The performance was spoken of as being hampered by the acting, ' which,' says ' The Porcupine,' for April 30, 1864, ' is shy , but the effect of good mountings and stage management goes far to make up for the deficiency, even in this essential particular.' William Champion, father of E J. Lonnen, was stage manager of the theatre at this time.   On May 9, Master John Boulton, an infant prodigy of four, appeared as Richard III, and sustained the character throughout the fifth act.

Dick Turpin's Ride to York was played on March 15, 1865, with Walter Edwin as Dick.   On Thursday, September 14, Matt Robson, Robert Power, Beaumont Kelly, T. Mead, and Mrs. W. H. Dentith played in *Transformed* and *The Bargeman of the Thames.*

On May 20, 1867, the Leno family (including the afterwards celebrated comedian, Dan Leno), were engaged.   Mr. and Mrs. Leno were comic duettists, and the Brothers Leno, clog, boot, and pump dancers.   In ' Hys Book '* Dan Leno relates an amusing story in connection with one of his visits to the Adelphi :—' When we arrived, in order to maintain the dignity of our little company, I got some money from the manager to pay for our luggage being taken to the theatre instead of taking it ourselves.   I called a man with a handcart, whose respectfulness touched me deeply because he was a good deal better dressed than I was.   He loaded his cart with our curious assortment of baggage.   There was a trick bedstead which, bundled together and tied round with rope, was not at all an object of beauty suitable for a nobleman's furniture, and an old tin tray tied in with string formed the bottom of one of the baskets, so that when the cart was piled up with the things it looked more like a cheap eviction than the arrival of a troupe of respectable professionals.

' We were to open at the Adelphi Theatre in Christian Street, and we told the man to take the things to the Adelphi. He touched his cap and went, while I decided that, as I had plenty of time, I would have a walk round the town before going to the theatre, and still reach there as soon as the porter; so away I went and bought some cakes with twopence of the money that the manager had given me to pay the man with. I have a vivid recollection of those cakes, which were of extremely obstinate nature with a speck of jam in the middle. I remember hammering one on a doorstep in order to chip a piece off, and I gave the other to some little girls, who licked off the jam and played hopscotch with the rest.

' When I arrived at the theatre in about an hour's time I found no porter and no luggage.   I spread myself all over

* Pp. 42-6.

the town to look for him, and you can imagine my surprise
when I discovered the man with the bedstead on his back
engaged in violent altercation with two liveried servants on
the steps of the Adelphi Hotel in Lime Street.   He insisted
on putting the luggage in, and the hotel was in a state of siege.
The basket, with the tin tray false bottom had been pitched
out by the hotel people so energetically that it had fallen to
pieces, and the " props " were scattered all over the muddy
street.   My porter was undaunted   He had been told to
put the things in the Adelphi, and he would have them in if
it killed him.   It was a noble and sublime spectacle, but our
belongings were being seriously depreciated.   Some small
boys amongst the interested crowd had found a stuffed dog
which had come out of the basket, and they were playing
football with it, and when I went to rescue the poor, dumb,
stuffed creature they played football with me.

' At last, with the dog under my arm and my clothes
covered with mud, I succeeded in getting near enough to the
porter to explain things.   He was disappointed.   I shall
never forget the look on that man's face if I live to be ninety-
nine.   I never saw a man look with such an earnest desire
to take a human life as he did, and had he raised the bedstead
and brained me where I stood I should not have been at all
surprised.   I should have been sorry, but not surprised

' Well, we collected the scattered property in the face of
a withering fire of criticism from the crowd, and then the porter and I, with the cart, headed a long procession marching to
the theatre.   Liverpool mud is very muddy indeed, and I was
not happy.   Even then our troubles were not ended, for when
we reached Christian Street, one of the wheels came off the
confounded cart, and once again our poor " props " were upset
in the slimy road   For the fourteenth time our porter repeated his entire vocabulary of obscene and profane terms
of general abuse and condemnation, and sent me into a cold
perspiration at the fearful language he used.

' And when at length I reached the theatre, tired, hungry,
muddy, almost in tears, I held out my hand to reward the
honest labourer for his toil.   I gave him all the money I had
left—*one shilling*.   It was a thrilling situation.   The man
staggered ; there was a wild glare in his eyes ; his breath came

and went in short snorts ; he clenched his fists, and—like the heroes of romance—I knew no more.'

In the autumn of 1867 the company included Montague Smythson, H. McDonald, G. H. Pedder, T. C. Davies, Bella Richardson, Fanny Marshall, and Clara Wood.   Mr. Charles Wood was the musical director.   The pantomime of that Christmas was *Harlequin Prince Primrose and Cinderella ; or, Goody Two Shoes, Her Twelve Fairy Daughters, and the Little Magic Glass Slipper*.   The principal characters in this were sustained by H. Munroe, William Champion, W. Morgan (clown), G. Honeywood (harlequin), and G. Sullivan (pantaloon) ; Misses Munroe, Laura Collins, Marion Jones, and Mr. Charles Wood's daughters, Polly and Kissy Wood.   The last-mentioned lady is now Mrs. H. C. Arnold.

In April, 1868, Mr. and Mrs. Charles Sullivan came on a visit.   Sullivan's real name was Charles Gaskin.   Prior to his *début* on the stage at the Queen's, in Dublin, he had been an ostler in Farrell's yard opposite to the theatre.   Later on he changed his name to Charles Sullivan, and as such he lives in the memory of the middle-aged playgoer as the ideal Conn the Shaughraun and Shaun-the-Post.

Poor Charley ! What a fund of wit and humour he possessed !   Once when he was playing in the pantomime of *Daniel O'Rourke and the Eagle* at the Queen's, Dublin, the eagle, a large property bird, lost one of its wings as it soared aloft.   The audience tittered, but Charley turned the incident to good account by exclaiming, 'Begorra, the bird is moultin.' He was witty to the last.   Shortly before he died, the doctor who did not expect the end so soon, left him with the remark, ' Well, Mr. Sullivan, I'll see you in the morning.'   ' Ah yes, doctor,' answered Charley, ' but will *I see you* ? '   And he never did !

In 1868, a number of alterations were carried out in the interior of the Adelphi, which was also redecorated.   The piece with which the season was inaugurated on Saturday, August 22, 1868, was *Macbeth*.   In this, Tulloch appeared as the Thane and Branson as Macduff.   The ' Liverpool Courier,' for August 24, mentioned that Mr. Branson's patrons attended in strong force, 'and made their presence known by demonstrations more real and decided than pleasant or desirable.'   In his address to the audience Branson appealed to his gallery friends to show some consideration for his interests by behaving themselves better than was their wont, at the same time assuring them that their conduct theretofore had done him great injury by preventing the attendance of persons who would otherwise have patronised the boxes.

Though the ' gods ' and ' goddesses ' at the ' Delly ' were nearly always frolicsome, it was from sheer high spirits and natural exuberance.   Few of them could read or write, yet most of them knew Shakespeare off by heart.   Woe betide any unfortunate player who made a slip in the text of a well-known part !   Upon his unlucky head the wrath of the ' Gallery King ' and his satellites soon descended.

For years at the Adelphi it was the practice to give small discs, made of bone, to those entitled to free admission   This custom is said to date back to the ancient Roman theatres, where those entitled to free admission were given small ivory or bone tokens (specimens of which are to be seen in the museum at Naples), on which was depicted a death's head—hence our word ' dead-head.'

At the Adelphi on Saturday evening, March 26, 1869, Osmond Tearle made his professional *début* in the character of Guildenstern in *Hamlet*.   He was then only seventeen   His ' first appearance on any stage,' as the familiar legend has it, had, however, taken place on the occasion of the performance of *Julius Cæsar* by the students of St. Francis Xavier's College, Liverpool, when he undertook the part of Trebonius.   Osmond Tearle was not a native of Liverpool, having been born in Plymouth, on March 8, 1852. His parents migrated to Liverpool when he was quite young.   As a boy he was very fond of reciting, and frequently figured at penny readings in conjunction with the youthful Hall Caine, now the well-known dramatist and novelist.

On Thursday, July 8, 1869, James Carr and Peter Grant took a joint benefit, the former making his first appearance as Tom in *The Dumb Man of Manchester*.   Pantomime, or non-speaking parts, were Mr Carr's particular line of stage business.

It was about this time that Leonard Boyne made his first appearance on the stage   He arrived in Liverpool in 1869 fresh from an army crammer's in Dublin, eager and anxious to learn the art of the stage.   His little stock of sovereigns was spent freely wherever actors congregated, but his prodigality failed to procure for him the right of exhibiting his talents.

'From the theatres to the south of the London Road,' says Henry Herman,* 'Boyne wandered northward to the old Adelphi ; but even there star parts were out of the question. . . . . . . They offered Boyne general utility, at a salary of fifteen shillings a week ; and the budding tragedian did not shine even in that.   Somehow or other things always went wrong with him on the stage.   He would give his letters to the wrong person ; he would go out at the wrong entrance and dash against the *ingénue*. . . . . Then they thought they would try him in another sphere, and he was made prompter.   They carefully explained to him the working of the gas-taps in the prompt corner.   All being marked in plain letters, " Battens," " Floats," "Wing Lights," etc., he could not possibly make a mistake.   " You turn to the right," they said to him, " to turn off, and to the left to turn on."   " I understand" Boyne replied.'   Mr. Boyne tells me that in those days the prompter at the Adelphi always worked the lights.

Night came, and Boyne was at his post with his fingers on the gas-taps.   The play submitted was a short-lived melodrama.   The end of an act had been reached, and the stage was in semi-gloom.   All the lights were out, except the footlights.   The villain had crept into the room and was about to steal the sleeping child from its cradle, when the mother made her appearance, lamp in hand.

'Floats up,' whispered the stage manager.

'Up where ? ' asked Boyne.

'Lights up ! ' was the reply.

'Up where ? ' asked Boyne rather scaredly.

'Turn up the lights, you owl ! ' cried the stage manager. Boyne made a dash at the tap marked ' Floats ' and turned it swiftly.   Out went the lights altogether.

'You d——— fool ! ' cried the stage manager, ' what are you going to do now, you blithering idiot ? '

Boyne drew himself up proudly.

'Yer language is not poloite,' he said, 'an' yer manner is

* ' Between the Whiffs,' p. 16.

not gentlemanly ; besides, I don't think yer know me sufficiently well to swear at me.'

There was some hissing in front, but most of the audience
roared.   Boyne, however, was not again entrusted with the
working of the gas-taps.   After leaving the Adelphi, he
obtained an engagement at fifteen shillings a week at the local
Theatre Royal.   ' The Dramatic Peerage ' (1891), says that
he was engaged for ' responsible business,' with incidental
turns at prompting.   His first appearance on the stage of
the Royal was made as Leybourne in Buckstone's *Flowers of
the Forest*.   After being there a month or two his salary was
increased to eighteen shillings weekly, but he was expected
to play from 12 to 18 parts per week.   In 1871 Mr Boyne
went to the Theatre Royal, Newcastle-on-Tyne.   His subsequent and present success, is, I think, sufficiently well-
known.

When Mr. Branson retired from the management of the
Adelphi in 1869 he was succeeded by Thomas Theodore Heath,
of the Colosseum in Paradise Street, who introduced variety
entertainments.   The following year, the establishment was
known as the Adelphi Music Hall and Theatre of Varieties.
Mr. Isaac de Frece was the lessee, and Mr. Harry de Frece,
the manager.   In the same year the house was called the
People's Concert Hall and Theatre of Varieties In October,
1870, the Lupino Troupe appeared, as did also Unthan, the
armless wonder. On October 18, 1871, the theatre was opened
by Mr. Lindo Courtenay, who brought for his opening attraction Fred Wright's company in *A Quarter of a Million of Money*.
In 1873, Mr. J. Pitney Weston, formerly of the Royal, was
the lessee, and called the house the New Albert Theatre.
On December 26 of that year he produced a pantomime of
the good old-fashioned sort, entitled *Little Bo-Peep* On Friday,
January 16, 1874, Weston took a farewell benefit, upon
which occasion he played Hamlet, and Branson the Ghost
and Laertes.   In 1875 the theatre was under the management
of James Carr.   In the stock company were Edmund
Tearle, Basil Henry, George D. Clarance, George Whyte, E.
V. Campbell, Clara Reed, and Clara Henderson.   ' Hague's
Journal,' for July, 1875, said that ' the company at the Adelphi
is meeting with the success they deserve.   With careful
management a new era seems in store for the old place.'

Towards the close of 1875 the Adelphi was under the management of Henry Leslie and Lindo Courtenay.   Afterwards Edward Trevanion became proprietor and manager.   He inaugurated drama here on the two-houses-a-night principle. Mr. Trevanion had at one time, in addition to the Adelphi, the Prince's Theatre, Blackburn, and the Circus in St. Helens. In 1883 a novelty was introduced in the shape of five Richards in one night—five gentlemen playing an act each in *Richard III.*

On January 22, 1884, W. S. Branson died at his residence, Caxton House, Fairfield, Liverpool, and was buried in Smithdown Road Cemetery.   He was 74 years of age.   Edward Trevanion successfully directed the destinies of the theatre down to his death in May, 1887.   During his illness he found a loving comforter and assiduous nurse in his wife, professionally known as Clare Eversleigh.   After his death the theatre was carried on by his executors, with the assistance of the late Barry Stuart as business manager.   Mr. Stuart was always a favourite with Adelphi patrons, as were Basil Henry, Maggie Stuart, and Clara Scott.   In the autumn of 1887 Barry Stuart was the sole responsible manager of the theatre.   Afterwards he became the lessee and manager with a willing and worthy lieutenant in Mr. G. D. Clarance, who later on became manager, with Mr. Frank Wilson as the lessee.   In its latter days the Adelphi was run as a variety theatre on the two-houses-a-night principle.   Since the magistrates refused to license the house for dramatic entertainments the theatre has been occupied by the Liverpool Gymnastic Club, Limited.

THE LIVER THEATRE.

In the latter part of the eighteenth century the site of the Liver Theatre was occupied by an orchard and garden, belonging to a Mr. Brooks, great-uncle to Rector Brooks, after whom Brooks' Alley was named.   Church Street was not paved until 1760, and the parapet not ;flagged till 1816. Few houses had been erected in the street up to the close of the eighteenth century, but, after the dawn of the nineteenth shops and houses sprang into existence very quickly.

One of the new buildings was opened about the 'twenties with the high-flown designation of ' The Dominion of Fancy.' Its walls were adorned with mirrors and ornate decorations, and it was used principally for balls, parties, and the exhibition of dioramas.

It is a far cry, I know, from Church Street, Liverpool, to the Black Forest in Germany ; but, if Mr. John Scott—who kept in the early part of the last century, an oil and colour shop in the Strand—had not amassed a large fortune by the sale of an indigo dye, which he named the ' Old True Blue ' (the basis of which he had discovered by chance in the Black Forest, from noting the deposit left by a particular kind of wood), the probability is that there would have been no Adelphi Theatre, London, or Liver Theatre, Liverpool.   Having bought property extensively in the metropolis, Mr. Scott built the Sans Pareil (afterwards converted into the Adelphi), for the exhibiting of his daughter's special talents—those of authoress and actress.   In 1816 he disposed of the theatre— which cost him £10,000—for £25,000.   He then lived retired for some years, but about 1824 migrated to Liverpool.*

In response to a generally expressed desire on the part of the inhabitants for a second theatre in Liverpool, Mr. Scott decided to turn ' The Dominion of Fancy ' into a theatre Accordingly a small stage—which was situated at the Church Street end of the building—was erected, a useful company engaged, and new scenery and machinery provided.   The name also underwent a change, ' The Dominion of Fancy ' being altered to the Pantheon Theatre.   The reason, doubtless, why Mr. Scott chose that title was because he had acted at the metropolitan theatre of the same name in Catherine Street where, it is interesting to note, the great novelist, Charles Dickens, had also performed, the manager of the establishment being no less a personage than Mr. Davenport, the prototype of the famous Vincent Crummles.

The Pantheon, which was situated on the first floor above some shops, extended to Brooks Alley, and the entrances to the boxes and pit were in Church Street.   The gallery and stage entrances were in Brooks Alley.   The theatre was tastefully decorated, and held from 800 to 1,000 people.   At

* In 1829 he built the unlucky Adelphi Theatre in Dublin.

the beginning of its career the Pantheon was only open from November to Easter.

The theatre was not exclusively devoted to the regular drama as, early in 1829, Madame Tussaud exhibited, her waxwork figures there for some considerable time. These included ' counterfeit presentments' of Dan O'Connell, and Burke and Hare. Another attraction was the centrifugal railway.

About the end of 1829, or the beginning of 1830, the Pantheon came under the direction of Richard Malone Raymond * and W. J. Hammond.† Prior to this both had been popular performers at the Theatre Royal, in Williamson Square. They re-christened Scott's theatre the Liver. For many years there was placed over the main entrance in Church Street a handsomely carved and gilded representation of the fabulous bird from which Liverpool is supposed to take its name. This emblem is still to be seen over the present shops.

Under Messrs. Raymond and Hammond's spirited management the Liver gained great popularity. In 1830 Paulo and Ellar appeared in pantomime ; and Mrs. Douglas Jerrold in *The Maid of the Inn.* On April 28, 1830, there was produced a new local drama, written by a Liverpool lady, entitled *The Siege of Liverpool ; or, the Days of Prince Rupert.*

In 1831 a popular burletta here was *Mr. Thomas Tomkins; or, 56 Ranelagh Street.* T. P. Cooke made his first appearance here on May 9 of the same year, as William in *Black-Eyed Susan.* He frequently acted on this stage.

On November 12, 1832, Madame Céleste appeared here for the first time, the pieces being *The French Spy* and *The Wizard Skiff.* Céleste was a frequent visitor at the Liver. Mons. Leclerq was the ballet master and pantomime director at this time. January 5, 1835, saw the first performance of that phenomenal success, *Tom and Jerry,* which had an uninterrupted run of eight weeks. It was at the Liver in the late 'thirties that the famous Sims Reeves obtained one of his first engagements—that of ' singing walking gent '—the emolument being thirty shillings weekly. It was also at this theatre that my good friend, the late James Carr, made, when

* Died January 13, 1862, aged 62.   † Died August 23, 1848, aged 49.

three months old, his first appearance on the stage, the piece
being the farce of *Mr. and Mrs White.*

Early in 1836 Messrs. Raymond and Hammond arranged
to present the drama *Sarah, The Jewess*, which had
previously been played not only at the Royal, but also at the
Amphi' and the Queen's.   Be it noted that the piece
had never been licensed by the Lord Chamberlain for
representation.   The management of the Royal no sooner
heard of the intended performance at the Liver than they
decided to put their powers into force, and stop the production.
Messrs. Raymond and Hammond wrote to the ' Liverpool
Mercury,' and complained of the repressive attitude of the
Royal management   They said, ' the patent granted to the
Royal empowers its owner to play only such pieces as are
licensed by the Lord Chamberlain. . . . . The monopoly is
wielded against the public, and they are told that they shall
not have rational entertainment at a moderate price, nor
any such as an individual may please to give them, when, and
at what charge he thinks proper '

Commenting on this the ' Mercury,' for February 12,
1836, said—' The case seems to be one of great hardship, so
far as the managers of the Liver are concerned, and the public
have good reason to complain, not, perhaps, against the lessee
of the Theatre Royal, but against the system of monopoly
which shuts out all competition, and gives them the exclusive power to provide such theatrical entertainments, and at
such prices as they may think proper.   It is high time that that
monopoly should be put an end to, and we cannot help thinking that the mode in which it has been exercised in the present
instance will contribute something towards bringing about
its abolition.   We have some reason to believe that the
bill for the regulation of dramatic performances, which passed
the Commons, and was thrown out by the Lords, last year,
will be again brought forward during the present session.
If it be, we trust that the hands of the mover will be
strengthened by a petition from the inhabitants of Liverpool '

In 1836 Mr. Hammond dissolved partnership with Mr.
Raymond, who remained in possession of the Liver   Mr.
Raymond, in response to a generally expressed desire on the
part of the inhabitants to have a second patent theatre in
Liverpool, decided to petition the Government to grant the

P

same rights and privileges to the Church Street house as were
held by the Theatre Royal.   The petition had the support
of the Corporation, and it was signed at the theatre, as well
as at the newspaper offices, by 11,000 persons.   The petition
was forwarded to Parliament on July 14, 1841, one copy
having been lodged at the Lord Chamberlain's office on the
twenty-ninth of the preceding April.   The following is a
copy :—

‘ To the Queen's most Excellent Majesty.

‘ May it please your Majesty, We, the undersigned, your
faithful subjects, gentlemen, merchants, bankers, manufac-
turers, and other inhabitants of Liverpool, and strangers constantly resorting thereto, humbly beg to approach Your most
Gracious Majesty with sentiments of the utmost loyalty and
attachment to Your Majesty's Royal Person, Family, and
Government.
‘ We humbly beg to represent to Your Majesty, that about
the year 1771 a patent was obtained from one of Your Majesty's
Royal predecessors to establish a theatre in the town and port
of Liverpool.   That when such patent was granted the population of Liverpool was little more than 34,000, whilst it now
amounts to about 250,000.   That although there are numerous
licensed theatres in London, two in Dublin, and two in Glasgow,
affording the inhabitants of those cities the advantage of fair
competition in dramatic representations, the inhabitants of
Liverpool (the second town in England) and its visitors, are
still subject to the exclusive management of only one patent
or licensed theatre.
‘ That the monopoly enjoyed by the present holders of
the patent granted in 1771, deprives the inhabitants of Liverpool and the numerous persons resorting thereto of the advan-
tages which would result from just competition, and we are
humbly of opinion that a second patent or licensed theatre
would tend to improve and elevate the character of the drama
in this great commercial town.
‘ We therefore humbly request that Your most Gracious
Majesty will be pleased to direct letters patent to be issued
to the   Right honourable the Earl of Sefton, Sir Joshua
Walmsley, knight, of Wavertree Hall, near Liverpool, and

James Aspinall, esquire, of Liverpool, Your Majesty's justices of the peace for the county of Lancaster, and their assigns, in trust for and on behalf of the community of the town of Liverpool, and its charities, for an additional patent or licensed theatre and company of players in the Town of Liverpool, suburbs, or neighbourhood thereof. And we humbly pray that Your most Gracious Majesty may long live to reign over a free and happy people.'

Mr. Clarke, the lessee of the Theatre Royal, naturally objected to the petition.   In a letter, dated August 10, 1841, to the Marquess of Normanby, he stated that any other patent house would injure the Theatre Royal. He even offered to forego the tenancy of the theatre, and place the patent at the disposal of the trustees named in the petition.

The trustees for the proprietors of the Theatre Royal also objected to the petition.   They said ' that the shares in the said property have become greatly depreciated, and that Mr. Clarke, who was for a number of years the manager of this theatre, has been induced by a great outlay, and a reduction of the rent, to enter into an agreement with Your petitioners for a lease of the said theatre for seven years, and he has recently given notice, that in consequence of the application for a second patent theatre, he will, in January next, quit the theatre, and submit to the consequences of a breach of his agreement, alleging that to hold the theatre for the remainder of his term would be absolute ruin to him, if a patent for an additional theatre is granted ; and he alleges that, although he has performers of the first talent from the metropolitan theatres, the receipts of the theatre up to this period have not cleared his expenses.'*

It was also pointed out by the proprietors of the Theatre Royal that, although the population had increased threefold since the Theatre Royal had been erected, a change in the tastes of the inhabitants of the town had discouraged theatrical enterprise. In addition they had also to contend with religious objections on the part of no inconsiderable portion of the community. Further, the second patent would be an infringement of the patent rights secured to the Theatre Royal by the Act of Parliament of 1771.

* Mr. Clarke retired from the management of the Theatre Royal about the end of 1841

The petition for licensing a second theatre in Liverpool was granted, and the warrant signed at Windsor on September 1, 1841. The Lord Chamberlain ordered the patent to be drafted, but afterwards had doubts of the power of the Crown to grant the request of the petitioners and communicated with Sir James Graham, Secretary of State, who placed the matter before the Attorney General. The latter gentleman was in favour of the grant, and the Lord Chamberlain was notified that no objection existed in that department to the issue of letters patent for a second theatre, and orders were accordingly given that the patent should proceed in the usual manner. The applicants considered the matter substantially concluded ; Mr. Raymond paid £100 towards the fees, and in addition entered into several important contracts.

When the matter was placed before the Patent office, the same doubts occurred to the head of the department as had already assailed the Lord Chamberlain. The application was returned to the Lord Chamberlain who considered it his duty to forward it again to the Home Office. On October 4, 1841, Mr. Raymond was informed that ' Sir James Graham does not propose to recommend the grant of letters patent for a second theatre at Liverpool.' And there the matter ended.

In the face of this, however, Mr. Raymond was obliged to open the Liver in order to try and meet the heavy engagements he had entered into upon the faith of the Royal order. On January 30, 1843, he informed Sir James Graham, the Secretary of State, that he was ' beset with informers, and many of the artists engaged in the theatre are being at this moment prosecuted. Appeals to a jury at Westminster must follow, to prevent the infliction of heavy penalties (which many are unable to pay), and before we resort to such a tribunal, I must earnestly, but respectfully, request you to reconsider the subject. . . . . The subject is at this moment causing a strong sensation in Liverpool. My theatre is prosecuted by the proprietors of the present Theatre Royal, who have frequently acted unlicensed pieces themselves, and now try to make me suffer for what they, or their agents have been repeatedly guilty of. Thus situated, Sir, I appeal to your sense of justice to consider the unfortunate position in which I am placed.   My means, my liberty are at stake, as well as the fate of others.'*

Mr. Raymond was subsequently fined £50.   A similar penalty would have been enforced against three of the principal performers engaged at the Liver Theatre had not Mr. Raymond compromised the matter by paying a further sum of twenty five pounds to the different charitable institutions in the town.

The repressive attitude adopted towards Mr. Raymond by the proprietors and lessees of the Theatre Royal was primarily the cause of the passing in 1843 of ' The Act for Regulating Theatres,' whereby the patent houses lost all their ancient privileges, save that of being exempt from a yearly renewal of the license to act.   The Liver Theatre was the first theatre in England to be licensed under the new Act, under which statute the theatres of this country are now licensed. It is also worthy of note that the Act abolished at one fell swoop the invidious enactments, under which actors and actresses had long been designated ' Rogues, Vagabonds, Sturdy Beggars, and Vagrants,' epithets which were severely felt by every member of the profession.

The re-opening of the Royal Liver† took place on Monday, October 9, 1843, under the direction of Mr. Raymond, the *pièce de résistance* being *The Rivals*, followed by *Cramond Brig or, The Gude Man of Ballangeich* (in which *the* Mackay played Jock Howieson), and *High Life Below Stairs*.

In his opening address Mr. Raymond said :—' I take this opportunity to return grateful thanks to the inhabitants of Liverpool and vicinity, who have on so many occasions honoured with their signatures and support, the various petitions to Government, to legalise this favourite establishment.   I am happy to announce that, chiefly owing to their kindness as well as an arduous struggle on my own part, this theatre is at length placed on a footing second to none, either in or out of the metropolis, being now legally authorised by the magistrates of Liverpool, according to Act of Parliament, to represent and perform the legitimate drama in all its various forms, including tragedy, comedy, opera, farce, interlude,

* Parliamentary Papers, 1843, Vol. 44.
† The use of the prefix ' Royal ' was one way of getting even with the proprietors and lessee of the Theatre Royal, as previous to the passing of the ' Act for Regulating Theatres,' no playhouse (save the patent theatres), dare use the term. Mr. Raymond's playbills also bore a large-sized drawing of the Royal Arms.

pantomime, and every other entertainment of the stage with-out restriction.'

In the autumn of 1843 Phelps, the great tragedian, com-menced a ' starring ' engagement at the Liver. During his visit he played Hamlet, Shylock, Gloster, the Stranger, Sir Edward Mortimer, Sir Giles Overreach, and Jaques.

Towards the end of 1843, the house was designated the ' Theatre Royal, Church Street,' afterwards going back to its old name—the Liver. Mr. Raymond's first dramatic season under the new order of things terminated on March 16, 1844.

In 1844, Sam Collins, vocalist and comedian, from the Covent Garden and Haymarket Theatres, performed for six nights as Paul Clifford in *Paul Clifford ; or, the Lost Heir*. This favourite performer (whose real name by the way, was Samuel Vagg), opened in 1862, Collins's Music Hall in Islington Green, London.

Commencing August 12, 1844, the theatre was, for a short time, under the management of the celebrated tragedian, Gustavus Vaughan Brooke, who leased the house from Mr. Raymond, and while here performed a variety of parts.

J. B. Buckstone, Mrs. Fitzwilliam, John Liptrot Hatton,* ' Jimmy ' Lunt (father of the Milton family), H. Bedford (nephew of Paul Bedford), and Tom Thumb also appeared about this time. Miss Emmeline Montague (afterwards Mrs. Henry Compton), performed Desdemona to Charles Pitt's Othello on June 26, 1845.

In 1845 the theatre came under the management of Mr. C. F. Marshall. In September of the same year Mrs. H. P. Grattan, of Covent Garden and the Princess's Theatres, opened the Liver.

Mrs. Grattan, who was a native of Liverpool, left the Liver in March, 1846, and was succeeded by Mr. James Mackenzie, junr. After being closed for a time the theatre re-opened in January, 1847, as the Grand Casino de Naples, under the dir-ection of Mr. Julian Adams, who brought his famous band.

In 1847 the attractions comprised the Ethiopian Seren-aders (February) ; a panorama, by Telbin (April) ; and from

---

* The celebrated musical composer who was born at 31 Whitechapel, Liverpool, on October 12, 1809.

May to July ' Baron ' Renton Nicholson's* *tableaux vivants* and *poses plastiques.*

The theatre was re-opened on August 30, 1847, by Mr. J. C. Hay with *Richelieu* and *The Turnpike Gate.* In September of 1848, Robert Houdin, the conjurer, made his appearance. On October 9, Mr. James Rodgers, lessee of the Theatres Royal, Hereford, Stafford, and Ludlow, assumed control. He gave dramas and ballets, but soon had to reduce his prices.

In 1849 Isabel Dickinson fulfilled a starring engagement. There was a good house on the opening night. Towards the close of the performance Miss Dickinson abruptly left the stage, followed by the other players The curtain was lowered, but the audience still retained their seats, unable to grasp the situation. A cry of ' Fire ' was raised, but, fortunately, it did not create any serious alarm. As a matter of fact the ' pittites ' only shouted ' Turn him out ! ' Afterwards the audience quietly left the theatre, only to find on reaching Church Street that the front and shutters of one of the shops underneath were in flames, with firemen and police in full and busy attendance.

In April, 1849, an operatic season was inaugurated. In July Madame Warton opened the theatre with her original and classical Walhalla entertainment. Mr. Robert Edgar was the last manager of the theatre. He did not hold it long, as by May 11, 1850, the theatre had been converted by Mr. J. Carmichael into the Liver Drapery Establishment, which it remained until taken as a music warehouse by Mr. William Lea, who, a little while ago, made two additional shops out of the premises.

THE SANS PAREIL THEATRE.

In the second week in June, 1825, there was opened at what was then No. 18, Great Charlotte Street, a large circular wooden building known as the New Rotunda. Stonehouse in his ' Streets of Liverpool,'† states the building was erected by a Mr. Marshall, and that it was known as ' Marshall's Moving Panorama.' At any rate, in the early part

---

* ' Baron ' Nicholson was the moving spirit of the infamous Judge and Jury Clubs.
† Third edition, p 80

of its career, panoramas were frequently exhibited.   At the opening in June, 1825, the panorama of the Bay and City of Naples was exhibited. This was succeeded in February, 1826, by a panorama of the City of Venice.   Later in the same year the place was converted into a theatre and opened by Mr. W. J. Holloway as the Sans Pareil.

Mr. Holloway came of a well-known theatrical family, one of whose members had gained celebrity by playing Richard III on horseback at Astley's. Others of the Holloways had ' portable ' theatres.   There are still some members of the family in the profession.

Success must have crowned Mr. Holloway's efforts, as in the following year (1827) he made the theatre more commodious and comfortable.   Messrs. Blanchard and Baker were two of the leading actors.   There were two performances daily, the first commencing at half-past five o'clock (doors opened at five), and the second at seven. The theatre boasted a pit and gallery, admission being sixpence and threepence, respectively.   The performances were ' by permission of the Worshipful the Mayor.'

Good acting was the rule, not the exception ; and the pantomimes at Christmas are said to have been excellent. The patrons of this theatre were drawn from the poorest classes, yet so prosperous was the house that the number of copper coins taken at the door by Holloway and his wife was truly prodigious.   Mr. Holloway used to stand at the pit door, and ' Missus ' attended to the gallery entrance. Afterwards the former would go into the pit to pack the people so that no space should be lost.   To expedite the ' packing ' process Holloway thought nothing of giving a boy a box on the ears to emphasise his remarks.   This type of showman has vanished into the dim and distant past.

In 1831, Holloway decided to rebuild his theatre, and during the recess the company performed in the spacious hall adjoining the King's Arms* in Castle Street.   Mr. Holloway christened his temporary theatre (the entrance to which was through an arch-way in Cook Street), the Sans Pareil. The opening performance took place on November 28, 1831, and the programme consisted of *Trial by Battle; or, Heaven Defend*

---

* The site is now occupied by the branch Bank of England.

the Right ; a sailor's hornpipe (in character) by Miss Holloway; the comic vaudeville *Paul the Rich, and Peter the Poor*, with a rustic ballet ; a comic extravaganza by Mr. Watson and a favourite song by Mr. Chickeley.   The evening's entertainment concluded with a grand serious piece, entitled *The Fall of Algiers in 1830 (by sea and land).* Boxes were 2s. ; pit, 1s. ;   and gallery, 6d.   There was half-price at a quarter to nine.

Here, as at Great Charlotte Street, Holloway set forth his plays in an attractive manner.   On the production of *The Ice Witch* on December 26, 1831, the ' Liverpool Mercury ' said :—' The scenery (entirely new), is highly picturesque, gorgeous and beautiful, surpassing all the former efforts of the artists of this establishment. . . . . The dresses and decorations are at once correct and costly ;   the dances tasteful and the music (original and selected), is characteristic and pleasing.   We advise those who may not have been able to obtain admission this week in consequence of the crowded state of the theatre, to take the earliest opportunity of gratifying their young friends and remunerating the spirited proprietor for the immense outlay that must have been expended on its production.'

In January, 1832, R. Bradbury, junr. (nephew to Grimaldi's great rival, Robert Bradbury), played clown in a pantomime here.   Cony and Flynn's performing dogs were seen in March.

After Holloway left the Cook Street ' Sans Pareil,' it was taken by a fanatic named Aitken, who converted it into a chapel, where he conducted so-called religious services. His fanatical ravings had the effect of obtaining for him thousands of disciples.   They afterwards migrated to Hope Hall.*   Samuel Warren, author of ' The Diary of a Late Physician,' drew public attention to Aitken and his flock in an article in ' Blackwood's Magazine.'   The scenes which took place, especially in the vaults beneath, were extraordinary.   The fanatics would meet to pray, jump up, tear their hair and clothes, leap over the forms, throw themselves down on the floor, and literally ' lick the dust.' The shrieks of the poor creatures were fearful.   The women in

* Opened in 1836.

their excitement were worse than the men, and they became so exhausted by their violence that they often lay on the floor as if dead.   But to return to the New Sans Pareil in Great Charlotte Street.

The opening performance took place on Monday, November 26, 1832, when *Eugene Aram, Damon and Pythias,* and *Wallace, The Hero of Scotland,* were submitted.   During the recess the theatre was fitted with boxes (1s. 6d.), pit (1s). and gallery (6d.)   Cartlich was the acting manager.   He was succeeded by Mr. Charles Leclerq, who was for many years favourably known in dramatic circles as a skilful ballet-master, pantomimist, and stage manager.   He was father of the accomplished Carlotta and Rose Leclerq, the latter of whom was born in Liverpool.   Monsieur Leclerq was a little stout man, while Madame was tall and stately with *prononcé* features.

In the early 'forties T. C. King, the afterwards celebrated tragedian, played leading parts for 18s. per week.   He was then about eighteen, and Mr. Holloway took a liking to this painstaking young actor.   Whatever the reason, King was not a favourite with the patrons of the Sans Pareil.   Towards the conclusion of the season Mr. Holloway offered him the increased terms of 25s. weekly to return, but King declined with thanks.

Holloway was astounded at what he termed the foolishness of refusing such an offer, especially as young King had just taken unto himself, or was about to take, a wife.   He asked for an explanation.   ' Well, sir,' replied Tom, ' the fact is I don't like your audience, and, what's more, they don't like me.'   ' Nonsense ! ' exclaimed Holloway, ' you come back next year, and you will prove a big favourite.   You'll have another audience altogether, as by that time all these beggars will be either hung or transported ! '

It is highly probable that some of the patrons of the Sans Pareil had, more than once, seen the inside of a prison.   The Government enquiry into juvenile delinquency in Liverpool showed as much.   In fact the proportion of male juveniles to the whole number of male prisoners committed to the Liverpool Borough Gaol was four per cent. more than the average proportion in the six metropolitan prisons.   In the course of his enquiry, the Inspector from the Home Office examined 91 boys of various ages who were then incarcerated in the Liverpool Borough Gaol.   From his report I cull the following :—' Perhaps in no other town in the United Kingdom has the demoralising influence of low theatres and amusements upon children been so decidedly experienced as at Liverpool. The number of children frequenting the Sans Pareil, the Liver, and other theatres of a still lower description is almost incredible.   The streets in front, and the avenues leading to them, may be seen on the nights of performances, occupied by crowds of boys, who have not been able to possess themselves of the few pence required for admission.'

In order to obtain the necessary admission money the boys stole from their parents and others.   The Sans Pareil and Liver were not their only favourite resorts, as they bestowed their patronage upon the Royal, the Amphi', and the Queen's, as well as upon the Penny Hop, in Hood Street, and the shows opposite the present Custom House.*

One youth in the Borough Gaol deposed that he ' first met with bad companions at the Sans Pareil.   The first thing I did at the Sans Pareil was when the place was loosing ; we used to put our hands over the rails when the people were going down stairs, and take off shawls, hats, or anything else ; the people that had lost them could not get back, the crowd was so strong.   If the hat was a good one, we used to put our own inside, and put it on our heads ; we also used to creep under the seats ; strangers would have their pockets hanging down (men or women), we used to cut them off sometimes. I have found bottles with liquor in them, copper, oranges, and other things ; in the women's we sometimes found purses. My father has often said those cursed places have been my ruin.'†

In the ' Liverpool Mercury ' for April 7, 1843, Holloway announced that ' after 15 Successful Seasons in this Establishment, and three previous in another part of the town. . . . .

* These shows were located on the site of the Old Custom House in Canning Place. An advertisement in the ' Liverpool Mercury,' (January 17, 1840), stated that there could be seen alive, ' A Child without either Legs or Arms ; also his Wonderful Brother, with Two Heads, Four Hands, and Three Legs—natives of Hertfordshire.   A Colt with only One Eye in the middle of its Forehead.   Also the Hampshire Pig, with Two Heads, Three Eyes, Two Mouths, and Three sets of Teeth, with a Wonderful Crown on its Head.'
† Parliamentary Papers, 1852, Vol. VII.

In consequence of New Streets' Improvements, he relinquishes the present Building after this week, as it is to be taken down.' And so ended the career of the Sans Pareil.

THE AMPHITHEATRE AND THE ROYAL COURT.

In 1824, a sewer burst under the Olympic Circus, in Christian Street, causing the foundations to become insecure and necessitating expensive alterations. The financial responsibility for the repairs bred a quarrel between Mr. John Cooke and the proprietors of the Olympic. The former personally decided to start an opposition circus of his own, and cast about him for a suitable site.

On Thursday, February 10, 1825, Mr. Cooke, through the medium of 'Gore's General Advertiser' informed the inhabitants ' that he had purchased all that piece or parcel of land situate in Gt. Charlotte Street and Roe Street, in or near Queen Square, for the erection of a New Olympic Circus ; the present one in Christian Street not being large enough for the very magnificent spectacles Mr. Cooke has in contemplation to produce in future.' The land purchased by Cooke is stated to have belonged to a Mr. John Leigh, whose residence was situated thereabouts. Great Charlotte Street which takes its name from George the Third's consort, was not laid out until about 1785, about which period Queen Square was projected. It was not, however, until about 1796 that Great Charlotte Street was actually made a thoroughfare.

The first stone of the new building, which was built by subscription, was laid on November 27, 1825, and in the short space of three months ' Cooke's New Circus,' as it was styled, was ready for opening. In dealing with the initial performance on Monday, February 27, 1826, the ' Liverpool Mercury,' for March 3, says :—' This place of amusement, the rapid erection of which under no very favourable auspices has astonished everyone, opened with great *éclat* on Monday evening. When completed, for as yet, it is only partially decorated, and altogether in a very unfinished state, it will be a credit to the town, and a lasting monument to Mr. Cooke's

persevering industry.   It is very spacious, much larger, indeed, than the Theatre Royal, and exhibits even now indications of ultimately ranking amongst the most elegant theatres
in the kingdom.   The enthusiasm of the audience on this,
to the proprietor, truly gratifying occasion, exceeded all
bounds.   Scarcely were the members of the orchestra (which
by the way, is very numerous and efficient), seated to play
' God save the King,' when the whole house arose simultaneously
in cheers, long and loud, which were repeated at intervals
during the evening ;   particularly as the splendid scenery,
incidental to *Timour the Tartar*, presented itself.   An address
was delivered by the stage manager, Mr. M'Gibbon, which, as
well as the speaker, was warmly applauded.   He read, also,
the certificate of three eminent surveyors, appointed by the
Mayor to examine the strength of the building, from whose
report it would seem, that, in the erection of his theatre, Mr.
Cooke had not been less mindful of its stability than of its
splendour.'   The prices of admission ranged from 3s. 6d. to 1s.

Opposite the stage-door in Rose Street, on a spot now
covered by the north-end of the premises occupied by Messrs.
Ryland and Sons, Limited, was once situated the ancient
Fall-well.   To this well ' Ye whole towne in generell,' says
Sir Edward Moore in his ' Rental ' (1667), had to send ' for
each drope of water (to) wase with, or boule pease.'*

The Circus had not long been opened when the lessees
of the Royal prosecuted Cooke for performing a stage-play,
Rob Roy, to wit, without a license.   Despite this, dramatic
and equestrian performances became the staple attraction.
Diddear and Elton appeared here in March, 1827, as Tom and
Logic in the very successful play of *Tom and Jerry*.   On
April 6 following, Cooke took a ' bespeak ' when Herring
played Paul Pry in *Paul Pry at Dover*.   The same month
saw performed *Harlequin and the Magic Punch Bowl ; or, the
Fairy Revels*.   Ellar, a prince among harlequins, was the
spangled hero, and Signor Paulo, clown.   The burletta announced for Ellar's benefit was prohibited by the lessees
of the Royal, as it was an infringement of their rights and

---

* ' When the well was filled up (about the year 1790), the water was diverted to the
residence of William Roe (after whom Roe Street was called), the site of which is
now occupied by the Stork Hotel in Queen Square.'   *Vide* Herdman's ' Pictorial Relics
of Ancient Liverpool.'   During some recent alterations at the Royal Court Theatre the
situation of the old well was laid bare.

privileges.   Batty, of equestrian celebrity, came in October. Towards the close of the year the Circus was leased by Messrs. Wyatt and Farrell.   It was then called 'Cooke's Royal Amphitheatre.'

In January and February, 1828, a curiously entitled entertainment, *Striking Characters ; or, A Hit if it Pleases*, was submitted.   In it, Dick Cortes ' the pet of the fancy,' Young Dutch Sam, Jem Ward, the champion of England, and Stockman were announced to give pugilistic exhibitions. *Paul Jones* followed.   On May 2, 1828, John Cooke, ' the late proprietor and manager,' took a benefit.

Andrew Ducrow opened the Amphitheatre on December 26, 1828, with a dramatic and equestrian company.   He had the theatre again in 1829 and 1830.

The author of ' Stage Reminiscences by an Old Stager '* gives some interesting particulars of Ducrow's visit to Liverpool in 1829.   The writer of the little book referred to was a clever stage machinist, formerly in the employ of Ducrow, and also with Madame Vestris at the Olympic in London.

' I have already mentioned,' he tells us, ' that he (Ducrow) acquired a lease of the Amphitheatre at Liverpool ; and about the middle of November, when we were playing at Newcastle-upon-Tyne, I was despatched to the former town to prepare the house for opening on Boxing Night.   The managers of the Theatre Royal there, Messrs. Lewis and Banks, were aware of our intention, and had made up their minds to hurt our business, if possible.   Accordingly, when I arrived in Liverpool, I found the dead walls of the city covered with posters announcing the forthcoming appearance of a then fashionable " star," no other than the celebrated trained elephant of Siam, " Mdlle. Dejeek," as she was called.   This ponderous performer had been introduced to the London public by Yates at the Adelphi, and it was now announced that she would make her first bow to a Liverpool audience on Easter Monday evening, in a piece prepared for her.   I at once determined to apprise the governor of the pachydermatous opposition with which we were threatened.   Before writing to him, however, I discovered that Wombwell was in the town with his menagerie, that the latter included a performing elephant, and that business was very queer with old Jerry.

* Glasgow : James Hedderwick and Sons (1866), p. 153.

Putting this and that together, I had glimmerings of a plan to forestall our opponents, and I communicated the idea to Ducrow, asking him at the same time to come over himself, as soon as possible, and take stock of the position on the spot. With characteristic promptitude he came to Liverpool by the first mail after receiving my letter, and we at once had an interview with old Wombell. The upshot was that, business being so bad with him, Jerry agreed to let Ducrow have the loan of every animal in his collection if he liked, on the latter's own terms. This bargain having been struck, Andrew turned to me, and, rubbing his hands, remarked that no pair of Englishmen living should beat him if he knew it; he would shew them what Andrew, the tight-rope boy from the old Circus* could do, now he was a manager. " You go to London to-night " he added, " get two of the best scene painters you can find, and bring them down with you by the first mail. Tell the tailor and the property-man to send everything Eastern in the house—go to Fairbrother's (the printer) and tell him to send down 1,000 of the four-sheet elephant posters—and there's fifty pounds for you till we meet next week ! "

' That night I left by the mail for London, and next day was fortunate enough to get through my commissions so expeditiously that I was able to start for Liverpool in the evening, having managed to secure as an artist the celebrated Mr. Danson, the very man whom I knew the governor would be best pleased at having. Mr. Danson brought down his own assistant with him as second hand, and between the two they soon covered the canvas in a manner in every way satisfactory. In the other departments the work was pushed forward with equal vigour, a good dramatic company was engaged to *support* Wombell's lot, and on Boxing Night (?) we produced the Grand Eastern Spectacle, entitled *The Elephant of Siam*, thus, to their intense disgust, having the start of the Theatre Royal folks by nearly three months (?). The piece was a triumphant success, and we played it three times a day during the Christmas holidays, and twice a day for a month afterwards. So great was the hit made, that offers of engagements came pouring in on every hand, and the result was that we made a tour of the three kingdoms with it. Thus Andrew took the wind out of his rivals' sails completely, and when the real Simon

* The Olympic Circus in Christian Street, Liverpool.

Pure followed (Mdlle. Dejeek), that unfortunate quadruped was in almost every case a dead failure.'*

In 1830 the Amphitheatre was under the management of Mr. R. Armistead. The handsome front of the building in Great Charlotte Street consisted of stucco-work, and was erected by Mr. Armistead. The exterior comprised three stories, of which the lowermost one was rusticated. Four Corinthian pilasters supported the pediment. According to J. G. Underhill's MSS,† in the Liverpool Free Library, the Amphi' at that time was capable of accommodating from 3,000 to 4,000 persons. The length of the building was 135 feet by 76 feet wide. The stage was 51 feet long, and the proscenium opening $41\frac{1}{2}$ feet.

' The front of the three tiers of boxes and galleries,' says Underhill, ' presents to the eye a prevailing mass of crimson ground enriched with burnished gold mouldings and ornaments. A large and splendid movable gas chandelier suspended from the ceiling and numerous subsidiary ones ranged round the front of the boxes, serve to shed over the whole of the place, the glow and radiance of an Oriental palace. During one part of the evening's performance, while the various displays of horsemanship were exhibited in the circle, the whole opening of the proscenium is occupied by an admirably executed representation of the Death of Nelson, on the deck of the " Victory," painted as a large picture in a gigantic gilt frame, richly ornamented with emblematical devices. The passages and entrances are judiciously contrived, and the avenue leading to the boxes is adorned with busts, paintings, and other appropriate ornaments. The extensive stabling required for the accommodation of the large stud of horses is ingeniously formed under the side wings of the stage.'

On December 27, 1830, Ducrow presented *Harlequin and Tom Moody*. Montgomery was harlequin, and Tom and George Ridgway clown and pantaloon, respectively. Mons. Leclerq was the stage manager. On January 3, 1831, Ducrow announced ' that the very flattering reception experienced by himself and the whole of the company on Monday night will stimulate him to added endeavours to contribute

---

* According to the advertisements *The Royal Elephant of Siam* was first performed at the Amphi' about the second week in February, 1830, while the *Elephant of Siam* was not produced at the Theatre Royal until June 14, 1830.
† Mr. Underhill was a bookseller and stationer in the London Road. He died in 1835.

to the comfort and convenience of the public.   A new stove is placed at the back of the pit, and additional curtains to exclude the draught of air. The box passages will be carpeted, and every possible effort to render the Amphitheatre unequalled in its accommodation.'

A laughable incident occurred at the period of one of Ducrow's visits to the Amphi'. At the Theatre Royal, while the circus was in full swing, a learned scientist was nightly lecturing on the starry firmament, with pictorial illustrations. On one evening, when the professor was dwelling on the beauties of the heavens there came into the pit a group of sailors, who sat for some time patiently enough, but they soon made it evident they had visited the wrong theatre, for one of them got on to his legs, and addressing the astonished astronomer, said : ' Look here, mister, we've had enough of this 'ere stuff ; take your d—— stars away, and bring out the blooming horses.'

On October 31, 1831, Signor de Begnis and his Italian Opera Company were here.   Their principal production was *Othello*.   The visit did not prove a financial success.   De Begnis was a fine harpist.   Although deeply pitted with small-pox, he was a great favourite with the ladies.

Mr. Davidge, proprietor of the Royal Coburg Theatre, London, opened the theatre on November 5, 1832.   Watkins Burroughs was the stage-manager.

Early in 1833 Batty's Equestrian Company commenced an engagement.   In the company was Mr Hengler, who not only acted as director of the circle but also performed on the tight-rope.   February 4 saw Pierce Egan, the author, as Bob Logic in his own *Tom and Jerry*.

On May 5 and 6, 1834, Paganini fulfilled an engagement. On October 13 of that year Batty re-opened the theatre.   It was advertised that ' backs have been added to the seats in the pit, the interior redecorated, and to the elegant chandelier has been added a number of brilliant gas jets.'

In February, 1835, Batty's company presented *Joan of Arc ; or, the Maid of Orleans*.   The titular part was played by the afterwards famous Mrs. Stirling, whose husband, Edward Stirling was the stage manager of the theatre.   Few, if any, could approach Mrs. Stirling in comedy ; for she combined every qualification to produce a matchless embodiment of the piquant, the high-bred, and the witty heroines of old comedy. She was about nineteen when she played at the Amphi'.

The theatre re-opened under the management of Mr. R. Armistead on December 21, 1835. Edward Stirling was still the stage manager. Ducrow came in January, 1837; and in April of that year Mr. Bates was proprietor. On September 29, Madame Pasta took her farewell of the Amphi' patrons. For the benefit of Mr Hughes, manager of the equestrian department, the spectacle entitled *Queen Elizabeth; or, The Princely Sports of Kenilworth Castle* was brought out on November 19, 1838. Mr. Hengler played the Earl of Essex. Master and Miss Hengler and Master and Miss Ginnett also took part. Corry and Blanchard, with their performing dogs, were here in June, 1839, and Jem Ward was announced to ' set to,' for the last time in public, with Mat Robinson, Peter Taylor, and Tom Watson.

In the first week in February, 1840, T. D. Rice, the celebrated negro comedian, performed as Jumbo Jum in the piece of that name. He also gave his renowned ' Jump, Jim Crow ' song and dance, together with ' Sich a-gettin up Stairs.' How the song ' Jump, Jim Crow ' came to be introduced is told in ' Theatrical Anecdotes.' Rice was an actor in a Western American theatre, and in a new piece that was about to be brought forward he was persuaded to enact the character of an old negro, much against his will. He consented only under the stipulation that he should have permission to introduce a negro song of his own. Rice had seen a very droll negro ostler, who used to dance grotesquely, and sing odd fragments of a song about one Jim Crow. He easily contrived to throw together a few verses with witty local allusions, and to heighten the extravagance of the dance to its greatest extent of grotesque absurdity. The new play proved a failure, but ' Jim Crow ' emerged triumphant to delight Europe and America.

Early in 1840 the establishment was known as Ducrow's Royal Amphitheatre of Arts. Towards the end of the year it was simply called the Royal Amphitheatre. Mr. Egerton (late of the Queen's, Manchester) opened the theatre on Monday, November 16, 1840, with a varied bill comprising the spectacle, *Jane of the Hatchet; or, the Woman of Beauvais*, the burletta, *The Railroad Station*, and the extravaganza, *Don*

Giovanni ; or, a Spectre on Horseback. The principal performers were W. J. Hammond and Miss Daly. Carter was here
with his lions and other animals in December.

In January, 1841, Gomersall gave his famous portrayal of Napoleon in *The Life and Death of Napoleon.* In
appearance Gomersall was the exact counterpart of 'the
little Corporal.' Ducrow was here in January, 1842. In
April of that year the establishment was known as the American Circus. The Liverpool Temperance Dramatic Association took the theatre in 1842 for the exploitation of temperance
dramas. They also had it the following year for a similar
purpose. Mrs. Stebbing was the lessee in 1843 , and in the
autumn of that year William Robert Copeland commenced
his memorable reign.

On February 19, 1844, Copeland revived *Richard III*,
with himself and Watkins Burroughs in leading *rôles.* The
tragedy of *Antigone* was played on June 23, 1845. On September 6, the pantomimic spectacle, *Don Juan*, was produced
by Howard Payne, his wife playing the principal part.
Payne, the quondam American Roscius, is credited with the
authorship of ' Home, Sweet Home ' The song was first
sung in his melodrama, *Clari, the Maid of Milan*

That fine tragic actor, James Bennett, gave a noble impersonation of Macbeth in May, 1846. On November 23,
1846, Henry Betty (son of the Young Roscius), made his first
appearance in Liverpool in playing Macbeth. He was also
very successful in *King Lear* ; and had a good engagement.
The pantomime of *Harlequin Tee-to-Tum ; or, the Fairy of
the Silver Stream and the Demon of the Golden Mine* was produced on January 1, 1847. The spectacle, *The Campaign of the
Punjab*, was also in the bill. On January 11, a man fell
from the gallery into the pit, a height of 29 feet 6 inches, but
without sustaining any very serious injury. A French equestrian company was here in December. On April 10, 1848,
Jullien's orchestra commenced an engagement. Then came
Charlotte Cushman to play Meg Merrilies (*Guy Mannering*),
Wolsey (*Henry VIII*), and the Stranger in the drama of that
name. W. J. Hammond was Miss Cushman's principal support.
The performance on June 5 was in aid of the fund for a perpetual curatorship of Shakespeare's house The plays submitted were *The Merry Wives of Windsor*, and *Love, Law, and*

Physic. In the former piece were Mark Lemon (Falstaff), Charles Dickens (Swallow), John Leech (Slender), G. H. Lewes (Sir Hugh Evans), George Cruikshank (Pistol), and Emmeline Montague (Mrs. Ford).   The receipts amounted to £451 5s. 6d.   On June 12, W. J. Hammond took a farewell benefit and spoke an address.   On August 24, the Brothers Brough (William and Robert) played in *Box and Cox* and *Twelfth Night*.   On December 26, *The Mountaineers* was followed by the pantomime of *Mother Goose ; or, Harlequin and the Golden Egg.*

Jenny Lind was here on January 6, 1849, and gave her services free of charge.   The performance was in aid of the Southern and Toxteth Hospital.   J. R. Anderson played Othello to Mrs. W. R. Copeland's Desdemona on January 22.   *Coriolanus* was also performed that week.   Commencing February 2, a series of operatic performances were given, including *Fra Diavolo, Maritana* and *The Bohemian Girl.* In May and June the principal visitors were G. H. Lewes,* Mr. and Mrs. Sloan, and T. P. Cooke.   On July 27, 1849, Barry Sullivan, the afterwards eminent tragedian, played in *The Lady of Lyons*, as did also Basil Baker, who was always a favourite locally.   In September Buckstone and Mrs. Fitzwilliam came on a visit.

Easter Monday, 1850, witnessed performances by Barry Sullivan and   J. F. Cathcart.   Ballets were given nightly at this precise period.   On July 1, J. R. Anderson commenced an engagement of twenty-four nights.   'Here I found,' he tells us in ' An Actor's Life,'† ' my old friends Cathcart and Basil Baker—both very good actors—who had been with me at Drury Lane.   There was also Barry Sullivan, an immense local favourite, and I believe most deservedly so, though to my mind he fell short, in comparison with James Bennett, in his rendition of Iago.   At this time there was an opera company at the Theatre Royal, with Messrs. William Harrison, Weiss, and Corri ; Louisa Pyne, Mrs. Weiss, etc., at the head of it, playing to empty benches ; so that we did not consider this much of an opposition.   Poor Harrison told me, with tears in his eyes, that he had been losing money heavily.

* The celebrated dramatic critic, a descendant of Charles Lee Lewes, the comedian. He was seen here as Shylock.
† Pp. 184-5.

He had given an entirely new opera on his own benefit night to £18 !   After that " he put up the shutters ! "

' When I had run through my Shakespearian plays, I resolved on the production of Schiller's *Fiesco*, notwithstanding its partial failure at Drury Lane   It was better liked in Liverpool than in London, and drew fine houses.

' I myself had made an adaptation of this play in prose before giving it in the metropolis, but, deeming it better policy to employ an author of recognised reputation for the task, I gave Mr. Planché my MS , together with one hundred guineas, as a remuneration for smothering the play in heavy blank verse.   The weight of the poetry, and the want of punctuality of my painters, who failed to be ready with the scene for the last act, together with the unfortunate title of the play, which the facetious critics would insist on calling " *Fiasco*," were the main causes of its non-success in London.   Of this I had proof positive ; for when I relinquished Planché's poetry for my own puny prose, the play was everywhere successful, and afterwards I made lots of money by it, in England and the States, under the title of *The Republican Duke*.'

In May, 1850, David Prince Miller was in Liverpool. Shortly after he had appeared in his entertainment, ' Never Despair ; or, the Ups and Downs of Life ' at the Concert Hall in Lord Nelson Street, Copeland gave him a benefit. ' Upon my benefit,' he tells us,* ' I made an appearance as General Damas in Bulwer's play of *The Lady of Lyons*. The good nature of the audience restrained their remarks, but I must have cut a most ludicrous figure. I am, unfortunately, much above the average size of men, being twenty-two stone in weight, and in figure something like a walking butt of beer, and it was with great difficulty the costumier could supply me with the required military suit ; at length this was accomplished, somehow, but I know I must have looked the most scarecrow looking general that ever made an appearance upon real or mimic field ; and in the scene after Damas is supposed to be promoted to a general, where he and poor Claude Melnotte meet—the latter in a most pensive mood— Mr. Barry Sullivan (who was playing Claude Melnotte), when he saw the comic figure I cut, laughed outright, and enough to

* ' The Life of a Showman,' p. 155.

make him.   My cocked hat was too little for me—my coat
was too big.   The audience also had a hearty roar.   I looked
at them and at myself, as much as to say, I well know what
you are laughing at—and the laugh was followed by a round of
applause.'

On May 19, 1851, Barry Sullivan made his first local appearance as Sir Giles Overreach.   On May 30, young Mr.
Hengler played a dramatic character for the first time, and
was audacious enough to begin with Hamlet. G. V. Brooke
performed on June 6, and Samuel Phelps came ten days later.
Commencing July 21, the leading members of the company
were John Vandenhoff, Barry Sullivan, and Miss Vandenhoff.
Céleste and Webster performed on September 25 and 26 ; and
the following month saw Mrs. Stirling, Mrs. Fitzwilliam and
J. B. Buckstone here.   Kate and Ellen Bateman, ' the great
wonders of the age,' made their Liverpool *début* on November 17.   They were then eight and six years old respectively,
and were seen in *The Young Couple*, *The Swiss Cottage*,
Macbeth, and *The Merchant of Venice*.   The sisters returned
here on June 4, 1852.

On September 3, 1852, the concluding item of the evening was the Haymarket farce, *Keeley Worried by Buckstone*,
which was called here *Baker Worried by Buckstone*.   ' Baker
by himself, Buckstone by himself.'   On October 15, *Off to
the Diggings*, a one-act play by G. J. H. Nightingale was
produced.   Mr. Nightingale was a member of the Liverpool
Literary and Dramatic Society, and one of the authors of
' Bloomerism.'   Charles Dillon (from the Queen's Theatre,
Dublin), appeared on October 25, and made a great hit as
Belphegor.

The famous Pyne and Harrison Operatic Company commenced an engagement on November 1, and towards the
middle of the following month the American tragedian,
McKean Buchanan, came for five nights.

George Vandenhoff arrived in Liverpool, from America,
on February 6, 1853, after an absence of eleven years.
Immediately upon his arrival Copeland made known to him
his intention to produce *Henry V*. Copeland had prepared
new scenery and appointments for the piece, which he
designed to produce with great care, and at a considerable
expense.   Vandenhoff agreed to Copeland's terms for a five

weeks' engagement, and arranged to play Hamlet on Monday, March 28, 1853. Copeland asked Vandenhoff how he would like to be billed, whether it would be as the ' eminent tragedian,' or the ' distinguished tragedian,' or the ' classical tragedian,' or the ' highly-popular tragedian,' or the ' Shakesperian tragedian.' Vandenhoff said ' None ; simply announce that Mr. Vandenhoff will make his first appearance in *Hamlet* ; and let the audience find out what degree I am entitled to in the Dramatic College.' The modesty of this answer seemed to please the manager.*

Following the production of *Hamlet*, Vandenhoff appeared during the week as Shylock, Claude Melnotte, and the Stranger. Uniformly good houses prevailed. On April 4, *Henry V* was revived with great care and attention to scenery, costume, and appointments. George Vandenhoff played the titular part for the first time. The play ran twenty-three successive nights to excellent houses ; ' though,' mentions Vandenhoff, ' I believe, they scarcely paid for the extraordinary expenses incurred by Mr. Copeland in his production of the piece— another proof that Shakespearian revivals, when got up with new and appropriate scenery and appointments, never remunerate the management.'

A little incident happened to George Vandenhoff during this engagement. ' I walked,' he tells us † ' into a well-known establishment called " The Crooked Billet ;"‡ and, finding the large dining room full, I entered a little side room, where I found a plainly dressed country tradesman, as he appeared, waiting for his dinner. I ordered mine ; and, after a few minutes, he said to the girl who waited—in a tolerably strong Lancashire accent—" Come, come, lass ; make haste ! time's munney (money)." Then, turning to me, he added, "Isn't it, sir ? " Now it was the breathing time of day with me, and I answered, " To you it may be : I'm sorry to say it is not so with me."

' " Ha," said he, after taking my measure with his eye " I dare say you don't *trubble* youself wi' business mooch."

' " Why ? " I answered, "*what* would you take me to be ? "

' " Oh," said he, " I should take you to be aboov all business ; not to need it, I mean."

'To give him a surprise, and see how he would take it, I replied : " How wrong you are, I am an actor."

' " Are you ?" said he ; " then " (slapping his hand on his thigh) " I can tell you *who* you are.   You are George Vandenhoff."

' " How do you know ? "

' " By the voice. I saw you play Henry the Fifth t'other night, and mightily pleased I was."

' " Well," said I, " are you surprised to find that I'm an actor, instead of a man of fortune, which you took me for ? "

' " Not a bit," he answered ; " you might as well be one as t'other ; and," he added, " I don't know that anyone can do more than *look* like a gentleman, and *behave* like one, whether he has a fortune or not." '

Josh Silsbee, the American comedian, performed on June 6, and J. R. Anderson, the tragedian, came seven nights later. The charming and talented *danseuse*, Rosina Wright, whom everybody loved, appeared on July 4. She was engaged for the season and gave great pleasure in the grand ballets produced.

Copeland always kept an efficient staff of ballet ladies and pantomimists. The two Misses Goodall were members of the dancing corps, and they as well as many others have to thank poor Copeland for their success in life. If a man or woman showed promise he gave them every opportunity of coming to the front. The stock pantomimists were the well-known Lauris, and the family at that time included Charles, Ted, Harry, John, Fanny, and Fred. Charles was the stock pantaloon, and Fred one of the best of clowns. Copeland kept the troupe in constant employment all the year round, supplementing his weekly dramatic productions with a comic ballet, ballet pantomime, or grand *ballet d'action*.

T. Lenton, whose speciality was ceiling-walking, came in July. When *Cato* was submitted on July 30, George and Henry Vandenhoff were in the cast. On October 3, Fred Wright, the clever comedian, made his first appearance in Liverpool. He was at that time billed as from the Theatre Royal, Adelphi, London. On the occasion of Henry Loraine's benefit (November 22), Fred Maccabe of ' Begone, Dull Care ' fame, presided at the pianoforte.

Barry Sullivan performed in August, and G. V. Brooke in November, 1854. On August 27, 1855, the English Opera Company was here, and had Herr Meyer Lutz as conductor. Mr. Webster and Madame Céleste commenced an engagement on September 8, 1856. On the occasion of Madame Céleste's benefit (September 12), an attempt was made by a drunken carpenter named John Ball to blow up the theatre. Ball, it appears, had cut away a large portion of the gas-piping beneath the stage, and had not a prompt discovery taken place, a large volume of gas would have ignited, and the building would, doubtless, have been burnt to the ground. Ball was committed to the assizes, but at the hearing in December, he was discharged with a caution.

On September 22, 1856, Henry Loraine gave the first of his farewell performances previous to his departure for the United States. Before he left England his friends entertained him at a public dinner at Whiteman's New Brunswick Hotel, in Clayton Square, and presented him with a testimonial. Mr. and Mrs. Barney Williams appeared on November 3, for the first time before the Liverpool public. Their engagement extended over three weeks, and the house was crowded nightly. In November, Sims Reeves was announced to appear in *Guy Mannering* and *The Bohemian Girl*, the latter to be conducted by Balfe the composer. Reeves, however, did not appear, as he was lying ill in Dublin. Commencing December 3, Professor Anderson played Rob Roy for three nights. He was succeeded by Barry Sullivan, who played Falstaff in *Henry IV* for his benefit on the 12th.

On May 25, 1857, T. C. King played Hamlet. On May 11, 1858, John Vandenhoff celebrated the fiftieth anniversary of his appearance on the stage. During the same year William Henry Rignold performed 'general utility' parts here. He had previously been a violinist in theatre orchestras. During the week commencing November 8, 1858, J. B. Buckstone and Miss Jane Reynolds appeared in *The Way to Keep Him* and *The Husband of an Hour*. Miss Reynolds was at that time leading actress at the Haymarket, London, where under Buckstone's management she was seen in the majority of the productions there. In 1887 she married Sir Henry Hawkins, afterwards Lord Brampton, and died twenty years later at a ripe old age. She survived her husband only by six weeks, but inherited the bulk of the deceased judge's fortune, which was proved at £141,674. She was possessed of very considerable means in her own right, and was a very charitable woman, particularly to the Church of her adoption—she was a devout Roman Catholic—and to any deserving theatrical cause which was brought to her notice.

In January, 1859, Copeland entered into an arrangement with Elliott Galer for the purpose of establishing an English Opera season. The principal artistes included Fanny Reeves, Madame M. Bishop, Charles Lyall, and E. Corri. Herr Meyer Lutz was the conductor. *Martha* was performed for the first time in Liverpool on January 10 ; and on February 14, Meyer Lutz's romantic opera, *Zaida ; or, the Pearl of Granada.* Seven days later Lady Don, who was accompanied by her husband, Sir William Don, made her first appearance in Liverpool.

In 1859, Henry Neville was a member of the stock company. Another gifted player, J. C. Cowper, was also here. It was in Liverpool that Cowper first acted Virginius, a character in which he was generally considered to excel. His clever and finished impersonation of Badger in *The Streets of Liverpool* was also greatly admired by local playgoers. Some of his most popular characters at this period were Hamlet, Richard III, Macbeth, Iachimo, Ingomar, Iago, Henri de Lagadere, Tullus Aufidius in *Coriolanus*, and Paragon, in the farce of *Perfection.* He also acted with success as Ion in Talfourd's play of that name, and as the Dei Franchi in *The Corsican Brothers.* This fine range of parts proved him a most versatile actor. He was equally at home in light comedy characters as in romantic lovers, and his tragic powers were by no means to be despised. It is interesting to note that when acting with Barry Sullivan he alternated the characters of Othello and Iago.

The following is a curious instance of Cowper's presence of mind. He was acting Richard one night at the Theatre Royal to the Richmond of John Warner (son of the celebrated Mrs. Warner), who insisted on wearing and using a cavalry sword with a sharp point. In the last act Warner struck Cowper a terrible blow on the right temple, the sword descending and cutting the cartilage of his nose. When

Cowper was picked up his face was bathed in blood, but thanks to his firmness and presence of mind, the audience remained unaware of the accident.

The theatre was closed on June 27, 1859, for structural alterations, and the company migrated to the Royal, where Amphi' prices ruled for the time being. The theatre re-opened on August 22. During the recess a new stage had been laid, the pit reconstructed, and the gallery enlarged so as to hold one thousand persons. On November 28, Miss Marriott played Hamlet for the first time in Liverpool.

About 1860, J. G. Swanton was a member of the Amphi' stock company. He shone best in the performance of heavy characters; and in later life his Jacob McClosky in *The Octoroon* was a most finished and consistent assumption. For many years he was one of the principal members of J. F. Warden's stock company at Belfast. After the decline of the stock system Swanton retired and opened a hostelry in Belfast. He died in 1886.

During the time Swanton was a member of the Amphi' stock company, Madame Céleste visited the theatre. Swanton informed my friend, Mr. W. J. Lawrence, that he 'remembered seeing Céleste one night as Harlequin *à la* Watteau in a pantomime, which had been played initially at the London Adelphi under her own management. She was supported in the harlequinade by the Lauris. She dressed the character thoroughly *à la* Watteau, with powdered wig, three-cornered hat, the half-mask, etc. He thought he never saw anything more graceful. It was the very poetry of motion.

'Some time after Céleste had paid that visit to the Amphi',' said Swanton, 'a member of the stock company called McCart took his annual benefit, and his wife (whose stage name was MacGregor), played Harlequin *à la* Watteau. I was in the house that night, and was inclined to feel bored before the curtain went up in anticipation of what I considered would be a very poor imitation. When Miss MacGregor bounded on the stage I gave a start of surprise, an action which tapered off into an ejaculation when the graceful *danseuse* had executed several steps and poses. "Surely!" said I, looking at the bill again and again, "there must be a mistake somewhere. That face, that figure, that graceful airiness—it must be Céleste!" All through that memorable performance I sat as one entranced, in a dilemma of delight. I had expected so little and gotten so much. The surprise was terrible. I forgot to tell you that Miss MacGregor was Mr. Copeland's stock Columbine, and I don't suppose a better one ever executed a trip. The next morning, or perhaps it was a couple of days after, I happened to meet McCart, and in the course of our confab, related my experience regarding his wife's dancing on the benefit night. The mystery was at once cleared up. "My dear Swanton," replied McCart, "didn't you know that my wife was retained at the Adelphi for many and many a day as Madame Céleste's double ? There were times of indisposition, little suppers, etc., etc., when Mrs. McCart stepped into Madame's shoes and passed herself off upon Céleste's most ardent admirers as the true Arabian bird. I don't want to blow, but there must have been a remarkable similarity of style about the two to cause this deception." I quite agreed with McCart and made a mental note of the whole matter. That's why I am able to be so explicit, although unfortunately I can't go into dates—never could—they are my abomination.'

' Ben McCormack, the clown, was connected for the best part of his days with the Amphi'. How he came to play clown is an interesting story. In those days a drama was always played before the pantomime, but on ' Children's Evenings,' the order was reversed, so as to let the kids home early. Well, on one of these juvenile nights, Foster, the clown, failed to turn up in time. He had evidently forgotten about the arrangement. What was to be done ? No one could find Foster, and the stage manager ran about distracted. Ben McCormack, who was the sprite of the pantomime, and had seen all the comic business rehearsed, offered to play clown. He was laughed at at first, but upon the audience getting impatient, he was allowed to don the motley. One of Foster's old clown's dresses was found in the wardrobe. He was a big burly man was Foster, and his togs didn't fit Ben. You would have split your sides laughing, if you could have seen them folding and pinning the costume round Ben, with the hope of making his slim figure recognisable. At the close of the panto. came the transformation scene, the old-fashioned transformation scene, in which the Fairy Queen addressed herself separately to each character. Well, McCormack had been thinking what funny thing he would say when he first bounded on. There was a wheeze then current in Liverpool, "There's always sure to be a row in the house when you ask for the loan of a bob." Well he came out with it, and it took immensely. So did his clowning. He absolutely revelled in the business. But meanwhile a messenger had been despatched for Foster, who on being found, lost no time in coming to the theatre. He was horrified to find McCormack doing all his pet business. "Come off, come off," he whispered to Ben from the wings. "Not me," replied Mac, "not while I'm enjoying myself." But Foster was not to be denied, and went on in the next scene. But that finished Ben's career as a contortionist. He clowned it next season, and was popularly hailed by the Liverpudlians. He then played a couple of seasons at other theatres, at Newcastle-on-Tyne and elsewhere ; and just as he was making a name fit to carry him to London, he took ill and died.'*

'Lal' Brough tells a funny story about McCormack in Routledge's by-gone Christmas Annual called 'The Stage Door.' 'In Liverpool some few years ago we had a very popular clown (now, alas! gone over to the majority), one Ben McCormack, "a fellow of infinite jest." On the occasion of his benefit he asked Mr. S. M. Harrison, a well-known local author, to write a speech for him. The speech began with "Motley is my only wear," etc., etc., and through the speech the word "motley" occurred very often. After the benefit, Ben was asked by the author how the speech went. "First rate, Mr. Harrison," said Ben; "they liked it very much, but there was a deuce of a lot about Mr. Motley in it, and not a word about poor Ben McCormack."'

At that time the clown was the best paid man in the company. That was why so many first-rate dancers, men better adapted for other lines, donned the motley. They would have made excellent harlequins, but there was no money in the mask and spangles.

Louisa Keeley made her first appearance in Liverpool on June 25, 1860. Barry Sullivan paid a visit in the following October. On March 11, 1861, he played, for the first time, the *rôle* of Henri Desart in Montague Williams and F. C. Burnand's drama, *A Tale of the Channel Islands ; or, the Isle*

* Unpublished memoranda of Mr. W. J. Lawrence, from conversations with the late J. G. Swanton.

of St. Topaz.   April 1 saw Madame Céleste in her picturesque impersonation of Miami in *The Green Bushes.*   *The Colleen Bawn* was acted for the first time in Liverpool on May 6.   Mrs. John Sloan was Eily O'Connor; John Drew, Myles-na-Coppaleen; and Sam Emery, Danny Man.   Winifred Emery (Mrs. Cyril Maude), is a daughter of Sam Emery.   The Christmas pantomime was entitled *The Old Woman who Lived in a Shoe; or, Harlequin Child of Childwall, and the Choice Spirits of Dingle Dell.*

In January, 1862, G. V. Brooke and Avonia Jones were here.   Their performances were supplemented by the panto-mime.   On February 24, Edwin Booth made his first appear-ance in Liverpool.   He played Hamlet and other *rôles*, and was engaged for twelve nights.   Edmund Falconer's *Peep O' Day Boys* was performed for the first time locally on May 26. In the cast were Miss Heath, Stanislaus Calhaem, and William Champion.   Oscar Byrne superintended the performances. In July Miss Cleveland was engaged for leading business.   At that time Fanny and Carlotta Addison were members of the company.   The latter, who was the youngest daughter of Edward Phillips Addison, comedian, was born in Liverpool, in July, 1849.   G. V. Brooke came in July and was here for several weeks.   He returned again in October.   When *The Relief of Lucknow* was presented on November 16, Mrs. Boucicault played Jessie Brown.   Mr. and Mrs. Charles Kean commenced an engagement on June 8, 1863.   G. V. Brooke and Avonia Jones performed during July and August.   On October 5 *The Ticket-of-Leave-Man* was played for the first time in Liverpool.   Wybert Rousby was the Robert Brierly. The Christmas pantomime was *Harlequin and the Child of Hale; or, the King of the Red Noses and the Liver Queen.*

On January 18, 1864, Kate Saville was seen in her original part of Miriam in *Miriam's Crime.*   On February 10, *The Poor of Liverpool* was given under the direction of the author. The Tercentenary of Shakespeare's Anniversary was celebrated on April 22, by the performance of *Hamlet* with Miss Marriott as the young Prince to Miss Millicent Palmer's Ophelia.   The theatre was thrown open to the public, free of charge, by the Mayor, Mr. Charles Mozley.   The following evening J. C. Cowper played Macbeth to Kate Saville's Lady Macbeth.   The bard was honoured the following week by representations of *Macbeth, As You Like It, Romeo and Juliet,* and *Much Ado About Nothing.* Miss Marriott appeared in the titular part in *The Duchess of Malfi* on May 30   She also was seen during the week as Bianca in *The Italian Wife,* and Meg Merrilies in *Guy Mannering*   Fechter's company in *The Monastery of St. Just* was engaged for twelve nights, commencing August 22.   Kate Terry portrayed the leading female *rôle.*   On September 9, Mrs. Burkinshaw (from the Theatre Royal, Dublin), played Orpheus in *Orpheus and Eurydice.*   Ten days later Henry Neville was seen as Robert Brierly in *The Ticket-of-Leave Man.*

On July 24, 1865, Charles Wyndham, ' from the United States Theatres,' made his first appearance as an actor in his native town.* He played Howard Ormsby in a new drama from his own pen, entitled *Her Ladyship's Guardian.* The following *critique* appeared in the ' Liverpool Mercury ' the day succeeding the production :—

' It is the production of Mr. C. Wyndham, who also takes the part of the principal character in the piece, though he has not committed the mistake, which author-actors are apt to fall into, of making himself figure too prominently in the performance.   The plot is not remarkable for novelty, but there is sufficient mystery about it to make the audience wait anxiously for the *dénotement.* . . . . . Mr. Wyndham as the hero of the piece, played his part with all the nonchalance which the character required, and some of the dialogue between him and Miss Vining (who made her first appearance at the Amphi'), as Lizzie Hope furnished the best specimens of acting in the piece.'

Wyndham remained at the Amphi' until December 6, 1865.   During his engagement, which had originally been for twelve nights only, he appeared as Captain Murphy Maguire (*The Serious Family*), Mephistopheles (*Faust and Marguerite*), and as Shaun-the-Post in a revival of *Arrah-na-Pogue* on October 25.

Adah Isaacs Menken, of Mazeppa fame, performed during December, 1865.   The 1865-6 annual was produced by John Coleman, and was entitled *The Yellow Dwarf ; or, Harlequin King of the Golden Mines and the Beautiful Mermaid with the Golden Hair.*

* Wyndham was born at 19 Tithebarn Street, Liverpool, on March 23, 1837.   The house has long since been demolished and a shop built on the site.

To 'The Theatre' magazine, of July, 1893, John Coleman contributed an article on Thomas Higgie, who was his stage manager at the Amphi'. Higgie, I may mention, was not only a good actor, but a skilful and prolific dramatist. Augustus Harris the elder and Charles Mathews both said Higgie was the best stage manager of his time.

In the article referred to, Coleman mentions that they had only a fortnight in which to get up the pantomime. 'At the eleventh hour our ballet-master failed us, but at the instigation of Higgie, our harlequin (E. W. Royce), got up our dances to the admiration of everybody. Our chorus-master left us in the lurch, but again at the instigation of Higgie, our *prima donna* (Marion Taylor), came to the rescue, and pulled us through splendidly. To crown all, at the last moment our drunken property-man struck, and his drunken subs followed suit; again the indomitable Higgie rose to the occasion. "I have never been licked in my life, sir," said he, " and I don't mean to be licked now! no, sir! damme no!" With that he placed a couple of stalwart policemen at the stage-door, subsidised half-a-dozen intelligent supers to assist, then he stripped to his shirt sleeves, so did I; he mounted guard at one side of the stage, I at the other, and the panto-mime went without a hitch; in fact it beat the record, and was played right up to Easter.*

' Having other theatres elsewhere, I was seldom in Liver-pool, hence Higgie was left " monarch of all he surveyed." During my absence his most intimate acquaintance was a young actor, whom he had previously met during the run of *Ivy Hall* at the Princess's. This gentleman was at the Prince of Wales's with the late Mr. Henderson, who did not appre-ciate his ability at its proper worth. Higgie, however, stoutly maintained that his young friend needed only time and oppor-tunity to become a great actor, and Higgie was right, for his young friend was Henry Irving.'

On October 13, 1866, William Robert Copeland was presented with a silver epergne on his retirement from active theatrical life. The presentation was made by Mr. Burkin-shaw on the stage of the Amphi'. Copeland had successfully directed the destinies of the theatre for 23 years. No one was

* The last night of the pantomime was February 24, 1866.

more respected in theatrical circles, or more straightforward in his dealings with both profession and public.

Henry J. Byron commenced his management of the theatre on October 15, 1866, with Barry Sullivan as the star. Byron's grandfather was the Rev. Henry Byron, who was first cousin to Lord Byron. Byron was partly of Jewish descent. His mother was the daughter of Dr. Bradley, of Buxton, and Bradley had married a daughter of that Liverpool worthy, Dr. Solomon, of ' Balm of Gilead ' fame. Solomon's once renowned specific is perpetuated locally in Balm and Gilead Streets.

Harlequin Blue Beard was the title of Byron's first annual. R. H. Kitchen was clown, and Charles Paulo harlequin. David Fisher, senior, was H J Byron's stage manager. On January 28, 1867, John Ryder appeared in *Henry IV*. Mrs. Stirling who had not been seen here for some years played Peg Woffington in *Masks and Faces* on February 4. Charles Dillon came on March 25. The Ryder-Reinhart revival of *King John* took place on April 1. Three weeks later J L. Toole came on a visit. On October 26, 1867, Byron produced, for the first time on any stage, his sensational realistic play *The Lancashire Lass*, with a real ferry steamer, which was a marvel of mechanical ingenuity. When the play was reproduced at the Queen's, London, on July 24, 1868, Henry Irving played Robert Redburn. On February 24, 1868, J. C. Cowper gave his well-known impersonation of Badger in *The Poor of Liverpool*.

Although Byron's managerial reign here was as artistically brilliant as it was regretfully brief, it was asserted that the Alexandra Theatre, which had proved unfortunate to Mr. Henderson, had been a disastrous speculation to Mr. Byron The actor-dramatist got the newest and best pieces, and put them on the stage in the most complete style ; but the nett result of his managerial enterprise was the loss of some £15,000 or so. Some time after throwing up the sponge, Byron took advantage of a professional engagement at the Amphi', to deliver a speech in the course of which he intimated his intention to pay every penny of the debt he owed to the Copeland family.

Of Byron numerous tales are told At a time when it was the custom locally to charge a shilling for securing a

reserved seat, or booking a stall in advance, he noticed a
number of persons buying tickets and paying the extra
impost. Going up to the box-office, he wrote conspicuously
above the window, a parody of Richard the Third's
exclamation :—' Off with his bob ! So much for booking-
'em.' The obnoxious custom did not long survive after
this. ¶When theatrical affairs in Liverpool were not pros-
pering with him he was accosted by a friend and asked
why he looked so glum. . ' I've just had a nasty dose of oil '
he replied. ' Oil ? ' queried his friend. ' Yes, Theatre
(R)oyal,' replied Byron, as he wended his way theatre-
wards. Once when he met poor Frank Musgrave, the latter
told him that he was ' going to Piccadilly.' All right,' said
Byron, ' mind you pick a *good* one.' These were manifestations of sheer high spirits. Even on his death-bed his love
of a joke betrayed itself. He said to little Toole, who was
sitting by him, ' I have just answered a letter from my groom ;
he says one of my horses is ill, my favourite mare, and he
wants to know if I should give her a ball. I told him "yes" ;
but not to ask too many.'

After Byron got into financial difficulties the theatre was
run from March 30, 1868, by Miss E. Copeland, with Henry
Leslie as director. On April 3, a benefit performance was
given for H. J. Byron. Ten days later Barry Sullivan commenced an engagement. *Under the Gaslight* was submitted
on May 4, when performances were given by Lady Don
and Shiel Barry. T. C. King came on August 10. Exactly
a week later King and Benjamin Webster played in Dickens
and Wilkie Collins's drama, *No Thoroughfare.* On September
28, W. Sidney was seen in his drama of country life, *The Light
in the Dark ; or, Life Underground.*

It's Never Too Late to Mend was presented on July 26,
1869, when Stanislaus Calhaem played Jackey, his original
character. On Saturday, August 28, J. Palgrave Simpson's
drama, *The Watch Dog of the Walsinghams,* was produced for
the first time on any stage. The principal parts were interpreted by Madame Céleste and James Fernandez. On November 13, Fernandez played Shaun-the-Post in a revival of
Arrah-na-Pogue. He was highly praised by the ' Liverpool
Daily Post ' for his performance. *Formosa* was played, under
the direction of Dion Boucicault, the author, on December 20.

The company included Catherine Rogers, Maggie Brennan, and Mrs. Billington

Barry Sullivan and Kate Saville came on February 5, 1870. They were succeeded by the Italian Opera Company. On April 4, a French Opera Bouffe Company commenced an engagement. May 2, saw Creswick the tragedian here. He played in *Ambition*, *Othello* and *Macbeth*. James Fernandez and Miss Eliza Rudd supported The managers of the theatre at that time were the executors of the late W. R. Copeland. On June 2, Henry Leslie took a farewell benefit, when Osmond Tearle played Frank Sterne in *Under a Ban*. Miss Bateman was here early in September, and was seen in *Leah* and *Mary Warner* Helen Faucit commenced a four nights' engagement in December, and appeared as Lady Macbeth, Pauline (*The Lady of Lyons*), and Rosalind.

In April, 1871, Edmund Falconer played Mickey Free in *Charles O'Malley*. Mdlle. Beatrice and her company came on June 19 Barry Sullivan and Miss Marriott were here in November. The latter, on November 27, played Rebecca in *Ivanhoe* She was supported by an able company which included Rachel Sanger, Grace Edgar, Osmond Tearle, and James Lunt. Edmund Falconer played Bryan O'Farrell in *Eileen Oge* on February 5, 1872. On March 30, Henry Leslie commenced his reign as sole lessee of the theatre. Barry Sullivan was the star. Places could now be booked for the pit, as well as for the stalls and dress-circle. Miss Heath and Wilson Barrett presented *Fernande* on July 8. , Barry Sullivan paid a return visit on October 21. Early admittance through the stage door could now be obtained on payment of sixpence extra.

Mdlle. Beatrice and her company visited the Amphi' again on February 10, 1873. Prominent in support were those capable players, John Dewhurst and J. Carter Edwards. In September the theatre was under the joint management of Henry Leslie and Lindo Courtenay. On September 10, Charles Reade's drama *The Wandering Heir* was performed with J. C. Cowper and Mrs. John Wood in the cast. On November 13, Miss Pilkington played Pauline to Barry Sullivan's Claude Melnotte. Miss Pilkington's *nom de théâtre* was May Douglas. She was a Liverpool lady. Of her the ' Liverpool Daily Post ' said : ' The representation was full of promise for the future, and on the whole an excellent one.'

A painstaking young actor named Harris was about this time engaged to play juvenile and light comedy parts. ' During this engagement,' says Pascoe, ' Mr. Mapleson engaged Mr. Harris as assistant stage manager for his Italian Opera Company, and after a fortnight appointed him stage manager, in recognition of the way in which some operas had been by him placed on the stage of the Theatre Royal, Bath, under more than ordinary difficulties.'* The young man referred to subsequently attained distinction as Sir Augustus Harris.

The Carl Rosa Opera Company commenced an engagement on February 2, 1874. Among the principals were J. W. Turner, Blanche Cole, and Rose Hersee. *The Wandering Heir* was brought forward on June 8. Philippa was played by Ellen Terry, who was prophetically described in the advertisements as ' the great rising star of British Comedy.' Charles Dillon and Bella Mortimer came on August 24, and the Carl Rosa Company returned on September 7. Mr. and Mrs. Aynsley Cook were then in the latter organisation. Commencing on February 8, 1875, Mdlle. Beatrice and her company played for 24 nights. They also performed for a similar number of nights in the following year. When the Chippendale Comedy Company came here on September 27, Hermann Vezin was a member of the company. Joseph Hatton's *Clytie* was performed on November 29, with Henrietta Hodson† as the heroine. The Yuletide attraction was the Carl Rosa Opera Company. It then included Rose Hersee, Julia Gaylord, Charles Santley, Henry Nordbloom, F. H. Celli, Ludwig, and Mr. and Mrs. Aynsley Cook.

In 1876, Frank Cooper (who is descended on his mother's side from the great Sarah Siddons), was tentatively engaged as a low comedian at the Amphi'. Mr. Cooper was then in his twentieth year. ' The contract,' he tells us in ' M.A.P.,'‡ ' was made without their having seen me, and I shall not readily forget Leslie's face when I presented myself at his office. " Good gracious ! " (he was not quite so mild in expression as that) he exclaimed ; " there must be some

---

* '.The Dramatic List,' p. 159.   ‡† Mrs. Henry Labouchere.
                    ‡ June 15, 1907.

mistake. I thought you were a low comedian." I told him that at all events, I was supposed to answer to that description, and after a deal of talk he emphatically expressed the conviction that his audience would not "stand" a low comedian who measured over six feet in his socks, and spoke in a deep baritone, and suggested that I should remain with them as "Juvenile lead," or as the French say, *jeune premier*, which I accordingly did'

Salvini, the celebrated tragedian, commenced a three nights' engagement on March 20, 1876. He played Othello and Hamlet. On May 8, Genevieve Ward made her first appearance in Liverpool in playing Lady Macbeth *Si Slocum* was the title of a sensational American border drama, in which Mr. and Mrs. Frank Frayne sustained leading parts on June 12. On October 2, Miss Marriott gave her splendid portrayal of Queen Bess in *Elizabeth, Queen of England* On November 6, Arthur Garner reappeared at the Amphi' as Tom Spiril in Paul Merritt's play, *Stolen Kisses,* which was its first production on any stage. When *Liz; or, that Lass o' Lowrie's,* was produced on July 9, 1877, R. C. Carton (the prospective dramatist), created the part of the Rev. Alfred Lonsdale. The opera of *The Merry Wives of Windsor* was performed by the Carl Rosa Company on December 29, 1877, when Aynsley Cook gave a finished impersonation of Falstaff. Charles Reade's drama, *Joan,* was introduced on September 2, 1878, with Rose Leclerq in the leading character.

On April 28, 1879, *The Tempest* was performed. Ethel Castleton and Jennie Lefevre appeared alternately as Miranda, while John Wainwright and Robert Brough also alternated the characters of Caliban and Trinculo. Julia St. George played Ariel, and on the occasion of her benefit (May 9), took her farewell of the Liverpool stage.

The partnership between Messrs. Leslie and Courtenay lasted until May, 1879. Lindo Courtenay then became sole lessee, with Charles Courtenay as his acting manager.

A comic Irish pantomime entitled *The Man in the Moon* was produced on November 10 The company included Mr and Mrs. Charles Sullivan, Guilfoyle Seymour, Adam Leffler and Thomas Nerney. Richard Hicks played clown.

On April 26, 1880, the English Opera Company commenced a six nights' engagement. Prominent among the principals were J. W. Turner, Aynsley Cook, and Ludwig. On May 6, W. S. Branson was accorded a complimentary benefit. The T. P. Cooke prize drama, *True to the Core*, was revived on August 16, with Osmond Tearle as Martin Truegold. Fred Gould and H. Vernon's *Black Flag* Company came on September 20. Barry Sullivan was here during the week commencing November 15. The Carl Rosa Opera Company occupied the bill at Christmas.

In 1880 the theatre was put up for auction, and bought by Sir David Radcliffe for £20,000. The last performance took place on February 28, 1881, when the bill was exactly as follows:

' ROYAL AMPHITHEATRE.

Liverpool.

Sole Lessee   ..   ..   ..   Mr. Lindo Courtenay

Doors open at 7. Commence at 7.15.

Prices of Admission.

Private Boxes £2 2s. and £1 1s. New Omnibus Boxes £1 11s. Single seats in same 4s. each. Dress Circle 3s. Side Circle 2s.6d. Pit Stalls 2s. PIT ONE SHILLING. GALLERY SIXPENCE.

Box Office open from 10 till 3.

On Monday next, February 28

Benefit

of

Mr. Lindo Courtenay,

and

Last Performance at the Amphitheatre

prior to alterations, etc.

On which occasion

Mr. and Mrs. Edward Saker

Alexandra Theatre

Mr. Frank Emery

Prince of Wales Theatre

Mr. F. C. Packard,

Madame Joyce Maas

By permission of Mons. Van Biene, Bijou Opera House

Mr. Arthur Ricketts,   Mr. Owen Dacroy,

Mr. L. S. Dewar

Miss Florence Courtenay,

Miss Polly Poland,

Miss May Douglas, etc.

Have kindly consented to appear.

The performance will commence at 7.15 with the Celebrated Comedy Drama in Four Acts by Mr. Frank Harvey, entitled :

JOHN JASPER'S WIFE,

By permission of Mr. F. H. Paget, in whom the Provincial right is invested.

Sir Archibald Grimely   ..   .. Mr. L. S. Dewar.
Philip Forrester ..   ..   .. Mr. Owen Dacroy.
Mr. Quillet, a Lawyer ..   .. Mr. Vincent.
Adam Jasper, a Farmer..   .. Mr. Arthur Ricketts.
John Jasper, his Son, a wealthy Iron Founder
                          Mr. Lindo Courtenay.
Lady Alice Harborough ..   .. Miss May Douglas.
Grace Forrester, her Cousin   . Miss Florence Courtenay.
Betty Jasper   ..   .. Miss Polly Poland.
Lady Grimely   ..   .. Miss Lizzie Harris.

Act 1. " Rough Billows."   Act 2. " Calm Waters."
Act 3. " Drifting Back."   Act 4. " At Anchor."

To be succeeded by

A MUSICAL MELANGE

In which the following distinguished artistes will appear :
Mr. and Mrs. Edward Saker, Mr. F. C. Packard,
Madame Joyce Maas, &c.

Address by Mr. Lindo Courtenay.

To Conclude with the First Act of
ROBERT MACAIRE

Jacques Strop	..	Mr. Frank Emery
Robert Macaire	..	Mr. Lindo Courtenay

Supported by a Powerful Company.'

On the last night, the Amphi' patrons were particularly
lively, the gods and pittites especially so ; for I am told that
there was a continuous fusilade of popping ginger-beer
corks and veritable showers of nut shells from the gallery.
A gentleman who was in the house mentions that he
was nearly blinded by a hat, which was repeatedly tossed
from pit to gallery and gallery to pit, always hitting someone,
and finally reaching its owner in a hopelessly battered
condition.

Afterwards Sir David Radcliffe had the interior of the
Amphi' entirely gutted, and the house rebuilt from the
designs of Mr. Henry Sumners, an eminent local architect.

The new theatre was named the Royal Court, and the
opening performance took place on Saturday, September 10,
1881, Captain R. B. Bainbridge (then controlling the fortunes
of the Theatre Royal, Manchester), being the lessee. The first
musical director was Mr. John Crook ; Mr. Sidney, the first
general manager ; Mr. E. Edmunds, the stage manager ; and
Messrs. Hall, Spong, and Muir, the scenic artists.

The inaugural performance consisted of a new and
original opera in three acts, entitled *The Lancashire Witches ;*
or, King Jamie's Frolic, written by R. T. Gunton, and
composed by F. Stanislaus.   The cast was as follows :

King James the First	..	.. Mr. Aynsley Cook.
Hopkins (the ' Witch Finder ' and Sir Ralph's Lawyer)		
		Mr. T. F. Doyle.
Sir Ralph Ashton (Lord of the Manor of Whalley)		
		Mr. J. Furneaux Cook.
Richard Ashton (his Son), will be played alternately by		
		Messrs. Henry Walsham and W. H. Woodfield.
Captain of Soldiers	..	.. Mr. Lynch.
Mayor of Blackburn	..	.. Mr. Montigne.

Innkeeper ..   ..   Mr. R. Bell
Hodge   ` ..   ..   ..   Mr. T. Worsley.
Stodge   ..   ..   ..   Mr. G. Hart.
Alizon (beloved by Richard), will be played alternately by
Madame Cave-Ashton and Miss Constance Loseby.
Dame Alice Nutter (a Witching Widow) Miss Alice Cook.
Mother Demdyke ⎱ Witches   ..   ⎰ M'adlle. Mariani.
Mother Chattox ⎰   ..   ⎱ Miss Juliet Smythe.
Sally   ..   ..   Miss Marie Buxton.

Act 1. Whalley Abbey.   Act 2. Pendle Hill.
Act 3. Hoghton Towers.

The first and only Court pantomime submitted by Captain Bainbridge was *The Babes in the Wood*, which was produced on December 24, following It was written by J.F. McArdle. In the cast were Alice Cook, Aynsley Cook and Richard Hicks. Strangely enough, no Christmas pantomime was afterwards produced at the Court until December 24, 1895, when the Drury Lane annual *Dick Whittington* was performed.

The year 1882 saw two new plays.   The first was on April 26, the operatic burlesque *Merry Mignon*, by Wilton Jones, with music by John Crook of the Royal Court, and the second on November 6, when for the first time in England, a play in six acts, called *Almost a Life*, was produced

In the following year visits were paid by D'Oyly Carte's Opera Company and John Hollingshead's Gaiety Burlesque Company , and in June the Rentz-Santley Burlesque Company appeared in an extravaganza founded on Longfellow's 'Evangeline.'   On the twenty-fifth of the same month came Nellie Farren and company in *Blue Beard*.   On July 30, Charles Dornton and William Rignold played in *The Two Orphans*, and David James was seen in *Our Boys* on September 17.   Other visitors were Florence St. John, Mr. and Mrs. Kendal and John Hare, Hermann Vezin, and Charles Warner.

In the March of 1884, Captain Bainbridge severed his connection with the Court, the last play under his *régime* being *Blow for Blow*. On March 29, he took a farewell benefit.

About this period the theatre was sold by Sir David Radcliffe to Carl Rosa for £40,000. The new proprietor opened the theatre on March 31, 1884, with a revival of *The Ticket-of-Leave Man*, Alfred B. Cross playing Bob Brierly. J. D. McLaren was Mr. Rosa's general manager, John Atkinson the acting manager, and J. O. Shepherd, musical director, a position which he still worthily retains. Mr. Shepherd came originally from the Opera House, Leicester.

The late H. A. Bruce (' Daddy,' as he was endearingly termed), succeeded J. D. McLaren as manager of the theatre. Mr. Bruce was manager of the Court until June, 1896, when he transferred his energies to the local Shakespeare. During the last six months of 1890, Mr. Bruce had Sir Augustus Harris as co-managing director of the theatre.

On June 30, 1884, J. B. Howard (of Messrs. Howard and Wyndham) appeared as Rob Roy. Commencing August 25, Carl Rosa secured for three nights the services of Sims Reeves, who appeared in *Guy Mannering* and *The Beggar's Opera*. The Christmas of 1884 saw the appearance of Mr. Rosa's popular opera company, which included Marie Roze and Georgina Burns ; and Ludwig, Crotty, Snazelle, and Barton McGuckin. For over a dozen years afterwards the Carl Rosa Company provided the Christmas attraction at the Court.

A drama called *The Game of Life*, written by Howell-Poole, was produced on August 15, 1887. On May 5, 1890, a farcical comedy by J. H. Darnley, entitled *The Solicitor* was brought out. Commencing July 21, 1890, the Liverpool Opera Company gave six performances of popular operas. On Thursday, October 22, 1891, Wilson Barrett essayed for the first time the part of Othello, and with the happiest results. The sustained beauty and power of his performance called forth the highest laudation from the critics, one, perhaps, the most accomplished of them all—Mr. (now Sir) Edward Russell—saying : ' Mr Barrett is thoroughly possessed with the sentiments of the part. . . . . In all he is most convincing and powerful, carrying the audience thoroughly, rapidly, and excitedly with him. . . . . The whole of the third act is very masterly, all the vigour of the actor's physique supporting a strong and sound Oriental conception . . . . . In fact, the ferocity of the Moor, combined with his intense agony, is realised from the moment when the poison first works, with a sincerity and absorption of the whole man which places Mr. Barrett's Othello in the first rank.'*

On August 3, 1896, Mr. Robert Arthur became lessee and manager of the Court, and opened with Mrs. Bernard Beere's Company in *Masks and Faces.* Just twelve months later, the theatre passed into the hands of the Robert Arthur Theatres Company, Limited, under whose management the first production was *The Trumpet Call,* given on August 2, 1897.

Mr. Arthur's first Liverpool annual was *Cinderella,* which ran into a second edition. Prominent in the cast were Marie Montrose, Amy Augarde, Flo Wilton, Bert Gilbert, Bertie Wright, and Newman and Downes. The second pantomime (1897-8) was *Robinson Crusoe,* with Frances Earle, Florrie West, Hetty Dene, the Sisters Levey, Stratton Mills and Harry Wright. Tuesday, April 12, 1898, saw the *premiere* of the four-act opera *Diarmid,* written by the Marquis of Lorne, and composed by Hamish MacCunn. It was performed by the Carl Rosa Opera Company. The 1898-9 annual, produced on December 21, was *Aladdin,* written by Walter Summers, and the cast comprised Claire Romaine, Austin Melford, and Little Tich.

On December 21, 1899, *The Babes in the Wood* was produced. The 'book' was by Walter Summers, and the principal parts were played by Nell Hawthorne, Sybil Arundale, Eva Dare, Mrs. Stanislaus Calhaem, J. F. McArdle, George Mozart, Walter Groves, and Paul Cinquevalli. Alfred C. Calmour's *Mistress of Craignairn* was produced by Frank Cooper and Murray Carson's company on February 26, 1900 ; and on October 18 following Mr. and Mrs Kendal were seen in Mrs. W. K. Clifford's new play *The Likeness of the Night.* The last Court annual of the century was *The Forty Thieves,* written by Walter Summers, with Mabel Nelson, Sybil Arundale, the Sisters Levey, Tom E. Murray, and Little Tich in the cast. The following Christmas saw the production of a very pretty extravaganza, entitled *Oberine,* written by Walter Summers. Victor Widnell's play, *A Woman of Impulse,* was produced on March 24, 1902. Another beautiful extravaganza, *Santa Claus, Junior,* from the pen of Walter Summers,

* 'Liverpool Daily Post,' October 23, 1891.

was brought out in the following Christmas. Ellen Terry appeared in Miss Clo. Graves's new play, *The Mistress of the Robes*, on November 4, 1903. *The Scarlet Goblin*, written by Frank Dix, was the succeeding Yuletide attraction. On Saturday evening, December 3, 1904, Sir Henry Irving made his last appearance on the Liverpool stage, when he played in *Waterloo* and *The Bells*. *Dick Whittington* was the annual for 1904-5. On November 15, 1905, Martin Harvey essayed Hamlet for the first time in Liverpool. *The Queen of Hearts* was the next pantomime ; *Aladdin* the subject for 1906-7 ; and *Cinderella* for 1907-8.

THE ' HOP.'

The ' Hop,' or the ' Penny Hop,' as it was not infrequently called, was for many years a house of entertainment of very considerable popularity. It was situated at 140 Dale Street, almost facing Fontenoy Street. The ' Hop ' was opened about 1830 by Mr. John Caloe as a Theatre of Arts. Here were to be seen mechanical working models of ' The Storm at Sea,' ' The Bay of Naples and the Eruption of Vesuvius,' and an allegorical representation of ' The Birth of Venus,' while a beautifully modelled figure of Napoleon told the fortunes of ladies and gentlemen. Other entertainments consisted of negro minstrelsy, legerdemain, marionette performances, dissolving views, and the centrifugal railway. I must not omit to mention the wax-work figures, which included ' Sir John Franklin Lost in the Arctic Regions,' ' Andromache and the Lion,' and ' Gold Diggers at Work in California.' All these figures, as well as their mechanical parts, were made in the work-shop behind the stage of the ' Hop.'

Apropos of the model of ' Sir John Franklin Lost in the Arctic Regions,' Mr. Caloe's son* tells me that one morning a jolly Jack Tar strolled in and duly paid his penny. After looking round he came to the Franklin group, before which he paused, and ejaculated ' Poor fellows ! Poor fellows ! ' Addressing the figure of a sailor he said ' I can't shake yer flipper, messmate, so give us a wag of yer foot.' Thereupon,

* Mr. John Caloe, of Old Basford, Nottingham, to whom I am indebted for some of these particulars.

he heartily shook one of the model's supposed frozen feet, but much to his dismay it came off in his hand. ' Well, I'm blessed, if that there frost ain't gone and eaten your foot off as well !   Poor fellows !   Poor fellows ! '   And out he went.

In the summer of 1846 a dwarf named Joseph Astill was on exhibition here.   He was then, according to his memoir, in his thirty-sixth year.   ' It is very difficult,' we are told by his biographer, 'to form a proper idea of the personal appearance of this extraordinary person.   When standing upon the floor, or walking about the room, which he does, dressed in the most elegant and fashionable manner, with all the grace and dignity of a finished gentleman, all his lines are of the most elegant proportion ;   his head is of the proper size and beautifully developed.   He is of a dark complexion, dark hair, fresh rosy cheeks, large beautiful eyes, a fine forehead, a handsome mouth, covered with a graceful and effective pair of mustachios.   A great vivacity of expression, and hilarity of behaviour ;   he is altogether free from deformities which generally disfigure such minified species of manhood.'

After this glowing account of Mr. Astill's charms, we cannot be surprised that he should have entered the bonds of holy matrimony, which he did at St. Peter's Church, Liverpool. The dwarf lady of his choice was Elizabeth Mansfield, of Manchester.   ' This lady,' says the memoir ' is equally symmetrical, of an intelligent mind and intellectual abilities.'   They were married on August 7, 1846, by the Rev. Thomas Halton, M A., in the presence of John and Sarah Caloe, of the Mechanical Exhibition Rooms, as the ' Hop,' was first styled.

' After this,' says my informant, 'we took a plunge into real legitimate drama, and played three shows a night, and *five* on Saturday.'   A small, but good working company was got together, under the direction of the proprietor's brother, Mr. William Caloe.   The   company   included   Messrs. R. Goodman, Luke Sharples, and Mr. Williams, junr., Mr. and Mrs. Williams, Mr. and Mrs. Sandy Keir, and Mr. and Mrs. W. Henderson.   They were certainly not a big crowd, but as there were generally a few professional gentlemen wanting to fill up an extra week or two, the gaps were commonly filled by birds of passage.

Friday evening was the fashionable night of the week, and on one of these occasions *Richard III* was presented.   The

performer of the title part was a past-master in the art of what
he called ' steaming ' it.   That is to say, if he had a part of
many lines, which he had not completely studied, he used to
mix up with it scraps of all kinds from his memory ! Upon the
occasion referred to above he had imbibed ' not wisely, but
too well.'   However, he managed to get on all right for some
six lines, after delivering ' Now is the winter of our discontent, &c.'   Then, ' without turning a hair,' he spouted a
bit from *The Fire Raisers*, something from *The Warlock of
the Glen*, and, finally wound up with a few stirring lines
from *The Seven Charmed Bullets !*

There was another favourite performer named Jack
Matthews, whose speciality was the enactment of Hamlet.
He had a large black dog, which followed him all through
the tragedy.   It was trained to ' bay the moon ' when the
Ghost appeared, and throttle the King in the closet scene,
thus terminating the performance about half-an-hour after
its commencement !

Another performer was a gentleman who hailed from the
Emerald Isle.   On the night of his first appearance he had
not spoken a dozen words of his part when he suddenly ' dried
up,' and not being used to ' steaming,' or ' gagging,' he gazed
wrathfully at the audience.   The silence, however, was broken
by someone in the gallery shouting out ' Wax ! Wax ! Wax ! '
One cannot say why that word should have been flung at him,
but it was evident that the new actor grasped the allusion,
for, on coming to the front, he looked daggers at the house,
and exclaimed ' Is it a dirty cobbler ye be after taking me for,
ye blackguards ? ' That was enough ! The whole house
roared with laughter, mingled with cries of ' Wax ! Wax !
Wax ! ' In fact, that was his greeting whenever he appeared
ever after, with one exception.   This was on an occasion
when the play was *The Wood Demon*, which was generally
performed on a Saturday night.   Mr. ' Wax ' was cast for
the Demon, and it was arranged at rehearsal that he should
make his appearance standing upon an eleven inch plank that
was placed across the front of the frame used for the Theatre
of Arts.   Two wings were bolted to the plank, which, upon
being released, fell to the right and left, disclosing the Demon
' in his habit as he lived.'   It was explained to the actor that
he must be very careful in making his exit.

Saturday night came round, and the first house was crowded. As the luckless player was garbed in Demon dress and mask the ' gods ' did not pierce his identity, hence his usual greeting was conspicuous by its absence. This so elated Mr. 'Wax' that he forgot all about the plank upon which he stood, and, stepping back, disappeared from view in the twinkling of an eye. This ' vanishing ' trick was greeted with loud applause, but, unfortunately, he could not be got out from amongst the lumber in time to respond

During the filling of the second house he was prevailed upon to do the same again, as it would increase his popularity. It was arranged that he should fall upon a straw bed used for pantomime business, but, unfortunately, he did not clear the plank sufficiently, with the result that his lower jaw caught the edge of the plank.   The poor fellow was unable to appear any more that night, all the demon being effectually knocked out of him.

Another amusing anecdote of the ' Hop,' and that the last :—A troupe of acrobats were engaged, and one of their number gave a ' single turn,' in which he displayed his skill as a champion weight-lifter. Somebody, however, on mischief bent, changed one of the fifty-six pound weights for one made of cardboard. The strong man's vision was impaired by the loss of one eye, but in this instance not unfortunately so. He took the first and second weights, and after having manipulated them he took the third—the one made of cardboard. Realising in an instant what had been done, he as quickly decided to turn it to his own advantage by throwing three ' flip-flaps,' while holding the dummy weight He was greeted with a perfect round of applause, and the audience declared it to be the greatest feat they had ever witnessed !

Mr. Caloe assures me that from the opening of the ' dear old " Hop," ' as he endearingly terms it, up to its final close in 1860, there was nothing put forward of a degrading, or immoral tendency, the plays and exhibitions being of a highly intellectual and instructive nature, affording enjoyment to thousands at a cheap rate

THE ZOOLOGICAL GARDENS THEATRE.

This establishment, which occupied a prominent place in public favour for many years, was situated in the beautifully

laid out Zoological Gardens, West Derby Road.   Vaude-
villes and farces, like *'Twas I ! The Swiss Cottage, The Loan
of a Lover*, etc., interspersed with singing and dancing, were
given by a number of talented performers.   Mrs. Burkinshaw,
the Leclerq Family, the Deulins, Stanislaus Calhaem, and
Fourness Rolfe all appeared on this small stage.   Admission
to the performances was free, except to the gallery,
where a small extra charge was made.   I am unable to say
when the theatre was first established.   In all probability it
was soon after the gardens were first opened by Mr. Atkins
in May, 1832.   The gardens closed about 1865.   Their site
is now occupied by Boaler, Goldsmith, Bourne, and Empire
Streets.   It is to be regretted that no effort was made to retain
the gardens for public use, as they could have easily been
converted into an ideal pleasure resort.

THE PRINCE OF WALES THEATRE,
VAUXHALL ROAD.

In 1842, nearly a couple of decades before the historic
' little house in the square ' was opened, there was situated
in Vauxhall Road, a Prince of Wales Theatre.   In that year
representations were apparently made to the Mayor that the
performances at the theatre were *contra bonos mores*.   The
house was therefore closed.   An investigation, however,
into the nature of the performances took place, and it was
found that the theatre had been well conducted, and the
performances above reproach.   The Mayor accordingly
granted full permission to the proprietor to re-open the
theatre ; and the inaugural bill after all the fuss consisted of
Vasha, the Slave Queen, and *Nicholas Nickleby*.   All other
details concerning this long forgotten house have been
devoured by ' Time's insatiable maw.'

THE ' PENNY HOP.'

This establishment was located in Hood Street during
the 'forties.   The interior consisted of a spacious room fitted
up in the rudest manner, with a stage and seats on an inclined
plane.   The entrance was through a dark passage and up a
ladder staircase.

Plays were given twice, and sometimes thrice, nightly. The patrons were of the lowest order, and many were without shoes and stockings.   Once the performers attempted to play *Jack Sheppard*, but in consequence of the frequent interruptions of the audience, who seemed to wish to take part in the play, the actors had to cease in the middle.*

THE ROYAL COLOSSEUM AND QUEEN'S THEATRES.

Let us imagine that we are living in Liverpool in the seventeenth century and that we have sauntered out for a breath of country air as far as the old bridge, which spanned the Pool at the foot of Lord Street, then the extreme end of the town eastward   Resting awhile, we gaze upon the eddying waters of the Pool coursing their way through what is now Whitechapel and Paradise Street, and lapping the shore upon which, in after years, the theatres under notice were situated.

Some years passed, and the waters of the Pool were diverted by the opening of Liverpool's first dock (the Old Dock as it was called), the position of which is now occupied by the Custom House   As the town developed eastward, there was amongst other buildings erected in Paradise Street a farmers' inn and livery stables, kept by one James Dimoke, who, for some considerable period both before and after the year 1750, kept the only carriage (a one-horse chaise, with a leathern top), that could be hired in the town   Hackney carriages were then unknown, and the only private carriage was that belonging to Miss Clayton, of Clayton Square.

Towards the close of the eighteenth century the Unitarian congregation in Liverpool, finding the chapel in Key Street too small, cast about for a suitable site for the erection of a newer and more commodious conventicle.   This they found on the site of Dimoke's old inn and livery stables, previously referred to   The lease bears date 1788, and the new chapel was opened for public worship in 1791

' In form,' observes ' The Stranger in Liverpool,'† ' the structure is octagonal ; open at one of the sides, in which is

---

* Parliamentary Papers, 1852, Vol VII.   † Ninth edition (1829), pp. 144-5.

S

the principal entrance.   Each side of the octagon exhibits
two windows :   an attic balustrade runs round the whole,
ornamented with vases at each angle : in the centre is a large
octagonal lantern, with small vases at the angles.   A handsome iron gate* and railing enclose a small area, which gives
an additional ornament to the building.   The inside is
well lighted, and in every respect commodious.   The seats
are lined and ornamented ; the pulpit supported by six columns,
with a double flight of stairs, makes a very pleasing appearance.   The gallery is well constructed, and in the front is
richly inlaid and veneered with beautiful woods.'   The chapel
also possessed a well-toned organ.   At the rear of the building
in Manesty's Lane (where the stage now is), a day school
for boys and girls, and the schoolmaster's house were
situated.†

During his sojourn in Liverpool, Dr. Martineau (brother
of the celebrated authoress, Harriet Martineau), preached
some of his most excellent sermons within. the walls of
Paradise Street Chapel ; and here also have worshipped,
on more than one occasion, Thomas Carlyle, ' the Sage of
Chelsea,' and his wife.

In 1849 the Unitarians migrated from Paradise Street
to. a handsome edifice in the Gothic style of architecture in
Hope Street.   Paradise Street Chapel was put up for sale and
bought privately on behalf of Mr. Joseph Heath, who, about
1850, opened the building as the Royal Colosseum Theatre
and Music Hall.   It is only fair to mention that the Unitarians did not know for what purpose their former chapel had
been bought.   When Mr. Heath first opened the theatre the
pews of the chapel were requisitioned for seating accommodation.   The dramatic entertainments which Mr. Heath
gave his patrons, the youthful and ancient mariners from the
Wapping and other contiguous docks, were of a full-flavoured
description, while the variety performances, which were given
in that portion of the building fronting Paradise Street,‡
were well suited to the taste of those for whom he successfully
catered through a number of years.

---

* This gate only a few years since was still to be seen in front of the theatre in
Paradise Street.
† It was either in the house formerly belonging to the schoolmaster, or one adjoining
t hat Mr. James Kiernan, the well-known *entrepreneur*, was born.
‡ This lesser hall was afterwards used as a dancing saloon.

When Mr Heath first opened the ' Colly,'—as it was familiarly called—the audience, in order to enter the theatre, had to pass through the graveyard which partly encircled the building. Amongst a number of youthful frequenters of the ' Colly ' the belief gained ground that some ' spirit doom'd for a certain term to walk the night ' haunted the vicinity of the theatre. Be this as it may, there is no doubt that prior to the removal of the remains for reinterment elsewhere, ' Props' of the theatre was never at his wit's end for a skull for *Hamlet*. Indeed the actor could help himself, for when in the dressing-room (which had previously been used as a grave vault), he had, it is said, only to put his hand through a thin division wall to lay hold, even as Hamlet did, of the grisly relic itself.   My friend, the late James Carr, told me he remembered that on one occasion when *Eugene Aram* was played at the ' Colly,' a real skeleton from the adjoining graveyard was requisitioned to do duty for the bones of Aram's victim !

In 1857, Mr. Heath's manager was George Ware, who afterwards officiated in the same capacity at the Whitebait Music Hall, Glasgow.   Mr Ware, who was born in 1829, was the author of several popular ditties   These included ' The Whole Hog, or None,' popularised by the great Mackney, ' The Squire and Maria,' and ' Up Goes the Price of Meat.' He also wrote several of Sam Collins's successes, including ' The Fiddler's Wife,' and ' The House that Jack Built.'

After amassing considerable property in the neighbourhood, Mr. Heath joined the majority, and yielded up his possessions to his son, Thomas Theodore Heath, who carried on the theatre with undiminished popularity and success.

It was in the ' Colly ' pantomime of *Fortunatus ; or, the Magic Wishing Cap*, produced at Christmas, 1866, that Mr. and Mrs. Leno, and Master Dan Leno played   Mrs. Leno was principal ' boy.'   Mr. Leno was clown, and little Dan, who was then about four years old, appeared as a juvenile clown. In 1867, Mr. James Elphinstone, one of the members of the well-known theatrical family of that name, was the acting and stage manager of the theatre.   On November 1, 1867, there was produced a drama from his pen, entitled *Prince's Park and Scotland Road ; or, Vice in Liverpool*.   In 1869, G. H. Macdermott, of ' We don't want to fight, but, by Jingo, if we do ' fame, was a member of the stock company, and played in that year's pantomime of *King O'Toole's Goose*, as did also Clara Wood. While the great Tichborne case was occupying the attention of the public a new drama, entitled *Robert Richborne ; or, the Disputed Title*, was brought forward on July 31, 1871. In 1875 Mr. C. H. Duval took the theatre, opening on September 27 with *The Ticket-of-Leave Man*. After Mr. Duval came Mr. Jacob Goodman. It was during the latter's tenancy of the theatre, that, on October 11, 1878, a panic occurred resulting in the loss of thirty-seven lives, not to speak of the many injured. This was primarily due to the fall of a portion of the ceiling into the pit, a mishap that occasioned a false alarm of fire. The late Fred Coyne was on the stage, singing ' You don't mean what I mean' when the panic broke out. Mr. Goodman offered £20 reward for the discovery of the miscreant who raised the false alarm of fire, but apparently without success. Afterwards considerable alterations were made in the theatre, the wooden pillars under the balconies being replaced by iron ones, and the roof materially strengthened. The 'Colly' at that time was capable of holding 3,000 persons. After being closed for some time it was re-opened in the December of 1879 as the Royal Colosseum Temperance Concert Hall, when a series of concerts was inaugurated by a committee of local gentlemen, under the presidency of Mr. William Simpson, who endeavoured to revive the old popularity of the ' Colly,', but, unfortunately, their efforts were not crowned with success. In 1880, Mr. Dan Saunders, formerly manager of the New Star Music Hall, in Williamson Square, took the theatre under his care and had the license re-established. He opened the house on April 26, 1880, as Saunders' Theatre of Varieties. Jolly John Nash was the star. In June of the same year Charles Godfrey appeared, and in November Jenny Hill came, followed by Pat Feeney. At Christmas Mr. Saunders presented Frank Green's pantomime, *Jack and the Beanstalk*, in which Charles Godfrey played the Dame, and the Leopolds were responsible for the comic scenes. Mr. Saunders was succeeded in 1881 by Mr. P. Wilcocks. During this gentleman's proprietorship Marie Loftus and Pat Feeney appeared. Wilcocks christened the establishment the City Theatre of Varieties. Messrs. Butler Stanhope and J. Vowles were the next tenants. They named the establishment the Royal

City Theatre, and it became a dramatic house once more. The following year (1883), during Mr. Sam Sweeney's management, it was again known as the City Theatre of Varieties Early in 1884, Mr. J. H. Wood was the lessee   The house was then styled the City Theatre and Royal Colosseum   On August Bank Holiday, 1884, the theatre, after being renovated, was opened by Mr. W. Potter as the Grand Theatre of Varieties.   Mr. E. Jonghmann was the musical director. The following year saw Messrs Wilmot and Roach, of the Grand Theatre, London, installed as lessees.   Afterwards Mr. Roach was the sole lessee and manager.   Commencing Monday, February 26, 1894, the house was opened by Mr. Elphinstone as the Grand Theatre.   *The Diver's Luck : A Story of the Great Eastern* was his initial attraction.   On Whit Monday, June 3, 1895, the theatre was opened as a dramatic house under the title of the New Grand Opera House, and, strangely enough, by two of the grandsons of the original founder of the theatre, Joseph Heath.   Determining to revive the glories of the old place, they burnished up its tarnished beauties, sweeping out every nook and corner, so that within and without it was hardly recognisable, so great was the transformation.

During the first twelve months of Messrs. John Edgar Heath and Albert Heath's tenancy, the New Grand was compulsorily known as a ' teetotal theatre,' and, after being conducted by them for two years, it was bought by Messrs. Elliston and Machin for about £18,000.   The theatre remained in their hands until about the end of July, 1901, when Mr. T. Morton Powell became the lessee.   Mr. Powell re-opened the theatre on August Bank Holiday of that year, and down to December of 1903 held the managerial reins. During several months in the following year the theatre remained closed.   Then the work of demolition and reconstruction was commenced with a will, and in a little while, as by the hand of an enchanter, a new and handsome playhouse named the Queen's arose on the site.   Of the old building there remains the front elevation in Paradise Street and School Lane, and portions of the old walls.

The opening took place on August Bank Holiday, 1904, with the drama entitled *Bigamy*, and under circumstances which gave the lessees, Messrs. Carson and Granville, every hope for the success of their venture.

The Queen's seats 2,000 persons at popular prices. The ceiling and the fronts of the boxes, circle, gallery and proscenium are in decorative fibrous plaster work of a unique design. Cream and gold, picked out with crimson, are the prevailing tints. The stalls and circle (horse-shoe shaped), are fitted with the most approved tip-up seats in crimson plush. The pit, which is several feet below the street level, is also fitted with seats in crimson plush, and there are several commodious refreshment *buffets*. There are eight boxes in all on either side of the stage, each of which will accommodate six persons. The proscenium opening is 27 feet wide and 26 feet high, or 22 feet up to the iron screen. In width it is .53 feet wide, and 38 feet from the footlights to the back cloth. The handsome entrance hall and vestibule has an ornate ceiling, mahogany screen and doors, Italian mosiac pavements, and oxydised silver electrical fittings. There are nine dressing-rooms situated where the old court-houses used to be, and two ' star ' dressing rooms in close proximity to the stage. There are no dressing-rooms under the stage as in the old theatre. The theatre is lighted throughout by electricity. The present proprietors of the Queen's are the Granville Theatres, Limited, of which Mr. Fred Granville is the popular managing-director.

THE BIJOU OPERA HOUSE.

At 65 Bold Street—called after the Bold family, who held property thereabouts—there stood a conventicle known as Dr. Thom's Chapel. About the early 'fifties of the last century it was converted into an elegantly fitted-up chamber, with a small stage, and re-named the Queen's Hall. The hall was also known as the Queen's Operetta House.

The late Valentine Vousden, who recently passed away in his eighty-fifth year at Bexhill-on-Sea, performed here on more than one occasion. Thirty years ago his annual income reached £3,000, and for many years it never fell below four figures.

In 1863-4 Mr. and Mrs. Drayton gave their popular musical entertainments, the conductor being the well-known musical composer, F. Stanislaus.   In the company was Fourness Rolfe, a very able actor, whose widow is still living and keeps a tobacconist and newsagent's shop in the Whitefield Road.   Charles Christy's Minstrels were here in May, 1865.   Mr F. Burgess was the acting manager of the company, which also included ' Pony ' Moore.

Mr. J. S. Lofthouse, who had the Oxford Music Hall in Lime Street, and the Cambridge at the corner of Warwick and Mill Streets, was the proprietor and manager of the Queen's in 1866.   In November of the following year those clever little people, the Aztecs, were on exhibition January 27, 1868, saw W. S. Woodin of ' Carpet Bag ' celebrity, and the following September witnessed those versatile entertainers, Mr. and Mrs. Howard Paul.   Maccabe of ' Begone, Dull Care,' fame sojourned here in December.   Mr. William Snodgrass was proprietor of the hall at this time.   In 1870, Mr. J. W. Bullock was lessee.   September of that year witnessed Mr. and Mrs. German Reed, and Messrs. Corney Grain and Arthur Cecil in their always enjoyable entertainments.

This was Corney Grain's first experience of touring. While in Liverpool opportunity was afforded him of observing the odd ways of an eccentric ' Dresser.'   ' One day, ' he tells us,* ' I noticed a paper bag on a shelf.   I thought it contained buns or biscuits.   Suddenly it moved slightly, as I thought.   Was it so, or an optical delusion ?   I heard a slight rustling ; it couldn't be the bag.   I remembered a silly old riddle about making a-bun-dance ; it couldn't have come true.   Again the bag moved.   I felt frightened.   Suddenly the bag seemed to jerk itself along the shelf.   I cried out to the dresser to come quickly.   " Lor, sir," he said, " it's only a little linnet as I bought cheap to-day off a man in the market ! "   Poor little linnet !   The dresser painted some of its feathers green and red, made a little perch that fitted into his button-hole, and the poor bird was taken round the country with us, fastened to this perch by a loop round its body.   I forget the linnet's fate, but I fear it was sad.'.. .

* ' Corney Grain,' by Himself, pp. 47-52.

. ' Liverpool seems to possess a curious race of dressers. There was another one three years later who rejoiced in the name of Sexton.   He had the faded appearance of an operatic chorus-singer by daylight, one of those unemployed peasants who are always asserting and exercising their rights of meeting on the stage, whether it be in the King's Counsel Chamber, the Queen's Boudoir, or a Woodland Glade.   His hair was shaved off at the temples, worn rather long, and a soft wide-awake was perched insecurely on the side and back of his head, like unto the manner of the unemployed operatic peasants aforesaid.   He had once been to Knowsley, and everything he saw brought back vividly to him the memory of the late Earl of Derby.

' " Ah ! sir," he would say, ' if the late h'Earl of Durby 'ad but seen this performance, 'ow 'e would 'ave apprusshiated it." '

' There were queer people we met in Liverpool. We asked a gentleman to recite on one occasion in our lodgings. He looked round ; the room was very small, and he said, " I am perfectly willing, but my voice is so extraordinarily powerful I am wondering if the room would stand it."

' Then, again, there was the timorous and o'er modest lady who let lodgings which gentility terms apartments ; she was about sixty, and her sister sixty-five, but they refused to let their apartments to Mr. Cecil and myself—they doubted the propriety of the step, as they were two lone maidens.

' Then there was the cheery gentleman who entertained us one Sunday, and insisted that Mr. Arthur Cecil should see his pigs.   In vain poor Mr. Cecil pleaded his ignorance of the pig in its raw state ; in vain he protested !   " Harry," said the impulsive gentleman, " take Mr. Cecil out and show him the old sow ! "   And out Mr. Cecil had to go and see the old sow.'

A popular favourite at the Queen's Hall was C. H. Duval, who performed here during February, 1871.   Charles Duval was originally intended for the bar, but he abandoned Blackstone to follow Thespis.   He made his professional *début* in Dublin, where he opened as a monologue entertainer.   The Great Vance (Alfred Peck Stevens), was here in April.   Some time previously Vance had opened a dancing academy in Liverpool, but as it did not prove particularly lucrative, he made up his mind to take an entertainment of his own through the provinces.

The lady who sang solos and duets and danced on two or four legs, the ' two-headed Nightingale ' as she was styled, made her first appearance on August 17, 1872.   In February of the following year the Great Tom Maclagan commenced an engagement.   In April of that year he was succeeded by Harry Liston, who gave his always acceptable ' Merry Moments '   Mr Liston was born in Manchester in 1843, and began life as a commercial traveller.   When George Leybourne, the celebrated comedian, used to drive about the metropolis in a carriage with four horses, Liston, by way of burlesque, went about the streets in a cart drawn by four donkeys.

A popular entertainer was Barry Aylmer who performed here in October, 1873.   He was succeeded by the Wardropers, Henry and Walter.   Herr Dobler, a very excellent conjurer, came in February, 1874   On one occasion when Herr Dobler was strolling through the market in Cork, he encountered a woman selling oranges.   He took one out of her basket, and slit it with a knife, when, lo and behold, out dropped a sovereign.   A second was put under the same process, with the same result, the old lady staring aghast at the oranges, the sovereigns and the professor   On the professor offering to buy the lot, the vendor sturdily refused to have any dealings with an emissary from the nether regions, as she conjectured Herr Dobler to be.   However she subjected her oranges, one after another, to a similar operation, with evident disgust at the non-success of her efforts   But the mysterious stranger begged of her to cut in two one of the halves, when to her great delight out dropped half-a-crown.

On September 19, 1874, Cooper's original Virginia Female Christy Minstrels commenced an engagement.   These artistes gave a performance as varied as it was attractive.   On September 20, 1875, Charles Duval gave a performance in aid of the Captain Webb testimonial fund   The Hero of the Channel was present during the evening and received quite an ovation.

On January 24, 1880, a new comic opera in two acts, entitled *Blue and Buff ; or, the Great Muddleborough Election,* written by ' E. V. Ward,' with music by W. L. Frost, was

produced for the first time on any stage. This pleasing little
piece, which was played by local amateurs, was much better
rendered in Liverpool than when performed by professionals
at the Haymarket, London, in September, 1882. The name
' E. V. Ward ' was an anagram compounded of the initials of
the two real authors, Mr. William Archer, the well-known
dramatic critic, and Mr. E. R. V. Dibdin, now the esteemed
curator of the Walker Art Gallery.

On May 3, 1880, the hall was opened by Messrs. Bell,
Woolrich, and Brown as the Bijou Theatre and Drawing-Room
Opera House, a cumbersome title truly, but one which was
afterwards shortened into the Bijou Opera House. The initial
performance was given by the Liverpool Amateur Operatic
Society.   On November 14, 1880, Messrs. Bell, Woolrich,
and Brown obtained a fourteen years' lease of the Bijou from
the owner, Mr. Booker. They laid out about £2,000 on the
house, and the landlord spent close on another £1,000.

Afterwards Mr. Bell became sole lessee at a rental of £310
per annum.   In 1882 he took in an adjoining house for the
purpose of improving the entrance and providing increased
accommodation for a new crushroom, a ladies' cloak and retiring-room, and refreshment bars, as well as for providing better
access to Back Bold Street. The gallery staircase was also
greatly increased in width. Altogether he spent about £500
on the building. The additional premises were subject to a
yearly rental of £110. Behind them was the railway belonging
to the Cheshire Lines Committee. The railway was laid about
1868, the lines being carried under Bold Street by means of a
tunnel, and opening out therefrom close to the little Opera
House, in an excavation 32 feet below the level of Back Bold
Street. The formation of the ground at that particular part
of the street was partly rock and partly made ground, and it
was necessary in carrying out the cutting to have a retaining
wall to keep Back Bold Street in its place. The wall erected
fell down on December 26, 1882, and the theatre had to be
closed.   Mr. Russell, Q.C., M.P. (afterwards Lord Russell
of Killowen), was leading counsel for Mr. Bell at the Liverpool
Assizes (held in May, 1883), in his action against the railway
company, when the jury returned a verdict for the plaintiff,
damages £500.

Early in May, 1883, Mr. Haldane Crichton produced here for the first time on any stage a drama by Messrs. Palgrave Simpson and A W A'Beckett, entitled *From Father to Son*. The theatre at that time was under the management of Mr. A. Gordon. In 1886 Mr. A. L. Baron held the managerial reins. Two years later Mr. Montague Roby, proprietor of Roby's Midget Minstrels, was the lessee He commenced his season at Christmas, 1889, and did wonderful business for upwards of seventeen consecutive weeks. Mr. T. T. Brindley was Mr Roby's resident manager with the Midget Minstrels. Among the latter was a very talented little lady who has since gained note as Louie Freear.

There is little more to mention of the history of the Bijou —which was made into shops in the early 'nineties—except to record that the theatre was always a favourite one with amateur dramatic societies. Time was when this city could boast of a number of amateur clubs, but now alas ! they are few indeed. In the old days we had the Barry Sullivan, Irving, Terry,Compton, Sheridan, Fairfield,Cambridge, Phœnix and West Derby Societies, besides several others. Many who have since achieved distinction in the world of the theatre acted with local amateur clubs, notably James Welch, Walter de Frece, H. C. Arnold, J. James Hewson, R A. Roberts, Fred Volpé, Melville G. Bickford, A. T. Crawford, Miss May Shirley and Miss Nellie Thierry.

THE ROYAL PARK THEATRE.

The first playhouse opened in the south end of Liverpool was the Royal Park. It was situated in Parliament Street. It was opened on Monday, September 27, 1852, by Robert Edgar (husband of the clever tragedienne, Alice Marriott), with all the fittings and scenery which he had purchased on the closing of the Liver Theatre in Church Street. The building had originally been a guano store, but under Mr. Edgar's superintendence it was converted into an attractive place of amusement. It held at popular prices about £90.

Mr and Mrs. Charles Pitt were here in October, 1852, and in December Miss Marriott appeared as Miami in *The Green Bushes*. On December 27, Charles Millward's first pantomime *Ye Siege of Liverpool ; or, Harlequin Prince Rupert, and Ye Fayre Mayde of Toxteth* was produced. In it Miss Marriott performed, supported by the entire strength of the company. Harry Boleno was specially engaged to play clown.

The 1853-4 annual was *Ormshead the Great ; or, Harlequin and Jenny Jones, The Flower of Snowdon.* It was also written by Mr. Millward. Miss Marriott played Snowdrop, and was announced to give ' a few airs, which the author has thrust on her.' The pantomime was preceded ' By a grave episode, in which the shades of Joe Miller and the Author will have very lively representatives.'

In October, 1859, Mr. John Campbell was the lessee of the house. After passing through several vicissitudes the building terminated its career as a theatre some few years ago, and like its Thespian neighbour, the Stanhope Theatre in Beaufort Street, is now used as a warehouse.

THE PRINCE OF WALES THEATRE.

Two hundred years ago what is now Clayton Square was a rural spot. A mansion dating from that time ultimately became the home of Miss Clayton,* whose garden was the prettiest and most productive in the town. Equally famous with the garden was Miss Clayton's closed carriage, at which, we are told, the inhabitants used to stare with the greatest wonderment, it being such a novelty. And had we lived in 1745, we might have watched preparations for the laying out of Clayton Square. In 1769, in this quiet and retired square with its grass grown pavement, three more houses were erected close to Miss Clayton's. Afterwards other houses followed in due course, to be turned in after years into shops and offices. Clayton House eventually became Clayton Hall. This hall, which was used at irregular intervals, possessed a good organ, inaugurated by Dr. Wesley on January 23, 1854. Among those who appeared here were John Coleman in his drawing-room entertainment (January, 1854) ; Julia St. George in her entertainment, ' Home and Foreign Lyrics,' the writer of which was Amelia B. Edwards, and the composer, J. F.

---

* Miss Clayton was the daughter of William Clayton who represented Liverpool in Parliament, with intermissions, from 1698 to 1714.

Duggan (December, 1856), and Gordon Cumming, the lion hunter (July 9, 1857) Carter's American Panorama, and the Indian giant and the little Texas lady formed the attractions in September, 1858.

'On a cold and dreary evening in December, 1859, a young man who had lately landed from Australia was roaming through the streets of Liverpool in quest of some amusement. Attracted by a dim light glimmering through the fog in front of a building he read the following notice :—

"Clayton Hall. To-night............, Minstrel Troupe, Musical Varieties" This decided him. He paid his shilling and walked in.

'The entertainment not being of a particularly lively nature, his eyes wandered listlessly over the interior, which was a large square hall with a gallery at the end. Suddenly he thought :—' The situation is good, why not take the hall, reconstruct the building, and form a pretty little theatre ?' By the time the performance was at an end he had formulated an oath *à la* Wilson Barrett. The young man was Alexander Henderson.

'Early the next morning Mr. Henderson called on Mr. W. Earp, proprietor of the hall, from whom he then and there secured the lease, with the option of purchase. Two days later he sailed for Australia, where he remained six months, at the expiration of which time, the hall becoming vacant, he returned to Liverpool to take possession, and to make the necessary alterations '*

Alexander Henderson's first wife, a Miss Moon, was connected with Liverpool. Originally he had been a clerk in the post-office in connection with the railway department. He first tried his hand at theatrical management in Victoria, Australia. Henderson afterwards made the acquaintance of the Nelson family, the head of which, Sidney Nelson, was the once well-known composer. He joined in their ventures, and served a rapid apprenticeship to a business in which few succeed, but in which he was on the whole very fortunate.

The prospectus of the Prince of Wales Theatre was drawn up partly by a gentleman who took a deep interest at that time in Liverpool theatricals, and partly by Mr. Sam Colville,

* ' The Prince of Wales' Theatre Annual ' (1884).

the American manager, who happened to be in town, as his wife, the brilliant Mary Provost, was playing an engagement here. A considerable amount of money was spent in the reconstruction of the building, which was completed by Christmas, 1861, and christened the Prince of Wales Theatre. Early in 1862, the Brunswick Hotel adjoining was taken into the theatre, and an entrance hall and crush-room in Cases Street provided. Seven years later the Cases Street entrance to the theatre was abolished.

Describing the theatre, the late William Edwards Tire-buck in his novel, 'Dorrie,' wrote that it was 'A very cosy comfortable little house; so cosy that the stage seemed part of the orchestra, the orchestra a part of the stalls, the stalls a part of the little pit, the opposite boxes on familiar terms with each other, the dress-circle a friendly continuation of the boxes, and the gallery like a cap of liberty and fraternity capping them all.'* A truer or more pleasing description of the Prince of Wales could not be desired.

The opening performance took place on Thursday evening, December 26, 1861, with Buckstone's comic drama, *The Maid with the Milking Pail*, followed by H. J. Byron's burlesque on *The Colleen Bawn* entitled *Miss Eily O'Connor.*

The following were the respective casts:

The Maid with the Milking Pail.

Milly,	Miss Maria Simpson.
Lord Philander,	Mr. P. Granger.
Algernon,	Mr. Alexander.
Diccou,	Mr. Sheridan.

Miss Eily O'Connor.

Myles-na-Coppaleen,	Miss Maria Simpson.
Hardress Cregan,	Miss Proctor.
Kyrle Daly,	Mr. Alexander.
Daddy Mann,	Mr. Fitzpatrick.
Mr. Corrigan,	Mr. Sheridan.
Sergeant Tooralooral,	Mr. Franklin.
Eily O'Connor,	Mr. John Rouse.
Miss Ann Chute,	Miss Herberte.
Mrs. Cregan,	Miss Barrowcliffe.

* Chap. XXXIII, p. 291.

Prior to the commencement of the performance Mr. Fitzpatrick came forward, and delivered the following opening address —

   ' The Manager with mighty woes oppress'd,
A heavy weight of light fun on his breast,
Requests that I should ease him of his care,
Presents his *carte*—I mean his bill-of-fare.
No five-act tragedies, we bring to tease you,
We'd rather *live* than *die*, kind friends, to please you.
Hard *feat* to gasp through ten poetic *feet*, or
Meet our fate in dull lines of long *metre*.
We'll catch the " humours of the age," and show
How far the charms of harmless mirth can go ·
Give every novelty we can afford—
Upon these *boards* you never shall be *bored*.
Cram but our little house from floor to rafter,
We'll cram the stage with fun,and crack your sides with
     laughter !
" Laugh and grow fat ! " I've come to this decision—
That Dr Fun's the very best physician.
Have you the blues ? Look here, a Clayton pass is,
We recommend at once a dose of *Farces*.
You're bilious ! cure you ? Yes, I think I can, sir ;
Take a decoction of *Extravaganza*.
Indigestion ! What ? Go take a blue pill ?
Take nothing of the sort—go take a vaudeville.
You're wearied with your 'counting-house and desk ;
Require a change—come to our new *burlesque*
Ladies, you fear a slight attack of vapours—
We recommend a trial of our capers.
Here all your trifling ills shall be appeased,
For we " can med'cine to a mind diseased."
Rely, to-night shall be the earliest token
Of promises, unlike pie-crust, *id est*—unbroken.
We throw ourselves to terminate these verses,
Not in the *Mersey*, but upon your *Mercies* :
We trust our many faults, errors, you'll forgive,
For only in your smiles can our little theatre live ;
And if, as now, we see around, good humour, youth, and
     beauty,
'Twill cheer us on when led by you—each one to do his
     duty.'

Alexander Henderson had the gift of doing the right thing at the right time.   His plan was to have a first-rate stock company, chiefly consisting of rising young players, content with modest salaries, and thus to afford good support to stars, who rapidly found in Clayton Square pecuniary profit and social consideration.   Other things in which he showed great judgment were his scene painting and stage furniture. For his scenic work Henderson secured the services of poor Dalby, whose gift it was to prepare with magical celerity, even at a day's notice, stage pictures of remarkable beauty. As for upholstering, Henderson struck out a new line altogether and arranged with the best firms to stage piece after piece with new furniture, making his stage look like the *milieu* of real luxurious life.

The earliest important engagement was that of J. L. Toole.   It took the little comedian three whole days to settle in his mind whether he would close with Henderson's offer of £30 per week certain, or accept the alternative of sharing the profits after the expenses had been deducted.   Finally, he decided on the latter course, with the result that his pro-portion of the profits at the end of his month's engage-ment amounted to nearly £600.   His first appearance here was made on January 20, 1862, when he played Simmons in *The Weavers*, and Spriggins in *Ici on Parle Français ; or, French Before Breakfast*.   In the former piece he gave ' A Norrible Tale.'   During his visit he also played the titular part in H. J. Byron's burlesque, *Blue Beard*.

On February 15, 1862, H. J. Byron's fairy burlesque, *Aladdin* was presented.   Another of Byron's burlesques, *Lurline*, was produced on the Easter Monday following. Those favourite performers the Nelson Sisters (Carry and Sara), appeared on August 18, in *The Invisible Prince ; or, the Island of Tranquil Delights*.   Phelps played in November and Lady Don in December.   Byron's *Ivanhoe* was the Christmas piece.

Miss Marriott attracted large houses in February, 1863. About this time Henderson issued a paper for free distribu-tion in the theatre.   It was called ' The Curtain,' and contained notices of the plays performed.   The title of the publication was afterwards changed to ' The Foot-lights.'

On December 26, 1863, a drama entitled *Stolen Money*,
from the pen of Mr. (now Sir) E. R. Russell was produced.
The play was founded upon a story which appeared in Charles
Dickens's Christmas Number for 1860, called ' A Message
from the Sea ' ' The Porcupine,' for January 2, 1864, said,
' there is much in the drama to admire, ... and the
author may be warmly congratulated on the heartiness and
cordiality with which the drama was received.'

The Tercentenary of Shakespeare's anniversary was
commemorated by the revival of *Hamlet* on Thursday, April
21, 1864. The titular part was played by Alfred Wigan. 'As a
Tercentenary commemoration,' says ' The Porcupine,' for April,
30, ' the *Hamlet* of the Prince of Wales was poor and mean.
We are not dwarfing Shakespeare by over-decoration nor
do we fear that lack of stage-management will ever destroy
the effect of his text ; but we have at least the right to expect
that a theatre which for common dramas and burlesques
weekly produces, at very short notice, the most exquisite
scenery, shall at least mount Shakespeare respectably. We
see no palliation for the offence of omitting to do so   Not
even the smallness of the stage excuses it, for we are continually
marvelling at the ingenuity with which, in burlesques, the little
stage is made almost unlimited by the clever illusions of the
artist, and no one can persuade us that what is done for *Ixion*
or *Rumpelstiltskin* could not be done to render the bastions
and terraces of Elsinore and the arrangements of the scene
at once *vraisemblables*, picturesque, so spacious looking as
to give freedom to the action of the actors and the imagination
of the spectators. The play was certainly very well
performed.'

Alfred Wigan essayed Hamlet on May 7, 1864. Then
came the Pyne and Harrison Opera Company. On August 1
following, the Brothers Webb (Henry and Charles), gave their
celebrated impersonations of the two Dromios in *The Comedy
of Errors*   Squire Bancroft played Antipholus of Syracuse.
The Webbs also acted in *The Courier of Lyons*. It was once a
popular fallacy that the brothers were twins. As a matter
of fact, Henry was two years older than Charles and was
much the better actor. Henry burst a blood-vessel while
playing Dromio of Ephesus, and died in London in January,
1867.

T

Lionel Brough portrayed Lavinia in *The Miller and His Men* on August 15, 1864.   Brough joined Mr. Henderson's company at the Wales in 1863, and remained a leading member for more than three years.   Subsequently he was at the Amphi' under the managements of W. R. Copeland and H. J. Byron.   In October, 1867, Brough went to London.

In the autumn of 1864, a youth bent on becoming an actor stood outside the Prince of Wales Theatre, fearful of making his *début*, and dreading the meeting with his future comrades.   That youth was John Hare.

'After considerable delay,' says Sir John Hare,* ' I was allowed to pass the sacred portals of the stage-door by the dirty Cerberus in charge, and groped my way on to the small and dimly-lighted stage, to find myself in the presence of the company assembled for rehearsal.   To my astonishment I was received with more than courtesy—with every token of respect.   A chair was considerately placed for me in the centre of the stage by the prompter, and, taking possession of it, I more calmly awaited the development of events. Apparently I was already " discovered."   Someone advanced to me respectfully with outstretched hand and his hat in the other, welcoming me to England, and hoped that my first appearance would meet with the success which my reputation predicted.   It had preceded me across the seas, he said, to my mystification.   I soon found, however, that I had been mistaken for a certain Mr. Raymond, an American " star," whose arrival was awaited in Liverpool.   Then, although the deferential attitude assumed towards me disappeared, I must say that, for a new recruit, I received extraordinary kindness and encouragement, especially from Bancroft, with whom I speedily made good friends and have remained so up to the present day.'

On Thursday, September 29, 1864, Hare made his *début* on the professional stage in a forgotten comedietta entitled *A Woman of Business*.   His part was that of a young dandy, the Honourable Shrimpton Smallpiece.   The 'star' was little Toole whose acquaintance Hare then made for the first time.

* 'Reminiscences and Reflections,' by John Hare. 'The Strand Magazine,' May, 1908.

Speaking of his first appearance Sir John Hare says :—
' My feelings of dismay on walking on to the stage for the
first time were such that my self-possession entirely deserted
me on becoming aware of the sea of faces in front, with the
result that I absolutely forgot every word I had to say.
Gaping like a fish out of water, I must have presented a
pitiable and ludicrous spectacle.   At any rate, I was not
left long in suspense—a burst of hisses greeted me from the
pit and gallery, harmonizing with the sound of refined but
derisive laughter from the boxes and stalls.   This reception
was my salvation   Indignation enabled me to master my
nervousness, so that I recovered my speech and was able
to finish the scene in an adequate, if not successful, manner.
Leigh Murray, who had accompanied me to Liverpool to
witness my first appearance, was clearly not much impressed
with the *début* of his pupil   He did his best, however, to
console me with encouragement, and himself with several
extra glasses of his favourite beverage.'

When Watts Phillips's comedy, *The Woman in Mauve*, was
produced on December 19, 1864, John Hare played the part
of Beetles, an ex-policeman.   This was Hare's first part of
importance, and he played it with great acceptance.   The
' Liverpool Courier' for the following day said, ' Mr. Hare
again manifested rare abilities in character parts.'   A few
nights later during the progress of the second act of *The
Woman in Mauve* the leading characters were joining in the
chorus to a song sung by Sothern, who played the part of
Frank Jocelyn, Hare meanwhile beating time with a telescope, which he used throughout the play as a kind of memory
of his former truncheon.   The song went splendidly, and the
audience roared with laughter at each successive verse.

' The shrieks of the audience,' explains Hare, ' led me to
indulge in extraordinary exertions with my telescope, which
I waved with the enthusiasm of a continental *maestro*.   In the
midst of my ecstasy Sothern astounded me by saying quietly
in an aside, " It's all right, old fellow , don't worry, but just
get off the stage as soon as possible ! " I then discovered to
my horror, that some towels with which I had stuffed myself
(in order to obtain a suggestion of *embonpoint* with which
Nature had not endowed me), had dropped from their moorings
and were making an untidy heap on the stage.   Need I say

I fled from the scene and left the others to finish without me ? '*

The following story is told concerning one of E. A. Sothern's visits to Liverpool:—Sothern was very fond of animals, especially of big dogs. He wanted one for his New York home, and commissioned his friend, Henderson, to buy it for him. This gentleman, like Messrs. Brooks, Dickson and Stetson of *Romany Rye* celebrity, advertised for one.

In answer to the advertisement, Mr. Wilkins, a retired actor, wrote to say that he had a suitable animal with which he would part for a consideration. The animal referred to had once been the chief attraction in canine dramas like *The Forest of Bondy ; or, the Dog of Montargis.* There was a time in the history of the stage when dogs were popular and meritorious performers. They were histrionic ' stars ' of a secondary magnitude. Dramas were written round the dogs, and the actors had to play up to them.

The usual preliminaries having been concluded, a purchase was made, and Wilkins received the sum of five pounds sterling for his dog. Cæsar was the dog's name, and he was supposed to be only five years of age. Examination by an expert revealed the fact that his age was three times five at least. Sothern, therefore, sued Wilkins for the recovery of the five pounds. At the trial, Cæsar was produced in court. He was admired for his fine appearance, but it was proved that he had been ' made-up ' for the occasion.

Wilkins acknowledged that Cæsar was a veteran. He also said that for many years Cæsar had been the principal attraction of the Harrison Family and their canine troupe. Wilkins pleaded impecuniosity as his excuse for parting with the dog, and the court decided in his favour. But Cæsar's legal guardian refused to have anything to do with him. The most pathetic part of the story remains to be told. Not long after the famous trial, Cæsar was observed in the streets of Liverpool, with a tin cup in his mouth soliciting money for a blind man. This was the end of the noble animal who had performed as a canine ' star ' before admiring thousands, who had seized celebrated actors by the throat, protected heroines from the wiles of stage villains, and had very nearly become the friend and companion of E. A. Sothern.

* ' The Strand Magazine,' May, 1908

On February 13, 1865, the notorious Davenport Brothers, fresh from their so-called spiritual manifestations in London, visited St. George's Hall, where their mysterious performances created great discussion. They were accompanied by a fellow conjurer called Fay, and a ' Dr.' Ferguson who acted in the capacity of lecturer. The brothers attributed their feats to spiritual means. This our townsmen could not stand, and some of them arranged such knots as no spirits could succeed in untying. The result was rebellion and riot. The mysterious cabinet was smashed to pieces by some of the audience, while others pursued the Davenports and their confederates to the stage door of the Prince of Wales, where revolvers in hand, they arrived in a bedraggled and breathless condition. Henderson gave them refuge from the infuriated crowd, and later on let them out by a private way, to reach their lodgings and catch the first train home.*

Henderson took advantage of the foregoing occurrence to produce an appropriate sketch entitled *The Knotting'em Brothers*, on February 17, 1865. In this Hare was capitally made up to resemble one of the Davenports.

Alfred Wigan commenced an engagement on March 20, 1865. During his visit he essayed two new parts, Shylock in *The Merchant of Venice* and Evelyn in *Money*. In the latter piece John Hare played the small, but effective, part of the old member, an asthmatical old gentleman with a penchant for snuff-taking. ' The scene in the club,' says Hare,† ' is so arranged that the old member makes his entrance alone. His " business " is to take his seat and call out, " Waiter, snuff-box ! " Then the other characters enter. I had, however, determined to seize this opportunity of making an elaborate character-study of the old gentleman. I do not know exactly what I did, but instead of going quietly to my seat, I gave a detailed delineation of an asthmatic old gentleman who grunted, coughed, and did everything except speak, to the apparent delight of the audience, who laughed immoderately at my efforts, much to my personal gratification. I, however, delayed the entrance of the principal characters for a considerable time, and was only brought to my senses by the sight and sound of the infuriated Wigan saying to me

* ' Mr and Mrs Bancroft On and Off the Stage.' Sixth edition, p. 78.
† ' The Strand Magazine,' May, 1908.

from the wings, "Now, sir, we've had enough of this. Be silent !" The impression made on the audience showed itself subsequently, for whenever the old member opened his mouth to say, "Waiter, snuff-box !" he received a round of applause, much to the indignation of Wigan.'

Society, which Tom Robertson had offered fruitlessly to Sothern, Alfred Wigan, and nearly all the London managers, was successfully produced here on May 8, 1865, for the first time on any stage. How Liverpool's good opinion of the comedy was afterwards endorsed at the metropolitan Prince of Wales Theatre in Tottenham Street, is now well known.

In December, 1865, Henry Irving commenced here his third engagement in Liverpool. On December 11, he played Archibald Carlyle in *East Lynne* to the Lady Isabel of Avonia Jones. Irving remained here for six months, play-ing utility and burlesque parts. On Whit Monday, in 1866, he sustained the female *rôle* of Œnone in an extravaganza, entitled *Paris ; or, Vive Lempriere!* while the twins, Castor and Pollux, were impersonated by Lionel Brough and Edward Saker. Of Irving's performance, the ' Liverpool Daily Post ' of the following day* said that he ' displayed as much his-trionic ability in the representation of an absurd burlesque part as he invariably does when he has an intelligent part to render.' There were other similar words of just praise and timely encouragement extended to him by his life-long friend, Sir Edward Russell, now the *doyen* of Liverpool dramatic critics. These early words of praise and encouragement were, I know, greatly prized by Irving, and never forgotten.

During the remainder of his stay at the Prince of Wales Irving rapidly improved in his art, and it seemed likely that the prophecies of a brilliant career were soon to be fulfilled. After the termination of his engagement with Mr. Henderson there came a temporary blank. ' I have many memories of Liverpool,' he said on the last night (October 6, 1883), of his engagement at the Alexandra, prior to his departure for his first American tour. ' One of them is of a time eighteen years ago, when I stood upon the steps of the Prince of Wales Theatre without an engagement, and wondered what on

* May 22, 1866.

earth I should do next.' Then came an offer from Dion Boucicault of a leading part in his new play entitled *The Two Lives of Mary Leigh*, afterwards known as *Hunted Down*. This marked the beginning of a new and important phase in Irving's career.

On June 4, 1866, H. T. Craven's new five act play *The Needful*, was produced for the first time on any stage. The part of Abraham Store was played by the author. The piece was afterwards produced in London.

Tom Robertson's comedy *Ours* was performed on August 23, 1866, for the first time on any stage. When it was brought out at the metropolitan Prince of Wales, on September 15, 1866, the cast was the same as on its representation here, with the exception that Frederick Younge then played the part of Sergeant Jones.

Of Robertson's great anxiety in connection with the piece, the late Charles Millward penned the following account:—
' Robertson was fearfully nervous at the rehearsals and not sanguine of success After the final rehearsal, on the day of the production, I persuaded him to join me in a sail on the river, and Clark and Dewar readily agreed to accompany us. We accordingly took the steamer for New Brighton, and on arriving there proceeded to the best hotel, and ordered the best dinner that could be provided. And how we all enjoyed that delightful impromptu banquet, the pleasant balcony (facing the sea), upon which we sat, and the exhilarating after-dinner talk ! Robertson was in his very best form, and no longer shaking with nervousness , but just as we were thinking about returning to the theatre, he fell asleep. I would not have him disturbed, poor fellow ! so he slept soundly until within one hour of the time fixed for the commencement of the memorable performance. It then became necessary to arouse him ; and the painful duty devolved on myself. We reached the theatre just in the nick of time, and then it was unpleasantly evident that Robertson's nerves were again unstrung. The theatre was crowded in every part ; but Robertson positively refused to occupy the box the manager had reserved for him. He would first take a smart walk, he said, "to blow the steam off." He must have accumulated a large quantity of superfluous steam, for he

was *non est* during the performance of the first and second acts, and although he had been vociferously called for by the audience, he was nowhere to be found. When the third act commenced, every soul in the theatre, save the author, knew that *Ours* was a thumping success. But where was Tom Robertson ? Surely not still blowing the steam off ? As we knew there would be a tremendous call for him when the curtain fell, we were bound to find the missing author, dead or alive.

'Messengers were despatched in all directions in search of him ; and as I had frequently seen him during his nervous attacks, I joined in the pursuit. I dreaded the prospect of the play terminating before the author turned up ; so I sought for him in the streets around the theatre. Ultimately I encountered him in Bold Street, walking at a furious pace, mopping the perspiration from his brow, in evening-dress, and *bareheaded.* He had been pacing the streets " blowing off,' more than two hours. With great difficulty I induced him to return with me to the theatre, where we found the last scene on. When the curtain fell, a tremendous shout arose for the author and Marie Wilton dragged him across the stage, pale as a ghost, as limp and flabby a specimen of a successful dramatist as one could wish to see.'*

The finishing touches to *Ours* were given by Mr. Robertson at Waterloo, Liverpool, where, in association with the Bancrofts, the Byrons and the Hares, he spent a delightful six weeks in the summer of 1866. Of those pleasant days the Bancrofts recount how at the Liverpool summer assizes held that year, the afterwards celebrated librettist Mr. (now Sir) W. S. Gilbert, attempted his maiden speech at the bar in prosecuting an old Irishwoman for stealing a coat.

' He was very anxious about his first essay, and we all assembled to hear it. Mr. Gilbert tried for a long time to speak, but the old woman interrupted him so persistently that he could not get a word in edgeways, with such polite remarks as, "Hold yer tongue !" "Shut up, yer spalpeen !" "Ah, if ye love me, sit down !" " It's a lie, yer honour !" " Hooroo for ould Ireland ! " etc. She jumped about and made

---

* T. Edgar Pemberton's 'Life and Writings of T. W. Robertson,' pp. 191-3.

such a noise every time Mr. Gilbert attempted to speak, that the judge ordered her to be taken down until the next day ; and as she left the dock, the prisoner made a grimace at Mr. Gilbert, which I will not attempt to describe ! So, after all, the maiden speech never came off, and I fear we were all immensely amused at Mr. Gilbert's discomfiture '*

The friends of the merry septenary party came down to Waterloo once every week, and the evenings were dedicated to improvised entertainments They had mock trials in which Mr. Hare was always condemned to act the part of the criminal in the dock. Clever speeches about nothing were delivered by rising young barristers Mrs Bancroft was the judge, and gave imitations of various gentlemen she had seen on the bench. Her robe was a pink wrapper, and her wig was made of cotton-wool. On one occasion a mock opera was performed. Mrs. Bancroft was the *prima-donna*, W. S. Gilbert, the lover, John Hare, his rival, with a large cloak, broad-brimmed hat, and knives and daggers all over him ; the late W. R McConnell (formerly Revising Barrister of Liverpool), was the *prima-donna's* father—a deaf old man—at whom they had to shout all their recitatives through an improvised ear-trumpet. The opera was sung throughout in Italian gibberish, and was a most amusing bit of nonsense I may mention that the method employed in the last act of *Caste,* to break the news to Esther that her husband still lived, was suggested to Robertson by one of the impromptu entertainments given at Waterloo. Their audiences were small but appreciative. ' We were all young then,' mention the Bancrofts, ' and the fun, perhaps, appeared greater than it would now, but it was a very happy time. Some of those pleasant friends are gone, alas ! never to return 't

For some five years Mr. Henderson successfully managed the theatre, but in 1866 he left to manage the New Prince of Wales Theatre and Opera House in Lime Street—a house which was said to have been ' built by the currant jelly for the currant jelly.' The Clayton Square theatre was taken by Mr. William Brough, who opened it as the Varieties on December 26, 1866, with *King Arthur ; or, the Days and Knights*

* ' Mr. and Mrs. Bancroft On and Off the Stage.' Sixth edition, p 99.
† *Ibid,* p. 100.

of the Round Table, in which piece those favourite performers Carry and Sara Nelson appeared. Mr. E. English succeeded Mr. Brough as manager, and opened the theatre as a music hall on February 11, 1867. Mr. Charles Benjamin Castle was the next manager. About this time a German troupe of ladies were seen in a series of classical poses. Their performances obtained for 'the little House in the Square' some rather undesirable notoriety.

Alexander Henderson returned to manage the Clayton Square house on September 2, 1867, upon which occasion *Our American Cousin* was performed with E. A. Sothern in his original part of Lord Dundreary. Madge Robertson (afterwards Mrs. W. H. Kendal), was also in the cast. When H. T. Craven's drama, *Meg's Diversion*, was presented on September 30, Henry Irving and Marcus Elmore were specially engaged for leading parts. Mrs. John Wood, who is a native of this city, made her first appearance on October 14, when she performed Anne Bracegirdle in *The Actress by Daylight*, and Jenny Leather-lungs in *Jenny Lind at Last*. In the latter she gave her popular imitations of Patti, Titiens, Mario, etc. That clever and distinguished player Hermann Vezin was seen in *The Man o' Airlie* on November 11. Mrs. Scott-Siddons, a grand-daughter of the great Sarah Siddons, was here on November 25, when she played Rosalind for the first time in Liverpool.

After Mr. Henderson left in 1868 the theatre was taken by Frank Musgrave, who opened it on February 10, 1868, with the burlesque of *The Brigand*, wherein vivacious Lydia Thompson (Mrs. Alexander Henderson), and diverting W. J Hill played. Mr. W. H. Swanborough was the acting manager of the theatre. Musgrave was also assisted in the management by his brother John. Toole and Mr. and Mrs. Billington performed during the week commencing November 9. Byron's *Not Such a Fool as He Looks* was produced for the first time in Liverpool on December 14. Principal parts were played by the author and William Farren. The Yuletide attraction was F. C. Burnand's burlesque, *The Rise and Fall of Richard III ; or, a New Front to an Old Dickey*.

On April 19, 1869, Fanny Josephs and George Honey performed in Byron's burlesque, *Lucrezia Borgia, M.D.* This was Miss Josephs' first appearance on the local stage. She afterwards became lessee of the Prince of Wales Towards the latter end of 1869 the theatre was under the joint management of Messrs. Eldred and Fairlie. On March 28, 1870, Edgar Bruce (who made his *début* on the stage here), Charles Dornton, Harry Paulton, and Mr. Billington played in *Aurora Floyd* and *Black-Eyed Susan*. Nellie Farren and Constance Loseby made their first appearance here with the Gaiety Company on April 4. The famous Vokes family performed on April 18. The theatre was opened under the management of Mr. H W. Pearson, on October 29, 1870, when the attractions were *The Coquette* and *The Idle 'Prentice*. In the last-mentioned play Arthur Garner made his first appearance on the stage. Mr. Garner remained at the Prince of Wales until the following year Mr. Henry Leslie succeeded Mr. Pearson, and opened the theatre on December 26, with *The Loving Cup*, and the Brothers Brough in *The Enchanted Isle*. A painstaking and able actor, J C. Scanlan, was the assistant acting manager.

Commencing March 6, 1871, James Bennett the celebrated tragedian was seen in a number of classic *rôles*. Another noted player, Julia St. George, performed in *The Princess of Trebizonde* on March 20. On April 10, the Billingtons came. The drama of *Smoke* and the opera bouffe of *The Princess of Trebizonde* were presented. The first week in May witnessed Madge Robertson and W. H. Kendal in *The Palace of Truth*. The company also included that excellent comedienne Lottie Venne, who then made her first appearance on the local stage. At that time the proprietors of the house were the Prince of Wales Theatre Company, Limited. On June 19, Mrs. W. H. Kendal, played Ophelia in scenes from *Hamlet*. On June 26, *Chilperic* was performed (for the first time out of London), by John Rouse, Emily Soldene, Bella Richardson, and Clara Vesey. A noteworthy rendering of Dan'l Peggoty in *Little Em'ly* was given by Sam Emery on August 7. Towards the close of 1872 the theatre was under the management of Mr. Sefton Parry.

On March 1, 1873, Nellie Bouverie (' Bouverie Bright '), made her first local appearance. In September, Mr. J. H. Addison was proprietor. Addison bought from Alexander Henderson the unexpired term of his lease, but subsequently

disposed of it for £3,000.   During his management a good
all-round stock company was maintained to support the
visiting stars   Mr. Addison brought *La Fille de Madame
Angot, Chilperic, Lurline, Genevieve de Brabant, The Happy
Land*, etc. In *The Happy Land* G. W. Anson was capitally
made up to represent the Grand Old Man.

In the summer of 1874 the theatre was under the management of Mr W. Sidney.   On September 21, Charles
Wyndham, R J. Roberts, Fred Marshall, Nellie Bouverie,
Caroline Elton, and Alice Ingram were seen in *Brighton*.
On November 30, Henrietta Hodson appeared in *Ought We
to Visit Her* ? Miss Heath and Wilson Barrett were here
on August 2, 1875. The following week came Alice Atherton
and Willie Edouin in Farnie's burlesque of *Blue Beard*.
Two of the ladies who impersonated peasant maids were charming Ethel and Maude Branscombe   I remember some years
ago seeing clever Willie Edouin and his talented wife intently
watching a Punch and Judy show in Lime Street.   They
seemed to thoroughly enjoy the performance, judging by the
smiles that wreathed their faces.   Fred Broughton's *Withered
Leaves* and *Pygmalion and Galatea* were performed on September 6.   In the company were Edward Smith Willard,
G. F. Leicester, and Edward Chessman.   The following week
brought versatile Nellie Power as Cherry in the burlesque
Cherry and Fairstar   The Kendals followed with *The Lady
of Lyons, A Happy Pair*, and *She Stoops to Conquer*.   On
November 8, Jenny Lee made her first local performance in
the titular part in *Jo*.

Mentioning Miss Lee reminds me that because she
was so frequently seen as Jo she came to be regarded as a one-
part actress.   A similar impression sprang up concerning
Joseph Jefferson and Signor Salvini because the one was
seldom seen save in *Rip Van Winkle* and the other save in
Othello. What short memories some persons have!   Miss
Lee was a most versatile artiste, as those can testify who
saw her as Myles in the burlesque of *The Colleen Bawn*,
when played at the Strand Theatre, in London.

In 1876, Mr. Thomas Kittle was lessee of the Prince of
Wales. On March 6, Boucicault's *Led Astray* was presented
Performances were given by Edward Compton, J. Elmore,
Ellen Barry, and C. A. Clarke, the dramatist.   Sir Randall

Roberts, Bart., made his first appearance on the local stage
on May 1. Nellie Farren played Young Rip Van Winkle in
the burlesque of that name on June 12, and sang that amusing
song, ' The Two Obadiahs.' The following week Joseph
Jefferson gave his famous impersonation of Rip Van Winkle.

On October 9, 1876, Mr. Frank Emery opened the theatre
with J. F. McArdle's opera burlesque *Zampa ; or, the Cruel
Corsair and the Marble Maid.* Mr. W. S. Gilbert wrote the
following dialogue for the occasion, spoken by the lessee and
G. W. Anson .—

Mr. ANSON—

' Ladies and Gentlemen—Upon my word,
I hardly like—tut, tut—it's quite absurd !
I've often pleaded for myself and never
Felt any kind of diffidence whatever ;
But now, somehow, it seems to me to-night
The words don't come so glibly as they might.
In point of fact, I'm pleading for another,
A gentleman who is (in law), my brother
I ought—your kindly wishes to engage—
To swear he means to elevate the stage—
To raise, at any cost, his noble calling
From the dark abyss into which it's falling.
Now 'twixt ourselves, I much regret to say
It's my belief he wants to make it pay :
He's just the kind of sordid man I fear,
Who likes a modest profit every year ;
And means to make one.   It's a thousand pities
The men who take good theatres in our cities
Should look upon it as their chiefest pride,
To set all money-making thoughts aside,
And by one rule, and one alone, be led,
" The piece is five acts, and the author—dead !"
But no—he wants, by his own sordid showing,
To pay his company and keep it going.
And, sad to say, has quite made up his mind
To play the newest pieces he can find !
You'll understand (for you are men of sense),
All this is in the *strictest confidence.*
When he comes on—he's waiting at the wing—
Of course you'll hear me say the usual thing.

He begged I'd make a speech—I couldn't *say* "no."—
But you'll take my word, of course, "*cum grano.*"
Mr. Frank Emery ! most charmed, I'm sure,
The British public ! Ah, you've met before !
A wandering stone—who, to the proverb's loss,
Has managed somehow, to collect some moss.
By dint of long and conscientious toil,
And comes to plant it in congenial soil.
A manager with views more truly sound
Could not in all the provinces be found.
His only aim is to improve the age
And elevate the sinking British stage ! '

Mr. EMERY—

' Ladies and Gentlemen—my worthy friend
Has smoothed my path and simplified its end ;
I don't deserve to be be-lauded so,
But "handsome is as Anson does," you know.
I'd gladly thank him but he isn't here—
Well, though he's thought it right to disappear,
He's still, "though lost to sight to Emery dear."
A truce to joking—this dramatic yoke
Upon my shoulders is indeed no joke !
No joke the fluttering hope and anxious fear
That surely season each succeeding year—
(And, what is still less like a joke indeed—
The hopes and fears of years that *don't* succeed).
Suffice to say, I'll do, with eager zest,
My very best to give the very best.
A manager with managerial " *nous*,"
Knows what is wanted in this " Little House."
There is a simple though a golden rule,
Well known to all dramatic Liverpool.
" Produce good pieces, well rehearsed and played,
Well dressed, well mounted—and your fortune's made ;
But mark this well—if you attempt to shirk
Your obvious duty and evade your work
By serving up third-rate dramatic messes,
With vamped-up scenery and dingy dresses,
And such unappetising kind of fare
Don't take the little Theatre in the Square ! " '*

* ' Liverpool Daily Post,' October 10, 1876.

Mr. Emery's first Christmas production was *The Sultan of Mocha.* His first pantomime, produced at Christmas, 1877, was *The Fair One with the Golden Locks,* written by Charles Millward. He was laughed at when he proposed to produce an elaborate pantomime on the small stage of the Prince of Wales. But he persevered, and his 'first' proved a big success. The musical director of the theatre at this time was John Bayliss.

On the last night (the sixty-second representation), of *The Fair One with the Golden Locks,* Mr. Emery spoke the following lines, from the pen of Charles Millward :—

'Ladies and gentlemen—kind patrons all,
Once more your Manager obeys Time's call.
Again, at your command, in rhyme, with reason,
He proudly notes the doings of the season.
In the first place, whate'er he said he'd do,
By Jingo, *was* done, and in fair style, too,
The "stars" announced throughout the bye-gone year,
Without exception twinkled brightly here.
(Curious to think how managerial bliss
Can be attained *without a single miss*)
The novelties he advertised—not few—
Proved for a wonder, absolutely *new*;
And finding rapid changes not alarming,
He made you own variety *was* charming.

'Some months ago, when by success much flurried,
Into wild schemes with reckless speed he hurried—
Forgetting that the house he ruled was small.
His notions—using an old Yankee term—grew "tall."
"What Drury Lane or Covent Garden do"
Said he "*my* little shop can do it too;
"And by my managerial troth, this time
"The 'little house' shall have a Pantomime!".
Friends stood aghast, advisers button-holed him,
And his "home ruler" plainly *her* mind told him,
'Tis even said this man of iron will
Was offered an asylum at Rainhill!
A Pantomime! the notion seemed absurd,
And yet the Manager has kept his word;
The "Fair One" is a fact, and not a scare,
A *real* pantomime in Clayton Square!

'How was it done ? It is not for me to say,
You have pronounced our piece a *merry* play.
Night after night, this house from floor to rafter
Has rung with hearty cheers and noisy laughter,
Our Manager is well-paid for his toil—
In fact, it may be said he has " struck oil " ;
To all the *artistes* from the " Fair One " down
To tiny Second , also to our Clown
And his belongings, hearty praise is due,
And grateful thanks, also, dear friends to you.
The critics' kindness we can ne'er requite,
You know we've had the *press* here every night !
For one and all, therefore your Emery prays
For Fortune's brightest smiles, and happy days.

Encouraged by the past, I now may mention
It is the Lessee's stern and firm intention
To offer you when next comes Christmas time,
Another—and a quite new—Pantomime.
And by your kind permission, Millward will
As author once more exercise his skill ;
Meanwhile, as Emery has shown great *nous*
By taking on long lease this little house,
He means to make improvements, and will strive
With might and main to keep the game alive.
For all this year you'll learn with satisfaction
He has secured each popular attraction ;
Your kind support he'll strive hard to deserve,
His motto : " You, my masters I'll well serve ! "
Stand by him, friends and patrons, and, be sure,
He'll do his best your favor to secure ;
No efforts, labor or expense he'll spare
To keep the " little house " well " *on the square.*" '

The 1878-9 pantomime was *Little Goody Two Shoes.*
During the first week in September, 1879, the Kendals, John
Hare, Albert Chevalier and William Terriss were here. The
plays were *The Ladies' Battle, A Quiet Rubber,* and *A Scrap
of Paper. Dora,* and *New Men and Old Acres* were performed on September 15, with Ellen Terry and Charles Kelly
in leading *rôles.* In the pantomime of *Cinderella,* produced

on December 26, Harry Fischer and T. F. Doyle performed. In the harlequinade the part of clown was played by Poluski, the Little, while Poluski, the Big, doubled the *rôles* of policeman and sprite.

On March 8, 1880, H. Beerbohm Tree made his appearance as the dandified old marquis in the comic opera of *Madame Favart*. On April 19, the first performance in Liverpool of *Carmen* was given by the Carl Rosa Opera Company. Carmen by Georgina Burns ; Don José, Fred C. Packard On May 11, Cora Stuart, made, in *Caste*, her first appearance here in comedy. In 1880 Emery stood as a candidate for one of the Municipal Wards, but without success. *Red Riding Hood* was that year's pantomime. It was written by T. F. Doyle, and in it appeared John S. Chamberlain, W. W. Walton, Miss Marie Stevens, and the author. On June 13, 1881, H. Beerbohm Tree played Lambert Streyke in *The Colonel*, a piece that was so successfully toured by Edgar Bruce for a number of years. August 1 saw something of a novelty, *Les Cloches de Corneville* being played entirely by children. This Lilliputian organisation was under the management of Charles Bernard. The 1881-2 pantomime was *Aladdin*. On February 27, 1882, Messrs. J. Comyns Carr and Thomas Hardy's *Far From the Madding Crowd* was brought out for the first time on any stage. That year's pantomime was *Robinson Crusoe*.

On March 31, 1883, Henry Pettitt and F. W. Broughton's comedy *Sisters* was produced. In this were George Walton and Alfred Hemming. May 2 saw the first production of the opera of *Foxglove*, written by Mr. Charles Dyall (then Curator of the local Walker Art Gallery), and composed by Dr. Röhner. May 14 saw Lila Clay's Company, consisting entirely of ladies (sixty in all), in the comic opera *An Adamless Eden*. On July 16, Sothern opened in *Our American Cousin*. A. W. Pinero's play *The Rocket* was produced by Edward Terry on July 30, for the first time on any stage. The comic opera, entitled *Captain Kidd ; or, the Bold Buccaneer*, written by G. H. Abbott, and composed by F. Solomon, was produced for the first time on any stage on September 11 On Monday, December 4, the Crown Prince of Portugal and suite visited the théatre and saw Edward Terry in *The Rocket*. On the entry of the Prince in the middle of the first act he met with a most enthusiastic reception from the audience. His Royal Highness appeared to thoroughly enjoy the performance. Few who were present on that occasion dreamt that the Prince was to end his life, (after he had ascended the Portuguese throne as King Carlos), by the hand of an assassin.

Beauty and The Beast, which was produced at Christmas, 1883, was the last of Emery's pantomimes. The annual was written by J. F. McArdle and F. J. Stimson. Miss Maude Branscombe, E. J. Lonnon, F. J. Stimson, and Fawcett Lomax were the chief exponents.

In April, 1884, Mr. Alexander Henderson returned to the Prince of Wales, which up to the end of August of that year was under the joint management of Messrs. Emery and Henderson. The theatre was improved internally and externally. The front, facing Clayton Square, was raised, and an ornamental model of the Prince of Wales's feathers erected. Above this the name of the theatre was lettered in gold. The acting manager of the theatre was the late Walter Hatton. From September 22, 1884, and for some months afterwards, Mr. Henderson was sole proprietor. His pantomime in 1884 was *Sinbad the Sailor*.

In the spring of 1885, Miss Fanny Josephs took over the theatre. The opening performance took place on Monday, April 6, when *The Candidate* was played by Charles Wyndham's Company. Mr. A. Mascard—afterwards succeeded by Mr. W. McNeill—was Miss Josephs' manager. On Monday, June 8, following, a local gentleman, Mr. Francis Drake, although wholly inexperienced in the ways of the stage, essayed to act Macready's great *rôle* of Richelieu. As might have been expected the experiment did not set the Mersey on fire.

Miss Josephs' first pantomime (1885-6), was *Dick Whittington and His Cat*. The following Christmas *The Babes in the Wood* was produced, the libretto by Fred Locke. The principal fun and melody-makers were Jenny Dawson, Minnie Byron, the Sisters Leamar, Johnny P. Dane, Patsy Harvey, Walter Andrews and Hal Forde. Miss Josephs' 1887-8 extravaganza was *Blue Beard*. J. L. Shine, Tom Bass, M. Girard, and Miss Vane Featherston were in the cast. On March 23, 1888, T. Edgar Pemberton's one-act comedy *Steeple Jack* was presented, in which Lionel Brough appeared. *Little Jack and the Big Beanstalk* was the feature of the succeeding Christmas, and in it were Billee Barlow, Agnes Hewitt, Nelly Navette, Edgar Granville, and Horace Wheatley.   Miss Josephs' fifth pantomime was *Aladdin* by F. W. Pratt, presented on December 23, 1889.   It proved to be her last, as she died in the following year.

Captain Wombell next took up the reins of management, opening on Monday, August 25, 1890, with Edward Terry and his company.   On September 1, Harry and Edward A. Paulton's three-act farcical comedy *Niobe* was produced, and seven days later *A Young Pretender* was performed by Yorke Stephens's company.   Captain Wombell's first annual was F. W. Pratt's *Robinson Crusoe*, produced on December 23, 1890, with Jenny Dawson, William Morgan, Fred Eastman, and Walter Passmore as principal artistes.   *Red Riding Hood* was the attraction of Christmas, 1891   The principal performers were Jenny Rogers, Amy Augarde, Marie Montrose, Topsy Sinden, and Vesta Victoria.   *Ali Baba and the Forty Thieves* produced on December 23, 1892, was Captain Wombell's third pantomimic venture.   In this were Fred Wright, junr , and Frank Danby.   The ' book ' was again by F. W. Pratt   In September of 1893, three weeks of variety entertainment were given, the late Jenny Hill being one of the ' stars.'   *Cinderella,* written by Geoffrey Thorn, and produced on December 23, 1893, made Captain Wombell's fourth Prince of Wales annual. The 1894-5 extravaganza was *The Babes in the Wood,* also by Geoffrey Thorn, produced on December 22.   Leading parts were sustained by Maud Boyd, Mabel Love, Russell Wallet, Fred Williams, and Wilfred Cotton.   December 21, 1895, witnessed Addie Conyers, Julia Kent, Nellie Christie, H. C. Barry, Harry Phydora, W. Vokes, Fred Williams, and Turle and Volto in Geoffrey Thorn's *Robinson Crusoe*.   The theatre was now under the joint direction of Captain Wombell and Mr Harold B Nelson.

On March 23, 1896, Mr. H. B. Nelson commenced his reign as sole proprietor and manager of the theatre in presenting *The Passport*.   Mr. Nelson's brother, Mr. H. Adair Nelson was the general manager, and Mr. E. Haslington Russell, the acting manager.   The 1896-7 annual was *Aladdin*.   Lottie Collins, Addie Conyers, J. F. McArdle, John Humphries, Fred Eastman, and George Mozart made up a strong cast.   The pantomime was from the pen of that clever dramatic author, J. James Hewson, who wrote all Mr. Nelson's annuals. Speaking of Mr. Hewson reminds me that he has now for many years been the esteemed local critic for ' The Stage.' He has also for some considerable time past exercised his acumen as dramatic editor of ' The Porcupine.' His honest and fearless criticisms are eagerly read and enjoyed in the theatrical world. He is also the author of a number of successful plays and books. Mr. Hewson is about the last of the Old Guard of local dramatic critics, which included able writers like the late J. B. Mackenzie and J. N. Petrie, both of whom were for many years on the staff of the ' Liverpool Mercury.'

Miss Marie Loftus succeeded Lottie Collins as the Princess in *Aladdin*. On March 16, 1897, Addie Conyers was accorded a benefit when Miss Loftus played Clown in the harlequinade, supported by Miss Conyers, and Messrs. Mozart and Eastman.

In Mr. Nelson's second pantomime (1897-8), *Red Riding Hood*, there were seen Minnie Jeffs, Mabel Love, Eugene Stratton, and W. W. Walton. Two first performances on any stage took place in 1897. The first on September 27, was J. H. Darnley and H. A. Bruce's *Shadows on the Blind*, and the second on November 29, the same authors' farcical comedy of *Guy Fawkes' Day*. *Dick Whittington* was the next Christmas annual. Vesta Tilley played Dick, supported by Olive Marston, Walter Groves, Freddie Farren, John Humphries, W. T. Thompson and Albert Christian. On May 16, 1898, Mrs. Brown Potter and Kyrle Bellew came. The following week saw Kate Vaughan here. On December 23, 1899, *Cinderella* was produced. Performances were given by G. P. Huntley, Fred Emney, Eugene Stratton, Tennyson and O'Gorman, Ida René and Lil Hawthorne. *Sinbad the Sailor*, produced on December 24, 1900, was the last pantomime given by Mr. H. B. Nelson, as he died, greatly regretted, in the spring of the following year. In this Claire Romaine, as principal ' boy,' had capable and efficient allies in Frances Earle, Frank Danby, Albert Le Fre, and John Humphries.

After H. B. Nelson's death, Mrs. Nelson ran the theatre for a short time, the last performance being given on Saturday evening, June 1, 1901, when *The Private Secretary* was played by Mr. Eugene C. Stafford's Company. In the following month an effort was made to dispose of the property by auction, but no sale was effected, the highest price offered being £13,000.   Incidentally, it was stated at the auction that during the thirteen weeks' run of the *Cinderella* pantomime, Mr. Nelson's takings had amounted to over £17,000

The theatre having remained without a tenant from June 1901, the property in the autumn of that year came under the control of Mr. G. C. Cleaver, who opened the house on November 25, with the North American Animated Picture Company.   On January 20, 1902, vaudeville entertainments were commenced, the Sisters Levey and the Follies being billed as the bright particular stars.   Other variety performances followed in due course.   On one occasion Hackenschmidt, the great Russian wrestler, was announced to appear, but owing to some dispute between the manager of the theatre and the muscular star, the former determined that no performance should take place, and not only disconnected the electric light installation, but to make assurance (as he thought), doubly sure, cut off the gas as well. Nothing daunted, however, the Russian lion managed to get the gas restored in the nick of time, and the wrestling contest took place after all !

A new era dawned for the ' little House in the Square ' when it was opened on September 1, 1902, by Messrs. C. St. John Denton and George Blunt.   Mr. George Mallet was the courteous general manager, and our townsman, Mr. William A. Armour, was the acting manager.   The theatre opened with the dramatic sketch, *All in the Family*, which was followed by the new farce, *Off the Rank*.   Leading *rôles* were sustained by Willie and May Edouin.   *Blue Bell in Fairyland* was presented on December 24, with Mabel Love in the title part.

When *Blue Bell in Fairyland* was withdrawn after a most successful run, it was followed in 1903 by Mr. Stanley Rogers' version of the *Babes in the Wood*.   Millie Lindon, Harry Randall, and Wilkie Bard took part in the pantomime.   The same year saw the production on December 24, of *Puss in Boots*, written by J. James Hewson.   In the early.part of the succeeding year *Goody Two Shoes* was presented.   This was the last pantomime given by Messrs. Denton and Blunt who shortly afterwards retired from the management.   In 1904 the Prince of Wales was taken by Mr. J. H. French, who presented *Red Riding Hood* on December 24. The following year the house closed, and since then it has not been utilised for theatrical purposes. What, one wonders, is to be the fate of the once famous ' little House in the Square,' with which so many bright histrionic memories are associated ?

THE ROTUNDA THEATRE.

Forty-five years ago, there stood on part of the site of the present Rotunda Theatre a public-house, wherein a ' free and easy ' was held nightly, the vocalists appearing on a small stage which has been described as ' about as big as a tea board.'   Afterwards Mr. Dennis Grannell, the proprietor, moved the concert hall business to an upper, and more commodious room.   About 1866 or 1867, sketches were given to supplement the light musical fare and a larger stage was built.   The stage, now located at the south end of the building, was, previous to the disastrous fire of July 9, 1877, situated at the opposite extremity.   In 1866 prices of admission were as follows :—' Boxes, 1s. 6d. ; stalls, 1s. ; body, 6d. ; by the new entrance in Stanley Road.'

In 1869, the first pantomime was given.   It was a condensed version of *Jack, the Giant Killer*.   Mr. and Mrs. Leno and little Dan Leno appeared in it.   Mrs. Leno played the giant-slaying hero of time-honoured memory.

On August 1, 1870, Charles Wood, who for five years had been at the Adelphi as musical director, came to the Rotunda in the dual capacities of musical and stage director. For over a quarter of a century Mr. Wood was associated with the theatre, and in later years in a managerial capacity.

At Christmas, 1870, the first ' full ' pantomime *Dick Whittington* was given, and from that date down to April 6, 1874— when the first stock season was inaugurated—the entertainments given were principally those provided by the concert hall and vaudeville companies, interspersed with occasional dramatic pieces.

In 1871, the first complete drama was played.   This was *Arrah-na-Pogue*, and it was performed by the Boucicault Amateur Dramatic Society.   The second dramatic performance was given in the same year by the Boucicault

Amateurs, when they submitted *The Colleen Bawn*. *The House that Jack Built* was produced at Christmas.

The first musical drama presented at the Rotunda was J. B. Buckstone's *The Daughter of the Regiment*. It was produced on August 19, 1872, with Lady Don in the part of Josephine, supported by the Rotunda Vaudeville Company. The play ran for six nights. *The Babes in the Wood* was presented at Christmas.

Little by little the old concert-hall business was abandoned, as Mr Grannell and Mr. Wood saw that for the popular taste the play was the thing. Therefore, to provide for the newer order of affairs, a new gallery, balcony, stage, and sixteen private boxes were erected in 1873, the theatre being kept open for performances during the alterations by the use of tarpaulins as a roof covering. The brass rail which encircled the gallery became, ultimately, an object of considerable dread to the ' galleryites,' as attached to it was an electric battery, so that any sacrilegious hand laid upon it received an electric shock. This proved an admirable way of keeping the rail untarnished.

Among those who appeared at the Rotunda from 1871 to 1873 were Basil Henry, Tom Maclagan, Edward Sennett, Barry Aylmer, T. F. Doyle, J. R. McLaren, Walter Searle, Herbert Campbell, George Vokes, Brinsley Sheridan, George Whyte, Edward Towers, Emily Randall, Ada Tisdall, Nelly Towers, Johanna Blake, Nellie Vezin, Rose Lucille, Alice Dodd, Mrs. Julia Lewis, and the Alexander Family.

On May 10, 1873, Adrian de Brescia and his company commenced a three weeks' engagement. *Guy Mannering* was played during the first week, *Rob Roy*, the second, and *The Octoroon* the third. *Little Red Riding Hood* was that year's Yuletide attraction.

The first stock season ran from April 6, 1874, to August 15, a period of nineteen weeks. The principal artistes were Messrs Arthur Lyle, Henry Vandenhoff, A. McPherson, Charles Dornton, C. J. Archer, J. C. Turner, Edward Courtenay, F. Harland, William Holston, Charles Kennion, James Elmore, Henry Percy, E. de Grisy; Misses Emily Forde (Mrs. Kennion), Lizzie King, Kissie Wood, Agnes Wood, Annie Morton, Eliza Gordon, Annetta Brown, Josephine Fiddes and Mrs. Henry Vandenhoff. On August 17

the concert-hall business was again resumed, and con
tinued down until December 26, when the pantomime
entitled *Puss in Boots ; or, the Princess Fair, the Ogre Rat,
the Miller's Merry Son, and the little Manx Cat* was produced.   Fanny Wiseman, Annie Richardson, and Ada
Luxmore were in the cast.

On the conclusion of the pantomime variety entertainments were given for four weeks, and for the last time in the
old Rotunda. Then followed the second stock season which
commenced on March 29, 1875, and ran for 39 weeks, beginning
with the *Lost Diamonds*, in which Ennis Lawson appeared,
and ending on December 23, 1875, with *Louis XI*, with
James Bennett in the *nom-rôle*.   In the company were
C. A. Clarke, James Carr, Arthur Lyle, John S. Chamberlain,
James Elmore, Robert Brough, C. J. McConnell, John
Vernon, J. S. Foote, W. Constantine, Mr. and Mrs.
Clarence Holt, Mr. and Mrs. Henry Vandenhoff; Misses
Eliza Gordon, Kissie Wood (now Mrs. H. C. Arnold), Agnes
Birchenough, Elise Maisey, Ellen Beaufort, Fanny Wiseman,
Jenny Hardcastle and Mrs. Charles Wood. Dion Boucicault's
drama, *The Colleen Bawn*, was produced on Monday, April 25,
with entirely new scenery, and was played for three weeks.
Charles Sullivan was specially engaged to play Myles. On
Monday, May 17, *Hamlet* was produced with Osmond
Tearle in the titular part.   Miss Eliza Gordon was the
Ophelia. The production was most successful, and had
an uninterrupted run of 18 nights. Mr. and Mrs. Saker,
from the Royal Alexandra Theatre, then fulfilled a fortnight's
engagement, and in their company was Arthur Wing Pinero,
the now well-known playwright. On December 27 was produced *Cinderella*. The annual ran for ten weeks. It was
from the pen of a local journalist, J. F. McArdle, who in the
same year had two other pantomimes running in Liverpool.

Mr. McArdle was the author of a host of pantomimes,
plays, and comic songs.   His pantomimes were always
eminently successful ; in fact it was frequently said with
truth that everything that ' Mac ' wrote made a hit. Some
of his earliest efforts first saw the light at the Rotunda.
Mr. McArdle died at his mother's residence in Liverpool on
February 21, 1883, and was interred in Ford Cemetery.

It was about the year 1875 that our townsman, James Kiernan, entered Mr. Grannell's services as a checktaker at nine shillings a week. Afterwards he rose to be bill inspector, and eventually succeeded to the position of assistant manager to Mr. Charles Wood. Mr Kiernan left the Rotunda after nine stock seasons, in order to open the Westminster Music Hall in partnership with Mr. Thomas Montgomery. Since then Mr. Kiernan has never looked back, his success in the entertainment world being as great as it has been well-deserved.

On Monday, March 6, 1876, the third stock season commenced. The opening attraction was *Clancarty*, with Walter Speakman prominently to the fore. The season terminated on December 23, when W. H. Pennington appeared as Othello. In that year's stock company were Messrs. E. D. Lyons, John S. Foote, George T. Minshull, Sydney Hazlewood, Mark Melford, Richard Mansell, Charles Morgan, Arthur Ricketts, W. S Branson, H. C. Arnold, Barry Stuart, T. H. Potter, Lionel Rignold, Osmond Tearle, Fred Selby ; Misses Maud Brennan, Ellen Beaufort, Kissie Wood, Henrietta Temple, Elise Maisey, Agnes Birchenough, Ada Neilson, Mrs. Charles Wood, Mrs. Robert Power, and Mrs. Charles Morgan. *Aladdin* was the 1876-7 annual, Lizzie Willmore being principal ' boy.' It ran for ten weeks

The fourth stock season opened on March 5, 1877, with *King Lear*, and terminated on Saturday, July 7, 1877. On the Monday following the theatre was destroyed by fire. The last play given in the old Rotunda was *The Shaughraun*, with Charles Sullivan as Conn. The final stock season in the old theatre comprised some notable performers, including Charles Dillon, Edward Smith Willard, Tom Maclagan, H. C. Arnold, T. Nerney, J. S. Chamberlain, Bella Mortimer (Mrs. Charles Dillon), Dora Usher, and Mrs. John Carter. A new and more commodious theatre, erected from the designs of Mr. C. J. Phipps, F S A , by Messrs. Haigh and Co., of Liverpool, was opened on Friday, December 20, 1878, under the patronage of the Mayor of Liverpool. The opening attraction was Benedict's opera *The Lily of Killarney*, presented by the Carl Rosa Opera Company, who were engaged for two nights. The following night they played Balfe's *Bohemian Girl*. On the ensuing Monday Charles Sullivan and company in *The Shaughraun* were the attraction, and for several weeks afterwards Irish dramas were played.

Then a stock season—the first in the new theatre—began. In this were Messrs. Henry Hampton, Arthur Lyle, Walter Speakman, Lionel Rignold, H. C. Arnold, William Gourlay (Scotch comedian), G. T. Minshull, Dora Usher, Caroline Elton, Annie Wilmot, and Kissie Wood. The first pantomime produced (December 26, 1879), was *Dick Whittington*. It was written by the late Charles Millward.

Down to 1888—when the proprietorship of the theatre was transferred to a limited company—stock seasons year by year were the rule. Those old stock days turned out many actors who are now in the foremost ranks of the profession ; and Charles Wood, in watching their early faltering footsteps with a fostering care, proved to be their ' guide, philosopher, and friend.'

In speaking of the old stock days at this theatre, ' Teddy ' Lewis once amusingly recounted to an interviewer* how on one occasion he was playing the old notary in *Elizabeth*—Miss Marriott being the ' star '—and in the chamber scene, when making his exit, unintentionally backed into a large fire-place, a quite delightful misadventure to those spectators with an eye for the incongruous. On another occasion John S. Haydon was playing Mathias in *The Bells*. At a critical moment a noise is heard which makes the guilty Mathias exclaim, ' What's that ? ' ' Instead of giving the correct reply,' says Lewis, ' I was inspired to shout " Somebody's dropped their socks." My life was in danger when the curtain went down.'

The roof of the present Rotunda, with its masts, spars, etc., somewhat resembles the deck of a ship. In the old stock days many of the actors went up aloft to learn their parts and be refreshed by the breezes.

On July 26, 1880, Kissie Wood played Jo for the first time in Liverpool. Miss Marriott came in November, and T. C. King in December. *Sinbad the Sailor*, by J. F. McArdle, was the Christmas piece. Leading parts were sustained by the Majiltons (Frank and Marie), Walter Andrews, and Bella Richardson.

* ' The Sunday Chronicle,' May 10, 1896.

Early in 1881, John Coleman and his company appeared in *Katherine Howard*.   Miss Marriott played good Queen Bess in *Elizabeth* on July 11.   Walter Groves performed the small part of Hudson.   The following week Miss Marriott portrayed Hamlet.   John S. Haydon was the Ghost, and Miss Kissie Wood Osric, and Fred Coles Francisco.   Joseph West was at that time a member of the stock company.   Mr. West, who who is now a member of the well-known Liverpool firm of Messrs. Simon Jude and West, joined the stock company on Easter Monday, 1881, and remained until the end of July when he left for the Theatre Royal, Plymouth.   Performances of *The Rivals* and *She Stoops to Conquer* were given during the week commencing August 22, by a company which included C. W. Somerset, and Mrs. Chippendale.   A special production of *Rob Roy* was given on September 26.   Prominent in the cast were John S. Haydon, J. K. Walton, Joe Bracewell, and Kissie Wood, Ellen Beaufort, and Myra Rosalind.   *Jack the Giant Killer* was performed at Christmas.

April 23, 1882, brought Jenny Willmore and company in the burlesque opera entitled *Little Pygmalion*.   Miss Marriott appeared as Romeo for the first time at the Rotunda on June 5, sustaining the part brilliantly for a week to good houses.   Alice Finch was the Juliet   *Cinderella*, played by a double set of performers, was produced on December 23.

Henry Loraine performed Richard III on May 7, 1883. A Liverpool lady, Miss May Douglas, portrayed Pauline in *The Lady of Lyons* on October 8.   John Dewhurst gave a finished performance of Richelieu on October 22.   *Little Red Riding Hood ; or, Harlequin Boy Blue, the Good Fairy and the Naughty Wolf*, written by F. W. Green, with local illusions by J. James Hewson, was that year's pantomime.   Kissie Wood played Boy Blue, and Florence Leybourne Irradianta, the Good Fairy , Major Crackles appeared as Simon Simple, and Fred Coles as Mother Shipton.   The pantomime also had a double cast, the morning performances being given by children, and the evening by adults.   Several of these juveniles afterwards achieved distinction on the stage.   One of them was Miss Maud D'Almaine, who played Irradianta. She is now Mrs. Thomas Barrasford.

Richard Mansell appeared in the titular part in *The Unknown* on March 3, 1884. On May 20, F. R. Benson made his first appearance in Liverpool, when he played Hamlet, supported by the stock company. In June, 1884, Mr. Grannell proposed to the Committee of the Liverpool Eisteddfod to give a prize of twenty-five guineas for the best libretto on the subject of *The Babes in the Wood* for his 1884-5 pantomime. The offer was accepted, and in October the prize was unanimously awarded to a local gentleman, Mr. Stanley Rogers.

Miss Bateman gave her well-known impersonations of Leah and Mary Warner during the first week in November, 1885. Katie Logan, Maud Haigh, Louie Scott, Payne Fletcher, H. C. Barry, Alfred Rousby and Joe Burgess were in that Christmas annual of *The Forty Thieves ; or, Harlequin Ali Baba and the Robbers of the Magic Cave.* It was written by J. Wilton Jones of the ' Leeds Post.'

Miss Marriott and Miss Bateman were the principal stars during 1886. The pantomime of *Robinson Crusoe* was produced on December 27. *Aladdin ; or, the Wonderful Lamp* was given the following year.

In March, 1888, the theatre joined the ranks of the limited liability companies under the style of the Rotunda Theatre Company, Limited. The directorate included Messrs. John Howard (Mayor of Bootle), Alderman Edward Grindley, Captain R. B. Bainbridge, and Mr. D. Grannell, with Mr. C. Wood as secretary. The share capital was divided into 25,000 shares of £1 each. Of these £5,000 were allotted to Mr. Grannell in part payment of the purchase money. Mr. Grannell on his part transferred the theatre, the billiard-room, and the American bowling alleys to the new syndicate.

The noted pantomime writer, Walter Summers, played in *Tempest Tossed* on May 28, 1888. Harry Nicholls and Arnold Bell performed in *Youth* on June 11. When *Round the Clock* was played the following week Walter Passmore appeared as Mr. Denby, and Arthur Ricketts as Gabriel Gadforth. John Glendinning, Edward Lewis, and James McWilliam were also here about this time. The Rousby Opera Company came on September 3. Maude Branscombe sustained the title-part in *Cinderella* at Christmas.

On Monday, April 1, 1889, a new musical comedy drama from the joint pens of Horace Wheatley and C. A. Aldin, entitled *Bright Days ; or, the Bride of Two Isles* was produced. An old Rotunda favourite, Valentine Smith, came with his opera company on September 23, 1889. *Sinbad the Sailor* was produced on December 26. Miss Minnie Rotchley was the sailor hero, and Louie Scott the Princess ; while comic parts were sustained by Fawcett Lomax, and Joe Bracewell.

Miss Katty King, daughter of T. C. King, appeared as Norah O'Sullivan in *Ballyvogan* on October 13, 1890. The author, Arthur Lloyd, performed Mr. McCrindle. Miss Minnie Mario, of the Sisters Mario, represented Robin Hood in *The Babes of the Wood* at Christmas. Walter Groves and Joe Burgess played the two robbers.

John S. Haydon performed as Rob Roy in a special production of that play on June 1, 1891. A fortnight later A. L. Baron appeared as Coupeau, and Eleanor Reardon as Phœbe Sage, in *Drink*. Misses Minnie Mario, Topsy Robina, and Amy Rogerson ; Messrs. Martin Adeson, J H. Booth, the Sisters Glen, and the Arlottis took part in that year's pantomime of *Dick Whittington*.

Performances of *Mary, Queen of Scots, Elizabeth*, and *Leah* were given during the week commencing May 23, 1892, by Miss Claire Scott. In the company was William Terriss, who was seen as the Earl of Leicester, Burleigh, and Lorenz. Fred Locke's *Little Bo-Peep* was brought out at Christmas. Miss Maud Stafford portrayed Boy Blue.

Late in May, 1893, Hermann Vezin gave notable performances of Hamlet, Othello, Shylock, and Richelieu. *Jack and Jill ; or, the Lancashire Witches and Mother Goose*, was that year's annual. It was from the pen of William Wade, the well-known journalist.

On June 4, 1894, Mr. and Mrs. A. B. Tapping played in *Jim the Penman, Money*, and *The Lost Paradise*. *Mary, Queen of Scots, Hamlet, Catherine Howard*, and *East Lynne* were performed by Mrs. Bandmann-Palmer and her company during the week commencing November 19, 1894. Wilton Jones's version of *The Forty Thieves* was produced in December. Miss Clara Bernard played the Prince in *Cinderella*, in the 1895-6 pantomime. Mr. and Mrs. Frank Harvey introduced *Brother against Brother*, and *The Land of the Living* during the third week in May, 1896. *Old King Cole* was given at Yuletide. Mr. Richard Flanagan's pantomime of *Aladdin*, from the Queen's Theatre, Manchester, was presented on February 8, 1897.

Down to 1898 the theatre was run by the Rotunda Theatre Company, Limited, but in that year the property was acquired by Messrs. Bent's Brewery Company, Limited. Mr. Matthew Montgomery succeeded Mr. Charles Wood as manager of the theatre. The Christmas pantomime for 1898 was *Robinson Crusoe*, produced by Messrs. Forster and Schaller. Miss Emily Stevens was 'principal boy.' In 1899, Messrs. Bent reconstructed the interior of the theatre to the best possible advantage, and so great was the transformation that the old Rotunda *habitué* had to rub his eyes in sheer wonderment. The re-opening took place on Monday, September 4, 1899, the attraction being Hubert O'Grady and company in *The Fenian*. *The Babes in the Wood* was given at Christmas, and on January 15, 1900, *Dick Whittington* was submitted with the late Minnie Mario in the title-part.

On September 5, 1902, Charles Wood, who was born in 1833, died at Bollington, near Macclesfield, where he had been for some time living in retirement. Mr. Wood was buried in Anfield Cemetery, Liverpool. At the time of his decease the following sympathetic acrostic was written by the late John S. Haydon :—

CHARLES WOOD.

' Charles, thy earthly cares are ended.
Heaven's house of rest is won.
All thy years with toil were blended,
Resolute life's path you wended,
Loved, esteemed by every one ;
Ever friendship's hand extended,
Sleep in peace !   God's will be done !

Well may youth thy precepts borrow
Old friends staunch to thee remain,
One, now pens these lines in sorrow,
Dreaming, sees thy face again !'

Upon Mr. Montgomery's retirement from the management of the theatre in 1903, he was succeeded by his son, Mr. Matthew Montgomery, who has done much to enhance the reputation of the Rotunda as one of the principal homes of melodrama in the provinces.

THE ALEXANDRA THEATRE
(AFTERWARDS THE EMPIRE).

The Alexandra Theatre* was erected in 1866, by Messrs. Jones and Son, of Liverpool, from designs by Mr. Edward Solomons, F.R.I.B.A., architect, of Liverpool and Manchester. The style is Italian treated in a free manner. The lower storey of the *façade* is composed of a series of five arches, with pilasters, surmounted by carved capitals. The space between two of the arches is now occupied by shops. When the theatre was first opened the arch to the left was used as the entrance to the carriage-drive, leading to the principal parts of the house. That to the right was the entrance to the pit-circle ; that in the centre for visitors to the stalls, dress-circle, etc. The two others formed shops, to one of which were attached extensive supper rooms. The lion heads in the above-named capitals serve for ventilation, the mouths being pierced for the purpose. In the tympanum are heads of Shakespeare, Schiller, Molière, Beethoven, and Rossini—emblematical of the   Drama and Music. The entablature is of a rich and ornate character, containing panels in the frieze which serve as windows   The cornice is supported by carved medallions ; and the whole is surmounted by a perforated and enriched balustrade. In fact the projectors of the building left nothing undone to render it one of the handsomest theatres in the provinces.

The proprietors of the building were the Alexandra Theatre and Opera House Company, Limited, registered on November 10, 1864. The first directors were Messrs. Benjamin Heywood Jones (chairman), James Glynne Bateson, Thomas Arthur Bushby, Thomas Gair, Thomas Dyson Hornby, Isaac L. Kohn Speyer, Andrew George Kurtz,

* The site of the theatre had previously been occupied by Charles Garner's Livery Stables.

William Langton, Edwin Latham, William Henry MacLean, William Marriott, George Melly, Gilbert Winter Moss, Frederick Barned Mozley, Francis Gerard Prange, Charles K. Prioleau, Philip Henry Rathbone, Charles Stoess, John Swainson, and George Henry Wakefield.

The foundation stone was laid by Mdlle. Titiens on January 13, 1866, and the theatre was opened not as the Alexandra but as the New Prince of Wales Theatre and Opera House on October 15, 1866. The performance commenced with the singing of the National Anthem by the Italian Opera Company, the solos being taken by Mdlle. Titiens and Mr. (now Sir) Charles Santley.* Afterwards Mr. and Mrs. Alfred Wigan spoke an original address written by Tom Taylor. Then followed *Faust*, with the undernoted cast :—

Faust,	Signor Mario.
Valentino,	Mr. Santley,
Mephistopheles,	Signor Gassier.
Wagner,	Signor Bossi.
Siebel,	Mdlle. Wiziek.
Marta,	Mdlle. Baumeister.
Margherita,	Mdlle. Titiens.

Il Don Giovanni was given the following night. Then followed performances of *Der Freischutz, Il Trovatore, Nozze di Figaro, Norma, Huguenots, Marta, Semiramide,* and *Lucia de Lammermoor.* The conductor was Signor Arditi ; and the ballets were arranged by Mr. J. Lauri.

Antony and Cleopatra, on February 18, 1867, was the first of a number of successful Shakespearian revivals brought out at this house. Leading characters were sustained by Walter Montgomery, Edward Saker, and Miss Reinhardt. Mr. and Mrs. Charles Kean made their *début* here on May 13 of the same year, when *Henry VIII* was presented. This was their farewell visit to Liverpool, and it turned out to be the period of Charles Kean's final appearance on the stage. The Keans were engaged for a fortnight. On Monday, May 27, Charles Kean electrified his audience with his rendering of Macbeth. The following night he performed Louis XI. This was his

---

* One of those who joined on the stage in singing ' God Save the Queen ' was a talented young lady named Miss Marie O'Beirne, who was studying for Italian Opera. Little did she think that she would one day direct the destinies of the theatre.

last appearance on any stage, for on the Wednesday night he was too ill to perform, and the part of King Lear had to be undertaken by J. F. Cathcart. Charles Kean died on January 22, 1868, and Mrs. Kean retired from the stage immediately afterwards.

In 1867 H. J. Byron became lessee of the theatre in succession to Alexander Henderson. During his short lessee-ship the acting management was in turn in the hands of Mr. English (who afterwards died in Calcutta), and Mr Alfred Whitty, son of Michael James Whitty, a gifted journalist and the founder of the ' Liverpool Daily Post.'

On Monday, July 29, 1867, the house was first opened under the name of the Royal Alexandra Theatre and Opera House. This was the title originally chosen for the theatre, and it was bestowed in honour of our present Queen, who was at that time Princess of Wales.

Commencing October 7, 1867, a series of Italian operas were given by a company which included such notable names as Mdlle. Titiens, Madame and Signor Trebelli-Bettini, Mdlle. Sinico, and Charles Santley. Another memorable Shakes-pearian revival took place on October 22, when *The Tempest* was performed. *Dearer than Life* was played for the first time on any stage on November 25. *Manfred* was produced by Charles Calvert on December 9, with himself in the titular part. New scenery was painted for the production by the Grieves.

A revival of *A Winter's Tale* took place on February 24, 1868, when the chief parts were played by Mr. and Mrs Charles Calvert. The following month they were seen in *The Merchant of Venice*. On March 6, H. J. Byron resigned his lesseeship of the theatre. Mdlle. Titiens and Charles Santley were again here in October with the Italian Opera Company. On Monday, December 7, the theatre was opened under the management of Edward Saker.* *As You Like It* was the attraction, in which Miss Beatrice Shirley, Gaston Murray, and the lessee played. Mr. Saker's first pantomime was *Ali Baba and the Forty Thieves ; or, Harlequin and the Magic Donkey*. It was preceded by *A Kiss in the Dark*.

---

* Shortly before Mr Saker undertook the management of the Alexandra he had the offer of an engagement with Miss Marie Wilton (now Lady Bancroft), as first low comedian at the old Prince of Wales Theatre, London.

W

On Monday, March 8, 1869, Miss Bateman performed in *Leah.* She was succeeded on April 9 by Mr. and Mrs Charles Mathews. On Easter Monday James Fernandez played the titular part in the *The King O'Scots.* June 7 saw *Extremes ; or, Men of the Day,* and *Paris ; or, Vive Lempriere !* In the latter piece Maria Saker and Kate Santley made their first appearance on this stage. E. A Sothern played during the week commencing October 11. J. L Toole was here in the following month.

One night when Toole was leaving the stage door of the Alexandra he was accosted by a bibulous rogue who in sober days had been a decent fellow and a respectable actor. ' For the Lord's sake, Mr. Toole, please lend me ten shillings ! My mother has just died, and I'm at my wit's end for money to bury her ' ' Dear me ! ' replied Toole, who was one of the most charitable and kind-hearted of men ' How sad ! Your mother dead, you say ? Poor fellow ! ' And half a sovereign changed hands. On his next visit to Liverpool, Toole, on a hot day in June was again accosted at the stage door by the bibulous one ' For Heaven's sake, Mr. Toole,' he said, please lend a poor wretched fellow ten shillings ! My mother is dead, and I don't know how to bury her ' ' My good man,' remonstrated Mr Toole, ' You told me that she died nearly *three weeks* ago, and now you say she isn't buried yet ! In this hot weather how can that be ? ' ' Look here, Mr Toole,' hiccoughed the toper, ' You're a great actor, I know, but who the deuce is to know better when my mother died, you or I ? ' ' The half sovereign did not change hands that night ' adds Henry Herman, who tells the story.*

On another occasion when Irving and Toole both happened to be playing at the same time in Liverpool they went out one Sunday to dine at an old-fashioned hostelry on the outskirts of Liverpool. After they had partaken of a good dinner they sat chatting over their wine and cigars until the time drew near for their departure. They then rang the bell for the waiter to bring the bill After he had gone, Irving and Toole for a practical joke, gathered up all the fine old silver off the table and placed it in the garden into which the room opened. They then turned out the gas, and crept under the table.

* ' Between the Whiffs,' p. 178-9.

The waiter after repeatedly knocking at the door looked into the room.   When he saw the lights out, the window open, and the guests gone, he cried out, ' Done ! They have bolted with the silver ; Thieves ! Thieves ! ' and went to alarm the house.   After he had gone, Irving and Toole came from their place of concealment, closed the door, lighted the gas and replaced the silver upon the table.   They had no sooner done this when the landlord and his family, guests *en déshabillé* and the servants of the house—some of them carrying pokers, etc —burst into the room.   The landlord and the others stood amazed, 'for there the two gentlemen sat quietly smoking their cigars.   Irving then asked them in his quiet gentlemanly voice : ' Do you always come in like this when gentlemen are having their dinner ? '   Their answer is not recorded *

Mrs. Stirling performed Peg Woffington in *Masks and Faces* on November 22, 1869.   Phelps played during the early part of December.   That year's pantomime was entitled *Robin Hood*. Miss Rachel Sanger played the principal part, G. W. Anson was the baron, and Walter Hildyard the clown. The pantomime was preceded by a comedietta.

In *Little Em'ly* and *The Princess* (April, 1870), were Misses Julia St. George, Fanny Addison, Rachel Sanger, and Sam Emery.   Commencing October 17, Toole played for twelve nights.   At the end of the month Sothern and Miss Amy Roselle commenced an engagement.   On November 28, Mr. and Mrs. Wybert Rousby appeared in *'Twixt Axe and Crown*.   *Apropos* of this visit, the following amusing story is told by Mrs Saker, who at that time was the leading lady of the Alexandra stock company.

' I was very young at the time,' she says, ' consequently when I was cast for Queen Mary in *'Twixt Axe and Crown* I had to be made up to look very much older.   Mr. Rousby thought a rather elderly lady would have been better for the part, but Saker said that Miss O'Beirne did not object to make up old, but she did not know how.   Mr. Rousby offered to make me up on the night, which he did in the following manner.   He darkened and lined my face, topped it with an iron grey front,·a long veil, and a crown.   I made a very stately entrance and was getting on well, until I came to the following lines in my part :—"They think to take the crown from off our royal head. Never ! " I gave my head a dignified toss, away went the crown, carrying with it the veil and front. There I stood revealed in my royal robes with a bunch of my own fair hair screwed up on the top of my head, a white forehead, and the rest of my face a deep grey-yellowish colour. Of course the audience revelled in the situation. However, I picked up the embellishment and put it on again with my back to the audience. When I turned round again the applause and laughter were immense '

On April 10, 1871, J. L. Toole and Nellie Farren performed in *The Princess of Trebizonde* and *The Pretty Housebreaker*. The first local performance of *The Two Roses* took place on May 29. In this appeared Henry Irving, George Honey, H. J. Montague, W. H. Stephens, and Amy Fawsitt, all of whom played their original characters Miss Julia Matthews, Howard Payne, J. D. Stoyle, and Aynsley Cook commenced an engagement on August 14, in *The Grand Duchess*. Mrs. John Wood, Lionel Brough, and the Royal St. James's Theatre Company performed in *Milky White* and the burlesque *Poll and Partner Joe* exactly a week later. *Ours* was given during the first week in September by a company which included John S. Clarke, John Hare, Charles Collette, and Miss Carlotta Addison. In October Dion Boucicault and his wife appeared as Myles and Eily in *The Colleen Bawn*. Shiel Barry was the Danny Mann. Commencing October 16, Mr. and Mrs. Alfred Wigan gave six farewell performances. The pantomime at Christmas was *Little Jack the Giant Killer*, with Miss Marie O'Beirne as King Arthur.

The following incident occurred during the run of a pantomime in the early 'seventies :—' I was sitting in our private box on the right-hand side of the stage with some lady friends,' says Mrs. Saker, who tells me the story, ' Mr. Saker being in his office, when suddenly a gentleman in one of the opposite boxes stood up and waved his arms frantically at me, at the same time shouting out " For God's sake, stand back." I could not comprehend the situation, but on looking into the pit I saw some people handing their children over into the stalls. I called out "There is no fire ! A false alarm!" At this moment large pieces of plaster fell on me, and to make matters worse a number of people left the theatre. .

' Mr. Saker rushed up to the gallery to see what was the
matter, and found that part of the gallery front had given way.
He made all the people turn out from that part at once, giving
no explanation in order not to create a panic.   They all moved
away with the exception of a sailor who refused to budge.
It was explained to him how very dangerous it was to remain.
" Oh," said he, " that's nothing.   I've been shipwrecked ;
besides, I've come many miles to see the pantomime, and I'm
going to see it."

' To quieten the fears of the audience, the late " Micky "
Roberts came on the stage and banged a big drum, singing
slowly the while.   Afterwards the audience began to return,
and the pantomime was proceeded with.   Before the next performance Mr. Saker had the defect rectified.'

Towards the end of April, 1872, the beautiful Adelaide
Neilson was starring at the Alexandra   On Friday, May 3,
she took a benefit, when she appeared as Rosalind, and as
Pauline in the fourth act of *The Lady of Lyons*.

At that time E. H. Brooke was the leading man of the
Alexandra stock company, and a great favourite.   On the
occasion of Miss Neilson's ' bespeak ' Brooke was not feeling
very fit, having suffered from a bad bilious attack, which left
him with a severe headache and a tendency to giddiness.
All went well,' says Mrs. Saker, who tells the story,
' until the great scene in *The Lady of Lyons* where Pauline
exclaims, " Claude take me, thou canst not give me
wealth, title, station, etc.," when Miss Neilson, with all the
power of her emotional enthusiasm, literally flung herself
into Brooke's arms.   Poor Brooke was still feeling very weak,
and he gradually subsided (I cannot say fell), with Miss Neilson
on to the stage.   Of course the audience roared with laughter.
They both got up and Brooke proceeded with the correct text,
" This is the heaviest blow of all," which seemed so appropriate at the moment that the merriment of the audience
prevented the progress of the play for several minutes.'

On June 10, 1872, Henry Irving was seen in *The Bells*
for the first time locally.   *Genevieve de Brabant* was given during
the first week in July by Miss Emily Soldene and company.
July 15 saw Mr. Buckstone and his players.   Ristori appeared on August 18, 1873, and in the following week was
succeeded by Henry Irving in *Charles I*.   A. W. Dubourg's

new play, *Bitter Fruit*, was produced for the first time on any stage on October 6 Miss Kate Bateman (Mrs. Crowe), for whom the piece was specially written, enacted the leading part. The Carl Rosa Opera Company was here on October 13, and included Blanche Cole, William Castle, Mr. and Mrs. Aynsley Cook, and Rose Hersee. The company performed *The Bohemian Girl*, *Maritana*, *The Marriage of Figaro*, *Lucrezia Borgia*, and *Satanella* On December 8, and the eleven following nights, James Bennett and Henry Talbot gave full-flavoured specimens of their quality as tragedians.

James Bennett had formerly been a member of the leading stock companies, and retained his popularity in most towns. He was at the City Theatre, Glasgow, about 1846. The manager of the theatre was John Henry Anderson (the 'Wizard of the North'), previously one of the lessees of the Theatre Royal, Liverpool In addition to Bennett, the other principal members of the company were Barry Sullivan, (who was at that time about twenty-two years of age), the young and majestic Laura Addison, and Ada Dyas. When Bennett accepted the Glasgow engagement he understood he was to have all the principal *rôles*, and Sullivan went there under the same impression regarding himself. Therefore, there were frequent rows. 'Bennett,' says John Coleman,* 'was the older and more experienced actor, and, though anything but a typical Claude, took the popular fancy. Sullivan ran his rival hard in Claude, Hamlet, and Romeo, but when it came to Macbeth, Othello, and parts of that class, he was proved to be an admirable walking gentleman actor of tragedy, while Bennett was proclaimed to be a tragedian. The result was (a cruel result too), that Sullivan was dismissed and Bennett remained "monarch of all he surveyed" This was a wrong which Sullivan never forgot, never forgave, even when time had reversed this unjust verdict. Only a few years ago, while dining *tête-à-tête* at the Savage Club, this subject cropped up, and instantly lashed him into a white heat.'

Bennett was specially engaged by Jarrett and Palmer to play Richard III at Niblo's Garden, New York, where he opened on April 10, 1871. On that occasion the present noted

* 'The Theatre,' June, 1891

actress, Mrs. Fiske (then Minnie Maddern), played the Duke of York. The tragedy was magnificently staged, all the scenery being imported from London. Charles Calvert's version was adopted in preference to that of Colley Cibber.

Colonel T. Allston Brown, the American stage historian, says ' Bennett was in person below the medium height, and in general appearance reminded one of Fechter He had the ungainly stage walk of Barry Sullivan (?) and Irving, the shrugging of the shoulders of Fechter, as well as the painful rolling of his eyes.' An odd description, truly ! There was absolutely no resemblance between the stage walk of Sullivan and of Irving. Sullivan's movements were the very poetry of motion.

Among the parts which Bennett ' created ' were those of Cromwell in E. L. Blanchard's *Aston Hall* (1854), and Creon in Watts Phillips's *Theodora* (1866). Bennett was a superb Iago, acting the soliloquies, not merely reciting them. His reputation as an actor could, if necessary, have rested on his performance of Louis XI alone. It was a masterly piece of acting, full of the most minute details, all showing the care and thought he had given to the part. The long drawn out death scene was the crowning piece of a most finished performance. Bennett died on March 9, 1885.

A play from the pen of the well-known novelist, Miss M. E. Braddon, entitled *Genevieve , or, the Missing Witness*, was produced, for the first time on any stage, on April 6, 1874. The Lyceum Company (including Henry Irving, Isabella Bateman, and John Clayton), was here in *Philip* on August 24. Irving played Count Philip de Miraflor. *Henry V* was revived on November 9.

The first week in March, 1875, saw Charles Mathews paying a welcome return visit. He played Dazzle in *London Assurance* to the Lady Gay Spanker of Mrs. Edward Saker and the Dolly Spanker of her husband.

Arthur Wing Pinero, the well-known dramatist, was at that time a member of the stock company at the Alexandra. On one occasion when he played Cool in *London Assurance* to Charles Mathews' wonderful Dazzle, he found himself on the right side of the stage, when his ' cue ' had been given to enter with a letter from the left hand. ' To work my way round,' says Mr. Pinero,* ' would have occupied two or three minutes ; there was no door on my side, so, without hesitating, I squeezed myself through a small opening in the scene, where two " flats " had been imperfectly joined. I stood before Dazzle flushed and breathless. He gave me a smile, and, turning to Charles Courtly, who was looking for me in the opposite direction, observed, " Here's Cool, *he has just walked through a brick wall.*"

' On the last night of his Liverpool engagement he passed me at the stage door on his way out. It was midwinter— and he—poor old gentleman—was to play in Dundee on the following Monday. I said " Good-bye, Mr. Mathews," and held out my hand. His thoughts seemed far away, perhaps in Dundee, where the snow lay rather thickly, but he absently gave me two fingers. I remember I wished at the time that they had been four, but, for all that, I look back on those two little fingers with pleasure, for I never saw their owner again.'

' Few people know,' says Henry Herman,† ' that the most popular of English comedy authors, A. W. Pinero, came to London simply through a fluke. Pinero was a stock actor at the Alexandra Theatre, Liverpool, receiving from the late Mr. Saker, a salary of some thirty to forty shillings a week, when Wilkie Collins's *Miss Gwilt* was produced, in which Pinero played a small character part. The author of *The Woman in White* had been struck by the clever performance of another actor ; but somehow or other, in reading from the playbill, he mixed up the names, and asked Miss Caven-dish's manager to engage Mr. Pinero for the London perfor-mance, thinking him to be another man altogether. Pinero came to London, with the result which is known to all ; and his luck at the start—of which, perhaps, he himself even is at this moment not aware—has followed him ever since.'

Charles Calvert's production of *Sardanapalus* took place on September 27, with himself in the title-part. Mr. Pinero represented Arbaces. Commencing November 8 a week of Italian operas was given, when Madame Christine Nilsson made, as Margherita, her first appearance in Liverpool. The Royal Italian Opera Company (under the

---

* ' The Era Almanac,' 1884, p. 87.   † ' Between the Whiffs,' p. 72.

direction of Sir Julius Benedict), was here on November 15. The company included Madame Albani. *Lohengrin* was presented on November 18, for the first time in Liverpool. On December 9, *Miss Gwilt* was produced. *Apropos* of this production the following story is told by Henry Herman :*

‘When Wilkie Collins's *Miss Gwilt* was rehearsed for the first time on any stage, at the Alexandra Theatre, Liverpool, it contained a part omitted at its production—namely that of the old gardener, Abraham Sage.   The *rôle* was allotted to a young man who was then the second comedian of the theatre, and who has since made a name for himself both in England and the Colonies.   The aspirant for stage honours was dissatisfied with his part—a very short one—and at one of the final rehearsals he interlarded his principal speech with a copious admixture of the word " sir."   When he had got through, Wilkie Collins looked at him over his spectacles and said sternly ‘ " Young man, I have written the word ‘ sir ’ four times. You have used it thirteen times.   Please understand that I want my words spoken as I wrote them."   " I am very sorry, Mr. Collins," replied the young comedian ; " but, you see, the part's such a poor one, and I wanted to give it character.’

" Thank you," Wilkie Collins replied quietly ; " I will look into this."

When the rehearsal of the act was finished, Wilkie Collins turned to Miss Cavendish's stage manager, who had charge of the production, and asked him for a pencil.

" I think, Mr. ———," he said, " if we put our heads together, we may do without Abraham Sage," and in the result every line of the gardener's part was struck out of the piece

‘ When the Alexandra Theatre Company, including Edmund and Robert Lyons, A. W. Pinero, and others, were engaged for the London production, that young comedian regretted his inconsiderate speech, and three years elapsed before he found a London engagement.   He has made up for it since.’

On March 20, 1876, Edward Saker and Charles Calvert produced, and played in, *Louis XI.* Mr. and Mrs. Charles Sullivan were here the following week in *The Colleen Bawn.*

The Italian Opera Company revisited the theatre on April 10. The stage manager for the company was Mr. (afterwards Sir) Augustus Harris, who, in later years, was familiarly known to many as ' Druriolanus.'   The first production in Liverpool of *The Shaughraun* took place on April 17.   Hubert O'Grady (who lies buried in Yew Tree Cemetery, Liverpool), was the Conn.   Mrs. O'Grady, Miss Rose Massey, and Thomas Nerney also sustained characters.   On June 26, Mr. and Mrs. E. H. Brooke appeared in *Gustave ; or, Life for Life.* In the supporting company was R. C. Carton, the now well-known dramatist.   On September 4, Mr. Saker produced *A Winter's Tale.*   Miss Violet Cameron, Mrs. Saker, Mr. Saker, and J. T. Dewhurst played Perdita, Hermione, Autolycus, and Leontes.   The production brought fame and pecuniary success to the manager.   After being performed for a month in Liverpool, *A Winter's Tale* was taken on tour.   On October 2, Henry Irving played Hamlet to Miss Isabel Bateman's Ophelia.   Other plays given subsequently were *Charles I* and *The Bells.*

In December, Mr. H. J. Loveday, the talented musical director of the theatre, left to join Henry Irving.   He was accorded a complimentary benefit on December 18.   Mr. Loveday was succeeded by a capable musician in Mr. John Ross.   Besides discharging the arduous duties connected with this office for a number of years, Ross also found time to act as conductor of the choir of St. Francis Xavier's Church, Liverpool.   He was one of the founders of the Liverpool School of Music, and was one of the prominent members of the teaching staff.   Ross died on November 22, 1897.

On December 18, 1876, Charles Mathews commenced a week's engagement with *My Awful Dad.*   On Saturday evening, December 23, he played in this and in *Not At All Jealous.*   This was his last appearance in Liverpool.   The following year he started upon a tour of the provinces, which was destined to be his last.   On June 8, 1878, he played in *My Awful Dad* at Stalybridge.   He never acted again.   At Manchester sixteen days later he closed his eyes in death, and was buried at Kensal Green.

Phelps visited the theatre on March 19, 1877.   The second week in May saw Edward Terry and company in *Weak Woman.*   The following week *Henry V* was revived.   On

September 10, Henry Irving appeared as Gloster in *Richard III* for the first time in Liverpool.   Calvert revived *Henry VIII* on November 12.   That year's pantomime was *The Children in the Wood*.

Edward Saker's revival of *Much Ado About Nothing* took place on April 22, 1878.   Mr. and Mrs. Saker played Benedick and Beatrice.   The part of Hero was sustained by Miss Monta Gainsborough 'with uncommon power and unimpeachable grace.'*   When *Maritana* was presented by the Carl Rosa Opera Company on May 20, Joseph Maas made, as Don Cæsar de Bazan, his first appearance in Liverpool. *Proof* was presented for the first time locally by Wilson Barrett's Company on August 19.   Henry Irving appeared on September 16, as Louis XI, and four days later played Jingle for the first time in Liverpool.   On October 21, Charles Calvert enacted Doctor Primrose ; Madame Cicely Nott, Mrs. Primrose , and Miss Florence Terry the titular part, in *Olivia*. The Christmas piece was *Robinson Crusoe*.

On May 12, 1879, *Les Cloches de Corneville* was performed by James Fernandez, George Barrett, Frank Darrell, James Danvers, and Miss Cora Stuart.   After having been reconstructed from the designs of Mr. C. J. Phipps, F.S A.,' the theatre was re-opened with J. L. Toole's company on October 20.   Charles Wyndham commenced a twelve nights' engagement on November 24, with *Brighton*   That year's Christmas pantomime was *The Forty Thieves*.   Miss Katie Seymour was in the cast.

Edward Saker's revival of *A Midsummer Night's Dream* —or as he quaintly styled it, *A Mydsomer Nyghte's Dreame*, was brought out on March 29, 1880.   The production was much enhanced by the substitution of children for adults in the fairy scenes.   The youngsters included Katie Barry and Addie and Rosie Blanche.   Saker had a congenial *rôle* as Bottom, and Joseph Burgess portrayed Snout.   On June 28 and 29, the great French actress Sarah Bernhardt made her first appearance in Liverpool.   She acted with enthralling magnetism in *Adrienne Lecouvreur* and *Frou Frou*.   Madame Modjeska was here for six nights commencing August 30. She was seen in *Heartsease, Adrienne Lecouvreur* and *Romeo*

* ',Liverpool Daily Post,' April 23, 1878.

and Juliet. Modjeska was succeeded by the celebrated Hanlon Lees in *Le Voyage en Suisse.* Ellen Terry and Charles Kelly commenced an engagement on October 4, appearing during their sojourn in *The Merchant of Venice, New Men and Old Acres,* and *Much Ado About Nothing.* D'Oyley Carte's Children's *Pinafore* Company came on November 8. W. H. Chippendale took his farewell of the local stage on December 18. The pantomime of *Robin Hood,* produced December 22, was by the author of ' The Piebald Possum of the Panting Prairie, and other novel and instructive works.' This was how J. F. McArdle then described himself. In the company were Harry Nicholls, Arthur Ricketts, Joseph Burgess, and R. J. Roberts. It was about this time that Mr. G. W. Harris first became associated with the theatre.

On June 13, 1881, Saker brought out his fourth and last Shakespearian revival. This was *The Comedy of Errors,* in which Lionel Brough played Dromio of Ephesus. Saker was to have performed the other Dromio, but he was forbidden to act by his medical adviser, so T. F. Doyle played the part instead. On August 15, that melodramatic success *The World* was seen here for the first time locally. Henry Irving played Eugene Aram on September 17. He and Miss Ellen Terry were also seen at this period in *Hamlet, The Merchant of Venice, Charles I,* and *The Belle's Stratagem.* Commencing October 10, Miss Alleyn displayed her skill in *Woman's Love, The Lady of Lyons, As You Like It,* and *Romeo and Juliet.* Modjeska followed. Mrs. Scott-Siddons (a grand-daughter of the famous actress Mrs. Siddons), came on December 12. She appeared in *As You Like It, King René's Daughter,* and *The Honeymoon.* Henry Kemble (grandson of the eminent tragedian, Charles Kemble), was in support. *Dick Whittington and His Cat* formed the Christmas attraction.

On February 20, 1882, the Italian Opera Company came for six nights, but only performed on Monday, Tuesday and Wednesday. On the Thursday, bills were issued by Saker which set forth that ' the manager of the Italian Opera Company having failed to complete his engagement by the non-appearance of Mdlle. Marie Marmon, Madame Demeric-Lablache, Signor Frapolli, and other principal artists, Mr. Saker is reluctantly compelled to bring the opera season to an abrupt termination.'   The Carl Rosa Opera Company performed Balfe's *Moro* for the first time in Liverpool, on April 11, 1882.   T. Edgar Pemberton's comedy opera, *The Chiltern Hundreds* was produced on April 17   The Drury Lane success *Youth* was performed for the first time in Liverpool on May 8. Mrs Langtry visited the theatre on June 5.   *La Dame Blanche* was given for the first time locally on August 31, by the Carl Rosa Opera Company.   The first Liverpool performance of *Boccaccio* took place on October 30.   Emily Soldene played the titular part.   Madame Ristori portrayed Elizabeth and Lady Macbeth in English during the week commencing November 20.   The following week Edwin Booth appeared in *Richelieu, Hamlet, Othello, King Lear,* and *Richard III.* Osmond Tearle played Hamlet, Othello, Claude Melnotte, and Richard III, during the week commencing December 11. *Blue Beard* was given at Christmas.   J. H. Milburn played the title part, and Nellie Bouverie principal ' boy.'   Comic parts were sustained by Harry Starr, and by the author, T. F. Doyle.   This was Edward Saker's last pantomime.

Lady Monckton and Sir Charles Young came on February 26, 1883.   They were seen in *Yellow Roses, The Wife's Secret,* and *Charms.*   On March 12, Lytton Sothern commenced a week's engagement and appeared in the characters formerly sustained by his father, viz., Lord Dundreary, and David Garrick.   Easter Monday saw Kyrle Bellew playing Romeo to Fanny Reid's Juliet.

On March 29, 1883, Edward Saker died at his residence, 118 Bedford Street, Liverpool, from a severe attack of gout. He was born in London, in 1831, and was the son of Mr. W. Saker, an actor of some note in his day.   Saker joined the theatrical profession at an early age by entering into the service of his brother-in-law, Mr. Robert H. Wyndham, of Edinburgh.   He made his mark in Liverpool both as actor and manager.   In conjunction with Lionel Brough, Edward Saker, before he came to manage the Alexandra, used to give an entertainment, entitled ' The So-Amuse Twins,' which was an exceedingly clever production.   Saker's Shakespearian clowns were wonderful examples of able comedy   During his fifteen years' management of the Alexandra his efforts for the elevation and advancement of the drama in Liverpool were unceasing.   His revivals were all pecuniary triumphs, and his pantomimes brought additional grist to the mill. The pantomime weekly salary list frequently ran into £600, but the annuals always realised from £9,000 to £12,000 profit, never less.   Saker was a member of the Masonic body, and took an active part in the formation of the Liverpool Dramatic Lodge.   He was interred in St. James's Cemetery.

After the death of her husband Mrs. Saker took up the reins of management.   With five young children to support and educate, the position was almost forced upon her.   Mr. Saker had, moreover, expressed a wish that his sons should eventually succeed to the management of the theatre, and it was Mrs. Saker's earnest desire to keep things going until they were old enough to assume control.   However, *l'homme propose, et Dieu dispose.*

On May 7, 1883, the Drury Lane success, *Pluck*, was performed for the first time in Liverpool.   In June a series of French plays were given by Madame Judic and company from the Théâtre des Varieties, and by the Gymnase company of forty artists.   Barry Sullivan commenced a fortnight's engagement on August 13.   During the first week the receipts amounted to upwards of £1,300.   It was about this time that Barry was asked by a number of our townsmen to represent them in the Nationalist interest in Parliament. He, however, declined the honour with thanks.   The end of August saw Mrs. Langtry paying a return visit.   *Esmeralda* was produced by the Carl Rosa Opera Company for the first time locally on September 3.   Then followed visits from Henry Irving and Miss Ellen Terry (September 24), Miss Kate Vaughan (October 8), and Miss Bateman.   *The Adamless Eden* Company of ladies (forty in all), performed during the week commencing October 22.   In the company were Ada Blanche and Belle Bilton.   Emily Soldene took her farewell of the local stage on November 24.   *Jack, the Giant Killer*, Mrs. Saker's first pantomime was produced at Christmas with Marie Loftus as Jack.

On February 25, 1884, T. C. King and Kate Read performed in *Othello, Ingomar, Richelieu*, and *Black-Eyed Susan*. Salvini, the celebrated tragedian, took his farewell of the Liverpool stage on May 3, when he gave his marvellous impersonation of Othello.   During his short stay of four nights he was also seen as Hamlet and King Lear.   Beautiful Mary

Anderson came on May 19. She played in *Ingomar, Pygmalion and Galatea, Comedy and Tragedy*, and *The Lady of Lyons*. On June 27, Sarah Bernhardt gave one performance of Lady Macbeth. The Alexandra re-opened on August 21 with *The Gascon*. During the recess the theatre had been redecorated. A new act-drop from the brush of John Brunton, who afterwards went to Australia, was shown for the first time. On November 20, Mrs. Saker played Pauline in *The Lady of Lyons* to Lewis Waller's Claude Melnotte. This was Mr. Waller's first leading part. *Aladdin* was the Yuletide attraction with Jenny Hill in the title part

Early in 1885, *Priest or Painter* was introduced to local playgoers by F. R. Benson's Company. Praiseworthy performances were given by F. R. Benson, William Mollison, and Mr. and Mrs. F. H. Macklin. It is worthy of note that Mr. Benson's grandfather, Robert Benson, was a member of the Liverpool cotton firm, Cropper, Benson and Company.* Miss Fortescue made her first appearance in Liverpool on May 11 in *Pygmalion and Galatea*. Miss Angela Fenton (Mrs. Colonel Greenall), and her company performed in *The Merchant of Venice*, during the week commencing August 10. Miss Fenton played Portia to James Fernandez's Shylock. The end of August saw Mrs Bernard Beere here in *Masks and Faces*. A benefit was given to Frank Emery on October 7 *Cinderella* was that year's pantomime with Miss Letty Lind in the title part.

La Fille de Madame Angot and *Les Cloches de Corneville* played by Warwick Gray's Children's Comic Opera Company came on April 19, 1886. A special production of *Rob Roy* was given on June 7, when leading *rôles* were sustained by Mrs. Saker and Walter Bentley. Barry Sullivan performed in November. *Sindbad the Sailor*, produced December 23, was Mrs. Saker's fourth pantomime. The authors were T. Edgar Pemberton and J James Hewson. Vesta Tilley played Sindbad.

On January 1, 1887, Miss Ellaline Terriss, daughter of the late William Terriss, made her first appearance on the

---

* Mr. Benson tells me that his grandfather rode in the first railway train between Liverpool and Manchester, when the Right Hon William Huskisson, M P. for Liverpool, was killed (September 15, 1830). Curiously enough there is an engine at the present time on the London & North-Western Railway called the ' Robert Benson.'

stage, and danced a hornpipe, with much success, in the first scene of *Sindbad*. Dion Boucicault's comedy of *The Jilt* was performed for the first time in the provinces on February 28, 1887. Edgar Bruce's Company were here in *Alice in Wonderland* on April 11. Mary Anderson played Juliet on May 9 for the first time in Liverpool. Five days later she appeared in the titular part in Dean Milman's tragedy *Bianca*, her first performance of the character in England. Barry Sullivan came on May 30, and brought his engagement to a close on Saturday, June 4, with an impersonation of Richard III. This was his last appearance on the stage. I was present on that occasion, and noticed that his acting was not as good as of yore. The sword combat in the last scene with Richmond (played by his son, Amory Sullivan), was not gone through in his customary effective style. It was fitting that Sullivan should make his last appearance on the stage in Liverpool, where his brilliant histrionic powers were first recognised, and so generously fostered. He died at Hove, Brighton, on May 3, 1891, and was interred in Glasnevin Cemetery, Dublin, where a public statue marks his last resting place.

Sarah Bernhardt played in *Adrienne Lecouvreur* and *Theodora* on July 11 and 12, 1887. The theatre re-opened on September 12 with Mrs. Bernard Beere in *As In A Looking-Glass*. Prices of admission to the stalls, dress-circle, and pit-stalls were reduced by sixpence. Irving came in October, and the Italian Opera Company in November. *The Forty Thieves* was given at Christmas, and was from the joint pens of T. Edgar Pemberton and J. James Hewson. Vesta Tilley was the principal 'boy.' This was Mrs. Saker's last pantomime.

On February 6, 1888, Vesta Tilley took a benefit, on which occasion the late Blanche Stoll (daughter of Mrs. J. G. Stoll), made her first appearance on the stage, and recited G. R. Sims's pathetic poem, entitled 'A Christmas Story.' Miss Tilley also sang a new song, written by Mr. Oswald Stoll, entitled 'How the Money Goes.' On March 12, *The Lady of the Lake* was performed by a stock company. J. B. Howard was the Roderick Dhu, and F. W. Wyndham the FitzJames.

Mrs. Saker retired from the management of the Alexandra on April 14, 1888, upon which occasion she took a farewell benefit. Two performances were given, one in the afternoon and the other in the evening. *Pygmalion and Galatea* was one of the plays selected to be given at the second performance, and Mr. W. S. Gilbert was announced to play the part of Pygmalion. But at the last moment his courage failed him, much to the disappointment of his various admirers, who were looking forward to seeing him in the dual *rôle* of actor and author   Galatea was charmingly played by Miss Julia Neilson, who on this occasion made her first appearance on the local stage. During the course of the evening Mr. Philip Rathbone, chairman of the Alexandra Theatre and Opera House Company, Limited, presented Mrs. Saker with a cheque on behalf of the subscribers.

In bidding farewell, Mrs. Saker. brought to a close a notable *régime* with which the name of Saker had been so long and ' honourably associated.   Mrs. Saker was always very popular in Liverpool.   Even the gallery boys who had saved up their coppers to go to the theatre, had been known to come to the stage door and give her their good wishes in a rich Irish brogue, which was all the more acceptable to her, as she, too, came from Dublin.

A noteworthy social feature of Mr. and Mrs. Saker's management was the ' At Homes ' given in the *foyer* of the theatre.   From time to time their friends were asked to meet Henry Irving, Ellen Terry, Sarah Bernhardt, Mrs. Langtry, and other leading artists.   Invitations for these distinguished gatherings were always keenly sought after.

Commencing August 6, the theatre was under the management of Mr. Richard Mansell, with Mr. Richard Flanagan as business manager.   The opening attraction was *The Demon*, performed by the Russian National Opera Company, which also gave later *The Patriot*.   On September 3, Miss Patti Rosa appeared in *Bob*.   Miss Mary Anderson played Perdita in *A Winter's Tale* for the first time in Liverpool on October 9.   On October 22, Robert Buchanan and Hermann Vezin's three-act comedy, *Bachelors*, was presented.   The *rôle* of Mrs. Lynne Loseby (a young widow), was played by a lady billed as Miss Stella Campbell. · This was Mrs Patrick Campbell's first appearance on the professional stage.   *Dick Whittington* was the Christmas annual.   Fanny Wentworth was in the cast.

The theatre remained closed from May, 1889 until December, 1894, when it was opened under the management of Mr. Ellis Brammall, junr., of the local Shakespeare Theatre, with *The Fair One with the Golden Locks.*

On March 11, 1895, the house was re-opened as the Alexandra by the Empire Theatre (Liverpool), Limited. John Hollingshead was the managing-director of the company, but even with ' Practical John ' at the head of affairs, that coy goddess, Success, proved difficult to woo. On August 5, the theatre came under the direction of the Alexandra Vaudeville Company, Limited. Our townsman, Mr. Sidney Bolingbroke Cooper, was the manager. In January, 1896, the property, which included the theatre and three shops, was put up for auction at the Law Association Rooms, Cook Street, and sold to Messrs. Moss and Thornton for £30,000.

Afterwards the theatre was reconstructed and beautified in a lavish manner, and the electric light installed throughout. The new proprietors, the Liverpool, Leeds, and Hull Empires, Limited, at the head of which was Mr. (now Sir) H. E. Moss, announced that ' the class of entertainment will be in strict unison with the building ; it will be as refined as it is excellent, a conspicuous feature being the absence of all that can be construed into vulgarity, the fixed determination of the management being to promote a class of entertainment which has made such rapid strides in public favour during the last few years. The company, therefore, trust that in their new endeavour to elevate the tone of variety entertainments they will command the good wishes of all classes of society.' How they, the present company, Moss' Empires, Limited, with which the Liverpool, Leeds and Hull Empires, Limited, was incorporated, have scrupulously kept their word with the public has long been a household word. In their hands the Empire has been a big success.

The new Empire opened on December 19, 1896, with the pantomime of *Cinderella.* Mr. James Aynsley Cook was the acting manager, Mr. E. Bosanquet, the musical director, and Mr. Kingston Trollope the stage manager. The first variety performance in the new theatre was given on February 15, 1897. In the following Christmas *The House that Jack Built* was produced. Mr. E. Bosanquet, the musical director, left the theatre in May, 1899. He was succeeded by Mr. Walter

Forrest Hague, a nephew of the late Sam Hague, who severed his connection with the theatre in October, 1908   To the regret of many Mr. J. A. Cook retired from the acting management of the theatre on November 29, 1899.   He was succeeded by his brother, Mr. Thomas Aynsley Cook. *Jolly Jack* was the Christmas attraction of 1899.   Leading parts were admirably sustained by Miss Bessie Cohen (Jack) and Joseph Alexandre and George Hughes.   The spectacle *A Hielan' Laddie ; or, His Twa Loves, His Lassie and His Queen* was performed on December 24, 1900.   *Cinderella* was the Christmas piece in 1901, and *Aladdin* was given the following year.   The next pantomime was *Puss in Boots*, which was produced on December 24, 1906.   On February 10, 1908, Laurence Irving and Mabel Hackney made their first appearance on the Empire stage, in a sketch called *Peg Woffington*   Mr Horace Cole is now the courteous acting manager of the theatre, and Mr. George M. Saker, son of the late Edward Saker, the talented musical director.

THE SEFTON THEATRE.

After the closing of the Royal Park Theatre in Parliament Street, the south end of Liverpool remained without a play-house until the Sefton, a rectangular hall in Park Road, was opened by Mr. C. H. Duval, for purely dramatic purposes, on September 21, 1875.   Previously the hall had been used for various kinds of entertainments.

Mr. Duval's reputation had preceded him to ' The Park,' and on his opening night he was patronised by an audience which completely filled the house.   A new stage had been erected, and everything fitting in the way of adequate scenery, dresses, and a good stock company provided. The performance opened somewhat unambitiously with the comedy *A Bird in the Hand is Worth Two in the Bush.*   The company comprised Misses Rose Mortimer, Grace Montford, and A. Powell ;   and Barry Stuart, Ben Schofield, and E. Fitzdavis.   The theatre accommodated about 1,100 persons —800 in the body and 300 in the gallery.

On the occasion of Mr. G. W. Edwards's benefit, which, took place on March 29, 1879, Messrs. H. T. Brickwell and James Carr played the respective parts of Valentine and

Orson in the romantic drama of that name. The former
gentleman afterwards appeared as harlequin in a laughable
pantomime, entitled *Fun, Frolic, and Mischief ; or, the Clown's
Holiday*. This was two years before Mr. Brickwell joined
Edward Terry as acting manager.

Although not a native of Liverpool, having been born
at Stroud in 1858, Mr. Brickwell was educated at the Liverpool
College, and in a small part, made his first appearance on the
stage at the local Amphi'.

In the 'eighties, the Sessions House Hotel, Kirkdale, was
occupied by Mr. Brickwell *père*. One Sunday when his son
and his daughter-in-law arrived at the hotel, they were surprised to find, massed in front of the house and stretching
along the footwalks and roadway leading thereto, a dense
body of people. On seeing Mr. H. T. Brickwell, the crowd
shouted ' That's im, that's 'im,' and then a very respectable
cheer was given. The younger Brickwell blushed becomingly,
looked dreadfully conscious, and bowed as gracefully as
possible. Apparently he had been taken for some illustrious
personage. Who could it be ? The mystery was solved
after he and his spouse had fought their way through the
demonstrative crowd (each one striving to shake him by the
hand), and were safely housed in the hotel. It then appeared
that Mr. Brickwell had been mistaken for Bartholomew
Binns, the successor of the ' long drop ' man, who was
expected to arrive that day to carry out on the morrow the
dread sentence of the law on an unfortunate criminal at the
adjacent Kirkdale gaol.

After directing the theatre for a few years, Mr. Duval was
succeeded as lessee by Mr. R. Mulvey, who re-christened the
house the Royal Sefton Theatre. Mr. Mulvey's stock company
used to give drama interspersed with variety turns. *London
by Night, Liberty, The Press Gang, Life's Devotion, Nobody's
Child, Blow for Blow*, and *Maria Martin* were some of the
plays submitted.

Mark Melford, the well-known actor-dramatist, John
Sheridan, Mr. and Mrs. W. H. Morton, Frank Fuller, and
William Tallon, were all formerly associated as players with
this house. The last-mentioned gentleman is still a resident
of this city. Mr. Henry Loydall managed the theatre for a
time, and after his *régime* Mr. Mulvey again took up the reins

of management. In 1895 Mr. James Kiernan opened the Sefton as a music hall. Afterwards it was converted into a billiard hall which it still remains.

THE ROYAL VICTORIA THEATRE

This theatre formed part of the attractions of the Liverpool Exhibition of 1887. Mrs. Edward Saker was the lessee ; Mr. G. W. Harris, manager ; Mr F. W. Walden, acting manager ; and Mr. Joseph Burgess, stage manager. Mrs. Saker did everything possible to maintain a varied series of attractions, and she made the pretty bijou theatre a place of agreeable resort. On Whit Monday seven performances of *Kenilworth* and a variety entertainment were given between the hours of one and ten p.m., during which time over 5,000 persons entered the theatre. Despite, however, every effort to achieve success a loss of some £500 was recorded in a brief period of six weeks.

THE SHAKESPEARE THEATRE.

This theatre, which is situated in Fraser Street, off London Road, was erected by Mr. Ellis Brammall, junr., and opened on Monday, August 27, 1888. It was the first playhouse in the provinces to be called after the immortal bard, the one in Shakespeare's own town excepted. Appropriately enough the opening performance (under the patronage of His Worship the Mayor of Liverpool, Mr. T. W. Oakshott), was *As You Like It*, given by the inaugural stock company, with the following cast :—

Banished Duke, ...Mr. Henry Moxon.
Amiens, ...Mr. Charles Stanley.
Jaques, ...Mr. T. W. Ford.
Duke Frederick, ...Mr. Charles Wybert.
Le Beau, ...Mr. Herbert Swindon.
Charles (the Wrestler), ...Mr. Arthur Lennard.
Oliver, ...Mr. Newton Ramsden.
Celia, ...Miss Susie Steele.

Adam, ...Mr. G. Lester Herbert.
Orlando, ...Mr. T. C. Bindloss.
Audrey, ...Miss Kate Hodson.
Jaques de Bois, ...Mr. Eustace.
Touchstone, ...Mr. Edward Chessman.
Corin, ...Mr. Henry Sainsbury.
Sylvius, ...Mr. Thomas Power.
William, ...Mr. F. Granville.
Phebe, ...Miss Adeline Evers.
                and
Rosalind, ...Miss Wallis
                              (Mrs. Lancaster).

The Songs and Choruses by the specially organised Shakespeare
Glee Union.

This palatial building will seat comfortably some 3,000 persons. The magnificent *foyer* through which approach is made to the dress-circle is luxuriously furnished with cosy lounges, and adorned with richly-bevelled mirrors, and chaste carvings in Dantzic oak of scenes from Shakespeare's plays, the whole surmounted by a tastefully pannelled ceiling. The rest of the theatre is quite in keeping.

The first manager was Mr. Charles Walters, who was afterwards succeeded by the late G. W. Harris, formerly associated with Mr. and Mrs. Edward Saker at the Alexandra Theatre. The acting manager and treasurer was Mr. John Gaffney, and the secretary, Mr. B. Henderson Howat. Of these gentlemen, only our townsman, Mr. Gaffney, remains connected with the theatre. He is now the esteemed resident manager. The first musical director was the late Fred Wright (formerly of the local Prince of Wales), and the first scenic artists were Messrs. Fred Dowling and J. A. O'Rorke. The late R. V. Shone, whose sad death by his own hand is a matter of painful memory, was the first assistant stage manager.

Edmund Tearle had the honour of being the first touring manager to visit the Shakespeare, and since then he has been several times on the same boards.

Notable amongst those who have appeared here since the theatre was opened are John Hare, George Alexander, Arthur Roberts, Dan Leno, Fred Terry, David James, H. Beerbohm Tree, Edward Compton, Forbes Robertson, Lewis

Waller, Wilson Barrett, Hermann Vezin, Leonard Boyne, Shiel Barry, Arthur Bourchier, W. L. Abingdon, Janette Steer, Minnie Palmer, Florence St John, Kate Rorke, Olga Nethersole, Sarah Bernhardt, Mrs. Langtry, and Mrs. Lewis Waller. The Carl Rosa and D'Oyly Carte Opera Companies have been frequent visitors.

At this theatre on Monday, December 3, 1888, the ill-fated Arthur Dacre and his wife, Amy Roselle, commenced a week's engagement, which proved to be their last visit to Liverpool. For four evenings of the week they played in 'Charles Reade's striking drama of *The Double Marriage*. Soon afterwards, it will be remembered, they proceeded to Australia on a tour, and there made their final exit from Life's stage by suicide.

Shakespeare pantomimes are always of excellent quality. The first annual was *The Yellow Dwarf*, an old theme now seldom discussed. It was written by T. F. Doyle, and presented on Saturday, December 22, 1888. Principal parts were played by Matt Robson, G. T. Minshull, Walter Groves, John S. Chamberlain, and Miss Amy Grundy.

A special feature for some years at the Shakespeare was the series of revivals by F. R. Benson and his Shakespearian Company. Each year a committee of local gentlemen of standing and repute was formed to give, at it were, a tone to the revivals, which were eminently successful, the classic season generally lasting for a month. Although Mr. Benson's visits do not now extend as long as formerly, they are still attended with good results. Mr. Benson first came to the Shakespeare with his company on April 29, 1889, the opening play being *A Midsummer Night's Dream*.

Among the first productions seen here there have been several notable successes. On May 6, 1889, William Duck's company gave, for the first time on any stage, *A Wife's Devotion*, written by J. H Darnley and J. M. Fenn. In collaboration with the late H. A. Bruce, Mr. Darnley afterwards wrote *Shadows on the Blind*, and *On Guy Fawkes Day*. Mr. Bruce also wrote a novel, ' From the Ranks to the Peerage,' which met with success ; and at the time of his lamented death was engaged on another, ' Amy Poigndestre.' Poor old ' Daddy ! ' May the earth lie lightly on him !

The second pantomime was *Old Mother Hubbard*, with T. F. Doyle again as author. It was produced on Saturday, December 21, 1889. *Humpty Dumpty* was the title of the next Christmas extravaganza. It was written by Wilton Jones, and principally interpreted by J. T. McMillan, Charles Seel, J. H. Milburn, and Nelly Leamar (the Hon. Mrs. Duncombe). Its first performance took place on Saturday, December 20.

Here on Easter Monday, March 30, 1891, for the first time in 'England, James M. Hardie and Miss Sarah B. Von Leer presented that phenomenal success *On the Frontier*, a stirring melodrama founded on Fenimore Cooper's novels ' The Last of the Mohicans,' and ' The Wept of the Wishton Wish.'

The fourth pantomime was *Aladdin*, the ' book' again by T. F. Doyle. It was produced on December 24, 1891. The anniversary of that night in the following year saw the first performance of *Blue Beard* by W. H. Risque, with Henry Wardroper, Martin Adeson, Victor Widdicombe, the Lorenzis, Florrie Robina, and the Sisters Phillips in the cast.

During the week commencing Monday, September 11, 1893, *Diplomacy* was played here by the following remarkable combination :—

Count Orloff,	Mr. Bancroft.
Baron Stein,	Mr. Arthur Cecil.
Julian Beauclerc,	Mr. J. Forbes Robertson.
Algie Fairfax,	Mr. Gilbert Hare.
Markham,	Mr. Gilbert Trent.
Antoine,	Mr. E. Mayeur.
Shepherd,	Mr. H. Vaughan.
Henry Beauclerc,	Mr. John Hare.
Dora,	Miss Kate Rorke.
Countess Zicka,	Miss Elizabeth Robins.
Marquise de Rio-Zares,	Lady Monckton.
Mion,	Miss Helen Luck.
Lady Henry Fairfax,	Mrs. Bancroft.

That year's pantomime was *Cinderella* (produced December 23), in which Martin Adeson, Huntley Wright, Harry Freeman, and Marie Kendal gave performances. The following year (1894), saw *Bo-Peep* by J. H. Wolfe. In it were Marie Lloyd and Belle Harcourt, Walter Sealby, Fred Sinclair, and James Chippendale On March 25, 1895, the 1892-3 annual of *Blue Beard* was revived. It was produced under the general direction of Fred Coles The 1895-6 annual was *Dick Whittington*, with Maggie Duggan in the title part, her first appearance in pantomime at the Shakespeare. Alfred Hemming, C. Guilfoyle Seymour, the Lorenzis, and Freddie Farren were chief among the fun-makers. The next annual was *The Babes in the Wood*, by J. H. Wolfe. Julie Mackey, Jennie Rogers, Sam Wilkinson, H. Gomer May, and J. P. Dane were the principal exponents. The 1897-8 pantomime was J. H. Wolfe's version of *The Yellow Dwarf*, in which G. T. Minshull, Nat Clifford, Marie Dainton and Gwennie Hasto appeared.

Mr. Ellis Brammall, junr., directed the destinies of the theatre until the property was leased in 1898 to Hardie, Von Leer, and Gordyn, who opened the house on April 11, 1898, with *A Night Out*. In the 1898-9 extravaganza *Dick Whittington*, by Percy Milton, were Arthur Milton, Herbert Lisle, Billee Barlow, and Nita Clavering.

In 1899 the theatre was turned into a limited company, with Mr H A. Bruce as managing-director. The company obtained a twenty-one years' lease of the premises at a yearly rental of £2,000, with the option to terminate the tenancy in 1909, together with a further option of purchasing the lessor's reversion in the property for a stipulated sum. The house opened under the new auspices on August 14, *Ma Mie Rosette* being the initial attraction.

Among the noteworthy productions of this period was that much discussed play *The Christian*, dramatised by Hall Caine from his own novel, and brought out here for the first time in England on Monday, October 9, 1899 Jay Hickory Wood's version of *Cinderella*, produced on December 23, was the next pantomime The performers included Amy Augarde, Adrienne Augarde, Lillie Belmore, Henry Wright, Fred Williams, Austin Lenton, Harry Lupino, and the Bostons.

On Monday, May 21, 1900, *The King's Password* by Mrs. Vere Campbell first saw the light, and on September 3, of the same year, George R. Sims's play, *The Scarlet Sin*, had its initial production. Boxing Night, 1900, saw the production of *Jack and the Beanstalk*, which was the first Drury Lane pantomime to be played at the Shakespeare. Principal parts were filled by Maggie Duggan, Ethel Haydon, George Robey, and Fred Zola.

On September 2, 1901, Mr. Charles Frohman asked the patrons of the Shakespeare to sit in judgment upon the *Sherlock Holmes* of Conan Doyle and William Gillette. A favourable verdict was given. On November 8, 1901, Edward Terry submitted a new three-act farcical comedy, written by Sidney Rosenfeld the American playwright, and entitled *The Purple Lady*. The Yuletide piece was *Robinson Crusoe*, written by William Wade, the talented author of many pantomimes. Lelia Roze figured in this as the shipwrecked mariner.

On Thursday, September 18, 1902, the theatre, subject to the existing lessees' rights, was put up for auction by Mr. William Thomson at the Law Association Rooms, Cook Street, but was bought in by Mr. Temple, of Liverpool and Warrington. Afterwards the property was acquired by Mr. Robert Arthur, managing-director of the Robert Arthur Theatres Company, Limited. The lease of the Shakespeare Theatre Company, Limited, has, however, still a number of years to run.

The romantic comedy in four acts, entitled *Monsieur Beaucaire* was produced by Lewis Waller for the first time in England on October 6, 1902.

Dick Whittington, from the pen of William Wade, was the Christmas attraction of 1902. Ada Blanche was the bold London 'prentice. *Cinderella* was played the following Christmas. On May 23, 1904, Wilson Barrett commenced an engagement of three weeks. On May 27, he submitted his own play *In the Middle of June* for the first time in Liverpool. On June 9, he appeared in another new piece from his own pen, entitled *Lucky Durham*, then performed for the first time on any stage. Saturday evening (June 11) was the last night of his engagement, and on it he played Wilfred Denver in *The Silver King*. This was his last appearance on any stage, as he died, greatly regretted, on July 22 following. A new play, entitled *Dr. Wake's Patient* was produced for the first time on any stage, on September 5. On December 24,

Aladdin was produced.   In the cast were Carrie Moore, Billie
Burke, George Graves, and Frank Danby.   William Mollis-
son appeared in *Beside the Bonnie Brier Bush* on the occasion
of its production on April 3, 1905   Mrs. T. P. O'Connor's
play *The Temptation* first saw the footlights here on June 1
following.   Another first production was William Gillette's
play *Clarice*, brought out on September 4.   The 1905-6
annual was *The Babes in the Wood*, and the succeeding
pantomime, *Mother Goose*.   On November 2, 1907, John Hare
took his farewell of the Liverpool stage in *A Pair of
Spectacles* and *A Quiet Rubber*.   The 1907-8 pantomime was
Cinderella.

THE NEW THEATRE ROYAL.

This establishment, which is situated in Breck Road, was
built by Mr. Thomas Montgomery, and opened on December
24, 1888, with Arthur Rousby's Company.   *The Bohemian Girl*
was the opening attraction, followed during the week by
performances of *Maritana* and *Figaro*.   Afterwards a capable
stock company was engaged for the exploitation of notable
plays.   Later on there came visits from travelling companies.
On May 13, 1889, a variety bill was provided with
Henri Clark as the 'star'   Afterwards resort was again
made to the employment of touring companies.   Among
those who appeared at that time on the stage of the Royal
were Walter Passmore, Lawrence Daly, Lester Collingwood,
William Calvert, Martin Adeson, Horace Wheatley, Walter
Groves, Butler Stanhope, Grace Edwin and Clara Cowper.
On August 3, 1891, the house was opened as the Theatre
Royal Palace of Varieties, and so remained until about a
couple of years ago, when up-to-date drama played by a stock
company on the popular two-houses-a-night principle, was
reverted to.   This has proved very successful, and Mr.
Matthew Montgomery is to be cordially commended for
having reintroduced the old 'stock' system into Liverpool.
Mr. Frank O'Toole is the acting manager, a position
which he has worthily filled for a number of years.

THE STANHOPE THEATRE.

On the east side of Beaufort Street there was erected in
1805 an ecclesiastical building of no great architectural

pretensions. It was tenanted for years by the Calvinistic Meth-odists, who christened it the Ebenezer Chapel. After their secession, Mr. Butler Stanhope, of the Theatre Royal, Birken-head, converted the building into a theatre, and opened it in November, 1894, with *The Shaughraun*. The part of Conn was cleverly played by Mr. Stanhope, who was ably supported by a stock company. In January of the following year, Mr. Stanhope brought travelling companies, the first being Mr. W. E. Langley's combination in *The Scarlet Brotherhood*, a play which had first seen the light at the Royal Muncaster Theatre, Bootle. When Mr. Stanhope severed his connection with the theatre he was succeeded by Mr. John Walters, who renamed the house the Queen's. Mr. Walters did not remain long, and now, (like its near Thespian neighbour, the Royal Park), the Stanhope is used as a warehouse.

THE LYRIC THEATRE.

The Lyric, situated in Everton Valley, was built by Mr. Ellis Brammall, junr., and opened by Mr. H. C. Arnold on Boxing Day, December 26, 1897, with J. H. Wolfe's panto-mime of *Blue Beard*. The following were the chief items in the cast :—

Blue Beard	Mr. W. H. Moss.
Ibrahim	Mr. John P. Dane.
Fatima	Miss Marie Free.
Sister Anne	Mr. James Norris.
Shacabac ⎫ Abradac ⎰	Messrs. Sandy and Carl.
Selim	Miss Laura Lyle.

An interior view reveals an attractive theatre, rich in crimson velvet, polished mahogany, and cream and gold adornments. The ceiling dotted all over with electric lights, is a beautiful piece of ornamentation. In the *foyer* there is a handsome carved oak centre-piece and an electric light candelabra. The theatre will comfortably seat nearly 2,000 persons. The *façade*, which contains all the doors of entrance, is in terra-cotta brick work, with stone reliefs.

Mr. Arnold, the lessee and manager, is a Liverpool man, bred and born, and first saw the light in Crown Street, about the middle of the 'fifties   Destined by his parents for a commercial career, he soon exchanged the prose of business for the poetry of the stage   After gaining experience in local amateur dramatic circles, he made his first appearance on the professional stage at the Amphi' in the autumn of 1871. As an actor he speedily won a name for himself, and in course of time successfully appeared on every stage in his native city. For a number of years he was a prominent member of the famous Rotunda stock companies.   After touring with his own company for some years, he decided to abandon the road and have a theatre of his own. Happily, his choice fell upon the Lyric, which from the commencement has been a credit to himself and to his native city.

Mr. Arnold is a P M. of the Liverpool Dramatic Lodge (1609), and also P.P J.G D , of the Province of West Lancashire.

During the time the Lyric was a dramatic house Mr. Arnold always placed before his patrons the best talent. Some of these attractions were :—*The Sign of the Cross, The Great Ruby, Pink Dominoes, Tommy Dodd, Morocco Bound, The Shop Girl, The Skirt Dancer, The New Boy, In Old Kentucky, Cheer, Boys, Cheer ! The Trumpet Call, Sweet Lavender, Tommy Atkins, The New Barmaid, Under the Red Robe, The Celestials, The Lady Slavey, A House of Mystery, Gentleman Joe, The Gay Parisienne, Woman and Wine, Betsy, The Lady of Ostend, Why Smith Left Home, The Brixton Burglary, The Bell-Ringer, La Poupée, Orlando Dando, The Prodigal Daughter* (Mr. Arnold's own company), *A Soldier and a Man, A Night Out, Charley's Aunt, The Middleman, The White Queen, Saucy Sally, The Circus Girl, The Lights o' London, The Geisha, A Woman of No Importance, Quo Vadis ? The Silver King, The Sorrows of Satan, Les Cloches de Corneville, David Garrick, A Royal Divorce, One of the Best, The Private Secretary,* and *A Runaway Girl.*

At this house there has only been one first production, viz. '—*The Principal Boy,* produced June 5, 1899.

Mr. Arnold has presented here three pantomimes, the first, that with which the theatre opened, the second, *Cinderella* (December 24, 1898), and the third (in conjunction with Mr. Sidney Cooper), *Robinson Crusoe,* produced on December 23, 1899.

Mr. Arnold ran his theatre as a dramatic house for over five years, but finding that the public taste was more for the variety business he converted the Lyric into a popular two-houses-a-night variety theatre. The opening performance under the new order of things, took place on Easter Monday, 1903. The Lyric has proved one of the most successful variety theatres in Liverpool.

Mr. Fred Coles was the acting manager from the time the theatre was first opened down to June, 1907, when he was reluctantly compelled to resign the position through ill-health. He was succeeded by Mr. H. C. Arnold, junr. Mr. James Hargreaves is the present musical director. His predecessors have been Messrs. George Chapman, junr., Arthur Workman, and James Taylor.

THE CONCERT HALLS.

THE MUSIC HALL, a plain brick edifice, stood in Bold Street at the corner of Concert Street. The hall, which was built in 1786 by Mr. Wilson on land purchased from Mr. Jonas Bold for £120, was opened in June of that year. It witnessed the triumphs of the greatest musical celebrities of the day—Braham, Salmon, Catalani, Pasta, and others; but it ultimately declined in popularity, and became converted to the prosaic purposes of trade.

THE PORTICO ROOMS. This establishment was situated in Newington, and was in existence prior to 1841. It was erected for panoramic exhibitions, concerts and lectures, and musical entertainments. On December 11, 1843, W. J. Hammond gave his popular entertainment, 'A Night with Punch.' Here, on February 10, 1844, General Tom Thumb made his first appearance in England. He was brought over by P. T. Barnum. Madame Céleste of the Theatre Royal placed her private box, immediately on his arrival, at the great showman's disposal. This was policy on Madame's part, as she had an eye to 'lifting the shekels' in America. In January, 1849, the name of the Portico Rooms was changed to Stiles' bowling saloon. Afterwards it was known as the Liver Bowling Hall.

HIME'S MUSIC HALL.   This building was erected on the site of the old Music Hall in Bold Street, and opened on October 24, 1853.   It was an elegant room, the decorations being rich and chaste.   There was seating accommodation for nearly a thousand persons.   The hall is now used for commercial purposes.

ROYAL ASSEMBLY ROOMS.   This establishment was first known as the Templar's Hall.   In 1842 the building was taken by Edmund Elliston,* son of Robert William Elliston, the comedian and patentee of Drury Lane Theatre, London. Elliston altered the place considerably and laid down a splendid floor.   He engaged a London architect, Charles Reid, to superintend the work.   The hall was opened by Elliston as the Royal Assembly Rooms, with a view to giving concerts and balls.   Here in January, 1844, Braham, the famous vocalist, sang   On May 17, of the same year, Samuel Lover, the Irish novelist, gave a series of readings.   In August, 1845, Signor Orsini conducted a number of concerts.   Mr. and Mrs. German Reed gave their celebrated entertainment here on November 4, 1856.   The rooms are situated on the east side of Great George Street, nearly opposite the Chapel.

THE PHILHARMONIC HALL.   The Liverpool Philharmonic Society was established to meet the want of a regular supply of high-class public musical performances   Meetings were held at first in a large room in Great Richmond Street, at the back of St. Anne's Church.   The members found the accommodation inadequate, and they decided to build a hall worthy of the object to which they were devoted.   The Philharmonic Hall in Hope Street was the result.   The cost of the building was about £30,000, and the money was raised by shares.   The first stone was laid on September 23, 1846, and the building opened on August 27, 1849.   The architect was Mr. John Cunningham of Liverpool.   The leading artists at the opening performance were Mesdames Grisi, Alboni, Catherine Hayes, Corbari, L. Corbari, MacFarren, A. and M. Williams, and Viardot Garcia ; Signori Mario, Lablache, Bartolini, Tagliafico, Polonini, Covas, and Herr Formes ; Messrs. Sims

---

* A daughter of Edmund Elliston resides in Canning Street.

Reeves, Lockey, Benson, and Whitworth.   Among the instru-
mentalists were Benedict, Piatti, Bottesini, Hallé, Ernst,
and Vivier.

It was in this fine hall on February 13 and 14, 1852, that
the Amateur Dramatic Society in connection with the Guild
of Literature and Art gave performances of Sir Edward Bulwer
Lytton's new four-act comedy *Not So Bad As We Seem ;
or, Many Sides to a Character*, and of a piece called *Mr.
Nightingale's Diary*.   The primary object of the performances
was ' to encourage Life Assurance and other provident habits
among Authors and Artists ; to render such assistance to both
as shall never compromise their independence ; and to found
a new Institution, where honourable rest from arduous labour
shall still be associated with the discharge of congenial duties.'
The performers included Charles Dickens, Douglas Jerrold,
John Forster, Mark Lemon, Charles Knight, Wilkie Collins,
John Tenniel, and Dudley Costello.

It was here that Thackeray lectured in September
and October, 1852 ; and it was here too, that the breakfast
was given in 1853 in commemoration of William Roscoe.
The artists engaged at this hall are always of the first quality
and the concerts give every satisfaction.

THE CONCERT HALL.   This building was situated on the
north side of Lord Nelson Street.   It now forms part of
Messrs. Cope's tobacco establishment.   The hall was projected by Mr. John Finch, senr., an extensive iron merchant
of the town.   It was erected for the use of the Socialists,
Mr. Finch being a disciple of Robert Owen.   The hall was
opened as ' The Hall of Science.'   It was a spacious building
with a gallery on three sides, and had a seating capacity of
2,700 persons.   The hall, which at one time was called the
Nelson Assembly Rooms, was one of the most popular places
in town for concerts in general, for the holding of public
meetings and the delivery of lectures.   The Saturday evening
concerts were very successful, the attendance being uniformly
large.   Sims Reeves was here on March 23, 1849, and in April
Samuel Lover came to give a series of readings.   On May
18 and 25, 1850, the hall was engaged by Harry Boleno for
his friend, David Prince Miller, author of ' The Life of a
Showman.'   Mr. Miller's entertainment was entitled 'Never

Despair ; or, the Ups and Downs of Life,' and was ' illustrative,' he tells us in his book,* ' of various exhibitions I had been engaged in during my checkered career, with anecdotes of celebrated actors I had met with on and off the stage. Much to my astonishment I was eminently successful '

In January, 1859, the celebrated Lola Montez gave a lecture on ' Strong-Minded Women.'   On April 30, 1860, the Terry Children, Kate and Ellen, appeared in a couple of drawing-room entertainments entitled ' Distant Relations,' and ' Home for the Holidays ' Ellen Terry was then in her thirteenth year, having been born on February 27, 1848. This was one of her first visits to Liverpool Mr Terry and his children when they visited Liverpool used to stay at a house of spacious proportions which stood at the corner of Birkett Street and Richmond Row.

In a recent number of ' M.A.P.'† Ellen Terry tells us that ' her mother took Kate to London and she was left with her father in the provinces for two years. I can't recall much about those two years except sunsets and a great mass of shipping looming up against the sky The sunsets followed me about everywhere, the shipping was in Liverpool, where father was engaged for a considerable time. He never ceased teaching me to be useful, alert, and quick. Sometimes he hastened my perceptive powers with a slipper, and he always corrected me if I pronounced any word in a slipshod fashion. He himself was a beautiful elocutionist, and if I now speak my language well, it is in no small degree due to my early training.'

Arthur Sketchley visited in 1867, and told about ' Mrs Brown on her Travels.'   Henry Russell was always a great favourite at the Concert Hall.   Large and appreciative audiences used to gather to hear him sing to his own accompaniment ' To the West,' ' The Ivy Green,' ' Man the Lifeboat,' ' Cheer, Boys, Cheer ! ' and other excellent items in his repertory

There was a large room beneath the hall in which, occasionally, public meetings were held   It was here the Parliamentary Debating Society (a mimic embodiment of the

---

* ' The Life of a Showman,' p. 155. ￭   † June 8, 1907

Parliament of St. Stephen's), held its meetings. Ultimately the hall was sold, and, as previously mentioned, is now devoted to commercial purposes

THE VARIETY STAGE.

THE 'FREE AND EASIES' AND CONCERT ROOMS.

To look at the magnificent Palaces of Varieties in Liverpool, and other places, one would hardly imagine that less than half a century ago the prototypes of these places of amusement were conducted on very different and vastly inferior lines. The impartial observer who chances to know the whole story cannot fail to note with satisfaction the wholesome revolution which has been accomplished in this class of entertainment

In Liverpool, as in other cities and towns, the protoplast of the music hall was the tap-room of the public house. These rooms were generally known as 'free and easies,' and they did not belie their title. In some of them there was no platform, and the singer had to ' take the floor,' and make the best of his opportunities.

In some of the concert-rooms performances took place upon a small platform erected at one end of the room, and upon this the artists did their level best to entertain their patrons as they sat at little tables partaking of refreshment. In the old days the generality of the performers seldom used any make-up, and had to stand or fall purely on their merits Several of the concert-rooms had their own particular vocalists, some of whom were clever enough in their way. If the comic singer had a song with a good rollicking chorus his success was all the greater. Everybody joined in the chorus, whether he had a voice or not, and frequently, someone who had imbibed 'not wisely, but too well,' would finish up a few bars behind, to the great amusement of the company. Any member of the audience was at liberty to give a taste of his quality, subject of course to the approval of the chairman, who sat in state. The chairman's insignia of office was a little wooden mallet, with which he rapped for order, or made signal taps when about to introduce an entertainer with a few complimentary and well-turned phrases. In those days it was considered a great honour to sit at the chairman's table, and an additional honour if the great man condescended to drink or smoke at the visitor's expense. Admission to the concert-rooms was invariably free, a small extra charge being made for the refreshments.

Although a number of the concert-rooms were respectably conducted, there were some, I regret to say, of a more or less disreputable kind In order to show how the music hall has progressed, let us see what the inside of a certain type of free concert-room was like about half a century or so ago.

The house selected is one which was situated in the neighbourhood of Williamson Square On the lamp over the door is the word ' Poses ' Congregated round the bar inside are a number of women and foreign sailors, all in various stages of intoxication After ascending a flight of very ricketty stairs we reach the concert-room—a long, narrow apartment in a filthy state. There is a stage about two feet from the floor , the drop-scene is tattered and dirty. Forms for the accommodation of the audience are ranged along each side of the room, leaving a passage down the centre for the waiters No charge is made for admission, but the visitor has to pay threepence for a refreshment ticket. There is a piano in the room presided over by a little hunchback, who is smoking—when he is not coughing. Seated by him is a gentleman who plays the violin—when, and how, he likes.

A bell is rung and the fiddler makes his appearance on the stage, as a violinist. He afterwards warbles about the joys of single blessedness, but finds himself persistently interrupted by the sailors who are audibly kissing the bare-necked, lightly dressed girls who have them ' in tow.' The singer refuses to continue, and reseats himself by the side of the pianist. He explains to the proprietress of the room that he can't finish the song, and that if she wants it finished she must do it herself, ' for I'm d—— if I can work, and I'm d—— if I do ' ' What's to do ? ' asks a gentle creature with several dinges in her face ' That's what you get for paying a fellow beforehand. Why he's —— cheeky now he's got his tin.' ' Oh ! let him go to ——' replies the lovely nymph.

After a brazen damsel had sung a couple of songs, the fiddler,—who certainly *was* drunk—jumped upon the stage, and announced that the next performance would be Adam and Eve, in three pictures.   Adam and Eve were in skin tights.   Eve wore a garland of fig leaves, or some other botanical equivalent, but saving ' the breeches ' the dress was strictly historical.   The *tableaux* were ' Adam and Eve in Paradise,' ' Eve's Astonishment at Beholding Adam,' and ' The Consummation of Bliss.'   The third *tableau* finished, Eve condescended to sit near and drink with a sailor ' half seas over,' and obligingly informed him that they performed also ' The Morning and Evening Star,' ' The Graces,' and other beautiful pictures when there was a good company in the room.*

In ' Playhouse Square ' (Williamson Square), as our forefathers called it, there were, as far back as the 'forties, several old concert-rooms.   Harry Boleno, the celebrated clown, used to hold ' a select harmonic meeting ' each evening at his hostelry, the Clown Tavern, adjacent to the Theatre Royal.   In 1854, he left Liverpool and migrated to the Catherine Wheel, in Windmill Street, Haymarket, opposite the Argyle Rooms, in London.

Jem Ward, a hard-hitting pugilist with some literary and artistic ability, held harmonic evenings when ' mine host ' of the Star and York Hotels.   In the large room of the York Hotel, which was situated at the corner of Williamson Square and Tarleton Street, ' Baron ' Nicholson, of the Garrick's Head, Bow Street, Covent Garden, established a Judge and Jury Society in September, 1843.   Nicholson, who was the originator of the Judge and Jury Clubs, advertised that ' the Entertainment is one of forensic display in costume, eloquence, and fun ; its features involve wit, learning, and oratorical excellence.'   The legal gentlemen of Liverpool were specially invited to attend.

The large room in the York Hotel was called by Nicholson ' the House of Lords,' and it was fitted up as a regular court. There was a bench for ' M'lud,' and on either side sat Counsel, all of whom were bewigged and gowned.   The entertainment consisted of mock trials dealing with Society scandals of the

---

* ' Liverpool Life : Its Pleasures, Practices, and Pastimes,' (1857), pp. 26-8.

day, and the humour displayed was of the broadest kind, frequently merging into rank obscenity

Musical evenings were also given at Evans's supper-rooms,* on the right-hand side of Upper Dawson Street; in the ' Square ' at Dick's Albert rooms; at the Shakespeare Tavern; and at the Black Bess Tavern, where a Judge and Jury Club used to be held.   At places like Evans's Song and Supper Rooms, hot suppers, admirably cooked and served up, were obtainable up till one or two a m., and gay and festive feeders could listen at the same time to the singing of comic and sentimental vocalists.   Liquid refreshments of all kinds and cigars were also to be obtained.

Several of the concert-rooms were situated in Lime Street. In the 'fifties and 'sixties there were in that thoroughfare the ' Hop ' Temperance Free and Easy; the Albany Concert Hall; the St. George's Concert-rooms, 50, Lime Street; and the Garibaldi Concert Hall, which was located on a portion of the site now occupied by the New Tivoli Palace of Varieties

The   Savoy   and   Vines'   Pavilion, in   Lime   Street, were   always   popular   places   of   entertainment   In 1886 Joseph Vines, son of Mr A. B. Vines, applied to the magistrates for a provisional license in respect of new premises to be called the Pavilion Theatre of Varieties.   Mr. Segar, who appeared for Mr. Vines, stated that it was intended to reconstruct the licensed vaults held by him, and to take in the licensed premises held by Mr. Vines, senior, at 81 and 83, Lime Street.   The projected building was to be capable of accommodating 1,100 people.   The scheme was opposed by Mr. Taylor, barrister, on behalf of the Adelphi Hotel Company, the Grand Hotel, the Real Property Company, and others. Ultimately the magistrates refused the application.

Among other concert-rooms were the Edinburgh Castle in Lime Street; the Queen's Arms in Richmond Street; and the Crystal Palace in Button Street.   Other concert-rooms were Farmer's, the Great Eastern, and the Blue Anchor. Then there was the London in St. Anne Street, kept by Mr. ' Bill ' Bailey, and situated where the Royal Liver

---

* A branch of the famous Covent Garden rendezvous.

Friendly Society has now its branch office.   In Scotland Road
there were the Great Northern Concert Rooms, and the
Rotunda.

THE STAR MUSIC HALL AND THEATRE.

Beneath the shadow of the Theatre Royal there stood
more than half a century ago, on the site now occupied by
the Star Theatre, a noted hostelry and concert-room called
the Star.

The exterior appearance of the Star was that of a dwelling-
house, the entrance being up some steps.   Inside, the concert-
room consisted of what at one time had been the front and
back parlours, made into one, and at the further end was
a small stage.   In the early 'forties the proprietor of the
Star was Jem Ward, who established harmonic evenings
there.   In 1845, Ward left to take the York Hotel at the corner of Williamson Square and Tarleton Street.   He was succeeded, in 1847, by Mr. Hamilton, who advertised that the
admission was free to the concert-room, and that he purveyed
chops, steaks, and wines in first-class style.

Emmanuel Braham was proprietor of the Star in the
early 'sixties.   He was succeeded, as proprietor, by David
Lazarus.   In 1866 it was advertised that the Star Concert
Hall would close on July 2, for the purpose of erecting the
New Star Music Hall.

The New Star Music Hall was opened by the proprietors,
Messrs. Ambrose, Fineberg, and Lazarus, on December 26,
1866.   Messrs. Joe Simmons and Dan Saunders were the
joint managers.   The New Star was capable of holding between 1,800 and 2,000 persons, and cost about £22,000.   The
interior of the house was designed after the Oxford in London.
The scenery was by Telbin, and there were seventeen performers in the orchestra.

The following is a copy of the opening bill :

THE NEW STAR MUSIC HALL,
Williamson Square, Liverpool.

Proprietors   -   Messrs. Ambrose, Fineberg, and Lazarus.

OPENING NIGHT.

Programme For This Evening.

God Save the Queen .. Madame Tonnelier, Mr. Busfield
and Full Band and Chorus
Overture "William Tell" (*Rossini*)..Orchestra
Song ....Miss Milnes
Serio-Comic Song ....Miss Julia Harcourt
Song ....Mr. J. Busfiel
Quadrille ....Orchestra
Comic Song ....Mr. Robert Fraser
Cavatina ....Madame Tonnelier
Serio-Comic Song ....Mrs. J. F. Brian
Fantasia-Violin ....Mr. H. C. Cooper
Patter Song ....Mr. J. G. Forde

Grand Selection from
Bellini's Tragic Opera
NORMA.

Introduction and Chorus ......Full Choir
Solo—" High on yon Mountain " Mr. D. Saunders.
Duet—" Cruel Norma " ....Madame Tonnelier and Mrs
D. Saunders
Finale and Cavatina " Gentle Goddess "
Madame Tonnelier and full Choir
Conductor ....Mr. H. C. Cooper
Fantasia—Pianoforte ....Signor G. Operti
Gymnastic Entertainments ....The Brothers Victorelli
Solo—Trombone ....Mr. H. Russell

Grand Ballet entitled
LA FÊTE DES FLEURS

Supported by the Misses Helen and Emma Gunniss, and a
double London *Corps de Ballet*
Serio-Comic Song ....Miss Julia Harcourt
Sensation Song ....Mr. R. Fraser
Subject to alterations by the Manager.'

The New Star was practically a success from the commencement. For the first six months admission to the entertainment was obtained by purchasing a check ticket which entitled the holder to certain refreshments of the amount specified on the check.

To the Star was always brought the best of talent; and to the variety stage the late Isaac Fineberg introduced more than one artist who afterwards won fame and fortune. For many years the Star, Liverpool, and Day's, Birmingham, ranked high among the leading music halls of the country and engagements at both were greatly coveted.

For many years the Star, with its one circle, its chairman, hammer in hand, and its small tables, around which the waiters dodged in and out in a marvellous manner, was a bright and alluring rendezvous for lovers of mirth and melody.

About 1872, David Lazarus severed his connection with the Star, and took the Theatre Hotel in the ' Square.' The proprietors of the Star then became Messrs. Ambrose, Fineberg, and Noah Lees. Afterwards, there were only two proprietors, Messrs. Fineberg and Lees, with Mr. Harris Fineberg, son of the former gentleman, as manager.

To give the names of all the talented artists of the variety stage that, in days gone by, graced the boards of the Star would take too long. To cite a few only, there have been the Great Vance, Tom Maclagan, Ethardo, Harry Liston, the Vokes Family, Jolly John Nash, Mackney, Blondin, George Leybourne, Sam Torr, J. H. Milburn, Pat Feeney, W. J. Ashcroft, Bessie Bonehill, Jenny Hill, etc., etc.

With increasing years Mr. Fineberg decided to throw off the responsibilities of management and eventually in 1895, sold his interest in the theatre to a company. The new company spent some thirteen to fourteen thousand pounds in reconstructing the house, and continued to run it as a music hall—under the style of the New Star Theatre of Varieties.

Success does not seem to have crowned the company's enterprise, and, in the spring of 1898, a dramatic license was applied for. This being obtained, the last variety entertainment was given on Saturday, May 28, 1898, and when the curtain was rung down, ' finis ' was written to its long and entertaining record as a music hall.

The following is a copy of the final variety bill —

'STAR THEATRE
Williamson Square, Liverpool.

IMPORTANT NOTICE.

A Full Dramatic License having been granted to the above Theatre, the Management have pleasure in announcing that, commencing Whit Monday, and week after week, will be presented First-class Dramatic and other Novelty Entertainments.

Monday, May 23rd, 1898, and every evening during the week.

The Whirlwind De Forrests ,
America's Sensational Dancers and Pantomimists.

Louise Agnes,
Ballad Vocalist.

Dagmar Wonders,
Acrobatic and Risley Performers.

Harry Kirk,
Tyrolean Vocalist and Facial Artiste

Mabel Kessler,
Comedienne and Post Horn Soloist.

Lily English,
Burlesque Actress.

Special engagement, direct from the Continent, of the
Kaiser Quintette,
Lady and Gentlemen Acrobats and Musicians.

Francois and Ricardo,
Equilibrists.

Flo Ross,
Serio-Comic Vocalist.

Burgoyne and Hilliard,
Acrobatic Posturers, Grotesques and Pantomimists.

Joe Wesley,
Negro Comedian and Dancer.

Arthur Ismay,
Eccentric Comedian and Mimic

Lena Trewey,
Characteristic Vocalist.

Elsa Joel,
High-class Operatic Vocalist.'

On the Monday following, May 30, 1898, the dramatic season was inaugurated under the proprietorship of Mr. Harris Fineberg by Mr. Rollo Balmain's Company, the opening attraction being *Hoodman Blind*.

As a dramatic house and people's theatre, under the able proprietorship of Mr. Harris Fineberg, the Star has prospered exceedingly. The Star holds 2,000 persons, and Mr. Harris Fineberg always caters excellently for the popular taste at popular prices.

THE PARTHENON MUSIC HALL.

It was in the early 'forties of the last century that the Parthenon in Great Charlotte Street first came into existence. In an advertisement for February 25, 1845, announcing a ball, the Royal Parthenon Assembly Rooms are described as being 'new and spacious.'

At first the place was used for various kinds of entertainments. The Iowa Indians were on exhibition in March, 1845, and Bianchi's wax-works in the following August. Exactly a year later the Rooms were under the direction of the proprietor, Mr. J. G. Stoll, who announced that 'an unrivalled company of dancing and vocal talent are nightly engaged.' There was no charge for admission, the 'open sesame' to the entertainment being the money paid for refreshments. Afterwards the hall was known as the Parthenon Music Saloon, and in 1850 as the Parthenon Rooms.

From a bill dated May 20, 1850, in 'The Variety Stage,'* I learn that *poses plastiques*, which of late have been such a 'boom,' are no new device, but simply a revival of a popular form of entertainment in vogue over fifty years ago. The following is a copy of the bill referred to :

'PARTHENON ROOMS

Great Charlotte Street, Six Doors from Ranelagh Street.

MODELS OF ART
Tableaux Vivants, and Poses Plastiques.

---

* P. 226-8.

The Proprietor has the pleasure to announce to his Friends and the Public the complete success of this truly Classic Exhibition ; and, in order to merit the patronage with which this Establishment has, since its opening, been honoured, begs to announce it will be his constant study to produce a

SUCCESSION OF NOVELTIES

of a superior character, which, he trusts, will meet with their universal approbation.

THE SPLENDID DECORATIONS AND APPOINTMENTS from Authentic Sources, are Entirely New.

MR. JOHN REED,
The Old Favourite Comic Vocalist.

MISS M. BAXTER,
The Celebrated Sentimental Singer, from the London and Glasgow Concerts.

Programme of Tableaux and Songs for

Monday, May 20th, 1850

and during the Week

Comic Song, " Mr. Brown and Mrs. Black," ....Mr. Reed.
Song,.......... " Single Gentlemen," ....Miss Baxter.
Comic Song,.. " Don't be Foolish, Joe,".......Mr. Reed.
Song, " I Hear Them Speak of My Fatherland," Miss Baxter.
Tableau—Jeptha's Rash Vow.
Sacred History.

Comic Song,........ " The Review," ....Mr. Reed.
Tableau—The Sultan's Favourite Returning from
the Bath.
Composition.

Song,...." The Peace of the Valley is Fled,"..Miss Baxter.
Tableau—Brutus Ordering the Execution of his Son,
In Two Tableaux.
Roman History

Comic Song,.... " Pity the Sorrows," .... Mr. Reed.
Tableau—Diana Preparing for the Chase.
A. Cooper, R.A.

Song,...... " I strive to Forget Thee," ....Miss Baxter.
Tableau—A Bacchanalian Procession.
From the Borghese Vase.
Antique.

Lady Godiva, in character, ...Mr. Reed.
Tableau—Daughters of the Deep.
Composition.

Song,...... " Who'll buy My Heart," ......Miss Baxter.
Tableau—Greeks Surprised by the Enemy.
Composition.

Comic Song,...... " Ruined Cobbler," ....Mr. Reed.
Tableau—Lute Player.
Praider.

Song,.. "Come and let us be Happy Together," Miss Baxter.
Tableau—Amazons' Triumph.
A. Cooper, R.A.

Comic Song,...............................Mr. Reed.
Tableau—The Grecian's Daughter.
Grecian History.

Doors open at Half-past 6 o'clock, to commence at 7, and the Performances will be one continued routine of Tableaux and Songs.'

This form of entertainment comprised the bill-of-fare at provincial halls, without any special development, until the 'sixties.

After directing the destinies of the Parthenon for some considerable time Mr. Stoll was succeeded by his son, J. G. Stoll, junr. Stoll *fils* married a lady who had been an actress. At the period of their union she was a widow with two sons, Roderick and Oswald, the latter of whom was born in Melbourne, in 1867, and educated in Liverpool. On the death of his stepfather, in 1880, Oswald Stoll left school in order to assist his mother in the management of the Parthenon. Oswald devoted himself principally to the clerical side of the business, while his brother Roderick was identified with ' the front of the house.'

There are many entertaining anecdotes told of Mr. Oswald Stoll's negotiations with artists in those early days. It is said he more than once offered a few pounds per week to 'stars' who were then commanding large salaries.   In his negotiations he had no experience to guide him, save his stepfather's record of payments

Mr. Oswald Stoll in his management of the hall showed wonderful astuteness, and was quickly recognised as an able caterer.   In after years when he came to control several vast enterprises, his novitiate here served him in good stead. He is now the managing-director of Moss' Empires, Limited.

The Parthenon boards have been graced by many well-known 'stars' in the variety firmament.   The popular favourite Vesta Tilley has been seen here more than once ; also the Leno family (including Master Dan), Marie Loftus, Harry Lauder, Bransby Williams, and   scores of other notables.

In the early 'nineties Mr. Oswald Stoll and his mother ceased to be publicly identified with the Parthenon.   It was in 1890 that Mr. Stoll, when twenty-three, made a bold bid for fame and fortune by opening at Cardiff the first of his many successful Empires.   Mention of Mrs. Stoll reminds me there is a tradition in the family that she must take the first money paid for admission at the opening of a new Stoll enterprise, in order to ensure success and good fortune.

In 1894 Mr. George Atkinson took up the managerial reins.   Later, the Parthenon came into the hands of a syndicate directed by Captain W. Slater.   Mr. Edwin W. Smith, its manager, afterwards became proprietor.   Early in 1904 the hall was reconstructed internally, and made more commodious.   In 1907 Mr. Smith severed his connection with the theatre.   Afterwards the hall was styled the Théâtre Moderne.   Recently the building was acquired by Messrs. Henochsberg and Ellis, and converted into a clothing establishment.

ST. JAMES'S HALL AND THE NEW TIVOLI
PALACE OF VARIETIES.

When Lime Street was widened in 1845 several dilapidated houses on the west side of the street were swept away, and on part of their site, in 1847, Mr. Edward Starkie Tuton erected the Teutonic Hall.

A decade later the ground floor section of the hall was known as Allsopp's New Crystal Palace, while the higher regions were called the Teutonic Upper Hall. In the latter in 1857, Hamilton's dioramas were exhibited. The wax-works in that year contained the recently added models of Palmer, Dove, Madeline Smith, Emile L'Angelier, and Captain Rogers and his two mates. General Tom Thumb was at the Teutonic Hall in December, 1858. The following year the hall was styled the Theatre Variété, afterwards changing its nomenclature to that of St. James's Hall. The proprietors were Messrs. Wilsom and Montague.

In April, 1863, Charles Christy's Minstrels were here. In the company was G. W. ('Pony') Moore. On Monday, October 30, 1865, Henry Irving commenced here his second Liverpool engagement. He was then a member of Mr. Swanborough's Comedy Company. Irving's first part in the bill for that evening was Mr. Woodcock in the farce *Woodcock's Little Game*, and although he had no part in the second piece, *The Bride of Abydos ; or, the Prince, the Pirate, and The Pearl*, he appeared as Heartycheer in the after-piece, *The Bonnie Fishwife*. In September, 1866, F. C. Burnand's burlesque *Sapho ; or, Look before You Leap* was presented. Performances were given by Jennie and Lizzie Wilmore, and Mrs. Caulfield. The following month saw Brinsley Sheridan here. The Leno family performed on April 20, 1867. The family included Mr. and Mrs. Leno, and Masters George and Henry Leno, 'American breakdown dancers.' The two latter were then aged five and seven years respectively. George afterwards became the celebrated Dan Leno. Maria Simpson (Mrs. W. H. Liston), inaugurated a dramatic season on June 15, 1867, with Foote's comedy of *The Liar*. The part of Jack Wilding was portrayed by Charles Wyndham, who also appeared as Count Roberto in the extravaganza, *La Vivandière ; or, True to the Core*. Other performers were Miss Goodall and J. D. Stoyle. The ballet which followed *La Vivandière* was under the direction of those clever devotees of Terpsichore, the Misses Gunniss. In October, Annie Thirlwall and Henry Corri commenced an operatic season. In the spring of 1868 the establishment was known as the St. James's Hall and Operetta House. On April 20, Walter Howard, a past-master in the art of banjo-playing, performed.

The Great Vance was seen here on October 31, and the three following nights. On March 29, 1869, Maskelyne and Cook commenced an engagement, and on April 26 following the Kiralfy Ballet troupe came. The hall at that time was under the management of Mr. Henry Coleman. The Siamese Twins, and Anna Swan, the Nova Scotian giantess, were on exhibition the week commencing May 31   Under the auspices of the British Operatic Association Madame Tonnelier performed Elvira in *The Grand Duchess of Gerolstein* on June 27, 1870. Madame Tonnelier afterwards opened a singing academy in Liverpool.

I now come to the period when Sam Hague and his minstrels made their first appearance at the hall. The Minstrels were organised by Mr. Hague in Macon, Georgia, U.S.A , in 1865, and came to Liverpool in the July of the following year, when they performed at the Theatre Royal. At that time they were known as the American Slave Serenaders, and were stated to be ' the only combination of genuine darkies in the world '

Their first appearance at St. James's Hall took place on October 31, 1870, and for over a quarter of a century Sam Hague successfully guided the destinies of Liverpool's home of Minstrelsy. His troupe of performers—numbering generally about 40—was always of the best, and the entertainments were not only bright, attractive, and amusing, but without the slightest tinge of vulgarity.

In connection with the hall there was published about 1870, ' Hague's Minstrel and Dramatic Journal.' The first series ran for some thirteen years under the editorship of Mr. W H. Lee (Mr. Hague's business manager), and subsequently of Mr. J. H. Stringer. The first number of the second series was issued in September, 1882. It was a small illustrated monthly of eight printed pages, and the price was one penny Mr. Henry A Duffy was the final editor.

During the course of his fifth or sixth season at the hall, Sam Hague was the victim of a dire calamity. All his property—for which a little before he had given the sum of £30,000—was destroyed by fire. This sad catastrophe took place on May 2, 1875. The fire, it is supposed, broke out in the Green-room, or in one of the dressing rooms. The whole of the roof, the scenery, dresses, and interior of the hall soon became a charred mass of ruins. The flames, however, were kept from spreading to the wax-works of Mr. Allsopp underneath, and to the adjoining County Court. Poor Hague when he saw the destruction of his popular hall cried like a child. Unfortunately the hall was only partially insured, the building for £5,000 and the fittings, etc., for £4,000. Another sad feature in connection with the fire was the destruction of Herr Schalkenbach's famous electric organ, which had taken a life-time to construct. It was insured for £900, but this did not by any means represent its value. The Mayor (Lieut.-Col. Steble), and a number of influential gentlemen then organised a benefit performance at the Amphi' for Hague and his minstrels, which was a great success. The minstrels then went on tour, Sam Hague dividing his attention between his troupe and the building of his new hall, which he had ready for opening on May 1, 1876.

The new hall was about the same size as the old building, but it held considerably more, as a new and handsome balcony had been added. The entrance hall and staircase were very much enlarged. Surmounting the ornate proscenium was an American eagle standing out in bold relief from the centre of a large wreath of oak leaves, at the back of which there was represented, in gold, the rays of the sun. Situated on either side of the proscenium were two figures, emblematical of Mirth and Dancing. The opening address was written by J. F. McArdle, and was spoken by Mr. Waldon. It ran as follows :—

> ' 'Tis just a year since fire destroyed our home,
> And forced Hague's Minstrels all abroad to roam,
> One fatal night the flames consumed each rafter
> That oft' had rung with peals of honest laughter.
> Our little stage once lit with wit's bright flashes,
> Was in an hour reduced to heaps of ashes,
> And Liverpool will be renowned for ages
> For burning down its big and little stages.
> Without a roof to shield our dusky band,
> We had to wander forth throughout the land :
> Though everywhere we roamed, as you may guess,
> We met with hearty welcome and success.
> Still, we are glad, after our rambling year,
> To come back home again and settle here.

But look around ! What transformation strange !
Aladdin's lamp could not work such a change !
Our house before was beautiful and bright ;
But who expected such a dazzling sight ?
We shouldn't know it, so transformed the place is,
But for your welcome cheers and friendly faces.
Thanks, patrons, friends—Sam Hague and all his troupe
Know that you're glad to greet our happy group
You see he hasn't spared time, labour, pelf,
But here he comes to thank you for himself.'

Mr. Hague then came upon the stage, and spoke the following lines :—

' Yes, friends ; my heart and home's in Liverpool—
But work, not talking, is my usual rule.
And if my tongue, my heart's best thanks could speak,
I should be talking for another week.
I'll do my best to please, as in the past,
And ever strive to make our friendship last
I know while I your faithful servant am,
Hague's minstrels you'll support, and still stand Sam.'

For a score of years afterwards Hague and his minstrels were honourably and successfully identified with 'the fortunes of St. James's Hall. In March, 1896, the hall was converted by Mr. James Kiernan—to whom Liverpool owes much for the advancement of the music hall—into the Tivoli Palace of Varieties, under which designation it was run as a variety theatre until about the close of the century After being closed for several years, the building was demolished and the present structure, the New Tivoli Palace of Varieties, erected by Messrs. Brown and Sons, of Liverpool and Salford, from the designs of Mr. Bertie Crewe. The opening performance took place on Monday evening, December 10, 1906. The theatre seats about 1,500 persons.

HENGLER'S CIRQUES AND THE ROYAL HIPPODROME.

Dale Street, or Dele Street, as it was anciently called, has always been one of our principal thoroughfares. On a portion of the site now occupied by the Municipal

Offices, there stood for many years a celebrated hostelry
called the ' Saracen's Head.'   From its sheltering portals
the old stage coaches, the ' Rob Roy ' and ' Tally Ho ! '
rolled away merrily to divers parts of the kingdom.   About
1855 the ' Saracen's Head ' was demolished. The ground, however, remained unbuilt upon until Charles Milton Hengler
chose the position for the erection of his circus.

This was not the first visit to Liverpool of 'Handsome
Hengler,' as he was called, he having previously appeared at
the Amphi'.   Charles Hengler was a Dane, and came from
Copenhagen. He was a versatile performer, being able to
dance upon the tight-rope and perform Hamlet the same
evening, and thus display what is aptly described as a ' fine
contrastive talent.'

Previous to the opening of the Circus in Dale Street, on
March 16, 1857, the following notice was published :—

' HENGLER'S GRAND CIRQUE VARIÉTÉ
Dale Street, Liverpool.

Mr. Charles Hengler, in announcing his intention of
(for the first time) catering for the amusement of the inhabitants of Liverpool and its vicinity, respectfully informs them
that he has been honoured by the especial patronage of Her
Most Gracious Majesty the Queen, Prince Albert, and the
Royal Family and suite, at Windsor Castle, February, 1845,
and in 1849 ; also by the nobility, clergy, and gentry of every
town he has hitherto visited—a sufficient guarantee that his
establishment stands pre-eminent for producing an entertainment of the highest order.

' The TALENTED ARTISTES engaged are the first in the
equestrian profession.   These combined with a matchless
STUD of FIFTY HORSES and PONIES, costly WARDROBE and
APPOINTMENTS, cannot fail to render the Cirque worthy of the
inhabitants of Liverpool.

' The splendid building, erected regardless of expense by
Messrs. Holme and Nicol(after the style of the Cirque Napoleon,
Paris), will be found replete with every possible arrangement
for the comfort of the vast audience it is constructed to
accommodate in its several spacious and distinct apartments.
The First and Second Class Boxes are carpeted throughout,
and furnished with cushioned seats. The spacious Promenade,

200 feet in length, encircles three-fourths of the building, from every part of which an uninterrupted view of the Arena is commanded. A magnificent Canopy will cover the interior of the building, which will be interspersed with flags of all nations and emblematical designs, red, white, and blue being the characteristics of the decoration. The whole brilliantly illuminated with gas.

' The bands will be found full and efficient, and the Entertainments will consist of SCENES of RIDING, STUDS of the MENAGE, BRILLIANT SPECTACLES, EQUESTRIAN PAGEANTS, etc., etc., enlivened by the Witticisms and grotesque Achievements of the Four Best CLOWNS of the Day

' Reserved Seats or Stalls (select), 3s., Half-price 1s. 6d.; Boxes (select), 2s , Half-price 1s, ;   Second Seats 1s , Half-price 6d. ; Gallery 6d., no Half-price ;   Promenade 1s., no Half-price.

' Leader of the Quadrille Band, Mr G. Jackman ; Leader of the Brass Band, Mr. W. Allen ; Master of the Horse, Mr. F. Brown , Treasurer, Mr. C. Fisher ; Architect, Mr. O'Hara ; Acting Manager, Mr. A. Henry;   Director, Mr. Charles Hengler, proprietor.'

This notice, together with the excellent troupe with which Hengler opened, had the desired effect, the stalls, boxes, second seats, and gallery being crowded at every performance, to the great discomfiture of Copeland of the Amphi'.

In 1861 the ground upon which the Cirque was erected was acquired by the Liverpool Hotel Company, and on Thursday, March 14, 1861, the final equestrian performance took place.

Hengler lost no time in establishing another circus, and on Monday, October 21, 1861, he opened, in Newington, a second Cirque Variété, erected for him by Messrs Holme and Nicol. The ' first and second-class entrance ' was in Newington, and the gallery entrance in Cropper Street. Prices here were the same as at the Dale Street circus, and ranged from sixpence to three shillings.

Charles Hengler in those days lived in Mount Pleasant, and his brothers Edward and John Milton Hengler in Elizabeth Street, where they had the riding-school, still known by the family name.

After the Newington Circus was demolished, and after achieving success in the establishment of equestrian arenas in London, Glasgow, Dublin, and elsewhere, Charles Hengler once more cast his eyes upon the scene of his early triumphs, and in fulfilment of a long made promise, to ' erect a Cirque worthy of this large and appreciative community,' he decided to build in West Derby Road a handsome and commodious hippodrome.

Mr. J. T. Robinson, the surveyor of theatres to the Lord Chamberlain, was the architect, and Mr. Samuel Campbell, of Liverpool, the contractor, the ceiling and general decorations being carried out by Mr. Thomas Rogers, the well-known scenic artist of London.

Hengler's business manager was courteous Alfred Powell, who was associated in a managerial capacity with the Cirque for more than a quarter of a century. George Clements was the first musical director, a position which he filled with conspicuous ability for many years.

Considerable interest was evinced in the opening of ' Hengler's Grand Cirque,' which took place on Monday, November 13, 1876, before a large and brilliant assembly. The principal attraction of the entertainment was the performance of the Jackley Troupe, eleven in number. The clowns were Astley, Le Quips and Willie Templeton.

The first morning performance in the new Cirque was given on Saturday, November 18, 1876, and the first Yuletide juvenile spectacle to be presented was *The Fairy's Garden Party in Honour of Little Red Riding Hood*, given the following Christmas.

A brief description of the exterior and interior of the building as first opened will doubtless be of interest. The Cirque occupied an area of 20,000 square feet, and was built of red brick. The front elevation, abutting on West Derby Road, was built of the best pressed red brick, relieved by ornamental drawings of a classical design. When the Cirque was first opened the bank and shops that now figure in front of the building were not then erected. The floor of the principal entrance in West Derby Road had a handsome tessellated pavement, and glazed folding doors were placed at the end of the entrance hall, whilst the entrance itself had iron ornamental gates of a bold chaste design.*   In all there were five private boxes, 200 reserved stalls, 600 seats in the parterre, 2,000 in the pit, and 1,600 in the gallery, making a total accommodation for 4,500 persons, though on several occasions, (particularly when the late W E Gladstone spoke here on September 24, 1895, on the Armenian question), this number was greatly exceeded.   The Grand Old Man said of Hengler's that 'few buildings give so noble a presentation of an audience,' and on another occasion he again described the place as 'the most agreeable, to the speaker of all those with which he was acquainted ' †

A great feature of the Cirque was that no matter where one was seated a free and uninterrupted view of the arena could be obtained, while the acoustic properties of the building were in every respect admirable.

At his death Charles Milton Hengler left to his sons a handsome estate running into several figures.   Both Mr. Hengler and his wife were well known in Liverpool and universally beloved.

As the years rolled by each successive Christmas found Hengler's echoing with the merry laughter of old and young. A visit at holiday time to the Cirque came to be eagerly anticipated, and the bare mention of the name Hengler's was sufficient to make youthful eyes sparkle with glee in joyful expectation of delights to come.   But the end was at hand; and came all too soon, for, on Saturday evening, February 9, 1901, when Mr. Albert M. Hengler was proprietor and director, the last performance took place, and 'finis' was written to a long and brilliant chapter in the history of equestrianism.

After this the Cirque remained unoccupied for some months ; in fact, until Mr. Thomas Barrasford acquired the property on behalf of a syndicate.

Of Hengler's Cirque only portions of the four main walls now remain.   The work of demolition and reconstruction was practically accomplished in about six months' time.

* These gates now fulfil a similar duty at the principal entrance to the Royal Hippodrome.
† Morley's ' Life of Gladstone,' Vol. III, p. 521.

The new building, which was opened on August 4, 1902, and christened the Royal Hippodrome Theatre of Varieties, is constructed of concrete and iron, the floors resting on iron supports on the cantilever system.   An interior view reveals a pretty and ornate structure, the prevailing tints being cream and grey, picked out with gold.   The ceiling, from which hang handsome electric pendants, is a beautiful piece of painted work (on canvas) by the clever artist, Mr. Sicard, of London, and is emblematical of Music and the Arts.   The base of the proscenium is in marble, and the arch itself is in yellow and reddish gold.   The latter is surmounted by five extremely artistic paintings depicting the Five Senses, also from the brush of Mr. Sicard; whilst adjoining are two attractive paintings of Arcadian beauty, by the same artist.   The 'stage dimensions are 90 feet by 40 feet; height to ' gridiron,' 55 feet; and height to ' flies,' 27 feet 6 inches.   The Hippodrome is to all intents and purpose square-shaped, and from any point the line of vision is free and uninterrupted.   The stage is fitted with an up-to-date fire-proof curtain, and the whole of the auditorium is lighted by electricity.   Both stage and auditorium are heated with hot-water pipes, and there are conveniently placed dressing-rooms for the artists.

By the provision of numerous exits the safety of the public and of the artists is carefully protected, each exit door being fitted with safety panic bolts.   The ventilation is another noteworthy feature.   In the main ceiling two air shafts of 4 feet in diameter, together with a 36 inch electric fan, are constructed, whilst at the rear of the gallery thereare two exhaust ventilators and two 18 inch electric fans.

.   The Hippodrome is conducted on teetotal principles, and the prices of admission are well within the reach of everybody.   The theatre will hold about 4,000 persons, and it has a seating capacity of some 3,500.   Two performances each evening are given.

The present proprietors of the theatre are the Liverpool Hippodrome Company, Limited, of which Mr. Thomas Barrasford is managing-director.   Mr. Walter Hassan (who comes of a family well versed in the art of the stage), is the popular acting manager.   The opening of the ' Hippo,' as it is familiarly termed, marked an epoch in local music hall annals, and Mr. Barrasford's spirited enterprise and excellent catering have met with great success.

MASTER HUMPHREY'S CLOCK.

This popular place of resort was situated at 10 Great Charlotte Street. Mr. Samuel Leatherbarrow was proprietor of Master Humphrey's Clock for many years. About the 'fifties the name was changed to the EUPHONIC CONCERT ROOMS. There was no charge for admission, and the establishment kept open until midnight.

THE MALAKOFF MUSIC HALL

The Malakoff Music Hall was brought into existence during the 'fifties, by the late Dan Lowrey. It was situated in Cleveland Square and was a popular resort for youthful and ancient mariners. In addition to variety performances, plays and pantomimes were also submitted. In one of Mr. Lowrey's advertisements (1864), he amusingly stated that there is ' a private box for captains *and gentlemen.*' Outside the Malakoff there is a statue of Mr. Lowrey in one of his favourite Irish characters. The building is still in existence.

THE ROYAL CASINO

This place of entertainment was located in Blundell Street, about four doors from Park Lane. It was in existence in 1851, in which year a series of *poses plastiques* were given.

THE APOLLO MUSIC HALL.

The Apollo Music Hall was situated in Park Lane, nigh unto the Custom House. It was in existence over forty years ago, and was successfully managed for a number of years by Mr. Anderson. A favourite vocalist and comedian here was 'Tom' Bennett, whose son, John was for a long period the *chef d'orchestré* of the Parthenon in Great Charlotte Street.

THE LIVER MUSIC HALL.

This establishment, which was located at 46 Mersey Street, was also known as Ceda's Music Hall. In the latter part of the 'sixties the manager of the Liver was Signor Antonio Devoto.

THE EAGLE MUSIC HALL.

The Eagle Music Hall was in existence in the 'sixties. It was managed by Mr. R. Ford, and afterwards by Mr. Levine. Outside the premises, 73 Old Hall Street, there still remains the old insignia of the Eagle.

THE VINE. (*HOTEL*)

Facing Master Humphrey's Clock in Great Charlotte Street was another favourite place of entertainment known as THE VINE. Mr. W. F. Naylor was long the proprietor of this establishment. At Christmas, 1863, a pantomime was given, entitled *Harlequin and the Magic Wreath; or, All that Glitters is Not Gold.*

THE CASINO.

The Casino, 23 Bevington Hill, was originally intended for a market. In the early 'sixties it was called the Princess's Theatre. Afterwards it was opened by Dan Lowrey, who christened it the Nightingale Palace of Amusement and Recreation. Prices of admission (which included refreshments), were threepence, fourpence, and sixpence. The Nightingale was run on similar lines to the Malakoff. In 1870 it was called the Victoria Music Hall. When Mr. H. Ambrose was proprietor in the 'seventies the establishment was known as the Casino Temperance Hall. Subsequently when John Tudor had it, the Casino blossomed into

Tudor's Varieties. After other mutations, it terminated its career as a place of entertainment some few years ago. The building, which is situated next to St. Bridget's Roman Catholic Chapel, is now used for commercial purposes.

THE ROYAL ALHAMBRA MUSIC HALL.

Mr. John Hill built and opened this hall at 226 (now 64), Derby Road, Kirkdale, in the 'sixties. It was for many years a popular resort at popular prices for the inhabitants of the north end of Liverpool, and of Bootle. The auditorium and stage were situated on the first floor, the ground floor being used as an hotel, an American bowling-alley, and a concert-room. The Alhambra could boast of a pit and gallery, the entrances thereto being in Derby Road and Esk Street. Mr. John Hill, junior, succeeded his father as proprietor, and from time to time sublet the music hall section of the premises to different managers. Among the latter were Mr. Charles Bishop, and Messrs. Hargreaves and Davis. 'The Stage' for August 14, 1885, states of the latter management that ' they have, with their unflagging perseverance, succeeded in improving the behaviour of the audiences who patronise the hall, and the entertainment is now conducted in a very respectable manner.' The Alhambra ceased to be a music hall about twenty years ago.

BELL'S ENGLISH AND AMERICAN HIPPODROME AND CIRCUS.

It was opened with the pantomime, *Harlequin and Tim Bobbin, or, The Lancashire Witches*, on December 26, 1862. The circus was built of wood and canvas, and was situated in Crosshall Street. Afterwards it was styled Myers' Circus, and in 1864 the American Opera House. The vocalists here were fined if they did not wear white kid gloves.

THE OXFORD MUSIC HALL.

This hall, which was situated on the position now occupied by Mrs. Egerton's hostelry in Lime Street, was in existence over forty years ago. In the 'sixties Mr. J. S. Lofthouse was the proprietor. He also had the Cambridge at the corner of Warwick Street and Mill Street, and the Queen's Hall in Bold Street. Lofthouse used to engage for the Oxford such people as Tom Croslin, the celebrated negro comedian, and Jenny Hill. Mr. Lofthouse, who also had a hall in Dublin, afterwards became manager for Mr. Hugh Jay Didcott, and later on started a variety agency in York Road, London. He was doing very well at the time of his premature death by a chill. The Oxford was afterwards managed by Mr. Emmanuel Braham, who was succeeded by Messrs. B. Walker and Jonas Cohen.

THE ALHAMBRA MUSIC HALL.

In January, 1865, this place of entertainment, which was situated at 46 Manchester Street, was announced to open every evening with a full dramatic company. It was then styled the New Royal Theatre. Plays and pantomimes were given. The theatre was situated on the first floor, above some shops. The entrance was up a flight of steps, and the prices ranged from 2s. 6d. (stage boxes), to 3d. (pit.) There was also a small gallery. The theatre was afterwards known as the Alhambra Music Hall. Mr. Harry de Frece directed its destinies for some time. The Alhambra was one of the first music halls in the provinces to be run on the popular two-houses-a-night principle. After Mr. de Frece left to take up the management of the Gaiety in Camden Street he was succeeded by Joe Travis. This was about 1876. At that time the theatre was styled the Alhambra Temperance Music Hall. The hall terminated its existence about the close of the 'seventies.

THE CAMBRIDGE MUSIC HALL.

This hall was located at the corner of Warwick Street and Mill Street. The entrance was in Warwick Street. The hall was situated on the first floor, and a balcony encircled the auditorium. It held from 800 to 1,000 persons.

The Cambridge was opened by Mr. J. S. Lofthouse on July 4, 1865, and was prettily decorated internally. The ceiling and walls displayed artistic pictures of ' Science,' ' Music,' ' Night,' and ' Morning,' and ' The Seasons.' The principal artists at the opening included Mr and Mrs. Leno, and the Brothers Leno, Lancashire clog, boot, and pump dancers They were succeeded by Jenny Hill, Harry Liston, and Fred Coyne. Other performers were Tom Croslin, the negro comedian, and Jem Mace, who gave a series of classical poses. Mace's trophies and belts were on exhibition at the hall during his visit.   In Mr. Lofthouse's time the Cambridge was run on the one-house-a-night system. Succeeding managers were Messrs. E. M. Davies, B. Walker, and Joe Travis.   Mr. Walker was at one time associated with the destinies of the Oxford in Lime Street, and Mr. Travis with the Alhambra in Manchester Street. In Walker's time the hall was run on the two-houses-a-night principle. On one occasion the front of the building was destroyed by fire. The Cambridge ceased to be a music hall about thirty years ago, and is now known as the Templar's Hall

THE CONSTELLATION MUSIC HALL.

The Constellation Music Hall was situated at 74 Whitechapel, at the corner of Charles Street. The opening night was December 24, 1866. Mr. Jonas Cohen was proprietor, and Mr. Harry de Frece, manager. Admission to the stalls and side gallery was 6d., to the body of the hall (with a refreshment ticket), entrance in Charles Street, 6d., back gallery (with a refreshment ticket), entrance from Whitechapel, 3d. The refreshments included wines, spirits, ale, porter, cigars, chops, and steaks. The doors were opened at half-past six, and the performance commenced at seven o'clock precisely.

THE GAIETY THEATRE.

Prior to 1867 Dr. F C. S. Corry, M.D., had entertained the town at the Concert Hall, Lord Nelson Street, with a dioramic entertainment. Success attended his efforts there so well that he decided to have a permanent place for the exhibition of his dioramas. This he found in Camden Street, where he converted a couple of dwelling-houses into the Prince Patrick Hall. He opened there on February 16, 1867, with a diorama entitled ' Ireland : Its Scenery, Music and Antiquities,' and a company of Hibernian minstrels. The hall then held about 1,500 people. One of the entrances was in Back Commutation Row. On May 29, 1867, General Tom Thumb, who was accompanied by his wife and Commodore Nutt and Minnie Warren, was here. Each day the party drove to the hall in a miniature equipage drawn by four small ponies. This was a splendid advertisement for the little people.

The Prince Patrick underwent a change of title on December 31, 1868, when it was re-opened as the Wellington Hall by a concert party. The following year the hall was under the management of Messrs. Craddock and Day, late of the Royal Alexandra and Prince of Wales Theatres. They did not hold it long as on November 1 of the same year Mr. Alfred Roe (late director of the Leeds Theatre of Varieties), succeeded them and opened the place as the New Wellington Varieties. On June 6, 1870, Lydia Howard, who was only six years of age, gave a musical and dramatic entertainment, in which she was assisted by a talented company. Towards the close of 1870 the hall blossomed into the Gaiety Theatre, with Mr. Frank Clive as managing-director. The following year it was again styled the Wellington Hall. In October, 1872, when Professor Anderson appeared, it was christened the Royal Temple of Magic.

On April 13, 1874, the theatre was again opened as the Gaiety. Mr. Naylor Roberts was proprietor, and our townsman Mr. (now Sir) Charles Wyndham was the manager. On the opening night *Committed for Trial*, and *Little Tom Tug* were performed. Wyndham played in the former piece. The theatre, which was redecorated for the occasion, could then boast of stalls, dress-circle, pit, and gallery.

The Gaiety was afterwards run by a limited liability company. Next came Mr. C. H. Duval, who opened it on September 22, 1874, with an opera bouffe company in *La Fille de Madame Angot*. After Mr. Duval left to manage the Colosseum in Paradise Street he was succeeded by Mr. Harry de Frece   This was about 1877.   In the early 'eighties the house was known as the Gaiety Temperance Theatre. One Monday evening in October, 1886, a fire broke out at the back of the stage, in the neighbourhood of the gas meter. Fortunately, one of the employees had the presence of mind to turn the gas off at the main and so prevented what might have been a serious conflagration.

About 1890 the theatre was styled the Gaiety Varieties. Mr. Harry De Frece still directed its destinies.   After he left the Gaiety changed hands more than once.   Subsequently, at a period when it had been closed for some time, Mr. Henry Newbold of this city applied to the magistrates for a license to open the theatre, but the application was refused.   The building is now used for commercial purposes.

THE LONDON MUSIC HALL.

After Mr. Joe Simmons severed his connection as manager with the Star in Williamson Square, he, in July, 1869, opened the London, 20 Richmond Street.   The establishment, which at one time was known as the Liver, was afterwards managed by Mrs. Joe Simmons.   In 1878 it was under the control of Mr. Murray.

THE CONTINENTAL MUSIC HALL.

This hall was located on the west side of Hotham Street, near the corner of Lord Nelson Street.   It was opened by Mr. F. W. Hoffmann on February 18, 1871.

THE PEMBROKE HALL.

The proprietor of this hall was Mr. H. Scott, and it was opened on December 14, 1874, by Mr. Randall Williams with his 'Hobgoblinscope' entertainment.   In 1875 it was known as the Pembroke Hall and Theatre of Varieties, in which year a Christy Minstrel Troupe gave performances.   In 1876 it was used as a skating rink, and subsequently for a variety of other purposes.   The hall, which is situated at 38, Pembroke Place, is now in the occupation of the Salvation Army.

THE HAYMARKET MUSIC HALL

This hall, which is located on the south side of Beau Street, was opened by Mr. William Kerr, with Mr. W. Thomas as manager and scenic artist, on Monday, November 27, 1882.

The Haymarket is capable of seating over 2,500 persons. The hall was designed for the purpose of giving two performances nightly, a special feature being the arrangement for the mode of entrance and egress of each audience.   All crushing and inconvenience is avoided by the first house leaving by doors opening at the back of the premises.

After Mr. Kerr severed his connection with the hall, he was succeeded by Messrs. Alfred Farrell and Fred Willmot. The last mentioned gentleman, who is a native of Liverpool, afterwards directed its destinies alone.   The prices in his time varied from one penny to a shilling.   Jovial Joe Elvin used to perform his sketches here, and the Star Comiques of London visited the hall in turns.

On one occasion Mr. George R. Sims, the well-known author, visited the Haymarket, and was courteously conducted over the establishment by Mr. Willmot.   'Dagonet' afterwards recounted his experiences in ' The Referee.'* 'I stayed,' he wrote, 'for two hours at the Haymarket.   I went up into the gallery, and sat among the penny boys.   I went down into the twopenny pit, and sat among a crowd that had to swing all one way when it laughed, because there was no room for a double movement ; and from first to last I found the entertainment clever and smart and the ' star ' turns of the West End order.

' During the evening a little incident occurred which shows that even in a cheap music hall class distinctions will assert themselves.   To go from the pit to the gallery I had to pass

* September 9, 1900.

the transfer box.   A young man stood in front of it inter-
viewing the manager.   His case was a peculiar one.   He had
paid a penny to go from the gallery to the pit, because he
thought there was more room.   Now, he had returned from
the pit, and this was the dialogue ·

'Man · "I don't want my money back, governor, but can
I go into the gallery again ?"   Manager (astonished) : "Whatever do you want to go back into the gallery for ? You paid
extra to get out of it !"   Man : " Oh, I aren't comfortable
down there ; they're too d——aristocratical for me."   The
manager gave the man his penny back and laughed aloud.
The aristocracy of the twopenny pit tickled him immensely.'

Mr. Willmot successfully managed the Haymarket until
1906.   Afterwards Mr. Edwin W. Smith, formerly of the
local Parthenon, was the lessee and manager.

THE WESTMINSTER MUSIC HALL

This popular north-end variety theatre, which had previously been a club, was opened by Mr. Thomas Montgomery
and Mr. James Kiernan on April 11, 1887, with J. H. Milburn
and a good variety company.   The following year the Westminster was altered and made larger.   The stage door of the
Westminster was situated opposite to some very small houses.
In one of them lived a horny-handed son of toil, who, on
every possible occasion used to breathe anathema against the
stage and all its works.   On one occasion a battery of guns
used in a certain play broke all the glass in this worthy's
windows.   This naturally annoyed him ; but the climax came
with the engagement of an elephant called ' Sheriff.'   ' This
elephant,' Mr. Kiernan recently told an interviewer in a local
journal,* ' took upon himself to avenge the wrongs of his
brother artists, and backing against the wall knocked the
whole house down.   The tenant's choice of adjectives after
that was an education to everybody.'

* ' Liverpool Theatrical News,' August 26, 1907

After Mr. Kiernan left the Westminster the late Matthew Montgomery directed its destinies. Mr. Montgomery was succeeded by his son, Mr. Matthew Montgomery. The theatre is held at present by Mr. Fred E. Weisker.

THE PADDINGTON PALACE.

This variety theatre was opened by Mr. James Kiernan on September 4, 1889. In 1891 it was altered and made larger. Variety business on the popular two-houses-a-night principle was successfully conducted here for a number of years. Latterly drama, twice nightly, has been the staple fare.

KIERNAN'S OLYMPIA HIPPODROME AND CIRCUS.

This place of entertainment was opened on Monday, February 29, 1892. It was situated in Overton Street, Wavertree Road, and the lessee and manager was Mr. J. Sidney Childs. The Circus, which was designed by Mr. J. Havelock Sutton, architect of the Shakespeare Theatre, was a handsome building internally. The performers on the opening night were James Newsome, Kennette, the Brothers Echo, Verdi, and Rossini, Mdlle. Marie, Mdlle. Ella Bertha, Miss Virginie, James Powell, Carl Anthony, Young Claude, Mdlle. Marguerite, James Hunt, and Le Quips. The building was destroyed by fire on May 28, 1892. The site is now occupied by Mr. Kiernan's New Kursaal, which was opened on November 2, 1907.

THE ROSCOMMON MUSIC HALL.

This hall, which is named after the street in which it is situated, was opened about 1892, and was constructed out of a couple of spacious dwelling-houses. Mr. John Hargreaves was long and successfully identified with the fortunes of the Roscommon. After undergoing other changes in management, the theatre passed recently into the hands of Mr. Fred Willmot. At first Mr. Willmot ran the Roscommon as a variety theatre, but finding that drama twice nightly was more suitable to the taste of patrons he has adopted that system.

THE PARK PALACE.

The Park Palace was opened by Mr James Kiernan on December 11, 1894, and was run as a variety theatre until recently. Latterly, dramatic fare on the two-houses-a-night principle took the place of vaudeville entertainments.

THE OLYMPIA.

The Olympia is a handsome and imposing building, and occupies an ' island ' position in West Derby Road and Boaler Street.

The site of the theatre was formerly occupied by the Liverpool Licensed Victuallers' Asylum, which was erected in 1852, for necessitous widows and orphans of deceased members   The original asylum was in St Anne Street, and is now part of the headquarters of the 5th T B.K.L.R.

In the late 'seventies the asylum and the land upon which it stood in West Derby Road were in the market to be sold.   Later on the asylum was demolished, and the land remained unoccupied, save when tenanted by itinerant showmen, until that vast syndicate known as Moss' Empires, Limited, bought the ground

The Olympia was opened on Easter Monday, 1904. The theatre is twice as large as the London Hippodrome, and it has a seating capacity of 3,750. Every kind of variety entertainment occupies the bill from time to time.

The exterior is designed in free Italian Renaissance style, faced with red pressed bricks with stone dressings, and the façade is well outlined with a central tower surmounted by a mechanical revolving sign, and flanked on either side with small minarets.   There are some thirty-six exits, each 6 feet wide, the doors being fitted with safety panic bolts.

The interior is handsome, the scheme of colouring being cream, blue and red, relieved with gold.   There are sixteen rows of comfortable tip-up stall seats, with a clear view of the stage.   At the rear of the stalls on either side of the cinematograph room, are situated ten private boxes, and there are four stage boxes.

The circle is immediately above the stalls.   The side elevation on the grand tier and balcony level is panelled out and divided by ornamental pilasters and Indian panelling, and between these panels full-length elephants support trusses carrying the main ceiling.   Curtains and draperies are of Indian design, being of brilliant Oriental scarlet plush, enriched by wide embossed upright bands, and further ornamented at the base and sides by borders of *appliqué* design in deeper shades of crimson and gold, finished with massive silk fringe, three feet deep.   The proscenium valance, surmounting the *tableaux* curtains, is prettily draped and embellished with *appliqué* designs in gold and silver, and deeper scarlet plush on a brocaded background.   The curtains and draperies of the private boxes are of the same materials.   The stage and arena constitute a distinctly novel feature.   The arena is 42 feet in diameter, and is worked by hydraulic power. At the pull of a lever the arena collapses and automatically disappears in twenty seconds, a lake for aquatic displays, containing 80,000 gallons of water, taking its place.   The arena-mat, some 42 feet in diameter and weighing some three tons, is entirely manipulated by mechanical means, being drawn on or off in less than a minute by the aid of electricity and without manual labour.   Formerly some twenty-six men were employed for this purpose.   Fountains are fitted in the water tank, which enables displays to be made.   The prime opening attraction was the equestrian sketch, *Tally Ho !* from the London Hippodrome.

THE NEW PAVILION THEATRE.

This handsome and spacious theatre is situated in Lodge Lane and Beaumont Street.   It was opened on February 24, 1908, by the proprietors, Messrs. W. H. Broadhead and Son. The Pavilion is the first theatre erected in the populous Lodge

Lane district. The building, which is constructed on the two tier principle, is capable of seating 2,050 persons. It is conducted on the two-houses-a-night system.

THE THEATRE ROYAL, GARSTON.

Less than a couple of decades ago the Garstonians were unable to boast of a permanent theatre, and had to be content with such dramatic fare as itinerant showmen occasionally brought. In 1891 there was the Britannia Theatre, under the proprietorship of Mr. J. W. Snape, who is, I believe, still touring. The Britannia was not a permanent structure, but it was Mr. Snape's intention at that time to build a regular theatre. But this he never carried out. The Royal Palace of Varieties was afterwards erected in St. Mary's Road, and the opening took place in 1892. Mr. John Hargreaves was the manager. After being run as a variety theatre it was converted into a playhouse. Closed since February, 1895, the theatre was re-opened on August 3, 1896, by Mr. David Barnard with *Parson Thorn* as the attraction. Mr. Barnard brought good companies, and successfully directed the theatre for a number of years. After he left the Royal it was converted into a billiard hall.

BOOTLE

Bootle has only begun to make theatrical history within a comparatively recent period.

Probably the first entertainer of repute to relieve the monotony of life there was Samuel Lover, the celebrated novelist, who gave an ' Irish night,' at the old Rimrose Hotel, in 1845.

The opening out of the north-end docks gave a special fillip to trade in this quarter, and provided an increasing number of inhabitants, for whose delectation itinerant showmen and others used to come and give specimens of their quality.

Entertainments used to be given in the Palatine Hall, Miller's Bridge, and musical evenings were held in several hostelries—notably the Jawbone and the Dolphin.

A theatre of some considerable pretensions was Mr. C. H. Duval's Royal Standard, which, was situated in the Derby Road on the site now occupied by a branch of the London City and Midland Bank. The performances here were of a full-flavoured description, and were greatly appreciated.

Then there was Cartland's Circus, which was opened about 1890. It was constructed partly of wood and brick, and stood at the corner of Strand and Irlam Roads. The site is now occupied by the Fire Station.

The pressing need of a permanent theatre in the Borough was obvious, and, to supply the long-felt want, the Messrs. Pennington decided to erect a suitable theatre. The site chosen was on the east side of Irlam Road, on ground which a few decades before had formed part of a wave-kissed strand.

In 1887 Mr. Harry Pennington (who is now the Earl of Derby's agent for Bootle), prepared the plans. Mr. Pennington was then in his twenty-third year, and at that time (according to his own confession), had no practical knowledge of theatre architecture. In 1888 Mr. Pennington, senior, who had been long in the service of the Earl of Derby, commenced the erection of the building, but in the August of that year he unfortunately died.   Consequently, building operations were suspended until 1889, when the undertaking was again put in hand, the Messrs. James and John Pennington carrying out the work until its completion.

The theatre was christened the Royal Muncaster, and it was let to Messrs. H. T. Denyer and Harris Fineberg, who opened it as a music hall on Monday, October 6, 1890.   The following is a copy of the inaugural bill :—

'ROYAL, MUNCASTER THEATRE,

Irlam Road, Bootle.

Proprietors and Managers .. H. T. Denyer & Harris Fineberg.

This Place of Amusement is the first Theatre built in Bootle. Pennington Brothers, Builders and Architects. The Building superintended by Mr. James Pennington.

The New and Magnificent Scenery painted by Mr. S. King and Assistants (By permission of Messrs. Fineberg and Lees, Star Music Hall, Liverpool). The Band of 15 Performers under the direction of Mr. E. Jonghmann.

Programme.

Monday, October 6, 1890, and during the week.

Overture   ..   ..   Band

Miss Cissy Trent,
Transformation Dancer.

Mr. Billy Seward,
Negro Comedian.

Miss Seaford,
Burlesque Actress.

The Cawellys,
Acrobatic Entertainment.

Grand Selection from Wallace's Opera
MARITANA,
Under the direction of Mr. E. Jonghmann.

Mr. Eaton Batty,
Baritone Vocalist.

Miss Lydia Yeamans,
Accompanied by Mr. F. J. Titus.

Mr. Fred Millis
Ventriloquist.

Sisters Wills,
Vocalists, Dancers, and Musicians.

Fish and Richmond,
Eccentric Comedians.

Mr. Walter Stockwell,
Comic Vocalist.

God Save the Queen.

The Artistes will appear according to Number exhibited at
· side of stage.

Prices of Admission :

Stage Boxes, £2 2s. to 10s. 6d. ; Stalls, 2s. ; Front Circle,
1s. 6d. ; Side Stalls, 1s. ; Pit, 6d.

Doors open at 7, Performance to commence at 7.30.

Early Doors at 6.30 to all parts 6d. extra.'

The Muncaster was run as a variety theatre down to the
time Mr. Denyer ceased his connection with the theatre. Mr.
Fineberg then proceeded to give dramatic performances. In
1893 the Messrs. Pennington took over the management of
the Muncaster, giving drama for three weeks out of the month
and variety entertainments the fourth week. Finding,
however, that drama was more suitable to the popular taste,
they decided to give theatrical fare only, and as a dramatic
house this theatre has been run ever since. The Muncaster
is a people's theatre at popular prices, and brightens the
lives of many. At the time of writing drama is being played
twice nightly by an able stock company. This innovation
was inaugurated on the August Bank Holiday of 1907.

The first assistant manager of the theatre was Mr. J. W.
Jones, who came here during Mr. Fineberg's management.
Mr. Jones was succeeded in the beginning of 1900 by Mr. Sam
Hill, who had been associated with the theatre for several

years in a minor capacity.   Mr Hill remained here until
April, 1900, when Mr. Albert E Wilson was made acting
manager.   Mr. Hill is a talented Lancashire dialect writer,
and has published a couple of volumes (' Foirewood,'
and ' Little Spadger's Dog '), besides numerous dialect
sketches.   Mr. Wilson first came to the theatre in
November, 1896, and, until the period mentioned above,
he was *chef d'orchestré.*   Mr Wilson is a capable musician,
and has composed the incidental music for several touring
successes.   In the latter part of 1906, he gave up the acting
management in order to resume his old position as musical
director.   In 1907 he severed his connection with the theatre.
He was succeeded as acting manager by Mr. Harry Young,
who fills the position with courtesy and tact.

Among the first productions at the Muncaster have
been *The Scarlet Brotherhood, The Gay Chaperon, Our Sailor
Lad, Between the Lights, Our British Empire, They All Love
Jack, The 10.30 Down Express, The Kaithough, The Mystery
of Desborough, When the Lights are Low, A Leap Year's Comedy,
From Washerwoman to Duchess,* and *The Pet of the Embassy.*

It is worthy of note that the proprietors of the theatre
are descended from a very ancient family.   Some years anterior
to the Norman Conquest mention is made of a Pennington
—variously written, Penyngton, Penington, and in the Domes-
day Book, Pennegton, probably from *Pennaig* in British meaning a chieftain, or great personage—Gamel de Pennington, to
wit.   Pennington, which is situated between Dalton and
Ulverston, in Lancashire, was the original seat of the family,
but Gamel de Pennington is supposed to have migrated some
forty years before the advent of William the Conqueror to
Mealcastre (now Muncaster), in Cumberland.   For centuries
Muncaster was the principal residence of the Pennington
family, and it is now with Warter Hall, Yorkshire, one of the
two seats of the present Lord Muncaster.   Until recently
a view of Muncaster Castle was depicted on the act-drop
of the Bootle Theatre.

THE ROYAL BRITISH CIRCUS.

This establishment, which was a commodious wooden
structure, was built and opened about 1898 by Mr. Edward

Paddock. It was located on the west side of Linacre Road, Litherland, opposite to the Catherine Hotel. The entertainments provided by Mr. Paddock consisted of equestrian performances interspersed with variety turns. Mr. Paddock afterwards let the building as a variety theatre to Mr. Fred Willmot. After Mr. Willmot left, the late Matthew Montgomery ran the house for a time as a music hall. Finally, the building was put up for auction, and the materials sold.

BIRKENHEAD

On April 5, 1847, Mr. W. J. Holloway, formerly of the Sans Pareil and Adelphi Theatres, Liverpool, opened a theatre in Birkenhead on the occasion of the opening of the Morpeth and Egerton Docks. On the same day the beautiful Park was inaugurated with great rejoicing

In the 'fifties Hendry's booth was something of an institution in Birkenhead. The booth, which was located near where the Market now stands, was remarkably well appointed. The scenery in particular, was beautiful, having been painted specially for the manager by an artist of note. Although the price of admission was small, goodly sums were often taken and the receipts regularly divided every night among the company, which was a numerous one. Most of the players were old stagers and very competent to perform their business. ' Business ' in Hendry's booth was quite different to ' business' in a theatre, because it was necessary that the plays should be given with lightning-like rapidity. For instance, Richard would run his wicked career—offer his kingdom for a horse— have his ' cut in ' at Richmond—and get killed off-hand in twenty minutes from the rise of the curtain. Another piece followed, with all those striking varieties of scene and character which delighted a mixed audience. Finally, there came a ' screaming farce,' and the whole was brought to a close in less than an hour. *The Castle Spectre* in tabloid form could be swallowed in twelve or thirteen minutes, whereas in a regular theatre it took nearly three hours. In addition to performing the players also had to ' parade.' This was usually done in that picturesque old style immortalised by Hogarth.

Hendry's booth, was as I have indicated, run on sharing terms. Hendry himself had six shares—two as proprietor, and one each as manager and actor, and the remainder for the use of the properties and for general wear and tear. The balance was allocated among the company as follows :—four shares for the ladies, six for the gentlemen, one for the supers, three for the band, and one for the two horses, making a grand total (including Hendry's six), of twenty-one shares, the general average of which was about eight shillings per head.*

In the late 'fifties Mr. John Milton Hengler, of the well-known equestrian family, was associated with the destinies of a Cirque Variété in Hamilton Street, the proprietor of which was Mr. John Henderson. *Harlequin O'Donoghue ; or, The Fairy White Horse of Killarney* was the title of a pantomime given at Christmas, 1859.

Another Temple of Thespis (made of wood), was situated in Market Place South, the proprietors of which were Messrs. Seagrave, Hurst, Johnston, and Francis. At this theatre a number of clever performers appeared. There was also another old theatre in the same street adjoining the present Birkenhead Market. This was managed by Mr. C. H. Duval, who afterwards was associated with the Theatre Royal. Other early places of entertainment were the Shakespeare in Chester Street (presided over, in 1869, by Mr. W. Weeks), and the Birkenhead Arms in the same street.

Another favourite place of amusement was Culleen's Circus, which was opened in 1883. The building, which was situated in Conway Street, adjoining the General Post Office, was capable of accommodating 3,000 people. It was held on a two years' lease, and the interior was handsomely decorated. The Circus was run for a time by Mr. J. Elphinstone, who was succeeded by Mr. Joseph Ohmy. In 1884 it was converted by Mr. Harry de Frece into De Frece's Variety Theatre, but was demolished in the succeeding year in order to make way for street improvements.

THE MUSIC HALL.

The Music Hall, so designated in the classic sense only, is situated in Claughton Road. It was inaugurated on January

* ' Behind the Scenes, being the Confessions of a Strolling Player ' by Peter Paterson, late Comedian of the Theatres Royal and Rural :' Edinburgh (1858), p. 75. .

21, 1862—the same year in which the foundation stone of the Birkenhead Borough Hospital was laid by the Marquis of Westminster.

THE THEATRE ROYAL.

Half a century ago the necessity of having a first-class Temple of Thespis of their own instead of ' crossing the water ' to Liverpool, was keenly felt by playgoers in Birkenhead.   Accordingly a company of well-known local gentlemen was formed, with Dr. J. M. Craig at their head.   Among others associated with the venture were Messrs. George Harrison, Robert Dean, Halsall Segar, Henry Kelsall Aspinall, and Lewis Hornblower, the last of whom was the architect of the projected theatre.

Land having been purchased in Argyle Street, building operations were commenced in July, 1863, and on October 31 of the following year Birkenhead's first Theatre Royal was opened.   The decorations were by Messrs J. and W. J. Jeffrey of Compton House, Liverpool, and the scenery was by Mr. D. Dalby.   The theatre would comfortably seat 1,850 people, and hold about 2,300.   There was an artistic proscenium, a pretty act-drop, and the stage was very commodious.

The opening address was written by William Brough, who in 1866 had the management of the Prince of Wales, Liverpool.   It was spoken by Alexander Henderson, the lessee.

After the National Anthem had been sung by a large and representative audience, the green baize curtain rose upon the comedy, *A Handsome Husband*, which was followed by F. C. Burnand's burlesque *Ixion ; or, The Man at the Wheel*, and the farce *Turn Him Out*.

The following is a copy of the playbill for the occasion :—

'THEATRE ROYAL, BIRKENHEAD,

Sole Lessee   ..   ..   ..   Mr. Alexander Henderson

GRAND INAUGURATION
AND
OPENING CELEBRATION.
Monday, October 31st, 1864.

ENGAGEMENT OF MISS LYDIA THOMPSON
and a most powerful company.

A New Act-Drop and Scenery painted by Dalby.

Monday, Tuesday and Wednesday,
October 31, and November 1 and 2, at Half-past Seven,
AN OPENING ADDRESS.
Written by William Brough Esq., will be spoken by Mr. Alex.
Henderson.

After which
"GOD SAVE THE QUEEN."
Will be sung by the entire Company.

The performances will then commence with the popular
Comedy, in One Act, entitled,

A HANDSOME HUSBAND.

Mr. Wyndham	Mr. E. Price.
Henry Fitzherbert . . .	Mr. A. Nelson.
Stephen	Mr. Brock.
Mrs. Wyndham . . .	Mrs. Agnes Ryder.
Hon. Mrs. Melford . . .	Miss Nellie Nesbitt.
Mrs. Twisden . . .	Miss Lewis.

To be followed by Burnand's celebrated Burlesque, entitled
IXION,
OR, THE MAN AT THE WHEEL.

CHARACTERS IN THE PROLOGUE—MORTALS.

Ixion { Ex-King of Thessaly, but though a King with a prefix of an X, it does not Alphabetically follow that he has a wise head on his shoulders. } Miss Lydia Thompson.

Trondapanieibomenos—Mr. Munro. Prosephe—Mr. Hill.
Podasokus—Mr. Thompson.

Queen Dia { Ixion's disloyal wife, who leads the Revolutionists and proposes to be a tanner of her husband as well as a dyer, and tramples on her regal diadem, in order to become a Dia-democrat. } Miss Procter.

IMMORTALS

Jupiter	{ King of the Gods, and the most fin-ished Gentleman in Olympus }	Miss Mary Huddart.
Mercury	{ the celestial Telegraph Boy—"With wings on his ankles, and wings near his toes, and no time he loses where-ever he goes" }	Miss Louisa Laidlaw.

CHARACTERS IN THE DRAMA

Ixion	{ who, being bankrupt, and sadly in want of change, is, in spite of his bad character in his former situation, "taken" up by Jupiter, and patronised by the "upper ten" }	Miss Lydia Thompson.
Juno	{ Queen of the Gods, and Jove's spouse, described by poets as the as ox-eyed lady, and consequently of a mettle-some temperament; fond of Peacocks that sing Peakens of Joy while driving her car }	Miss C. Elton.
Venus	{ the Goddess of Beauty ; still a spinster, although it has been said by a great authority that "Venus orto Mari" which, being translated is "Venus ought to Marry" }	Miss Nellie Nesbitt.
Cupid	{ the Son of Venus, who will be at once recognised as Love at first sight }	Miss Sidney Cowell.
Minerva	{ Goddess of Wisdom ; a very studious and quiet lady, though generally appearing with an owl ; Jupiter's housekeeper and keeper of the royal keys, but not on that account to be confounded with the modern Mother Bunch }	Mr. Walter Searle.
Apollo	{ Secretary to the Imperial "Sun" Fire Insurance Company (Limited), and out of his official capacity, author of several scientific works, art critic, adapter of dramas by any Foreign hand, and sporting member of the Four-in-hand Club. }	Miss Ada Coates.
Ganymede	{ Jupiter's beautiful "Buttons" a nice, active lad, the original Fat Boy, who may be described as a Gany-mede and Gany-pursey-un-to }	Mr. Alfred Nelson.

Bacchus { 'Promoter and chief Director of the Celestial Light Wine Association; Patron Deity of Newington Butts; Jove's Butler, with full power over the Imperial Pints, does not, in consequence of his occupation, lose his tun } Mr. G. P. Grainger.

Mars   .   .   .   .   .   . Mr. R. P. Sheridan

Diana......Miss Williams.   Vesta......Miss Jones.

Hebe (Clerk of the Weather)..............Miss L. Cowell

Winged Genii, Passing Clouds, Shooting Stars, Apollo's Grooms, Jupiter's Satellites, and other Heavenly Bodies.

The whole to conclude with the screaming Farce, entitled :

TURN HIM OUT

Nicodemus Nobbs (an initerant toy vender)

Mr. Walter Searle

Mr. Mackintosh Moke (a retired tradesman)

Mr. G. P. Grainger

Mr. Eglantine Roseleaf (an exquisite)   Mr. R. P. Sheridan

Julia   .   .   .   .   .   Miss Ada Coates

Susan   .   .   .   .   .   Miss C. Elton

Acting Manager, Mr. L. J. Sefton.   Stage Manager, Mr. Alfred Nelson.

Musical Director, Mr. Michael Connolly.   Machinists, Mr. Huby and Assistants.

Scenic Artist, Mr. D. Dalb

Properties, Mr. Scarbrow and Assistants.

PRICES OF ADMISSION—THE OPENING WEEK.

NOTICE—Owing to the immense expenses attendant on this undertaking, and with a view to keeping the Audience additionally select, the Manager feels it necessary to issue the following scale for the First Six Nights :

Dress Circle—5s. (Reserved); Boxes—4s,; Pit—2s.

Gallery—1s.

ORDINARY PRICE

Commencing the second Monday ;

Dress   Circle—4s. ; Boxes—3s. ; Pit—1s. 6d. ; Gallery—1s.

Doors open at Seven o'clock, the Curtain rising precisely
at Half-past Seven
The Box Plan will be open on Monday, the 24th instant, when
Seats can be secured and tickets obtained for any evening
during the Opening Week '

___

During the first week the Royal was opened, E. A. Sothern
appeared in *My Aunt's Advice*, and *Dundreary Married and
Done For*.   The following month (December), saw J. L. Toole
and Paul Bedford in *The Pretty Housebreaker* and *The Area
Belle*.   Mr. Henderson's first and only pantomime at the
Royal was Charles Millward's *The Jolly Miller of the Dee ; or
Harlequin Bluff King Hal and the Fair Maid of Leasowe*, produced on December 26, 1864, and preceded by the drama
entitled *Theresa's Vows ; or, the Cross of Gold*.

Mr. Alexander Henderson's association with the Royal
was not of long duration, as on Saturday evening, February 11, 1865, he retired from the management in order to
devote his attention to other enterprises, one of which was
the building of the New Prince of Wales Theatre and Opera
House in Lime Street, Liverpool.

He was succeeded as lessee and manager by Mr. Alfred
Nelson, with whom was associated as acting manager, Mr
A. B. Viner.   Nelson's opening attraction (Feb. 13, 1865),
was *The Poor of Birkenhead*, one of Dion Boucicault's ' bob-
tailed ' pieces under a new name.

Easter of 1865 saw another change of management, the
new lessee being Mr. C. Morrelli.   The Christmas of 1866
witnessed a further change, Mr. George Grant then assuming
control.   Mr. Grant opened with the pantomime, written
by Alfred Smith, and entitled, *Harlequin Alhambra ; or, the
Three Moorish Maidens, and the Spanish Knights*, with local
and topical ' hits ' plentifully interspersed.   The story was
founded on one of Lord Lytton's novels.   In 1868 Mr. H.
Montague of the St. James's Hall, Liverpool was the lessee.   In
March, 1869, the theatre was under the management of Messrs.
George Vining and E. H. Brooke.   About the middle of the
'seventies Mr. Charles H. Duval next had a try for fame and
fortune with the Royal.   In 1877 Mr. Butler Stanhope
took over the remaining portion of Mr. Duval's lease.

On March 4, 1878, Mr. Dennis Grannell acquired the theatre
on a three years' lease. At that time Mr. Grannell had also
the Prince of Wales (now the Argyle), Birkenhead, and the
Rotunda, Liverpool. Afterwards Messrs. Butler Stanhope
and J. Vowles became the lessees, and successfully carried
on the theatre for a number of years.

During Messrs. Stanhope and Vowles' first stock season,
which ran for nearly four years, the company included E. S.
Willard, T. Morton Powell, R. C. Buchanan, Harry Cullen-
ford, Henry Sainsbury, Horace Stanley, Sidney Hazlewood,
Walter Cameron, W. C. Shepherd, Marie Collins, and
Kate Kilpack. Among the ' stars ' engaged were : Charles
Dillon, J. L. Toole, Edward Terry, Henry Loraine, T. C. King,
and Kate Vaughan. The new plays produced at the Royal
during the Stanhope and Vowles *régime* comprised :—*The
Lighthouse on the Crimson Rock* (May 14, 1883), *Collars and
Cuffs*, musical farcical comedy by Henri R. French (November
30, 1883), *Creeping Shadows*, a drama in five acts, by
Butler Stanhope (April 18, 1887), and *Darkest London*, a
drama in five acts by Butler Stanhope (April 4, 1891).
In the last-mentioned play the author played the part of
Mark Collings, Mrs. Stanhope that of Jenny Bland, and little
Lalla Stanhope appeared as Dick Sparks.

On Friday, June 24, 1892, a fire broke out in the theatre,
when damage to the amount of £2,000 was done. Fortunately,
the premises were insured. The management afterwards
applied successfully to the magistrates for a temporary
license to act in the Circus in Conway Street until the
repairs had been completed.

After Messrs. Stanhope and Vowles severed their connection with the Royal, the theatre was taken over by Mr.
Ellis Brammall, junior. Next Mr. John Lawson of *Humanity*
fame and Mrs. Ennis Lawson became associated with its
destinies. They were followed by Mr. P. J. Singleton, who
in turn was succeeded in August, 1898, by Mr. W. W. Kelly,
who ran the theatre most successfully until the summer of
1905, when it was closed for extensive alterations.

After remaining closed for two months, the theatre was
re-opened by Mr. Kelly on August Bank Holiday, with *Peggy
Machree*. During the recess the theatre had been reconstructed, redecorated, and re-upholstered, and the electric

light installed throughout. While the alterations were in process an old spring well was found below the stage and covered up. This, doubtless, was one of the town's water supplies in the long ago.

THE ARGYLE THEATRE OF VARIETIES.

This favourite place of entertainment was opened as the Argyle Music Hall in 1868. It was built by Dennis Grannell and his brother-in-law, George Arundale, the latter of whom managed the hall until about 1873, when the partnership between Grannell and himself was dissolved. Grannell then ran the Argyle in conjunction with the Rotunda, Liverpool. The booking and general management from 1873 to 1893 were under the control of Mr. Charles Wood of the Liverpool Rotunda. A dramatic license was obtained about 1876, and the name of the house was changed to the Prince of Wales Theatre. The theatre was then run for some time with a stock company from the Rotunda Theatre, Liverpool. For some years a variety company from the Star, Liverpool, under the direction of Mr. Noah Lees, used to play during the summer on Monday and Saturday evenings. In 1889 the name of the house was changed back again to the Argyle. The theatre has been in the hands of the one family since it was built. The present proprietor, Mr. D. J. Clarke, is a nephew of Dennis Grannell, and worked under him from August, 1888, to May, 1893, when he took over the sole management.

THE THEATRE METROPOLE.

This theatre is situated in Grange Road. It was first opened as Ohmy's Grand Circus by Mr. Joseph Ohmy on Monday, December 17, 1888. The architect of the building was Mr. William Hesketh, of Liverpool; and the contractor, Mr. David Sumner, of Bootle. The building was designed and constructed so as to be convertible into either a theatre or a circus. The first intention was to set apart

four months of the year for circus entertainments, and the
remaining eight months for theatrical performances.   In
1890 the building was styled the Gaiety Theatre.   On
Monday, February 9, 1891, Mr. Ellis Brammall, junr., opened
it as a music hall.

On August Bank Holiday, 1891, Mr. Brammall turned
it into an orthodox Temple of the Drama, the opening attraction being *Our Regiment*.   The late John Riley was the resident manager, and the late B. Henderson Howat the secretary.
Riley was for many years associated with the Argyle under
Dennis Grannell, transferring his services to Mr. Brammall
on the opening of the Métropole.   On February 21, 1898,
Mr. W. W. Kelly became the lessee, and so remained until
February 21, 1905.   Since then the theatre has been closed.

INDEX

Lewes, Geo. H., 228.
Lewis, T. D., 131, 150, 163-4, 177, 186, 187.
Lewis, W. T., 67, 68, 107, 112, 126, 127, 131, 177, 187.
Lind, Jenny, 163, 228.
Liston, John, 128, 131, 144.
Lofthouse, J. S., 263, 362.
Loraine, Henry, 174, 175, 199, 232, 233, 299, 384.
Loseby, Constance, 249, 283.
Lover, Samuel, 335, 336, 372.
Lowrey, Dan, 359, 360.

M

Maccabe, Fred, 174, 197, 232, 263.
MacGregor, Miss, 235-6.
Mackay, Chas., 144, 148, 213.
Macklin, Chas., 51, 65, 69, 78.
Macready, Wm., 78, 103.
Macready, W. C., 78, 80, 134, 135, 140, 143-145, 147, 164.
Marriott, Alice, 195, 196, 235, 238, 239, 243, 245, 267, 268, 272, 298, 300.
Mathews, Mr. and Mrs. Charles, 82, 108, 113, 115-117, 127, 133, 143, 144.
Mathews, Chas. (the younger), 115-6, 146, 148, 149, 151, 155, 156, 165, 306, 311, 314.
Mattocks, Mr. and Mrs. G., 41, 43, 44, 53, 56, 57, 60, 61-2, 69, 74, 77, 81, 85, 107.
M'Ardle, J. F., 249, 285, 290, 296, 298, 316, 352.
McCormack, Ben, 236-7.
Mead, Tom, 157, 200.
Mellon, Harriot, 87, 88, 90, 99, 119.
Menken, Adah Isaacs, 239.
Miller, David Prince, 229, 336.
Millward, Chas., 267, 268, 279, 287, 298, 383.
Modjeska, Mme., 315-6.
Mollison, Wm., 319, 331.
Montez, Lola, 337.
Montgomery, Matthew, sen., 302, 303, 376.
Montgomery, Walter, 304.
Moody, John, 65, 69.
Morris, Mr., 41, 48.
Mountain, Mrs., 85, 109.

Mudie, Miss, 119.
Mullart, Miss, 35, 37.
Munden, Joseph, 67, 68, 85, 86, 107, 113, 114, 117, 124, 127, 128.
Murray, Chas., 99, 122.

N

Neilson, Adelaide, 309.
Neilson, Julia, 321.
Neville, Henry, 167, 234, 239.
Nicholson, 'Baron', 215, 340.
Nisbett, Mrs., 147, 151.

O

O'Grady, Hubert, 302, 314.
O'Neill, Elizabeth, 73, 80, 130, 132, 133, 135.
O'Neill, Shane, 130-1.

P

Packer, Mr., 41, 42, 44, 48.
Palmer, John, 31, 42, 44, 48, 49, 51, 57, 90-6.
Palmer, Millicent, 172, 238.
Palmer, Mrs. Bandmann, 301.
Parsons, Mr. and Mrs. William, 41, 42, 43, 45, 48, 49, 51.
Patti, Adelina, 169.
Payne, Mr. and Mrs. Howard, 128, 227.
Pennington, Harry, 372.
Pennington, W. H., 175, 297.
Phelps, Saml., 214, 230, 272, 307, 314.
Picton, Sir James A., 11, 13, 16, 21, 180.
Pinero, A. W., 289, 296, 311-313.
Pope, Miss, 41, 42, 43.
Pope, Mr. and Mrs. Alex., 85, 104, 105.
Powell, Mr. and Mrs., 86, 107.
Power, Tyrone, 127, 193.
Proctor, J., 198.

Q

Quick, Mr. and Mrs. John, 56, 61, 73, 75, 85, 105.

THE LYCEUM PRESS, 37 Hanover Street, Liverpool

Milton Keynes UK
Ingram Content Group UK Ltd.
UKHW022206281223
435087UK00004B/48